CANADIAN
TREASURY
MANAGEMENT

THOMSON

CARSWELL

CANADIAN
TREASURY
MANAGEMENT

Jeffrey D. Sherman, B.Comm, M.B.A., F.C.S.I., C.A.

THOMSON
™
CARSWELL

This publication is designed to provide accurate and authoritative information. It is sold with the understanding that the publisher is not engaged in rendering legal, accounting or other professional advice. If legal advice or other expert assistance is required, the services of a competent professional should be sought. The analysis contained herein represents the opinions of the author and should in no way be construed as being either official or unofficial policy of any governmental body.

The National Library of Canada has catalogued this publication as follows:

Sherman. Jeffrey D.
     Canadian treasury management / Jeffrey D. Sherman.

Includes index.
ISBN 0-459-27989-0

     1. Business enterprises—Canada—Finance. 2. Cash management—Canada. I. Title.

HG4028.C45S54 2003   658.15'0971   C2003-904584-6

One Corporate Plaza
2075 Kennedy Road
Toronto, Ontario
M1T 3V4

Customer Relations:
Toronto 416-609-3800
Elsewhere in Canada/U.S. 1-800-387-5164
Fax 416-298-5082

PREFACE

Enron, WorldCom, Livent, Cinar, Confederation Life, Equitable Life, Barings Bank, Bausch & Lomb — over the past two decades a steady stream of disasters and scandals has startled the business world. This is not a recent development: large businesses with sterling reputations have failed and impoverished their investors, employees and creditors since the seventeenth century. However, forewarned is forearmed: today's financial manager has access to a variety of tools to anticipate, control and measure risk. With the benefit of hindsight, it is clear that many of the catastrophes might have been prevented, if those involved had better analyzed and understood what was going on.

Canadian Treasury Management is a comprehensive guide to financial and treasury management in Canada. Its scope includes Canadian financial markets and banking, investment strategies, financial and cash management, and treasury and risk management.

This book provides in one convenient volume authoritative and practical information on a variety of topics vital to Canadian business managers. It is designed to be used as a convenient reference and resource guide for financial executives and managers, as well as a training aid.

The scope of *Canadian Treasury Management* is broad, so coverage of each topic is concise and to the point. It is divided into five parts:

- **Business Banking in Canada** provides a survey of the Canadian financial environment and financial institutions, including investor insurance and depositor protection. It also discusses banking from the perspective of the customer, and how to manage the relationship.

- **Corporate Investment Strategy and Analysis** is a primer on investment strategy, securities analysis and portfolio management in Canada.

- **Financial and Cash Management** covers the important elements of modern financial management including controls, budgets, managing cash, electronic payments and e-commerce, and credit. It also reviews cash management techniques as well as cash forecasting and budgeting.

- **Treasury, Risk Management and Derivatives** discusses analyzing and managing financial risk, using derivatives to manage risk, and other advanced topics including legal and accounting issues, and evaluating the performance of treasury operations.

- **Reference** information includes some historical Canadian statistics covering interest rates, exchange rates and other information. While it is easy to find current information through the Internet, it can be a challenge to find data going back over time, so a selection is presented here. This section also contains a glossary of treasury and financial terms, and information on the Treasury Management Association of Canada, and international treasury associations.

PREFACE

This book has been designed to be easy to use. Where appropriate, checklists and questionnaires are provided to make it easy to quickly diagnose issues and determine solutions. Detailed tables of contents and an index are also provided.

Two chapters have been written by experts in their field. Chapter 14, "E-Commerce and E-Payments," is written by Craigg Ballance, one of the leading experts on electronic payments and commerce in Canada. Chapter 21, "Legal Issues in Treasury Management," has been written by a team of experts at Aird & Berlis, LLP, Barristers and Solicitors. Further biographical information is noted in the following section, "About the Author and Contributors."

This publication is the successor to the *Canadian Treasury Management Handbook*, which has been the definitive reference resource for finance and treasury professionals in Canada since 1993. In response to requests from subscribers, after 10 years of publication as a looseleaf service it has been recast as a bound book, eliminating the need to file supplements. The material has also been substantially updated and revised with many completely new chapters.

This book owes a debt to those who contributed to its predecessor. Former contributors included Colin Haddock, Alison Manzer, Laural Ross and Melanie Russell. Over the years, many useful comments and suggestions have been received from the Treasury Management Association of Canada and its members. Thanks are due to the team at Thomson-Carswell who have helped create this book, including Julia Gulej, Product Development Manager; David Worthington, Marketing Manager; and especially Tim Yap, Editor. I am also grateful to my wife, Margaret Sherman for her support and encouragement.

We would like to hear from any readers with comments or suggestions to improve future editions of this book. Please e-mail *jdsherman@sympatico.ca*, or fax (416) 736-0881.

The art and science of treasury management is continuing to change quickly. We hope that this book will assist practitioners anticipate and cope with change.

Jeffrey D. Sherman
Toronto, August 2003

ABOUT THE AUTHOR AND CONTRIBUTORS

Jeffrey D. Sherman, B.Comm, M.B.A., F.C.S.I., C.A. has written extensively on contemporary finance, business and accounting issues for over 20 years. He has had experience with treasury and finance from several perspectives. He has been the Chief Financial Officer of both public and private companies, a consultant specializing in mergers and acquisitions and corporate finance, and has worked for a large chartered bank in various senior capacities. Mr. Sherman has lectured and conducted seminars for many organizations, and is the author and co-author of numerous books, including *Migration Canada* (published by Kluwer), a guide to the tax and legal implications of moving into or out of Canada, and *Financial Instruments, A Guide for Financial Managers* (Carswell).

Contributing writer **Craigg Ballance** (Chapter 14, "E-Commerce and E-Payments") has been managing technology and business convergence in the financial arena for over 20 years. He is recognized as an expert in the area of Electronic Business and Payments processes, and is the co-author of three books: *Electronic Commerce Relationships: Trust by Design* (Prentice Hall), *On-Line Profits: A Manager's Guide to Electronic Commerce* (Harvard Business Press) and *Electronic Commerce and EDI In the Financial Industry* (Lafferty Publications). Over the past decade, Mr. Ballance has provided consulting and design expertise to numerous banking and corporate organizations around the world, as well as in Canada, helping to apply technology and electronic payment methodologies. He is a Partner with E-Finity Group Inc. in Toronto, Canada.

Aird & Berlis LLP (Chapter 21, "Legal Issues in Treasury Management") is a prominent full-service law firm, with a large, diversified national and international presence of over 120 lawyers. Aird & Berlis LLP represents some of the world's largest corporations as well as a wide array of entrepreneurial businesses, associations, government agencies and individuals. The team that contributed to this chapter included the following lawyers: **Andy Ayotte** has practised in the financial services field since 1986; **Jeff Goldenthal** has practised corporate/commercial, corporate finance, lending and banking law since 1989; **Doug Palmateer** has practised in the financial services field, with an emphasis on bankruptcy and insolvency since 1980; and **Sonia Yung** has practised corporate and securities law, representing issuers and underwriters in numerous offerings of equity and debt securities, both by public offerings and through private placements since 1994.

TABLE OF CONTENTS

DETAILED TABLE OF CONTENTS

DETAILED TABLE OF CONTENTS

P A R T

Business Banking in Canada

We take for granted the structural strengths of the Canadian banking system. This section describes the features of business banking in Canada, and suggests ways of obtaining the maximum benefit from your bank.

C H A P T E R 1

The Canadian Financial System

Overview

Canada's financial system operates efficiently and effectively. It is the product of historical accident, government and social policy, the federal and provincial organization of the country, as well as the structure of Canada's financial industry and financial institutions.

The financial system achieves multiple objectives:

- medium of exchange and store of value;
- facilitating payments;

- matching savers and borrowers;
- managing risk.

This chapter provides an introduction to Canada's financial system.

Economic Perspective

The Canadian economy has grown remarkably over the last 40 years, but the rate of growth has varied considerably. In the 1960s and 1970s, growth in real Gross Domestic Product averaged about 4.7 per cent per annum. In the 1980s and 1990s, this figure was 2.8 per cent, reflecting lower growth rates each year as well as negative growth in real GDP in 1982 and 1991. In the 1970s, rapid growth was accompanied by inflation that averaged 8.1 per cent each year. Since 1991, inflation has been below 3 per cent per annum, and often much lower.

Large continuing government deficits were an important part of the Canadian economy from 1975 to 1996. In the mid-1990s, federal debt alone exceeded 70 per cent of GDP, provincial debt added a further 30 per cent. As a result of budget surpluses since 1997, federal debt is down to less than 50 per cent of GDP, and provincial debt a little over 20 per cent. While still a high level of debt in historical terms, the reduction in government borrowing requirements has a significant impact on the financial markets.

Canada's economy remains strong today, but is also vulnerable to developments in the United States. Employment growth has been one of the drivers supporting economic growth, but that may be expected to slow down in the future as the population ages.

A Brief History of Financial Markets in Canada

The beginning of the Canadian money market can be traced to the 1930s, when 91-day treasury bills were first sold by the Bank of Canada (the Bank). By 1937, tenders were held every other week and in 1953 a weekly tender was introduced. Most bills were purchased by the chartered banks, with occasional purchases by investment dealers on behalf of clients. During the 1950s, investment dealers started to carry small amounts of treasury bills in inventory.

Sales finance companies started to issue short-term commercial paper after the Second World War. In 1953, the Bank of Canada granted investment dealers lines of credit under which treasury bills could be discounted at the bank under a "repo" or purchase and re-sale agreement. In the mid 1950s, the chartered banks started granting day-to-day loans to money market dealers, so they could finance their inventories of these short-term government securities.

By the early 1960s, a market for non-government short-term money market instruments started to develop. Finance companies, as well as large non-financial corporations such as grain dealers, started to obtain short-term funds through the issuance of short-term notes. At that time, short-term funds were actually used to finance short-term needs. (Now, the relationship between the assets and liabilities on a balance sheet is not that straightforward. See Chapter 18, "Managing Interest Rate Risk and Derivatives.") Many entities in seasonal businesses were active in both sides of the market, issuing notes at one time of the year while investing surplus funds in the newly developing money market at other times.

The regulators (Bank of Canada and Department of Finance, as well as provincial securities commissions) fostered the growth of the money markets. Larger borrowers began to turn to the financial markets because they could obtain short-term funds at lower interest rates than the chartered banks offered. Similarly, investors could earn higher returns by purchasing money market securities rather than investing with chartered banks. The "disintermediation" that had a massive effect on financial institutions and their customers in the 1980s traced its origins to a quarter of a century earlier.

The 1967 *Bank Act* removed the ceiling of 6 per cent on bank lending rates, enabling banks to compete more effectively. This was followed by a reduction in the chartered banks' secondary reserve requirements, diminishing their need to purchase treasury bills. This reduced the downward pressure on treasury bill yields, and ultimately resulted in treasury bills reflecting "market" interest rates more accurately. Other developments were also occurring at this time, such as the "special call loan" market afforded by the chartered banks, which provided broader and more flexible sources of overnight funds for money market participants. As a result, the Canadian treasury bill market expanded significantly in the 1970s as the market became deeper and more resilient. Competitive yields for treasury bills resulted in a wide range of institutional and retail investors entering the market. Government of Canada outstanding treasury bills increased over 1,300 per cent from 1979 to 1996. At March 31, 1996, treasury bills outstanding totalled $166.1 billion. By June 2003 treasury bills outstanding were reduced to $12 billion as the Government of Canada changed its financing strategy.

The growth of the market in bonds and longer-term instruments paralleled that of the money markets. Government of Canada debt steadily increased as a percentage of Gross National Product to a post-war peak of 71.2 per cent in 1995-96 to finance the continuing budgetary deficits. For 1999-2000 this ratio declined to 59 per cent. The government is targeting a reduction to 40 per cent by 2005-06. There had been a marked growth in the corporate debt markets as corporations grew. In 1960, net new issues of corporate bonds aggregated $317 million. By 1989, this had grown to $22.2 billion and declined somewhat in subsequent years due to the recession. By 1995, net new corporate bond issues had grown to $19.9 billion and were $10.8 billion in 2002.

Functions of the Financial System

Medium of exchange and store of value

Throughout history, various societies have always used some commodity as a general medium of exchange and a store of wealth. In earlier societies, the medium of exchange has included items such as salt and precious metals like gold. The desire for convenience long ago resulted in the use of paper claims on physical goods rather than the goods themselves in settling transactions. The precursor to banknotes represented claims on stores of precious metal in goldsmiths' vaults. Today, banknotes represent claims against the Government of Canada. In general, today's liabilities of financial institutions (such as chequing and savings accounts) and governments (such as T-bills) also serve as money.

Payments

The financial systems in Canada effect payments quickly and efficiently. Two automated clearing systems operate to settle Canadian dollar transactions: the Automated Clearing Settlement System (ACSS) and the Large Value Transfer System (LVTS). ACSS is used for both cheques and electronic transfers. The volume and value of paper-based transactions such as cheques have fallen relative to electronic payments. In 1992, paper-based transactions accounted for 81 per cent of the volume and 99 per cent of the value of payments flowing through the ACSS. By 2002, these figures were 30 per cent and 81 per cent. For a discussion of e-commerce and the effect of the internet on payment transactions, please see Chapter 14.

Another element of the domestic payments system is its relationship to international foreign exchange markets. It is not difficult to transfer financial assets, and claims on assets, or buy and sell goods and services across national boundaries. Interestingly, foreign exchange never actually leaves the country. (Even when bank notes are physically tendered for payment in a foreign country, any financial institution receiving them will generally ship them back from whence they came.) Rather, international trade results in changes in the beneficial ownership of the assets — not movement of the assets. The Foreign Exchange markets are discussed in Chapter 19.

Matching savers and borrowers

The classic function of financial markets is to channel savings into investment. Financial markets — with or without financial intermediaries — permit the act of saving to be separated from the act of investing.

The so-called "law of supply and demand" really means that for any positively sloping supply curve and negatively sloping demand curve, there will be a point at which the two will intersect. Thus, the market rates that equalize the amount that savers save and the amount required for borrowers to spend (consume) or invest represents a point of equilibrium (albeit transient equilibrium) for the economy.

It has been argued by some economists that the convenience of saving in financial forms increases the amount saved, thus increasing the rate of capital accumulation. Whether or not this is true, it is clear that by increasing the efficiency of allocating savings among competing uses of capital, the well-being of savers as a whole is enhanced.

Providing information

A major consequence of the existence of the financial system is that information on risks and returns is widely disseminated through interest rates and securities prices. The information is voluminous and complex — and in fact, often contradictory — but it does permit savers and investors to make rational choices among competing outlets and sources of investment. Prices in financial markets are based on actual transactions so that they continually reflect investors' and savers' evaluations of investment and lending alternatives.

Sometimes the information is paid for explicitly. Investors and borrowers pay for market information in fees to security analysts, subscriptions to publishers as well as commissions or spreads between bid and ask prices paid to financial intermediaries for executing transactions. But this payment is for the reporting of information that is already in the market. The information is there, by virtue of the transactions being executed. This is a very powerful and often overlooked benefit of the free market system — and an argument for minimizing government intervention, other than to ensure the accuracy of disseminated information.

Managing risk

Various financial markets permit different sorts of risk management. The classic example is insurance, where, for a fee, the purchasers can eliminate risks that they do not care to endure. That is relatively straightforward, since the risk being insured is clearly set out in advance.

9

One theme of this book is the analysis and management of financial risk. Risk can be analyzed in many ways: credit risk, liquidity risk, interest rate risk and foreign exchange risk. Efficient financial markets ensure that those who are willing to risk adversity have choices to assess and manage (reduce) financial risk.

Forward foreign exchange contracts

Forward foreign exchange contracts permit an entity to determine today the proceeds it will receive for exchanging a quantity of a foreign currency some date in the future. Thus, the risk of an intervening fluctuation of foreign exchange rates can be eliminated.

Portfolio diversification

Diversifying investment portfolios of financial instruments can be a way to minimize risk and to maximize return at a particular level of risk. (See Chapter 8, "Securities Analysis and Portfolio Management.")

The Future

Rate of change

The only constant over the last few decades has been change, and the rate of change is accelerating. For example, interest rate swaps did not exist before 1981. The outstanding notional principal for interest rate swaps, interest rate options and currency swaps as at June 30, 2000, totalled $60.4 trillion compared to $52.7 trillion one year earlier. These markets could not have developed without powerful, fast and relatively inexpensive computing power. Market participants can now trade in "derivative" securities (swaps, futures contracts and options, for example), to achieve the same risks and rewards as trading in the underlying securities, but often with lower transaction costs and faster execution times. (For more information, see the International Swaps and Derivatives Association (ISDA) Web site at *www.isda.org* and Part D of this book.)

Global markets

Canadian financial markets are relatively small. But there are few barriers to dealing internationally. Canadian traders and investors participate in changes occurring in financial markets globally, either by investing or borrowing directly in the global markets or by dealing in Canadian instruments that exhibit greater or lesser degrees of correlation with those in foreign markets. For example, Canadian interest rates will be influenced by European and American interest rates, European views of the U.S. dollar and the Euro, and global capital flows.

Rather than being in a "reactive" mode when setting interest rates, beginning in November 2000, the Bank of Canada introduced a new system of eight fixed or pre-specified dates each year for announcing any changes to the official interest rate it uses for implementing monetary policy. Fixed announcement dates replaced the previous approach to announcing monetary policy actions under which the Bank can, in principle, adjust interest rates on any business day. With this new approach, the Bank joined many other central banks, including the U.S. Federal Reserve, the Bank of England, the European Central Bank, the Bank of Japan, the Swedish Riksbank, the Reserve Bank of Australia, and the Reserve Bank of New Zealand, all of which had adopted pre-set dates for announcing interest rate changes.

11

Intermediation and disintermediation

Global financial markets have experienced a long-term trend of disintermediation.

Until the 1960s, only the largest and best-known corporations could issue bonds or sell commercial paper. As a result, companies relied heavily on the chartered banks for financing. Since then, non-financial corporations have greatly increased the use of tradable financial instruments such as commercial paper, whether underwritten by securities dealers or directly placed into the markets. Thus the banks are bypassed for many market transactions.

Major U.S. banks now hold as many government bonds as they have loans to large corporations. In fact, many American companies have better credit ratings than their banks. Therefore, they can often borrow more cheaply than their bankers. In addition, they often have large treasury operations and access to the same international market information as securities and investment dealers. Thus, at least, the U.S. market may have reached a nadir of disintermediation, as many borrowers and investors deal directly with each other rather than through banks. To some extent, this is happening in Canada — it is likely to remain more pronounced in the U.S. because of its very different banking system.

Conclusion

With the fading of the dot-com and stock market boom, Canada's large chartered banks appear to be heading back closer to their core retail banking roots. Corporate lending and securities operations have led in the past to large profits — and, more recently, large losses. It now appears that the banks will more clearly differentiate themselves and their strategies as they focus on different core businesses.

We have seen a remarkable two decades as the banks acquired and built investment dealers, trust companies, and other financial businesses. Perhaps now the time has come for the more traditional core banking activities to become more visible.

Chapter 2 describes some major participants in the Canadian financial system, and Chapter 3 discusses the forms of institutional protection available to investors and depositors.

PART A

C H A P T E R **2**

Financial Institutions in Canada

Overview

The Canadian financial industry is comprised of a variety of institutions, with the combined book value of assets of almost $1.9 trillion (see Exhibit 1, page 19). They provide a number of different services (as opposed to selling "goods") and play a key role in the Canadian monetary system.

The primary function of financial institutions and intermediaries is to increase the efficiency with which savings are obtained from households, businesses, governments and foreign entities, and transferred to investors (i.e., to increase the flow of funds). Investors, including consumers, businesses, governments and foreign entities, presumably can put the funds to more productive and profitable use than can individuals. Financial institutions assist in increasing the flow of funds in the following ways:

- pooling small sums of funds which can be used for large projects and purchases;
- providing liquidity for investors which increases their propensity to save; and
- diversifying risk of default for investors as funds are invested in a number of investments rather than only a few.

In managing an enterprise's funds, interaction with financial institutions is required. Financial institutions offer a wide variety of techniques for managing funds, from simple deposit and chequing accounts to obtaining funds to start up a new business, to arranging a forward rate agreement to hedge foreign exchange risk arising from international trading activities. Therefore, to most effectively manage an enterprise's resources, it is important to have an understanding of what each type of financial institution does and the regulation to which it is subject.

Characteristics of Financial Institutions

Traditionally, the financial industry has been thought to be comprised of four pillars — banks, trust and mortgage loan companies, insurance companies and investment dealers. This pillar concept developed because government policies historically prohibited cross-ownership of these major types of financial services businesses. Also, government policies previously aimed to restrict foreign control of the financial services industry. The objectives of these policies were to:

- curtail conflicts of interest — for example, preventing a bank from underwriting and selling shares of a company having outstanding bank loans which are considered bad in order to repay the debt;
- prevent significant concentrations of financial power from developing which might strangle economic growth; and
- protect the industry from foreign domination.

Over the past two decades, the concept of the four pillars has become blurred and large banks carry out all four types of business as a result of acquisitions as well as new business development.

Identifying features of financial institutions include the following:

1. **Financial institutions are entrusted with funds from other than shareholders.** For example, banks hold funds from retail, commercial and corporate depositors and other banks; insurance companies receive premiums from policyholders; trust companies receive funds from depositors; and investment companies hold customers' funds and securities. The funds received from the public far exceeds the amount of capital from shareholders.

2. **A significant part of their income is derived from investing those funds.** For example, banks, trust companies and insurance companies make loans to personal, commercial and corporate customers, provinces, municipalities and other banks. They also purchase federal, provincial and corporate bonds, treasury bills, bankers' acceptances, commercial paper, corporate equity securities and real estate. Investment companies earn commission and fee income from investing others' funds as well as the firm's.

3. **Receipt of such funds may be incidental to business or the institution's primary function.** This function is the primary revenue-earning activity for banks; branch operations have historically been the most profitable part of its operations. However, profit from wholesale brokerage business is making up an increasingly large profit percentage. An investment dealer requires a margin deposit as security for trades made as agent for others. However, its primary source of income comes from commissions earned from trading securities on behalf of customers, not from interest earned. On the other hand, the primary business of a credit union is to take deposits from its members and lend this to other members. Its primary source of income comes from the difference between interest earned and interest paid (i.e., spread).

4. **Commitments are important to the institution's financial position.** The large pools of investment-available funds give financial institutions credibility as guarantors of third-party risks through such instruments as bankers' acceptances, stand-by letters of credit and guarantees.

5. **A risk of loss of confidence by contributors of funds (e.g., depositors) exists when funds can be withdrawn on demand or on short notice.** The best illustration of potential results of this concern is the "run" on banks during the 1930s when they did not have sufficient funds. As a result, there is a heightened need for liquidity and to avoid serious net withdrawals of funds.

6. **Financial institutions are subject to a significant amount of government regulation.** Because of the importance of the investment policy of financial institutions and the small margin of safety against loss resulting from their highly-leveraged financial structures, significant government regulation and industry self-regulation under government oversight exists.

EXHIBIT 1

**Combined Balance Sheet of Total Finance and Insurance Industries
(excluding funds and other financial vehicles)
At December 31, 2002**

	$ billions	%
Assets		
Cash and deposits	$31	1.6
Accounts receivable and accrued revenue	40	2.1
Investments and accounts with affiliates	202	10.6
Portfolio investments	471	24.8
Mortgage loans	457	24.0
Non-mortgage loans	491	25.9
Allowance for losses on investments and loans	(23)	(1.2)
Bank customers' liability under acceptances	39	2.0
Capital assets, net	35	1.8
Other	155	8.4
	$1,898	100.0
Liabilities		
Deposits	$937	49.4
Actuarial liabilities of insurers	133	7.0
Accounts payable and accrued liabilities	79	4.2
Loans and accounts with affiliates	62	3.3
Borrowings		
Loans and overdrafts from banks	7	0.4
Loans and overdrafts from others	11	0.6
Bankers' acceptances and paper	20	1.0
Bonds and debentures	63	3.3
Mortgages	2	0.1
Bank customers' liabilities under acceptances	39	2.1
Other	302	15.8
	1,655	87.2
Shareholders' Equity	243	12.8
	$1,898	100.0

Source: Statistics Canada, *Quarterly financial statistics for enterprises*. Fourth quarter 2002, catalogue no. 61-008-X1E.

Financial Services Industry

The various types of financial institutions are discussed below briefly. A later section ("Activities of Banks" on page 48) describes the activities of banks in greater depth.

At December 31, 2002, the industry had total assets of almost $1.9 trillion. (A combined balance sheet for the financial services industry is set out in Exhibit 1 on page 19.)

Banks

Banks are primarily in the business of taking deposits from individual savers under a variety of terms and conditions, and pooling the funds to be lent out to borrowers for a variety of purposes. There are two categories of banks established by the *Bank Act*:

1. **Schedule I banks** are Canadian-owned and widely-held. This group includes RBC Financial Group (generally called Royal Bank of Canada), CIBC (Canadian Imperial Bank of Commerce), BMO Financial Group (Bank of Montreal), Scotiabank (Bank of Nova Scotia), TD Bank Financial Group (Toronto-Dominion Bank), National Bank of Canada and several smaller banks.

   The smaller banks include Laurentian Bank of Canada, Canadian Western Bank and Manulife Bank of Canada. A single investor or an associated group cannot own more than 10 per cent of voting shares.

   Schedule I banks were originally founded by shareholders, and grew through mergers, by re-investing earning as well as by periodic share and debt offerings. Their principal activity is loaning funds to individuals, companies, governments and others at rates higher than rates paid on deposits and other borrowings.

20

2. **Schedule II banks** are foreign-owned and closely-held domestic banks. They are permitted to do the same types of business activities as Schedule I banks. However, they generally concentrate on commercial lending rather than retail banking due to the significant costs involved in establishing a branch network and the very competitive environment. Also, they must obtain approval from the Minister of Finance to open any branches beyond the first. In addition to obtaining deposits from corporations, they issue financial paper in the money market.

   Until January 1, 1995, total non-NAFTA Schedule II banks were limited to 12 per cent of domestic assets in the total banking system. This requirement was repealed and the growth of domestic assets of these banks is no longer restricted by a domestic assets limit.

   The presence of Schedule II banks in Canada has facilitated expansion of Schedule I banks abroad, provided a conduit for investment of foreign capital in Canada, and provided Canadian corporate borrowers with alternative sources of borrowings.

   Schedule II banks had assets of approximately $100 billion at October 31, 2002.

3. **Schedule III banks** are branches of foreign-owned banks. A branch can be either a full-service branch or a lending branch. Full-service branches, designed to accommodate foreign banks that want to carry out a wide range of financial activities in Canada, are subject to a legislative framework designed to minimize risks to the Canadian financial system. Full-service branches have powers similar to those of Canadian banks but are prohibited from taking retail deposits (defined as less than $150,000). Lending branches can provide loans, credit cards and other fee-based financial servic-

21

es, but cannot take deposits or borrow from Canadians other than financial institutions. As well, a lending branch is prohibited from guaranteeing any securities or accepting any bills of exchange that are intended to be sold or traded.

EXHIBIT 2

Key Figures of Selected Banks
Fiscal Years Ended October 31

	Total assets ($ billions)		Net income ($ millions)	
	2002	2001	2002	2001
RBC Financial Group	$377	$360	$2,762	$1,244
CIBC	273	287	653	1,686
BMO Financial Group	252	239	1,417	1,471
Scotiabank	296	284	1,797	2,169
TD Bank Financial Group	278	287	(76)	1,383
National Bank of Canada	75	76	429	563

Source: *Annual Reports*

Trust and mortgage companies

Trust and mortgage companies act as both trustees and financial intermediaries. As financial intermediaries, they offer a broad range of retail financial services, many of which are equivalent to banks' services:

- accepting savings funds, and issuing term deposits and other investment certificates;
- making personal and mortgage loans; and
- selling RRSPs and other tax deferred plans.

However, they are the only corporations permitted to act as trustees in charge of corporate or individual assets such as property and stocks and bonds, which entail fiduciary responsibilities. For example, trust companies frequently are appointed as executors and trustees of estates to administer them in the best interests of the heirs. They also administer charitable trusts and deferred income plans (RRSPs) and act as custodians of mutual funds. Their agency functions include managing and holding securities (custodial services); managing income properties on behalf of owners; arranging stock transfers for companies; acting as trustees of corporate bonds and debentures; and managing corporate pension plans.

Since most trustee funds are held on a medium- to long-term basis, investments tend to be longer term with residential mortgages favoured, though there is now a gradual shift out of residential morgages to portfolio investments. Many of the mortgage loan companies are owned by the large chartered banks.

Most trust companies are now owned by banks.

Insurance companies

Insurance companies act as trustees for policyholder funds. Total assets held by insurance companies at December 31, 2002, were $291 billion. There are two major types of insurance companies:

1. **Life insurance companies** are involved with life, medical and dental, pension and annuity insurance. These companies invest as much as possible in high-yielding, longer-term securities, since most of their insurance contracts run for the lifetime of a person. Therefore, they hold many mortgages and long-term corporate, provincial, federal and municipal bonds.

   During the past three years, several Canadian life insurance companies converted from mutual companies into publicly traded stock companies — a process referred to as "demutualization".

Policyholders of mutual life insurance companies own the company. In converting to a stock company, eligible policyholders became shareholders and the company has greater access to capital markets. Policyholders retain the contractual benefits of their existing policies and have the choice of either holding their shares or selling them on the open market.

2. **Fire/property and casualty insurance companies** are much more interested in safe, short-term securities since they may be called upon to pay out substantial sums at short notice. They protect individuals and businesses from risks relating to fire, accidents, automobile and health concerns. These companies have significantly fewer assets than life insurance companies.

Securities firms

Securities firms are also called investment dealers, stockbrokers, securities dealers, investment or brokerage firms or securities houses. The sharp distinction between these terms, which related to principal and agency activities, has disappeared. Few securities firms act only as principals or agents. However, provincial securities acts designate different levels of securities firms, each having different business powers and responsibilities.

If securities firms act as **principal**, they own securities at some point in the buying and selling transaction with investors. The profit is the difference between buying and selling prices. Firms commonly **underwrite** securities issues — most new securities issues are sold this way. The dealer acts as principal, using its own capital to buy the issue; therefore, the firm accepts market risk that prices will drop by the time of sale. However, the issuer assumes no responsibility since payment is guaranteed by the underwriter. Dealers minimize their risk from underwriting issues by:

- working closely with securities issuers to ensure the issue will be desirable to investors (key factors of the issue affecting marketability of securities include pricing and timing);
- inviting other dealers to co-underwrite a new issue; and
- having special clauses in the issue agreement permitting termination of the agreement under exceptional circumstances.

Dealers also act as principals in secondary markets by selling previously issued and outstanding securities. The dealer buys securities in the open market, maintains them as inventory, and then sells them. This gives dealers increased knowledge about secondary market conditions for advising investing clients. It also increases liquidity in the market and the speed of a firm's response to a client's buy or sell order.

A broker, as **agent,** acts for or on behalf of a buyer or seller without taking possession. The broker's gross profit is the commission charged.

Some securities issues, especially of unknown companies or highly speculative securities, may be placed on a **best efforts basis.** The dealer tries to sell as many securities as possible but does not take ownership; any unsold securities are returned to the issuer. Agency agreements are also common when a large issuer with a very good credit rating issues new securities. Since the dealer would not incur much risk, if any, the firm prefers the dealer to act as agent.

Securities firms are financed by original capital contributed by owners/shareholders and retained earnings. Most firms are incorporated as private companies with ownership of shares restricted to officers, directors and employees. However, the need for an increased capital base resulted in many securities firms going public in the 1980s, generally issuing shares restricted with voting rights, as well as many firms being subsequently acquired by large banks. Securities firms are highly leveraged, as they depend on borrowed funds to finance securities inventories, underwritten deals, trading commitments and client margin accounts.

The development of **discount brokers** has its roots in 1983 when fixed commission rates were eliminated and replaced by negotiated commissions on most trades at all Canadian exchanges. A discount broker does not advise clients, but acts as an order taker, to buy or sell, only. While discount brokers do not advise clients, up until 2000 they were required to review all client trades before the orders were forwarded to the appropriate exchange for "suitability". The purpose of the "suitability review" was to determine whether an order matched the client's stated investment objectives, including tolerance for risk. In 2000, securities legislation was amended to permit securities firms that do not offer advice to process orders without reviewing trades for suitability. This makes it possible to execute the trades in a more timely fashion. Most large banks provide a discount brokerage service.

Sales finance and consumer loan companies

Sales finance and consumer loan companies make direct cash loans to consumers who repay principal and interest in instalments. They also purchase, at a discount, instalment sales contracts from retailers and dealers when "big-ticket" items such as cars and appliances are bought on instalment plans by consumers.

Credit unions and caisses populaires

Credit unions and caisses populaires were originally formed to provide financial services to individuals with some personal or professional bond (i.e., individuals residing in the same community or belonging to the same profession), as chartered banks were seen to be too profit-oriented.

Pension funds

The assets of trusteed pension funds represent one of the largest pools of capital in Canada, second only to the financial assets of chartered banks. These funds hold 86 per cent of the assets of all registered pension plans.

Pension funds have experienced significant growth over the past 45 years due to longer life expectancy, earlier retirement, desire for financial independence during retirement, the view that the Canada Pension Plan and the Quebec Pension Plan (CPP/QPP) are inadequate, and tax laws permitting deferral of pension premiums paid by employers and self-employed individuals. Although assets were largely concentrated in high-quality debt and equity investments in the past, portfolios are now becoming more diversified, and include real estate and a broad range of securities, including some venture capital.

There are two major types of pension funds:

1. **Trusteed pension plans** which are offered to employees of corporations and organizations. Pension contributions normally are made by both employee and employer to a trustee, which may be a committee of the company or government body or, more commonly, an independent trust or life insurance company. The trustee is principally concerned with safety of principal and income.

   Since earnings of these plans are non-taxable, they tend to be large buyers of high yielding government and corporate debt and residential mortgages. Also, longer-term investments are sought because of the long-term nature of pension benefits.

2. **Government-operated plans** include the federally run Canada Pension Plan (CPP) and Old Age Security, and provincially run programs such as the Quebec Pension Plan

(QPP). These programs provide minimum retirement, old age, disability, death, widows' and orphans' benefits.

Investment funds

Investment funds are companies or trusts which sell their shares to the public and invest proceeds in a diverse securities portfolio. The funds employ professional money managers to administer the portfolio. The benefits of such an arrangement for the small investor include the ability to diversify by participation in a large and well-balanced portfolio, while having the services of professional money management.

There are two types of investment funds:

1. **Closed-end funds** which issue shares only at the beginning of the fund's life or, infrequently, at other times.

2. **Open-end or mutual funds** which issue shares to investors on an ongoing basis and redeem shares on demand. The asset base of these funds is significantly higher than that of closed-end funds, by a factor of more than 25 to 1.

Venture capital companies

Venture capital companies provide seed money for promising new enterprises. There are private and government agencies operating as venture capital companies. The largest public venture capital entity is the *Business Development Bank of Canada*, which is a Crown corporation responsible to the Ministry of Industry. It provides term loans to businesses, particularly smaller ones, which cannot secure funds on reasonable terms and conditions from other lenders. The BDC began operations in 1975 and its objectives are to assist in the development of Canadian business enterprises. It provides debt or equity financing as well as management assistance. The Business Development Bank of Canada (BDC) currently manages over $350 million in venture capital assets. Initial investments in "seed" stage companies range from $100,000 to $750,000 while investments in more advanced stages range between $500,000 and $5 million, with the average transaction between $1.5 million and $2 million. The Web site for the BDC is *www.bdc.ca*. Many provinces have established similar agencies.

Mortgage investment companies

Mortgage investment companies are established to raise large pools of mortgage capital. They offer reasonably safe investments, tax advantages and liquidity.

Banks

Regulators of banks include the following:

Office of the Superintendent of Financial Institutions (OSFI), which was created after a Commission of Inquiry into the failures of two Alberta banks in 1985 (the Canadian Commercial Bank and the Northland Bank), concluded that the system of bank supervision was not flawed but should have increased powers. It was established in 1987 and brought together the Department of Insurance and the Office of the Inspector of Banks. OSFI's legislation provides for a single regulatory agency responsible for regulating and supervising all federally chartered, licensed or registered banks, insurance, trust, loan and investment companies, cooperative credit associations and fraternal benefit societies with a view to maintaining public confidence in the Canadian financial system. OSFI also monitors federally regulated pension plans and provides actuarial advice to the Government of Canada. The supervisory activities of OSFI are conducted on a cost-recovery basis.

OSFI administers the following federal statutes, the *Bank Act, Insurance Companies Act, Trust and Loan Companies Act, Cooperative Credit Associations Act, Pension Benefits Standards Act, 1985* and it has obligation under the *Public Pensions Reporting Act* and the *Canada Pension Plan Act.*

Specific responsibilities applicable to banks include:

- Reviewing and licensing new bank charters;
- Monitoring issuance of bank securities;
- Annually examining each bank to assess its financial condition and adherence to the *Bank Act.* In August 1999, OSFI issued its revised *Supervisory Framework.* A cornerstone of the revised methodology is an evaluation of inherent risks associated with an institution's significant activities and the quality of the risk mitigation for those activities. This assessment will allow OSFI to use the work of an institution's internal management and control functions to focus OSFI's resources on activities that are likely to materially affect the risk profile of the institution. High-risk areas are subject to in-depth reviews periodically with an appropriate level of technical expertise;
- Issuing guidelines (with considerable consultation from the financial institutions). Recent guidelines have included such topics as credit derivatives, use of financial instruments, and capital adequacy.

OSFI's Web site is *www.osfi-bsif.gc.ca.*

Canada Deposit Insurance Corporation (CDIC) is responsible to Parliament, reports through the Minister of Finance and acts as an agent of the federal government. The original rationale for having deposit insurance was to ensure that the public could have as much confidence in a Canadian dollar on deposit in a bank or trust company as in a dollar under a mattress. CDIC was established in 1967 to restore confidence in the financial system after the failure of a major finance company.

Its objectives include the following:

- Ensuring the *safety of deposits made by small investors*. This is CDIC's primary objective. It insures Canadian deposits in 81 approved financial institutions (banks, federally incorporated trust and mortgage loan companies, and provincially incorporated financial institutions that choose to become members) up to $60,000 per depositor at one institution. (Refer to Chapter 3, "Investor and Depositor Protection".) At April 30, 2002, CDIC insured $347 billion of deposits held by Canadian deposit-taking institutions.
- Acting as a *lender of last resort* for financial institutions.
- Striving to *improve minimum financial standards of Canadian deposit-taking institutions to reduce failures*. The CDIC Act empowers its Board of Directors to set by-laws prescribing standards for member institutions. In this regard, CDIC developed, and made into law in 1993, eight *Standards of Sound Business and Financial Practices* (Standards) to reinforce the safety and soundness of deposit-taking institutions as follows: Credit Risk Management; Liquidity Management; Securities Portfolio Management; Real Estate Appraisals; Interest Rate Risk Management; Foreign Exchange Risk Management; Internal Controls; and Capital Management.

The Standards Assessment and Reporting Program (SARP) was subsequently developed in 1994. Under the provisions of SARP, CDIC members are required to report their compliance with the Standards as at April 30 of each year and to file their reports with CDIC and their primary regulator by July 31. Federal and provincial examiners review the self-assessments as part of their regular examination process and report to CDIC on member compliance.

In September 2000, CDIC released a consultation paper proposing an updating of the expectations of member institutions regarding the standards and the SARP process. The goal is to streamline the SARP process notably by eliminating most of the previous documentation requirements.

Differential premiums came into force in March 1999. Member institutions are "scored" according to a variety of quantitative and qualitative criteria including capital adequacy, profitability, income volatility, asset concentration and adherence to the CDIC standards. Depending on their score, members are placed in one of four premium categories: category 1 is the highest-rated (best); category 4 is the lowest-rated (worst). For the 2001 premium year, 67 per cent of member institutions ranked in the highest premium category. Ninety per cent were placed in categories 1 and 2.

In October 1999 CDIC implemented the "Opting-out by-laws" that permit banks that primarily accept wholesale deposits (defined as $150,00 or more) to operate without deposit insurance.

CDIC's Web site is *www.cdic.ca.*

The **Bank of Canada** is a Crown corporation with duties to regulate credit and currency in the best interests of the Canadian economy; control and protect the external value of the Canadian dollar; mitigate fluctuations in the general level of production, trade, prices and employment; and promote the economic and financial welfare of Canada. The Bank of Canada acts as the government's fiscal agent as well and, most importantly, manages Canada's money supply.

The Bank of Canada's Web site is *www.bank-banque-canada.ca*.

Financial Institutions Supervisory Committee (FISC) was established by the federal government and consists of the Superintendent, Governor of the Bank of Canada, Chairman of the CDIC and Deputy Minister of Finance. The purpose of this committee is to ensure effective and confidential exchanges of information among members so that all are current on matters related to supervising financial institutions. The committee focuses its attention on remedying solvency issues faced by financial institutions.

The Department of Finance's Web site is *www.fin.gc.ca*.

Sources of regulation include the following:

1. *Bank Act* (Act) — Regularly updated, with 2006 as the next target date for revision, governs all activities of banks including incorporation, corporate structure, reserve requirements, powers, disclosure requirements, supervision and winding-up of operations.

   Some important regulations under the Act are as follows:

   (a) *Ownership* — Currently, banks with capital to $750 million may be wholly-owned; exceeding that level, 35 per cent of their shares must be widely-held. No investor can own more than 10 per cent of any class of shares of Schedule I banks. Any "fit and proper" shareholder can have significant interest in a Schedule II bank for the first 10 years of its existence; thereafter, a maximum of 10 per cent of shares can be held and it would become a

Schedule I bank. With Ministerial approval, a widely-held financial institution other than a bank can own more than 10 per cent of Schedule II banks beyond 10 years if it owns more than 50 per cent of the shares and can elect the majority of the Board of Directors. Also, a foreign bank or widely-held foreign institution may own more than 10 per cent, if it meets certain criteria, and owns more than 50 per cent of the Schedule II bank's shares and can elect a majority of the Board of Directors. However, ministerial approval of acquisitions and significant increases in classes of Schedule II bank shares is required.

(b) *Business and Powers* — There is no definition of banking in the Act. The 1991 Act expanded activities in which banks can be involved. For example, investment counselling advice and portfolio management services can be offered. Banks can also network financial services offered by affiliates and subsidiaries, act as custodians of property, promote merchandise and services to holders of any credit card issued by the bank, act as receiver or liquidator, and enter directly into leasing activities (except automobile leasing).

(c) *Investments* — Generally, banks cannot have substantial investment in any enterprise (greater than 10 per cent of the voting rights or more than 25 per cent of shareholders' equity). Exceptions include substantial investments in companies which provide financial services and substantial investments acquired through realizations or loan workouts, or temporary investments. Banks may also, under certain circumstances, hold investments in companies in specified industries such as financial institutions, leasing (except car leasing), factoring, investment counselling and portfolio management, mutual fund distribution, merchant banking and real property.

2. *CDIC Act* — CDIC, under its Act, is accountable to Parliament and ultimately to the public.

3. *Interest Act* — Requires certain disclosures for customers, such as the borrowing cost of a loan, circumstances surrounding any prepayment right, and penalties from not repaying the loan on the due date.

4. *Bank for International Settlements (BIS) capital guidelines* — These guidelines are the basis for the OSFI capital guidelines. In July 1988, BIS's Committee on Banking Regulation and Supervisory Practices issued a paper setting out details of an agreed framework for measuring capital adequacy and the minimum capital standard. The Committee comprises representatives from the central banks and supervisory authorities of 12 major countries: Belgium, Canada, France, Germany, Italy, Japan, Netherlands, Sweden, Switzerland, United Kingdom, U.S.A. and Luxembourg.

In January 2001, the BIS released a new framework for measuring capital. The new framework better reflects a bank's risks, takes into account financial innovations that have occurred since implementation of the original framework, recognizes improvements in risk measurement and control, covers more of the risks that a bank is exposed to, and puts more emphasis on market discipline. It is estimated that this new framework will be implemented in 2004.

5. *Proceeds of Crime (Money Laundering) Act* — Bill C-22, which became law in June 2000, creates a centralized reporting agency, the Financial Transactions Reporting and Analysis Centre of Canada (FTRAC), to help deal with money laundering. With forthcoming regulations, the federal government will mandate the reporting of "suspicious transactions"

and the definition and reporting of a series of "prescribed" transactions, including large cost transactions, wire transfers and cross-border reporting, which are sometimes linked with money laundering. This bill replaces the former *Proceeds of Crime (Money Laundering) Act*, but will be known by the same name.

6. *Provincial securities acts* — Publicly traded companies must provide an annual management's discussion and analysis (MD&A) of financial condition and results of operations. These rules require disclosures about financial instruments; information must be provided about the nature and magnitude of financial instruments and their effect on the issuer's liquidity, capital resources and results of operations.

7. *Regulations of other countries* — Many financial institutions, particularly the large domestic banks, have extensive international operations, with many offices or branches in a number of different countries.

8. *Competition Act* — Applies to all takeovers and mergers of federal financial institutions.

9. *Numerous other acts* — Includes *Bills of Exchange Act*, *Canada Business Corporations Act*, *Income Tax Act* and environmental legislation.

Regulation of trust and loan companies

Regulators of trust and loan companies include the same as those involved with banks as well as provincial ministries which regulate provincially incorporated trust and loan companies.

Sources of regulation include:

1. *Federal Trust and Loans Companies Act* — Some important features of the Act include the following:

(a) Trust companies have full consumer lending powers. If the institution has capital of at least $25 million and obtains approval, it has full commercial lending powers; otherwise, commercial loans cannot exceed 5 per cent of assets.

(b) Extensive disclosure of service charges, borrowing costs and fees charged to consumers is required.

(c) Thirty-five per cent of voting shares must be widely-held for companies having more than $750 million of capital. (Legislation that was tabled in June 2000 contained an amendment that increased the capital requirement to one billion. It is largely expected that this bill will be re-tabled early in 2001.)

(d) Investment in mortgages cannot exceed a loan-to-appraised value ratio of 75 per cent unless insured by Canada Mortgage and Housing Corporation (CMHC) or a private mortgage company.

2. *Federal and provincial trustee acts* — Specify investments that can be made. This legislation is designed to protect guaranteed funds obtained from investors. Generally, investments are limited to first mortgages; federal, provincial and municipal bonds; and stocks and bonds of profitable Canadian corporations. Trustees must keep funds fully working and cannot keep them uninvested for long. Also, funds must be managed in a prudent manner, considering circumstances and interests of all beneficiaries.

3. *Provincial companies acts* (as some trust and mortgage loan companies are provincially incorporated).

4. *Various regulations* — Also cover banks including regulations passed by Parliament, OSFI guidelines, *CDIC Act*, provincial securities acts, *Competition Act*, *Bills of Exchange Act*, *Canada Business Corporations Act* (for federally incorporated compa-

nies), *Interest Act, Income Tax Act, Personal Information Protection and Electronic Documents Act* and environmental legislation.

Regulation of insurance companies

Regulators of insurance companies include the following:

1. Parliament and Minister of Finance for federal legislation; **provincial regulators** are in place for provincially incorporated insurance companies.

2. **OSFI** regulates insurance companies incorporated under the *Insurance Companies Act*. Of the approximately 180 life insurance companies, 135 are registered under federal laws.

3. **Financial Institutions Supervisory Committee** (as described under **Banks**).

    Sources of regulation include:

1. *Insurance Companies Act* **and Regulations under this Act**, which relates to insurance companies incorporated under this Act. Life insurance and property and casualty insurance business must be carried out in separate companies. The Act covers most aspects of insurers' operations such as incorporation; organizational matters relating to, for example, shares, dividends, directors, policyholders and the financial statements; rules regarding appointment of auditors, and winding-up and dissolution. In addition to requiring that investments be made in accordance with prudent portfolio principles, it restricts investments.

2. *Provincial companies acts* for provincially incorporated insurance companies.

3. *Various provincial acts* contain some rules covering federally incorporated insurance companies such as premium payments,

reinstatement, beneficiaries, proof of claim, how premium taxes are payable to the provinces.

4. *Other regulations such as the Competition Act*, the *Canada Business Corporations Act* (for federally incorporated insurance companies), the *Interest Act*, the *Income Tax Act*, provincial securities acts and environmental legislation.

Regulation of securities and investment dealers

Regulators of securities and investment dealers include the following:

1. **Provincial ministries**.

2. **Provincial securities commissions**, such as the Ontario Securities Commission. Regulation of securities and investment dealers is under provincial jurisdiction, although consideration in the past has been given to having this come under federal jurisdiction.

   Indeed, in December 1998, the Chair of the Ontario Securities Commission proposed a restructuring of the Regulatory Framework indicating that the blurring of the traditional distinctions between markets and intermediaries points to the need for more comparable regulatory treatment of similar market services and products, regardless of the way in which those products and services are packaged or the nature of the institution offering them.

   The proposal indicated that a more efficient regulatory framework for the financial industry will be achieved by dividing the responsibilities for supervision of the Canadian market along two lines — prudential regulation and market regulation. Such a framework would recognize and rely on the regulatory expertise and cultures of regulation that presently exist in the Canadian system.

PART A

Under such a concept, responsibility for prudential regulation of financial institutions that might pose a systemic risk to Canadian markets could be consolidated into a single regulatory body, such as OSFI. This agency would be responsible for setting appropriate standards and supervising the solvency of banks, insurance companies, trust and loan companies, and all other similar financial institutions. Market regulation would be assumed by an organization that would be responsible for oversight of market conduct, integrity of markets and consumer protection, with respect to financial services offered by all market participants, including banks, trust companies, insurers, investment dealers and pension funds.

The market regulatory organization would take a functional approach to the regulation of financial markets and products. This type of approach considers the economic functions served by financial markets and instruments and searches for the best regulatory structure to facilitate the performance of those functions. This would be achieved by focusing on activities rather than particular instruments or the nature of institutions which engage in the activities. Functionally equivalent or similar products should be afforded similar regulatory treatment.

Market regulation is essentially what securities regulators do. Through the Canadian Securities Association (CSA), provincial securities commissions in Canada have created a virtual National Securities Commission which administers a harmonized body of securities laws, which we have dubbed the "Canadian Securities Regulatory System". Under a new regulatory framework, the CSA would be the logical choice to be vested with responsibility for regulating the market activities of all financial institutions. Furthermore, within each province, existing regulators with responsibility for market integrity and consumer protection of provincial institutions (such as provincially incorporated trust and insurance compa-

nies) could either be consolidated with the securities regulator or remain separate with a coordinated approach to their
regulatory mandates.

For many reasons, little progress has been made since this proposal was made. However, the OSC believes that it is time for
tackling these questions.

Following are the Web sites of the provincial securities commissions:

Alberta Securities Commission
www.albertasecurities.com

British Columbia Securities Commission
www.bcsc.bc.ca

Manitoba Securities Commission
www.msc.gov.mb.ca

Newfoundland and Labrador Securities Division
www.gov.nf.ca/gsl/cca/s/about.stm

Nova Scotia Securities Commission
www.gov.ns.ca/bacs/acns/paal/ndxsecc.htm

Ontario Securities Commission
www.osc.gov.on.ca

Prince Edward Island
www.gov.pe.ca/caag/concorp

Quebec Securities Commission
www.cvmq.com/index_en.asp

3. **Self-regulatory organizations (SROs)**. The authority to regulate securities and investment dealers is delegated by securities administrators to SROs, which include the various
Canadian stock exchanges (Toronto Stock Exchange, TSX
Venture Exchange, Montreal Exchange) and the Investment

Dealers' Association (IDA). SROs are directly responsible for industry conformity with securities legislation and have powers to establish and enforce industry regulations to protect investors and to maintain fair, equitable and ethical practices.

The Mutual Fund Dealers Association (MFDA) was established in 2001 as a SRO to regulate distributors of mutual funds. In late 2002 it established an investor complaint service that can be contacted at (888) 466-MFDA (6332), or through its Web site at *www.mfda.ca*. The MFDA is in the process of setting up an investor protection fund.

Following are the Web sites of various Canadian stock exchanges:

Toronto Stock Exchange and TSX Venture Exchange
www.tse.com

Montreal Exchange
www.me.org

Winnipeg Stock Exchange
www.wse.ca/start

Sources of regulation include:

1. **Provincial securities acts** regulate the underwriting, distribution and sale of securities, and protect buyers and sellers of securities. Their underlying general principle is full, true and plain disclosure of all relevant facts by issuers, and they are designed to prevent fraud and deceit and to protect the investor from his or her own naiveté as much as possible. Examples of requirements under these acts are that anyone or any firm engaged in direct selling of securities to the public must register and meet certain requirements, such as minimum educational standards. There are different levels of registration for securities firms involved in different activities. For example, a **broker** can give advice and manage money; an **invest-**

ment dealer can give advice, manage money, and manage and sell mutual funds; **portfolio managers** can manage money; and **securities dealers** can only buy and sell securities and cannot manage money.

2. **National Policies** issued by administrators of all provincial acts. Examples of such policies issued to date relate to conflict of interest, the permitted use of derivatives by mutual funds, the investing in mortgages by mutual funds, simplified prospectus qualification, take-over bids, timely disclosure, advertising of securities on radio and television, violations of securities laws of other jurisdictions, and clearance of prospectuses nationally.

3. **Uniform Policies** which were adopted by securities administrators in Ontario, Manitoba, Alberta, Saskatchewan and British Columbia.

4. **Provincial Policies** which are applicable only in the relevant provinces.

5. **SRO Rules**.

6. **Other regulations** such as provincial securities acts, *Competition Act* and the *Income Tax Act*.

Pension funds

Private pension funds must comply with the *Insurance Companies Act* and provincial pension benefits acts (if provincially incorporated) or the federal *Pension Benefits Standards Act, 1985*, in addition to the *Income Tax Act, Canada Business Corporations Act* (if federally incorporated) or provincial companies acts. The *Income Tax Act* restricts the investments and loans the fund can make. *The Pension Benefits Standards Act, 1985*, covers such items as registration of the fund, taxation and the permissible investment policy.

Canadian Banking System

Since banks are the most commonly dealt with financial institution, the remainder of this chapter addresses the details of the Canadian banking system and the activities of banks.

Apart from the chartered banks, the key players in the Canadian banking system are as follows:

1. *Government of Canada* (Parliament and the Minister of Finance), whose legislative powers cover matters dealing with trade and commerce outside provincial boundaries, as well as currency and interest. It gives the *Bank Act* legal force.

   The Web site for the Government of Canada is *www.canada.gc.ca*.

2. *Department of Finance* and its head, the *Minister of Finance*, are responsible for the financial administration of Canada. One of its prime purposes is to advise the government on the country's economic and financial affairs. The Department's work is divided into nine branches. The Financial Sector Policy branch is responsible for policy analysis and advice regarding Canada's financial sector and the regulation of federally-chartered financial institutions. The Economic and Fiscal Policy branch is responsible for fiscal planning and forecasting the government's financial position and requirements.

   The Web site for the Department of Finance is *www.fin.gc.ca*.

3. *The Bank of Canada* (the Bank) is responsible to Parliament and reports through the Minister of Finance. The Bank is owned by the Government of Canada — its shares are issued in the name of the Minister. It is not a commercial bank and does not carry out ordinary banking business. It is theoretically autonomous of the government, but in reality, its policies

reflect those of the federal government. The Minister may direct it to follow government policy; however, such a directive has never been issued.

The Bank's activities are governed by the *Bank of Canada Act*. It has two main functions:

(a) To act as the government's fiscal agent, which entails the following activities:

- advising on financial matters;
- administering government deposit accounts and funds. All cheques written by the government and all receipts flow through these accounts;
- issuing and removing coin and currency;
- managing Canada's international currency;
- acting as a depository for gold; and
- acting as debt manager by issuing new government securities such as treasury bills, marketable bonds and Canada Savings Bonds, paying interest and redeeming securities at maturity.

(b) To conduct monetary policy to ensure sustained economic growth, high levels of employment and efficiency and stable currency and exchange rates. This is the Bank's most important role. In this regard, its prime function is to regulate credit and the money supply. It also controls and protects the external value of the dollar; mitigates fluctuations in the general level of production, trade, prices and employment; and promotes the economic and financial welfare of the country.

The Bank tries to achieve its objectives using the following methods:

- open market operations — selling and buying Government of Canada securities;
- draw-downs and re-deposits of the government's cash balances at chartered banks;
- changing the bank rate; and
- moral suasion on financial institutions to change their credit policies.

The Bank of Canada also acts as the bankers' bank, performing a key role in clearing banking transactions through deposit accounts maintained by banks and as a member of the Canadian Payments Association (see below). In addition, it acts as "lender of last resort" for banks.

4. *Canadian Payments Association* (CPA) was established under the *Canadian Payments Association Act* of 1980. It is a non-profit association of 126 deposit-taking institutions. Its objectives are to establish and operate a national clearings and settlements system, and to improve the national payments system. Basically, it is a means of settling accounts among the banks, the Bank of Canada and other members. All inter-bank cheques are cleared and processed through this system.

The Large Value Transfer System or LVTS enables individuals, businesses and governments to make final payments in a rapid, secure and efficient manner. LVTS incorporates real-time risk controls to ensure certainty of settlement of all transactions accepted by the system.

The LVTS significantly reduces the risk associated with making large-value Canadian dollar payments and should enhance the international reputation, the competitiveness and the stability of Canada's financial system. Payments over $25 million may only be made through the LVTS.

LVTS can transfer Canadian dollar payments between LVTS participants anywhere in Canada, in a matter of seconds. Because the financial institutions participating in LVTS are subject to risk controls, including the pledging of collateral to the Bank of Canada, the system provides these participants with certainty of settlement for every payment received. As a result, LVTS payments are final and irreversible. Once an LVTS payment reaches a customer's account, the customer can immediately withdraw, invest or forward the funds to another recipient. This is especially important to both the participants and their clients when the amount of the payment is substantial or when timing is important. Moreover, because of the real-time risk controls and certainty of settlement on a same-day basis, LVTS will greatly reduce systemic-risk — the risk that the failure of one financial institution to meet its payment obligations will cause one or more other financial institutions to fail. The LVTS, therefore, makes a significant contribution to the stability of the Canadian financial system.

All chartered banks must become members of the CPA; other deposit-taking institutions have the option of doing so. Members can either be directly involved in the clearing and settlement process or retain another member to represent them. Current membership categories include "banks", which account for more than 75 per cent of payments processed; "centrals", which are credit unions and caisses populaires; and "trust, loan and other financial institutions".

The Canadian Payments Association Web site is *www.cdnpay.ca.*

5. *Canada Deposit Insurance Corporation* (discussed in Regulatory Environment and Chapter 3, "Investor and Depositor Protection").

The Canada Deposit Insurance Corporation Web site is *www.cdic.ca*.

6. *Canadian Bankers' Association* (CBA) exists to support the aims of banks in all aspects of banking. It publishes the *Canadian Banker* periodical as well as position papers, and attends meetings to further its members' interests. The Association has a number of committees which address various current issues in banking, such as in legal, tax, government relations and credit areas. It collects and publishes market share information for its members. The Association also has an educational arm — the Institute of Canadian Bankers.

The Canadian Bankers' Association Web site is *www.cba.ca*.

Activities of Banks

Under the *Bank Act*, a bank cannot engage in any business that does not generally pertain to the business of banking; however, the Act does not define "banking". Other activities may also be carried out through wholly-owned subsidiaries.

Typical banking activities are set out below:

Deposit-taking

Deposit-taking is the core activity for many banks. Banks can offer a variety of term and deposit accounts and sell tax deferred savings plans. However, a bank must be a member of CDIC before it can take deposits.

Customers deposit funds with banks, sometimes on an interest-free basis, because banks provide safe custody of funds and other services such as free cheque-writing.

Lending

The *Bank Act* permits banks to lend with or without security and to charge the interest rate they choose. However, the cost of borrowing must be disclosed to the borrower as well as circumstances surrounding any prepayment right and late payment penalties. Banks may lend funds taking security against the following types of assets:

1. **Real estate.** A maximum of 75 per cent of the value of the property can be lent unless the mortgage is guaranteed/insured by Canada Mortgage and Housing Corporation (CMHC) or other appropriate insurer. In that case, up to 95 per cent can be lent.

2. **Conditional sales contracts — trade and other receivables.** The portion of the face value of receivables that a bank will lend depends on a number of factors, such as the type of receivables, strength of the borrower and economic conditions. However, banks generally lend approximately 75 per cent.

3. **Conditional sales contracts — inventory and equipment.** Banks can take inventory and equipment as collateral for advances and bankers' acceptances (BAs). Inventory and equipment taken as security can be of many types, banks' concerns being the constancy of market values and the saleability of the items. The portion of the stated value of the assets that a bank will lend depends on factors similar to those considered for accounts receivable. Banks generally lend 50 per cent of the value of inventory and 75 per cent of the value of equipment.

Investments

Except for specified types of companies and in certain circumstances, banks cannot own more than 10 per cent of a Canadian corporation. These exceptions include all types of financial institutions; factoring companies; financial leasing companies except car and personal household property leasing; information services companies; investment counselling and portfolio management companies; mutual fund distribution companies; real property brokerage companies; real property companies; and service companies. For some types of companies, a bank must control the enterprise. Also, acquisitions of companies as temporary investments or through security realization or loan workouts are exempted.

Real estate

Banks can acquire land and develop real estate as principal. Interest in real estate generally cannot exceed 70 per cent of the bank's regulatory capital. However, there are no restrictions on real estate acquired from taking security under a loan agreement or acquired as part of a workout. Banks also can own up to 100 per cent of a real property company. Land may be held for resale when it was acquired through disposition of a loan.

Dealing in securities

A bank can engage in the following securities-related activities:

- As *principal*, buy and sell bonds, debentures and other indebtedness of the bank (subject to prospectus requirements);
- *Underwrite debt and equity securities* (acting as agent) of another corporation, but only as a member of a selling group. However, a bank cannot underwrite securities as

principal in Canada. Exceptions to this general rule include certain government debt obligations, money market securities, and debt obligations of the bank or an affiliate. To overcome this limitation, banks have established separate subsidiaries for underwriting debt and equity securities as principal;

- Act as *agent* for certain mutual funds;
- Issue its own equity (subject to prospectus requirements) to raise capital;
- Offer *fiduciary services and other fee-generating activities*, including investment management, asset custody, business advisory services and private banking. However, a bank cannot directly act as a trustee; instead, it may own a trust company.
- Effect *private placements*; and
- *Purchase and sell certain securities* for other than the bank's own investment portfolio (i.e., speculative activity). Trading activities include money market (e.g., treasury bills, BAs, commercial paper (CP), government bonds), fixed income (e.g., bonds and debentures), capital market (e.g., forward rate agreements, interest rate swaps, interest rate options) and foreign exchange (e.g., currency, bullion). Banks cannot trade equities on the secondary market in Canada; therefore, banks own separate subsidiaries to undertake these activities.

Money market activity

Because the funds raised from customer deposits do not usually precisely match the loans made, either in maturity or size, the money market or treasury function is an important link to the bank's other activities. Surplus funds are invested, or funds are borrowed to make good any shortfall, on an overnight basis, and the overall liquidity and interest rate exposure of the bank is managed. This involves trading on money markets, taking or placing time deposits from or with other banks and major corporations. The purpose is to provide funds for the bank, enhance the market's long-term confidence in its liquidity and make a profit from the "interest turn" — the difference between borrowing and lending rates.

- **Trading and investing** — As part of their financing of international trade, banks exchange foreign currencies for customers. As a result, banks have developed extensive foreign currency trading activities, which not only involve customers, but include the large inter-bank market dealing in spot and forward currency transactions. Foreign exchange activities have resulted in the development of other closely related trading activities, such as futures, swaps and options — "derivative financial instruments". Banks also trade and invest money market instruments such as treasury bills, short-term bonds, commercial paper (CP) and BAs.
- **Brokerage** — Banks and other non-registrants are not allowed to directly own a stock exchange seat or provide many securities services. Banks are, however, permitted to own 100 per cent of a securities dealer.

Money transfer

All banking activities involve the need for money to be transferred. For deposits made by customers or cheques drawn by them in Canada, each branch collects its individual receipts and payments daily, which are processed through a central territorial clearing system by the head office of the bank in that territory. The net balance between each bank for the day is then cleared through accounts with the local central bank or a major domestic bank — the Canadian Payments Association controls this. For international customer transactions, these often have to be cleared on an item-by-item basis. For wholesale domestic activities such as money market or foreign exchange and large loans, a money transfer system is used which generally increases or decreases the bank's account with Bank of Canada. For international movements of funds, the transactions are usually processed to the bank's nostro accounts (foreign currency accounts held by a bank in the country of the foreign exchange).

Other activities

Banks can provide **information processing** services inside and outside Canada, such as payroll processing; provide services related to the design, development and implementation of management systems; and design, develop and market computer software (and special purpose computer hardware). In Canada, these activities generally have to be carried out through a subsidiary. Banks can also **issue letters of credit and guarantees/acceptances**. The guaranteed person or enterprise must have a complete obligation to reimburse the bank for the entire amount of the guarantee if the bank must make payments on guarantees it issued. Banks can also issue **credit and debit cards**. The bank must disclose the credit cardholder's cost of borrowing, all charges and penalties, and the rights and obligations of the cardholder. Banks are also authorized to promote their services to the holders of any of the bank's payment, credit or charge cards and are also authorized to sell lottery tickets on a non-profit basis, as well as transit tickets.

The following activities are specifically disallowed:

- selling goods, or engaging in any trade or business; and
- entering a partnership.

PART A

CHAPTER 3

Investor and Depositor Protection

Overview

With the uncertainty in the global economy and the past failures in financial institutions in Canada, it is important for the financial manager to be aware not only of the risks associated with different institutions and investment vehicles, but also of the protection available in the event of failure of a financial institution.

Deposit Insurance

The Canada Deposit Insurance Corporation (CDIC) is a federal Crown corporation which was created in 1967 to provide insurance against the loss of part or all of deposits made with member finan-

cial institutions in order to restore confidence in the financial system after the failure of a major finance company.

Member financial institutions display a sign at each at each
branch or office. If you are unsure as to the insurability of a deposit,
ask.

Insurance provided by CDIC

Insurable deposits include:
- savings and chequing accounts;
- term deposits such as guaranteed investment certificates
  (GICs) and debentures issued by loan companies;
- money orders;
- drafts;
- certified drafts and cheques; and
- traveller's cheques issued by members.

To be eligible for deposit insurance protection, a deposit must be
payable in Canada, in Canadian currency and must also have a
term to maturity of no more than five years.

Deposits and investments offered by deposit-taking institutions
that are not insurable include:

- foreign currency deposits (savings accounts, chequing
  accounts and term deposits);
- term deposits that are locked in longer than five years;
- debentures issued by a chartered bank;
- bonds and debentures issued by governments and corporations;
- treasury bills; and
- investments in mortgages, stocks and mutual funds.

Maximum protection

The maximum *basic* protection is $60,000 — *this is principal and interest combined.* The $60,000 maximum applies to **all** of the insurable deposits with the same member financial institution. Deposits are not insured separately in each branch office of a financial institution. (For example, the maximum insurance protection for three separate savings accounts held by the same person at three different branches of the Royal Bank of Canada, each with a deposit balance of $60,000, is $60,000 — not $180,000.)

CDIC also provides separate protection for:

- joint deposits;
- trust deposits; and
- deposits held in RRSPs and RRIFs.

For example, the maximum insurance protection for a deposit account held in one person's name, with a deposit balance of $60,000, as well as an account that is held jointly by the same person and another (e.g., a spouse), with a deposit balance of $60,000, is $120,000 — not $60,000.

Also, the maximum insurance protection for a deposit account held in one person's name with, a deposit balance of $60,000, as well as an account for which that same person is a trustee for another person (e.g., a son or daughter), with a deposit balance of $60,000, is $120,000 — not $60,000. A trust deposit can have more than one beneficiary. If the member financial institution has a breakdown of the interests of each person holding money in the deposit, each beneficiary is insured up to $60,000.

CDIC by-laws formalize the documentation required by CDIC for joint and trust accounts. Improper documentation affects the payout of insurance benefits in the event of a failure.

For a joint account, there must be a clear statement that the deposit is held jointly — reference to a right of survivorship is not sufficient unless both or all joint owners are identified. The address of each joint owner is also required — even if the addresses are the same. If the appropriate disclosure does not exist, CDIC will treat the deposit as part of the depositor's individual holdings — for a total of $60,000 of coverage, not $120,000.

Accounts set up "in trust" require a clear identification of the account's status, the trustee and the beneficiary or beneficiaries. As well, the addresses of each beneficiary is required and if there is more than one beneficiary, then the percentage due each beneficiary is required — even if it is split evenly. Again, if the appropriate disclosure does not exist, CDIC will treat the deposit as part of the depositor's individual holdings on the dissolution of an institution.

CDIC does not insure all moneys held in registered plans. To be insurable, the funds must be invested in *accounts or in term deposits that meet the five-year requirement, and must be payable in Canadian currency.* Key points to note with respect to insurable deposits held in registered plans include:

- the maximum deposit insurance for RRSPs is $60,000 — *principal and interest combined;*
- the maximum deposit insurance for RRIFs is $60,000 — *principal and interest combined;* and
- contributions made to a spousal plan are combined with other money held in plans under the spouse's name and are **not** combined with the plans belonging to the person making the contribution.

The total protection offered is, therefore, only limited by the number of combinations of accounts that a person can imagine.

In the event of failure

Since CDIC was created in 1967, 43 member institutions have failed. The first was the Commonwealth Trust Company in 1970, the latest was Security Home Mortgage Corporation in 1996. From 1990 to 1996, 18 member institutions failed, the more infamous included Bank of Credit and Commerce Canada (1991), Central Guarantee Trust Company (1992) and Confederation Trust Company (1994).

To collect a deposit held by a failed member financial institution it is not necessary to file a claim with CDIC. Provided that the failed institution has accurate address information, CDIC advises all insured depositors, in writing, of the particulars of the payout, which is done as quickly as possible after the closure of the financial institution. The payment includes principal and interest up to $60,000, although interest is not accrued from the date of closure of the financial institution. (It is therefore important to be paid out quickly.) To avoid collapsing registered plans, CDIC transfers insured funds to another member financial institution.

Caution

Money managers should be cognizant of the fact that some financial institutions have higher risk profiles than others — and accordingly often offer slightly higher interest rates on deposits. In 1995, amendments made the the *CDIC Act* provide incentives for financial institutions to manage the risk of their portolios in a prudent fashion including authority to:

- *provide supervisory intervention earlier* in the hopes of turning the institution around before failure;
- *levy premium surcharges* on a member financial institution that fails to follow certain practices (e.g., non-compliance

with CDIC's Standards of Sound Business and Financial Practices); and

- *charge risk-based deposit insurance premiums for CDIC member financial institutions* to provide incentives to members to reduce the risk profile of their portfolios.

For a more detailed overview refer to the CDIC Web site at *www.cdic.ca*.

Securities

In the Canadian securities industry, investment firms sponsor a number of organizations which oversee their activities. The *Investment Dealers Association* (IDA) and the various Canadian stock exchanges are regulators of the investment firms that "belong" to them. They are self-regulatory organizations — or SROs — which have the authority, the resources and the mandate to oversee their "members." Besides monitoring the sales, business and financial practices of their members, and oversee the stock, bond and money markets, they create rules governing everything from how the markets function to who can do business and how. They also collectively pay into the *Canadian Investor Protection Fund* (CIPF) which was set up in 1969. The fund was set up to protect investors from losses resulting from the bankruptcy of a member institution. It is not a government fund like CDIC; instead, the members of the investment industry insure each other. Contributions to the fund are made pro rata based on net revenues.

Insurance provided by the CIPF

Claims made on the fund are considered according to policies adopted by the board of governors. The board of governors also has discretionary powers concerning the validity of claims. It is a policy of the board to reject claims from those who were not dealing at arm's length with an insolvent institution and claims from those whose dealings contributed to the insolvency.

The CIPF only protects clients of SRO member firms and covers losses on stocks, bonds, treasury bills, mutual funds and derivatives. To determine the loss, a client's regular trading accounts — cash, margin, short sale, options, futures and foreign currency — are combined and treated as one general account. In addition, CIPF offers separate protection for joint accounts, registered plans such as RRSPs, retirement income funds and education savings plans, and trusts.

Maximum protection

The maximum coverage by the CIPF on the coverage for a customer's general accounts is $1 million for losses related to securities and cash balances. Separate accounts of customers are each entitled to the maximum coverage of $1 million. Losses in market value of securities are not covered.

General accounts

Accounts of a customer such as cash, margin, short sale, options, futures and foreign currency are combined and treated as one general account entitled to the maximum coverage. In addition, the proportionate interest of a customer in an account that is held on a joint or shared ownership basis is combined with the general account of the customer. For example, if spouses each has individual accounts in his or her own name and also has a joint account between him or herself, his or her proportionate interest in the joint account would be combined with his or her respective individual account. The result is that such accounts of each spouse are entitled to CIPF coverage to the maximum limit of $1 million for general accounts, and the joint account is not covered as a separate account.

Separate accounts

Separate accounts are accounts (or groups of similar accounts) disclosed in the records of the member that are treated as if they belonged to a separate customer and are entitled to the maximum coverage. Separate accounts include accounts for:

- Registered retirement plans such as registered retirement savings plans (RRSPs), life income funds (LIFs), locked-in retirement accounts or plans (LIRAs or LIRSPs) and locked-in retirement income funds (LRIFs). All such retirement plans or funds established with respect to a customer (excluding spousal plans) through the same or a different trustee are combined and aggregated into a single separate account;
- Registered Education Savings Plans (RESPs);
- Joint accounts (accounts that are owned on a joint or shared basis and for which each co-owner is authorized to act with respect to the entire accounts), except to the extent that the proportionate interest of a co-owner is required to be combined with a general account as described above;
- Testamentary Trusts;
- Inter-vivos Trusts and Trusts Imposed by Law;
- Guardians, Custodians, Conservators, Committees, etc.;
- Personal Holding Corporations (provided that the beneficial ownership of a majority of the equity capital of the corporation is held by persons other than the customer);
- Partnerships; and
- Unincorporated Associations or Organizations.

The protection provided by CIPF applies to the net equity remaining in a customer's account **after** all segregated securities, other securities and available cash are returned to the customer.

In the event of failure

CIPF covers the closing market value of a client's securities on the day the investment firm becomes insolvent. The Fund does not cover market losses incurred up to that date.

A client has 180 days from the date the firm is declared insolvent to file a claim for CIPF coverage. When a claim is filed, the client will receive a statement of their account and will be asked to verify the accuracy. Losses can be settled in cash or securities — at the Fund's option.

The CIPF Web site is *www.cipf.ca.*

Mutual Fund Dealers Association

The Mutual Fund Dealers Association (MFDA) was established in 2001 as a Self Regulatory Organization to regulate distributors of mutual funds. In late 2002, it established an investor complaint service that can be contacted at (888) 466-MFDA (6332), or through its Web site at *www.mfda.ca.* The MFDA is in the process of setting up an investor protection fund.

Insurance

The Canadian Life and Health Insurance Compensation Corporation (CompCorp) protects policyholders against loss of benefits in the event of the financial failure of its members. All companies licensed to write life or health insurance in Canada must be members of CompCorp. On April 1, 2002, 111 insurance companies were members of CompCorp.

Insurance provided by CompCorp

To be eligible for CompCorp protection, a policy must:

- be in Canadian currency;
- provide either
  - life insurance,
  - health insurance,
  - money accumulation (e.g., RRSP, pension plan),
  - annuity income (e.g., life income, term certain, RRIF), or
  - disability income;
- be written in Canada by a member company or shown on the books of a Canadian branch of a member company; and
- not be covered under any other similar plan.

CompCorp provides no protection where policy benefits are backed by assets that are segregated from the insurance company's general assets (if there is a guaranteed minimum benefit set out in the policy, that guarantee, however, is eligible) or where the insurer provides administration services only for an employee benefit or other group plan.

Maximum protection

Disability insurance and annuities

Payments of up to $2,000 per month are guaranteed for policyholders receiving income from disability insurance and annuities.

Health insurance

Health insurance benefits of up to $60,000 are protected.

Life insurance

Death claims covered under life insurance policies are protected up to $200,000. As well, the cash surrender value of life insurance policies is protected up to $60,000 per person.

Money accumulation plans

Unregistered money accumulation plans as well as money accumulation plans registered under the *Income Tax Act*, such as RRSPs and RRIFs, are protected up to $60,000 per person.

In the event of an insurance company being wound up, replacement policies would be available to policyholders wishing to continue their life, disability or health insurance protection.

In the event of failure

As with CDIC insurance mentioned earlier, in the event of failure the payment from CompCorp includes principal and interest up to $60,000 (for deposits) and $200,000 for insurance policies, but *interest or policy dividends are not accrued from the date of closure of the financial institution.* (It is therefore important to be paid out **quickly.**) To avoid collapsing registered plans, CompCorp also transfers insured funds to another member financial institution.

The CompCorp Web site is *www.compcorp.ca.*

C H A P T E R 4

Banking and Financial Services

Overview

This chapter discusses the more commonly used services available from banks and financial institutions in Canada, and how the treasurer may use them.

The banking services available cover a broad spectrum, and can be grouped into the following areas:

- Credit services (bank lending to the customer);
- Investment services (customer investing surplus funds);
- Non-credit transaction services;
- Risk management services; and
- Representation services.

Commercial and Corporate Banking

In Canada, there are 16 domestic banks (referred to as Schedule I banks), 31 foreign bank subsidiaries (Schedule II) and 21 foreign bank branches (Schedule III) operating. Most corporations use one of the larger Schedule I banks for most of their banking requirements. While this chapter is focused on those banks, this discussion also applies to other banks that tend to specialize in particular niches, rather than provide a broad spectrum of services.

Other types of financial institutions also provide many of the banking services set out herein. For example, leasing companies provide capital leases. While dealing with a corporation's main banker may be easy, it will often be appropriate to discuss requirements with other institutions.

The major chartered banks are very large, very complex organizations. The largest banks have thousands of branches, tens of thousands of employees, and well over $250 billion in assets. The banks have a complex hierarchy, a fairly arcane bureaucratic structure, and a bewildering variety of internal support personnel. Fortunately, most of this is invisible to customers most of the time. Customers generally deal with an individual account manager who can arrange for the services they require, or direct them to a specialist.

The largest customers are dealt with by corporate banking centres in the major cities. *Corporate* customers range from medium-size corporations (typically with sales in excess of $200 million) to large international companies with complex banking requirements and sales over $1 billion. A corporate account manager acts as the focal point to sell different banking services to customers, although he or she is primarily focused on credit-related products (such as loans) as well as cash management services. Corporate customers with large or complex requirements are often able to obtain special accommodations, such as direct telephone access to the bank's foreign exchange trading floor to book transactions and obtain market intelligence.

Smaller business customers are called *commercial* customers and are the specialty of commercial banking centres (also called business banking centres) located regionally where there is a high concentration of businesses. The commercial account manager is responsible for directing the customer towards the services required. Commercial accounts are also handled at ordinary bank branches.

Specialized corporate and commercial banking centres are available for various industry groups such as software, life sciences, and technology. This allows the account managers to specialize in particular industries to better service those sectors.

Other customers are dealt with only at local or retail bank branches which serve as a local contact point for corporate customers. Branches range from very small branches in small communities with as few as three employees to large branches with over one hundred staff. Automated banking machines have become the primary means that most customers use for their routine banking transactions: there are now over 17,000 automated banking machines in Canada and a total of 35,000 shared automated banking machines available through the Interac network.

Bank Credit Services

Bank credit services are services that expose a bank to credit risk: that is, bank loans and similar products. In addition, in the case of some non-credit transaction services, treasurers will find that the bank considers the service to be a credit service although the company is not really *borrowing* in the normal sense of the word, but the bank considers itself to be at risk. Spot foreign exchange contracts are considered credit services by banks even though the customer's account is debited the same day. From the bank's perspective there is a period, which can be up to almost 24 hours during the day, when the bank is at risk. In these situations the bank will apply some of the company's credit line to be earmarked specifically for the transaction.

Credit services are negotiated between a borrower and the bank, and the terms are set out in a written *term sheet*, an example of which is included in the Appendix to Chapter 5, "Maintaining Banking Relationships."

Types of bank lending include operating facilities, term financing, and mortgages.

Loans

Bank loans come in a variety of types, the most common of which are:

- Lines of credit;
- Overdrafts;
- Operating lines; and
- Term loans and mortgages.

Bank loans are generally for a fixed amount with specified repayment requirements. Interest accrues on the full balance of the loan less repayments. Loans may have fixed or floating interest rates, be secured or unsecured, and be repaid either in specific lump-sum amounts or by regular, usually monthly, payments. Monthly payments are usually blended, being a combination of interest and principal. An amortization schedule will show how the mix between principal and interest changes over the term of the loan.

Lines of credit

A line of credit is an approved overdraft, whereby the negative balance in the customer's account can reach an agreed amount. Alternatively, the line of credit may be set up as a loan that can be used as required, with the amount borrowed transferred to the customer's chequing account.

When the amount of financing required is likely to vary in the short term, or is not required in one lump sum, a line of credit is preferable to a straightforward loan because interest will accrue only on the amount used.

Overdrafts

Overdrafts may be approved or not approved. A pre-approved overdraft is essentially the same as a line of credit. Generally the bank has the right to refuse to honour transactions that create an overdraft that has not previously been approved, and very high rates of interest may apply.

Operating loans

Operating loans or lines of credit are designed as working capital loans. They may be structured as overdrafts, which fluctuate with each day's transactions, with an agreed limit for the overdrawn balance. Alternatively, the loan amount may be deposited in the borrower's chequing account. The overdraft arrangement is preferable because the borrower only pays interest on the outstanding balance. Typically, operating loans are margined or limited to agreed percentages of the borrower's current assets (usually accounts receivable and inventories).

Term loans and mortgages

Term loans and mortgages are designed for the acquisition of long-term assets, and the loan is expected to be repaid over an agreed period of time by means of periodic (usually monthly) payments. Payments may be interest only, or a blend of principal and interest. Term loans are likely to be secured by a charge on fixed assets or other tangible property.

Mortgages are a particular form of security, as the owner agrees to allow the lender to register a legal charge on the property, which prevents another person from obtaining title to the property without the lender's consent. The mortgaged property is generally owned by the borrowing company, but in many private companies real estate may be held by either a controlling shareholder or by a related company. The bank may in such circumstances require that the owner of the property guarantee the company's borrowing by giving the bank a mortgage on the property.

In most respects commercial mortgages operate in a similar manner to a homeowner's mortgage, except that the approval process requires more detailed information, and covenants (see below) similar to those for a term loan would be expected. Additionally, the early prepayment privileges given to homeowners do not automatically apply to commercial mortgages. For real estate companies and developers, the bank may insist on very specific conditions. A mortgage on an apartment building owned by a real estate company is often subject to a debt service coverage ratio whereby the rental income (net of operating expenses) must exceed the mortgage payments by a certain amount, often 1.15 to 1.25 times.

Covenants

Covenants are promises made by the borrower to the bank. They include an agreement to provide certain information regularly within a certain time limit, and that the business operations will be conducted in a certain manner. Covenants are generally contained in a Term Sheet.

Term sheets

For most loans, the bank and its commercial borrowers will need a written agreement covering the specific conditions surrounding the loan, as well as the legal documents. The term sheet sets out the agreement between the bank and the customer. It specifies the parameters under which the bank has agreed to provide the credit facility.

The treasurer should review the term sheet carefully, as a breach of any part of it may entitle the bank to cancel the facility and require immediate repayment.

The term sheet will generally include provisions for the following:

- Agreed amounts and purpose of the facility;
- Interest rates and fees;
- Repayment terms;
- Security provided — this will describe the legal agreements required;
- Margin requirements;
- Covenants (i.e., promises made by the borrower to the bank);
- Shareholder guarantees;
- Conditions relating to the borrower's operations;

73

- Reporting requirements; and
- Matters requiring bank approval.

The term sheet takes the form of a letter, signed by the bank's account officer. To be effective, the borrower's signature is required.

Chapter 5 contains an example of a term sheet and a detailed discussion of those particular items of the term sheet that are related to the bank's evaluation of the credit risk.

Other credit services

Other credit services provided by banks include money market securities. These securities are described in Part B of this Handbook generally from the perspective of the investor (lender), and may represent an alternative to bank borrowing. In many cases, a company will use its bank to assist it in issuing such securities.

Other credit services include:

- Commercial paper and money market instruments such as bankers' acceptances;
- Letters of credit (sight, documentary, and term);
- Credit cards;
- Factoring;
- Leases; and
- Loan syndication.

These are discussed below.

Commercial paper

Commercial paper is unsecured short-term promissory notes issued in bearer or registered form on a discounted or interest-bearing basis. Companies with good credit ratings can often access the commercial paper market through investment dealers or banks. Top-rated companies can borrow at rates that are usually below prime and that exceed the yield on treasury bills by 25 to 75 basis points.

Bankers' acceptances

A bankers' acceptance is a type of money market security that is issued by a corporation to a lender or investor (like commercial paper). Generally, the issuing company does not have the size or the credit rating to go directly to the commercial paper market, so it uses a bankers' acceptance that requires a bank's support. The bank agrees to accept or guarantee payment, if the borrower fails to repay the amount due at maturity.

Bankers' acceptances are really a bank-guaranteed form of commercial paper. Banks will review the creditworthiness of the issuer, and charge a *stamping fee* for the guarantee. The stamping fee is based on the corporation's creditworthiness, and is generally 50 to 100 basis points. In addition, the bank will probably require that the company apply for an issuing facility, whereby the company may issue bankers' acceptances, and the bank will accept or underwrite the borrowing, up to a certain limit. A *facility fee* is likely to be charged, payable regardless of whether the facility is used or not.

Bankers' acceptances are issued in bearer or registered form on a discounted or interest bearing basis. By agreeing to accept BAs for a customer, the bank is, in effect, providing a loan guarantee.

Once the bankers' acceptance is issued, investors in the money market may buy the security and view their investment as a loan to the bank, not to the company that issued the security. The bank reports bankers' acceptances as both an asset (a loan to the borrowing company) and an equal liability (the obligation to the holder of the security to pay on maturity) on its balance sheet.

The term of bankers' acceptances may run from a few days to a year, but the most common terms are 30 and 90 days. The yield to an investor is typically about 30 to 40 basis points higher than a treasury bill. The cost to the borrowing company is the yield at the time of issue, plus the "stamping fee" paid to the bank.

Letters of credit

The letter of credit is a commonly used instrument to facilitate international trade, used by importers and exporters. For example, a supplier in Taiwan may wish to sell to a customer in Canada, but wants to be certain that the customer will pay. The customer wants to be certain that the supplier will actually ship the merchandise. Neither the customer nor the supplier have any reason to either trust or mistrust each other. The purchaser will ask his or her bank for a letter of credit to be issued to the supplier, conditional on proof of shipment of the goods. The letter of credit is transmitted to the supplier who deposits the letter in the bank, together with an invoice and shipping documents. The supplier's bank will accept the letter of credit, and receive payment from the customer's bank.

The two banks are involved in assessing in the creditworthiness of the customer and the supplier. The customer that obtains the letter of credit will require a line of credit or have the full amount charged to its account as soon as the letter is issued. It may be some time before payment is actually required.

Letters of credit can also be useful in domestic situations. In a lawsuit, a claimant or defendant may be required to post funds as security for costs. A contractor may be required by the customer to provide a guarantee as to the successful completion of the work. In such situations, a letter of credit may be an efficient way to provide the security. In effect, the bank issuing the letter of credit is providing an irrevocable guarantee as to payment (and charges its customer for the guarantee).

Credit cards

a) For expenses — Businesses often use credit cards for business expenses, to simplify employee expense reporting, and to eliminate the need for cash advances to employees travelling on business. Banks provide the cards (through their Visa or Mastercard issuing divisions) and require that the company sign a cardholder agreement that among other things will provide that the corporation is liable for all charges to the credit card, whether or not authorized by the company. The business that uses corporate credit cards should have good control over the use of such cards, particularly to ensure that cards of former employees cannot be used. A clearly defined expense policy communicated in writing to all employees will reduce the potential abuses.

b) As a means of payment by customers — Credit cards have become the most popular means of payment for a large variety of goods and services. Businesses that accept credit cards in payment for their sales must be authorized by the credit card issuer. Terms of use are defined in an agreement that specifies responsibilities for the business, such as seizure and reporting of stolen cards, obtaining approval for purchases over a certain monetary amount, and accepting the credit card issuers' commission. Credit card receipts may be deposited electronically, using point of sale equipment, or the merchant copy of the slips may be deposited with the normal bank deposit of cash and cheques.

Factoring

Factoring involves the sale of accounts receivable to a third party for an immediate cash payment. Factoring is carried out by banks and factoring companies. Terms are negotiated between the treasurer and the factor who is accepting two risks — the risk of delayed payment by customers, and the risk of interest rates changing between the sale of the receivable and its collection.

Typical terms involve a discount that will reflect the creditworthiness of the business's customers, typical payment terms in the industry, and interest rates. The "security" for the financing is the integrity of the company making the sale and the ability to pay of the ultimate customer who has bought the merchandise or service.

Leases

Leasing involves the rental of an asset for fixed periodic payments, over a fixed term, with a predetermined termination arrangement that may involve the customer either paying a residual balance to acquire the asset or returning the asset to the bank at the end of the term.

Many leases are essentially loans: these are called capital leases. Instead of borrowing to acquire the asset, the lender (the lessor) purchases the asset and rents it to the borrower (the lessee), for an agreed monthly amount. At the end of the lease, the asset may be purchased by the borrower for a predetermined payment. Often, the asset may be acquired before the end of the lease as well, for a specified amount.

Because the bank owns the asset, it may be in a better security position, and be able to claim capital cost allowance for tax purposes. As a result, the interest rate implicit in the lease may be less than what the company could have arranged in the case of a conventional term loan. Applications for leasing are evaluated by banks in a similar manner to term loan applications, and in any event lease obligations are considered as liabilities when evaluating financial positions. Leasing can be attractive to a startup company that is not eligible for conventional bank financing. For accounting purposes, if the lease transaction is in essence a means of financing the asset, the company is generally required to treat it as a purchase and financing in its financial statements.

Loan syndication

Large business loans may be syndicated. This means that a number of lenders agree to take a portion of a loan. Such syndication may be desirable from the borrower's perspective in that better terms are obtained by introducing an element of competition for the business between lenders. Syndication may also be a means of enabling the borrower to obtain the desired financing in such a way that no one bank is taking a great risk that it views as inappropriate. From a practical viewpoint syndication is rare for loans under $175 million, because of the fees involved from lenders, lawyers and accountants. Banks do take an active role in syndication, and the borrower's main bank may be the lead bank that does the bulk of the administrative and organizational work.

Investment Services

Investment services provided by banks include:

- the purchase and sale of securities and other money market investments;

- bank term deposits;
- investment counselling;
- portfolio management and administration; and
- employee RRSPs and RRIFs.

Banks can offer a wide range of investment products themselves, through their investment dealer or through investment counselling subsidiaries.

Investment services used by treasurers will primarily be money market securities or other short-term investments, which are described in detail in Chapter 9, "Short-Term Investments." These investments will provide a means of earning interest revenue on surplus cash.

Interest on corporate bank accounts

Banks now often pay interest on corporate bank accounts, and the arrangements will typically be negotiated depending on the size of the balances and the volume of bank services used by the company. Interest is usually calculated at a rate below prime, and a certain portion of the balance may be non-interest earning. Interest is often tiered, so that the rate increases on higher balances. Where banks pay interest on corporate accounts, services charges will be assessed for cash management and related transactional services.

Money market investment

Banks act as suppliers of money market securities, and the treasurer of an organization that has surplus cash available for investment may acquire money market investments from the bank. There are other suppliers of such products, and treasurers should be well aware of the market. Short-term instruments are discussed in Chapter 9.

Long-term investments

Corporate treasurers may be responsible for longer-term investment management, for example, when responsible for the performance of corporate pension funds. While banks do provide the
ability to purchase and sell investments and to have investment
portfolios managed, those functions are also available through
other organizations such as investment dealers and portfolio managers. Long-term investments are discussed in Chapter 10.

Non-Credit Transaction Services

Virtually all organizations, whether businesses, non-profit organizations, or government bodies, require banking services to facilitate their transactions. After establishing the legal formalities and
appointing responsible officials, the opening of a bank account
may be the first activity undertaken.

A bank account may be opened with a non-bank financial
institution, such as a trust company, credit union (or caisse popu-
laire), or an entity such as the Treasury Branch of Alberta, or the
Province of Ontario Savings Office. For the purposes of this
Handbook, the term "bank" is used to mean any financial institution that provides banking services. The provision of banking services in Canada requires federal and provincial approval, and
involves membership in the Canadian Payment System (which
organizes the clearing function), and a deposit insurance organization such as the Canada Deposit Insurance Corporation.

The business current account is the standard account used, but
each bank has different products that may suit an organization
best. The choice of bank and account involves reviewing the treasurer function, the services needed, and the ability and willingness
of the bank to provide those facilities. The treasurer's flexibility to

change banks may be limited, either by the nature of the bank support during a difficult financial period, or by practical limitations
unrelated to credit services.

The review of banking products required should be based on an
assessment of the best way to manage the organization's cash
resources, collect incoming cash, and make disbursements. Other
chapters of this Handbook that relate to the use of non-credit bank
services as follows:

- Chapter 13 — Managing Cash;
- Chapter 14 — E-Commerce and E-Payments; and
- Chapter 15 — Credit and Collection.

Specific banking services that may be used include:

- Account management and information services:

  (a) Current accounts (the standard business accounts);
  (b) Consolidation or concentration of balances,
  (c) Electronic access to accounts,

- Account reconciliation;
- Cash management:

  (a) Cash collection products,
  (b) Cash disbursement products,

- Electronic data interchange;
- Foreign exchange;
- Payroll processing;
- Point of sale equipment;
- Safekeeping and custody; and
- Safety deposit boxes.

These are discussed below.

Account management and information services

Various account management and information services are available, ranging from the simple bank statement to direct electronic access to information of transactions. Current accounts are the standard type of business account and organizations may have numerous bank accounts for different purposes. Consolidation of balances is a valuable service, and is generally used to determine interest to be credited or charged. Electronic access to accounts has become increasingly popular and can save both time and bank service fees.

Account reconciliation

Banks provide a variety of reconciliation services. The extent to which they are accessible electronically continues to increase. The major banks allow customers to download transaction and balance information by telephone to facilitate monitoring of the accounts. The banks also have automated account reconciliation services available. As cheque fraud becomes a greater concern due to the ready availability of inexpensive high quality printers, timely reconciliation of bank accounts becomes a vital internal control. See "Cash disbursement products" below.

Cash management

Cash management products include cash collection products and cash disbursement products.

Cash collection products

Cash collection products and services range in sophistication from depositing cash and cheques manually at a teller wicket, to electronic funds transfers handled electronically from the treasurer's personal computer. Increasingly, banks are encouraging business customers to perform transactions away from traditional teller wickets. The objectives are to minimize transaction costs, minimize idle cash, reduce the risk of theft, and minimize errors. The easiest deposits to automate are recurring items.

The following is a list of products available from banks to assist companies to process incoming deposits.

- **Pre-authorized cheques and direct deposits** may be made to the recipient's account for items that the payors agree may be debited from their account. Magnetic tape or electronic transmission is generally used to reduce the time and cost of processing pre-authorized customer debits. This service is typically used where recurring amounts are agreed by an organization's customers in advance, such as monthly life insurance or mortgage payments.
- **Automatic transfer facilities** are used to allow operating units of a company to maintain local accounts and transfer excess funds based on predetermined instructions. It may also be used to transfer deposits made from a local branch to the head office account.
- **Lockbox** services are in effect a post office box maintained by the bank for an organization. Cheques from the organization's customers are directed to the post office box. Cheques are processed by the bank and the organization is provided with information in paper or magnetic form. The customer may request all envelopes, invoice and remittance advices, and photocopies of cheques. While common in the United States, such facilities are only used by the largest organizations in Canada because cheque clearing float is zero — cheques are credited the day they are deposited. However, lockboxes can be used to reduce mail float by providing local mailing addresses to customers.

They are also being used by organizations that wish to out-source their cash collections.

- **Bill payment** services are provided for organizations with large numbers of customers. This service is commonly used by utility companies. The company will need to have appropriate arrangements with other banks, so that the company's account can be credited directly at the end of the day. The company's principal bank will make the arrangements.

- **Electronic concentration** or *sweep* accounts, are used to centralize all balances in one account. This service may either be performed by the bank, or by the treasurer direct-ly using a personal computer. The company will need to set up the arrangements to participate in this service so that the appropriate passwords may be installed and the proper training provided. In many cases substantial savings in both bank service fees and staff time can be achieved. A down-load of transactions processed by the bank can be comput-er-matched to the company's cash receipts and disburse-ments records to automate the bank reconciliation routine.

- **Night depository** services involve the use of lockable pouches placed in the night depository vault. This service is useful for businesses collecting payment in cash.

Each bank uses its own brand names for its services. Treasurers may find significant differences in the cost and suitability of the services offered. The choice of which bank to use will depend on a number of factors, including convenience, on-going relationship with the bank, credit facilities provided, and cost. These issues are covered more fully in Chapter 5, "Maintaining Banking Relationships."

Cash disbursement products

Cheques — The most common disbursement product is the cheque, defined as an order in writing instructing a bank to pay a specific sum to a specified person, on or after a specified date.

While there have been interesting legal cases involving unconventional types of cheques (including a valid cheque written by a farmer on the side of a cow!), banks will not process cheques in the normal course unless they are on specified types of paper, of specified sizes, and with the required magnetic ink characters, or MICR (magnetic ink character recognition).

The MICR coding indicates:

- The account holder's bank and branch transit number — Each direct clearing member of the Canadian Payments Association has an institution number (three digits), and each branch of that institution has a transit number (five digits).
- The bank customer's account number — Institutions vary in their designation of account numbers but there are rules set by the Canadian Payments Association to determine the spacing and layout of the magnetic characters.

To reduce the possibility of cheque fraud, banks offer various services called "positive pay" or "negative pay" whereby they only pay cheques previously advised to them.

Direct debits — As noted under collection products above, a bank customer may authorize its account to be charged or debited for recurring items.

Direct deposits — Instead of issuing a cheque, many organizations directly deposit amounts to the accounts of recipients. One may argue that this service is not really a disbursement product, and should be included with Cash Collection Products. Treasurers will probably wish to consider this service as a means of disbursement when their company will be issuing a large number of payments. The company will provide the bank with a list of recipients, their bank accounts and amounts, together with one cheque for the total. The list will usually be an electronic file. This service ensures that recipients receive payment regardless of mail delivery. Direct deposits are commonly used for payroll disbursements, payment of dividends by widely-held public companies, interest (for example on Canada Savings Bonds), pensions, and annuities.

Wire transfer — The name has outlasted the technology, but the term wire transfer is used for same-day transfers of funds, and is commonly used for international transfers. In some countries, the term "telegraphic transfer" is used. Banks transmit messages for payments through an international bank payment network called SWIFT. Payment instructions may also be transmitted by telegram or cable, although this is relatively unusual now. In the latter case, special codes are used to establish the authenticity of the instructions. Fees for wire transfer services vary, but can be considerable. It may be cheaper but effective to simply courier a bank draft.

Electronic Data Interchange (EDI)

Banks provide a variety of services to facilitate electronic commerce, including EDI. EDI extends beyond funds transfer (a traditional banking product) to include the exchange of data.

EDI has typically been used between major manufacturers and their parts suppliers. Information covering purchase and work orders, inventory levels, and production schedules may be transmitted between vendor and customer so as to facilitate just-in-time delivery as well as prompt payment and simplified, automated accounting. The automotive industry has been the major user to date, but the scope of EDI is such that it can be expected to have a significant impact on the administrative functions of many organizations.

Various flexible web-enabled technologies are also available to facilitate electronic commerce. See Chapter 14, "E-Commerce and E-Payments," for a discussion of electronic banking products.

Foreign exchange

Canadian banks do a significant amount of foreign exchange business. Following is a brief summary of the types of foreign exchange transactions handled by banks. For more detailed information, please refer to Chapter 19, "Managing Foreign Exchange Risk and Derivatives."

- **Spot transaction** — This is an agreement between the bank and a customer to exchange one currency for another at a fixed rate with the exchange taking place within one business day (two if outside Canada and the United States).
- **Forward transaction** — This is an agreement between the bank and a customer to exchange one currency for another at a fixed rate with the exchange taking place on a specified future date. Forward exchange rates are reported in the financial pages of newspapers. The difference between the "spot" rate and the forward rate reflects the carrying costs (i.e., short-term interest rates) in effect for deposits in each currency. If short-term interest rates in one currency are high, it would appear to be profitable to buy that currency on the spot market, invest it in short-term money market securities in that currency, and sell the currency forward by means of a foreign exchange contract. The market removes this arbitrage opportunity when forward rates are priced.

A common misconception is that the premiums or discounts between spot and forward rates reflect the market's assessment of the likely future movements in the exchange rate. This is not the case: the premium or discount is only due to differences in the interest rates in the two currencies. If the market expects one currency to decline, it may indeed be mirrored in short-term interest rates, but the premium or discount itself does not predict changes in the exchange rate.

- **Option-dated forward transaction** — This type of contract is a variation of the standard forward contract in that the customer has a choice as to delivery dates.
- **Foreign currency swap** — A foreign currency swap is an agreement to exchange two currencies on both the spot and the forward date. Swap deposits are money market securities that involve the purchase of the foreign currency, the investment of the foreign currency in a foreign money market instrument, and the subsequent forward sale of the foreign currency proceeds when the money market instrument matures.
- **Future** — A futures contract differs from a forward contract in that the contract is in a standardized form and is governed by the rules of an options or futures exchange. In Canada, futures markets are administered by the Montreal Exchange. Futures are traded regularly and are usually unwound before the scheduled delivery date. Futures contracts are used by investors who wish to profit from currency moves, as well as by organizations trying to hedge their foreign exposures.
- **Option** — An option conveying the right, but not the obligation to buy (call option) or sell (put option) a specified amount of a currency at a specified price on or before a specified date. Like futures contracts, options may be traded, if they are traded on an exchange. Options may also be purchased or sold "over the counter" with a bank.

Forward exchange contracts, futures, and options are of considerable importance to companies engaged in international trade because currency fluctuations may have a major impact on profit margins. Banks tend to concentrate on the provision of forward contracts for customers, though for large organizations they may arrange futures and options contracts. Organizations wishing to undertake futures and exchange-traded options transactions may deal with an investment dealer rather than their bank.

Forward foreign exchange contracts involve two elements of risk to the bank and are normally treated as a credit service. They are included in this section because the treasurer may consider the service as a non-credit service, as the company purchasing the contract is merely making a transaction at the current market price. Banks do not see the contract in the same way. They recognize that they have a commitment to fulfil the sale or purchase of the foreign contract in the future, and that the amount of the settlement may change. Forward exchange contracts are regarded by a bank as being a use of the company's credit facilities, and will often restrict the company's ability to use its full authorized borrowing limits for regular transactions. The fact that the company is effectively extending credit to the bank in respect of its side of the transaction is not relevant to the bank. Various non-bank financial institutions have experienced significant credit risks with swap transactions when there was doubt about the ability of the other party (generally another financial institution) to honour the transaction. The bank may also monitor settlement risk, which occurs if the bank disburses currency before receiving the other currency from the customer.

Point-of-sale equipment

Banks are involved in the sale, leasing and rental of point of sale equipment, particularly to facilitate credit card sales (imprinters and authorization terminals). Debit cards are offered by banks as a means of expediting payment without cheques.

Safekeeping and custody

Organizations holding physical marketable investments may require safekeeping services. The standard arrangement involves the bank taking physical delivery of investments, or having the investments held by a depository (normally the Canadian Depository for Securities). The bank's safekeeping department will also monitor the receipt on a timely basis of investment income and credit the customer's account. A useful benefit of this service is that the bank will ensure that customers are advised of offers (take-overs, rights, and exchanges) made to shareholders, and will solicit the customer's instructions. When bonds are held for safe-keeping, customers need not worry about missing a maturity or having their bonds called for redemption. The lost interest from a missed redemption could significantly exceed the bank's safe cus-tody fees.

Safety deposit boxes

Safety deposit boxes are available in various sizes at many bank branches. Organizations may find a box useful for storage of sensi-tive and secret information. Safety deposit boxes may also be a convenient offsite location for computer backup storage and disas-ter recovery material.

Risk Management Services

Banks provide risk management products for managing and con-trolling interest rate risk (see Chapter 18) and foreign exchange risk (see Chapter 19). Foreign exchange products were summarized above.

Interest rate risk products include:

- **Interest rate swaps** — This is an agreement whereby one party agrees to pay a rate of interest determined in one manner on a notional amount of principal, and the other party agrees to pay an interest rate determined in a different manner, on the same notional principal. The most common type of interest rate swap is where one party pays or receives a fixed rate and the other pays or receives a floating rate.
- **Forward rate agreement** — This is an agreement to borrow or lend a notional amount of money at a rate that may be floating, but that cannot exceed or fall below certain predetermined agreed limits for a certain period of time. The agreement covers a predetermined period of time, and cannot be exchanged or sold (although it could be cancelled by entering into an offsetting transaction with the same bank).
- **Interest rate futures** — These are exchange traded contracts for a particular period of time, designated in units of a particular fixed income security.
- **Interest rate options** — Like options for any other security, they provide a right, rather than an obligation to acquire (call), or sell (put) a security at a given price, on or before a certain date.

  An interest rate option may be described as either a *cap*, i.e., an upper limit, a *collar*, with upper and lower limits, or a *floor*, whereby the interest rate may not fall below the agreed amount.

All of the above interest rate risk management products allow the purchaser to hedge a known future event that carries an exposure to changes in interest rates, or to take a speculative position as a conscious investment decision.

Both interest rate and foreign exchange risk management products are treated as credit services by banks. Organizations wishing to use them will require approval from the bank and be assigned a limit for these transactions.

Representation and Other Services

From the earliest days of banking, banks have acted as representatives in financial matters for customers. A bill of exchange, the forerunner of the cheque, became accepted as a means of payment because the person entitled to payment accepted the bank's promise as being equivalent to being paid in gold or currency. Many banks at some time in their early history actually issued paper currency that was accepted as legal tender, and banks in Scotland continue to do so.

A formal type of representation is the bank reference. Many customers require bank references to establish a relationship with a supplier, with another lender, or with a bank in a foreign country. Banks will limit their disclosure unless specifically authorized by the customer. Bank references are particularly useful for organizations trying to establish their business outside their home territory.

Using Bank Services

Banks need to know who their customers are so that they reduce their risk of being used as a conduit for illegal activities, including money-laundering. As a result, banks are increasingly cautious in how they establish accounts, and even a simple business chequing account will often not be permitted before the required paperwork is in place.

To establish any banking relationship (such as a chequing account), the company will be required to do the following:

- Establish the company's **authority to act** — Banks will always require legal authorization from their customers to use their services. A corporation's by-laws authorize the directors to make the banking arrangements. A banking resolution must be passed at a directors' meeting confirming the directors' decision to use a particular bank and to authorize the signing officers for each account. It is generally advisable for a large organization to have its directors pass a general signing resolution to enable senior management to authorize the appointment of new signing officers, so that staff turnover does not require a new board meeting.

- Accept the **bank's standard terms** of doing business — The bank will also want its customers to agree to its standard terms of business, usually described in an account operating agreement. These account operating agreements have been drafted by bank lawyers to protect the bank. Customers will usually have great difficulty in obtaining variations from the standard terms but they should try to negotiate for any changes they desire.

An example of the above is that banks generally require customers to acknowledge that no bank liability accrues if the bank honours a cheque that the customer has instructed be stopped. Clearly such a matter is contrary to the normal principles of a business agreement. It may be appropriate to write to the bank "without prejudice" setting out the issues on which your company has signed the bank's forms but stating the company's disagreement with a specific item.

94

Banks sometimes undertake credit checks, or other reference checks, before accepting a new corporate customer.

Conclusion

The large chartered banks in Canada offer a large variety of different services they offer their customers. This chapter has set out perhaps 30 of those services — the banks typically offer about 200. While it may not be desirable to obtain too many different services from one institution, the treasurer may find that considerable information is available through the company's banker.

Appendix 4A

Schedule I banks

Domestic Chartered Banks

Amicus Bank
595 Bay Street, 6th Floor
Toronto, Ontario
M5G 2C2

BMO Financial Group
First Bank Tower
1 First Canadian Place
Toronto, Ontario
M5X 1A1
(416) 867-5000

The Bank of Nova Scotia
Scotia Plaza, 7th Floor
40 King Street West
Toronto, Ontario
M5H 1H1
(416) 866-6161

CIBC
Commerce Court West
56th Floor
Toronto, Ontario
M5L 1A2
(416) 980-2211

Canadian Western Bank
2300-10303 Jasper Avenue
Edmonton, Alberta
T5J 3X6
(780) 423-8888

Citizens Bank of Canada
Box 13133, Station Terminal
Vancouver, British Columbia
V6B 6K1
(604) 708-7800

CS Alterna Bank
187 Bay Street
Ottawa, Ontario
K1R 5Y7

First Nations Bank of Canada
224 4th Avenue South
Saskatoon, Saskatchewan
S7K 5M5

Laurentian Bank of Canada
1981 McGill College Avenue
Montreal, Québec
H3A 3K3
(514) 522-1846

Manulife Bank of Canada
500 King Street North
Waterloo, Ontario
N2J 4C6
1 (877) 765-2265

National Bank of Canada
600 rue de la Gauchetière
Ouest
Montreal, Québec
H3B 4L2
(514) 394-4000

Pacific & Western Bank of Canada
Suite 2002, 140 Fullerton Street
London, Ontario
N6A 4M6

President's Choice Bank
P.O. Box 603, Stn. Agincourt
Scarborough, Ontario
M1S 5K9

Royal Bank of Canada
Royal Bank Plaza
8th Floor, South Tower
200 Bay Street
Toronto, Ontario
M5J 2J5
(416) 974-5151

TD Bank Financial Group
P.O. Box 1
Toronto-Dominion Centre
55 King Street West,
11th Floor
Toronto, Ontario
M5K 1A2
(416) 982-8222

PART A

Appendix 4B

Schedule II banks

ABN Amro Bank Canada
(The Netherlands)
P.O. Box 114,
15th Floor,
Toronto Dominion Centre
79 Wellington Street
Toronto, Ontario
M5K 1G8
(416) 365-6774

Amex Bank of Canada
(U.S.A.)
101 McNabb Street
Markham, Ontario
L3R 4H8
(905) 474-8000

Bank of America Canada
(U.S.A.)
200 Front Street West,
Suite 2700
Toronto, Ontario
M5V 3L2
(416) 349-4100

Bank Of China (Canada)
(People's Republic Of China)
P.O. Box 612,
Suite 3740,
161 Bay Street
Toronto, Ontario
M5J 2S1
(416) 362-2991

Bank Of East Asia (Canada)
(Hong Kong)
Suite 102-103,
350 Highway 7 East,
East Asia Centre
Richmond Hill, Ontario
L4B 3N2
(905) 882-8182

Bank of Tokyo - Mitsubishi (Canada)
(Japan)
Royal Bank Plaza,
Suite 2100, South Tower
Toronto, Ontario
M5J 2J1
(416) 865-0220

Bank One Canada
(U.S.A.)
P.O. Box 613,
Suite 4240,
161 Bay Street
Toronto, Ontario
M5J 2S1
(416) 865-0466

BNP Paribas (Canada)
(France)
1981 McGill College Avenue,
BNP Tower
Montreal, Québec
H3A 2W8
(514) 285-6000

Citibank Canada
(U.S.A.)
123 Front Street West, Suite
1900
Toronto, Ontario
M5J 2M3
(416) 947-5500

**Credit Suisse First Boston
Canada**
(Switzerland)
1 First Canadian Place,
Suite 3000
P.O. Box 301
Toronto, Ontario
M5X 1C9
(416) 352-4660

CTC Bank of Canada
(Taiwan)
1518 West Broadway
Vancouver, British Columbia
V6J 1W8
(604) 683-3882

Deutsche Bank AG, Canada
(Germany)
222 Bay Street, Suite 1100
Toronto, Ontario
M5K 1H6
(416) 682-8400

Dresdner Bank Canada
(Germany)
2 First Canadian Place,
Suite 1700
Toronto, Ontario
M5X 1E3
(416) 369-8300

Habib Canadian Bank
(Switzerland)
918 Dundas Street East,
Suite 1-B
Mississauga, Ontario
L4Y 4H9
(905) 276-5300

PART A

HSBC Bank Canada
(United Kingdom)
885 West Georgia Street
Vancouver, British Columbia
V6C 3E9
(604) 685-1000

ING Bank of Canada
(The Netherlands)
111 Gordon Baker Road
North York, Ontario
M2H 3R1
(416) 497-5157

**International Commercial
Bank of Cathay (Canada)**
(Taiwan)
150 York Street, Suite 910
Toronto, Ontario
M5H 3S5
(416) 947-2800

Intesa Bank Canada
(Italy)
P.O. Box 209
1 Adelaide Street East
Toronto, Ontario
M5C 2V9
(416) 366-0585

J.P. Morgan Bank Canada
(U.S.A.)
Royal Bank Plaza,
South Tower,
P.O. Box 80, Suite 1800
200 Bay Street
Toronto, Ontario
M5J 2J2
(416) 981-9200

**Korea Exchange Bank of
Canada**
(Korea)
Madison Centre
Suite 1101
4950 Yonge Street
Toronto, Ontario
M2N 6K1
(416) 222-5200

MBNA Canada Bank
(U.S.A.)
1600 James Naismith Drive,
Suite 800
Gloucester, Ontario
K1B 5N8
(613) 742-4800

Mizuho Bank (Canada)
100 Yonge Street
Box 29, Suite 1102
Toronto, Ontario
M5C 2W1
(416) 874-0222

PART A

National Bank of Greece (Canada)
(Greece)
1170 Place du Frère André
Montreal, Québec
H3B 3C6
(514) 954-1522

Rabobank Canada
77 King Street West
Royal Trust Tower, Suite 4520
P.O. Box 57, TD Centre
Toronto, Ontario
M5K 1E7
(416) 941-9777

Société Générale (Canada)
(France)
1501 McGill College Avenue,
Suite 1800
Montreal, Québec
H3A 3M8
(514) 841-6000

BCPBank Canada
(Portugal)
2nd Floor,
1102 Dundas Street West
Toronto, Ontario
M6J 1X2
(416) 588-9819

State Bank Of India (Canada)
(India)
P.O. Box 81,
Suite 1600,
North Tower,
Royal Bank Plaza
Toronto, Ontario
M5J 2J2
(416) 865-0414

Sumitomo Mitsui Banking Corporation Of Canada
(Japan)
P.O. Box 172,
Suite 1400,
Ernst & Young Tower
Toronto Dominion Centre
Toronto, Ontario
M5K 1H6
(416) 368-4766

UBS Bank (Canada)
(Switzerland)
154 University Avenue
Toronto, Ontario
M5H 3Z4
(416) 343-1800

UFJ Bank Canada
(Japan)
P.O. Box 525, Suite 4400
BCE Place
161 Bay Street
Toronto, Ontario
M5J 2S1
(416) 366-2583

**United Overseas Bank
Limited, Vancouver Branch**
(Canada) (Singapore)
Vancouver Centre
650 West Georgia Street,
Suite 310
Vancouver, British Columbia
V6B 4N9
(604) 662-7055

Appendix 4C

Schedule III banks

ABN Amro Bank N.V.
(The Netherlands)
P.O. Box 114,
15th Floor,
Toronto Dominion Centre
79 Wellington Street
Toronto, Ontario
M5K 1G8
(416) 365-6774

Bank Of America, National Association
Suite 2700,
200 Front Street West
Toronto, Ontario
M5V 3L2
(416) 349-4100

Bank One, National Association
P.O. Box 613,
Suite 4240
161 Bay Street
Toronto, Ontario
M5J 2S1
(416) 865-0466

Bayerische Landesbank
BCE Place
Suite 3210,
P.O. Box 814
181 Bay Street
Toronto, Ontario
M5J 2T3
(416) 815-4418

Capital One Bank
5650 Yonge Street,
13th Floor
Toronto, Ontario
M2M 4G3
(416) 228-5111

Citibank, N.A.
Citibank Place, Suite 1900
123 Front Street West
Toronto, Ontario
M5J 2M3
(416) 947-5500

Comerica Bank
Suite 2200, South Tower
Royal Bank Plaza
200 Bay Street
Toronto, Ontario
M5J 2J2
(416) 367-3113

Deutsche Bank A.G.
222 Bay Street,
Suite 1100, P.O. Box 196
Toronto, Ontario
M5K 1H6
(416) 682-8400

First Commercial Bank
Suite 100,
5611 Cooney Road
Richmond, British Columbia
V6X 3J6

HSBC Bank USA
70 York Street,
4th Floor
Toronto, Ontario
M5J 1S9

JPMorgan Chase Bank
P.O. Box 80,
Suite 1800, South Tower
Royal Bank Tower
200 Bay Street
Toronto, Ontario
M5J 2J2
(416) 981-9202

Maple Bank GmbH
Toronto Dominion Centre,
Suite 3500
P.O. Box 328
Toronto, Ontario
M5K 1K7

Mellon Bank, N.A. Canada Branch
P.O. Box 320, Suite 3200
Royal Trust Tower
Toronto Dominion Centre
Toronto, Ontario
M5K 1K2
(416) 860-0777

Rabobank Nederland, Canadian Branch
77 King Street West
Royal Trust Tower, Suite 4520
PO Box 57, TD Centre
Toronto, Ontario
M5K 1E7
(416) 941-9777

State Street Bank And Trust Company
30 Adelaide Street East,
Suite 1500
Toronto, Ontario
M5C 3G6

U.S. Bank National Association
130 Adelaide Street West,
11th Floor
Toronto, Ontario
(416) 306-3500

United Overseas Bank Limited
P.O. Box 11616,
Suite 310
650 West Georgia Street
Vancouver Centre
Vancouver, British Columbia
V6B 4N9

Union Bank of California, N.A.
440 - 2nd Avenue Southwest,
Suite 730
Calgary, Alberta
T2P 5E9

WestLB AG
Suite 1704, Box 52
95 Wellington Street West
Toronto, Ontario
M5J 2N7

Lending Branches

Credit Suisse First Boston
1 First Canadian Place,
Suite 3000
Toronto, Ontario
M5X 1C9
(416) 352-4501

National City Bank
Exchange Tower
130 King Street West, Suite 1800
P.O. Box 427
Toronto, Ontario
M5X 1E3

CHAPTER 5

Maintaining Banking Relationships

Overview

Many companies have a lead banker that provides most of the required banking services and is often supplemented by other financial institutions for specialized activities such as leasing. The large chartered banks have entered many areas beyond their core banking mandate, and some non-traditional banks, as well as non-banks, provide services traditionally thought of as banking.

This chapter discusses how to deal with your banker, whether he or she is in a bank or some other organization. It reviews how life looks from the banker's side of the table and also suggests alternatives to banks for some banking services.

The Banker's Perspective

To develop a successful banking relationship, it can be useful to consider the viewpoint of the banker. The large chartered banks are very large, very complex organizations. They each have thousands of branches, tens of thousands of employees, over $250 billion in assets, and $10–$20 billion in revenues per annum. The banks have a complex hierarchy, a fairly arcane bureaucratic structure, and a bewildering variety of internal support personnel. Fortunately, most of this is invisible to customers most of the time. Customers generally deal with an individual account manager who can arrange for the services they require, or direct them to a specialist. The banks are organized to deal with different customers by employing a variety of different resources.

The largest customers are dealt with by corporate banking centres in the major cities. "Corporate" customers range from medium-size corporations (typically with sales in excess of $200 million) to large international companies with complex banking requirements and sales of over $1 billion. A corporate account manager acts as the focal point when selling different banking services to customers, but is primarily focused on credit-related products (such as loans) as well as cash management services.

Smaller business customers are called "commercial" customers and are the specialty of commercial banking centres (also called business banking centres), located in many regional locations where there is a high concentration of businesses. The commercial account manager is responsible for directing the customer towards the services required. Commercial accounts are also handled at ordinary bank branches.

Other customers are dealt with only at local or retail bank branches. As well as dealing with individuals, bank branches handle commercial customers and serve as a local contact point for corporate customers. Branches range from very small branches in small communities with as few as three employees to large branches with over 100 staff.

Maintaining a Relationship

There are two key ingredients to maintaining a successful banking relationship: sharing information and honouring commitments.

More than anything else, the banker should always be kept informed as to what the company is doing. The banker will be in a very difficult position if he or she cannot obtain the information necessary to evaluate the company's financial situation in order to assess the risk to the bank's shareholders and depositors. The treasurer should provide the banker with timely information concerning the company's financial position and its strategic objectives. As in any relationship, the banker will be in a very difficult position if he/she first finds out about a major loss, the divesting of a certain division or a takeover bid through the media rather than directly from the treasurer. Bankers expect "no surprises" and the treasurer would be well advised to always keep the banker informed as to the company's situation. Even if the company's finance position is deterioriating rapidly, it is far better to keep the banker fully informed and work with them rather than to hide from them. A well-informed banker may be able to provide the treasurer with useful market or industry intelligence and an outsider's perspective (e.g., receivables look a little high). It will be very difficult for the banker to provide the treasurer with intelligent feedback in the absence of information.

The second key ingredient is honouring commitments. This involves not only making timely payments of principal, interest and fees, but also not impairing the bank's security in any way. For example, if a company takes a mortgage to make renovations to a property, the funds should not be used for another purpose, for example to buy another property. If the principal security of the company's line of credit is inventory and receivables, the company should be committed to maintaining the working capital and inventory turnover ratios set out in the term sheet. If a loan needs to be restructured, the company that has always made its payments will find a much more flexible, willing banker. The banker will be less willing accommodating a difficult or uncommunicative borrower. This issue becomes even more critical at annual review time where the terms and conditions of the banking services and/or loans may have to be altered.

In short, keeping the banker informed and living up to your obligations is the best way to maintain a positive banking relationship.

Annual Review

The purpose of the annual review is twofold: for the treasurer to determine how well the bank is performing in terms of service and cost effectiveness of the services, and for the banker to review the financial position and prospects of the company and to determine if changes need to be made to the banking relationship.

Some of the treasurer's concerns will be:

- Are services being provided on a timely basis?
- Is there backup provided for every item on the bank statement?
- Are errors resolved promptly?
- Are fees reasonable?
- Does the bank provide useful feedback with regard to the company's operations?

The banker will be concerned about:

- the company's financial position;
- its future operating plans; and
- how can the bank increase the profitability of the account?

The meeting should be held during a non-peak period (for example, three months after year-end), so that both sides can be prepared. The treasurer should outline the company's present financial position and its future business goals. The parties should discuss what additional banking services might become necessary as well as those that are no longer useful. Are the services being used efficiently? For instance, if the company is making numerous small foreign currency purchases, it may be more cost effective to group them into larger transactions.

The banker will want to review the bank's security position. Is the inventory balance net of returned (and unsalable) and obsolete inventory? Are accounts receivables net of provisions for doubtful accounts? Are machinery, equipment and premises being properly maintained? Are there signs that the company is poorly managed (for example, if delinquent accounts receivable are increasing, has the company hired a collections person)?

Ideally, the treasurer and banker can use the annual review process to make the adjustments necessary to improve service, to alter the mix of financial services provided and to arrive at a fee schedule for the next year. They should also discuss ways in which the company can improve its financial position. If nothing more, the annual review gives the treasurer and the banker an opportunity to meet and simply exchange viewpoints, ideas and information.

The Credit Review Process

The banker will have three major concerns about a relationship:

i) What is the risk to the bank?
ii) Does the return (i.e., interest rate and fees) justify the risk?
iii) Is there adequate security?

The banker will assess the risk from a number of perspectives:

(a) *Industry risk* — what is the present and future outlook for the company's industry? For instance, a regulated industry with a fixed rate of return and no competition has a significantly lower industry risk than a highly competitive, cyclical industry or an aging, contracting industry.

(b) *Business risk* — what is the company's position within the industry? What is its market share? Is it the industry leader or clearly a follower? Does it have capable management? How are its products regarded? What are they doing to enhance their situation?

(c) *Financial risk* — how sound is the company financially in comparison to its competitors? Is it already carrying too heavy a debt load?

(d) *Environmental risk* — what is the company's environmental record? Is the company likely to create environmental problems which could result in major clean-up expenses, fines or claims ranking ahead of the bank, or, in the worst case, a transfer of environmental liability to the bank?

Canadian bankers have considerable experience in virtually every industry and have the ability to analyze, assess and determine the perceived risk in each of these areas and to evaluate the risk/reward relationship on a given scale. This scale varies from institution to institution but is consistent within each institution.

The bank will also consider the security available. This can involve current assets as security (generally receivables and/or inventory), or fixed assets (land and/or buildings and/or machinery/equipment) and/or personal guarantees. Banks are able to take a pledge of accounts receivable and inventory, whereas trust companies and non-bank lenders have generally had to rely on fixed assets as security.

The banker will want to look at the ageing of accounts receivable, collection history, inventory turnover and work-in-process. If the company's product is new, the banker may want to see it, and review test results and quality control data. If the security offered is real estate or machinery, are these assets saleable, and are they in good condition? Are the personal guarantees worth anything (i.e., do the guarantors have substantial net worth **other** than their investment in the business itself)?

Finally, the banker will informally evaluate the treasurer and the principals of the company. Do they appear trustworthy? Does the presentation appear to be sensible? What is their past track record? Are they sincere? The quality of management is a critical factor in the bank's perception of the risk of a loan. Although it cannot be measured by objective benchmarks, the credibility will be tested over time, and the bank will want to know that the treasurer can be counted on to carry out those actions which have been promised, and to communicate in an open, honest, and timely manner.

The Negotiating Process

Commercial and corporate lending is an art, not a science. Therefore, there is no precise formula as to what the terms of the banking relationship will be. Naturally, the interest rate on the loan will be a function of the risk and security package. However, most measures of the risk (e.g., margin requirements and covenants) or security package (e.g., whether or not personal guarantees will be provided) are themselves negotiable.

The treasurer should be prepared to negotiate all aspects of the term sheet (see below) in order to reach a relationship that is favourable to the company yet practical to the point that the bank will approve it. If the treasurer is too passive, the banker will tend to charge more and ask for more security. If the treasurer is too aggressive, the banker may be left with no choice but to reject the application. The treasurer must be practical and seek a balanced term sheet that will be acceptable to both parties.

The Term Sheet

The term sheet will set out the parameters under which the bank has agreed to provide the credit facility. The term sheet sets out in business language the agreement between the bank and the customer.

The treasurer must review the term sheet with great care as a breach of any part of it will entitle the bank to cancel the facility, and require immediate repayment.

Typical contents of the term sheet are set out below:

- Agreed amounts and purpose of the facility;
- Interest rates and fees;

- Repayment terms;
- Security provided — this will describe the legal agreements required;
- Margin requirements;
- Covenants (i.e., promises made by the borrower to the bank);
- Shareholder guarantees;
- Conditions relating to the borrower's operations;
- Reporting requirements; and
- Matters requiring bank approval.

The term sheet takes the form of a letter, signed by the bank's Account Officer, and which to be effective, requires the borrower's signature (see example in Appendix to this chapter).

The most important item to be negotiated is the size and the purpose of the facility. Obviously the treasurer will want as much as requested, and the banker will want what is prudent from the bank's perspective. The treasurer should realize that if the bank is unwilling or unable to provide the facility at the requested amount, that this might not allow the company to carry out its business plan and as such, perhaps no amount should be borrowed. In this case, the treasurer should consider suspending the discussions in the interim while leaving open the possibility of returning at some later point with a scaled down business plan incorporating the reduced facility. This will also give the treasurer time to propose the package to another financial institution.

It is not unusual for a treasurer to ask for a larger facility than is expected to be needed so that the bank can reduce the amount. Assuming the amount of the facility is agreed upon, the next major area to negotiate is the interest rate and fees and the repayment terms. The proposed facility can be either a term or a demand loan. If a term loan, the interest rate will generally be fixed, with monthly principal and interest payments and a defined maturity date. If a demand loan, the interest rate will generally be on a prime plus basis, with monthly payments of interest only and an undefined maturity date (on demand). This area is highly sensitive as the rates and fees will determine the cost of the facility to the company and also give an indication of how risky the facility is viewed (i.e., if prime plus 3 per cent, this indicates that the company is a highly marginal customer, whereas at prime this indicates that the company is highly regarded). The treasurer must consider the financial aspects in the light of alternatives, i.e., the difficulty in trying to borrow from another source if the bank is charging prime plus 3 per cent. The nature of the bank's security is an important element of the negotiating process. In smaller companies, the bank may request a personal guarantee. This is often not appropriate, and the treasurer may be successful in negotiating the requirement away. However, banks have tended to take a harder line on this in recent years, particularly when the owner is active in operating the business.

Other elements of the term sheet will be:

- **Margin requirements,** such as limiting the loan to a percentage of certain assets, for example, 75 per cent of accounts receivable;
- **Covenants,** which may be financial measures, (e.g., not to exceed certain debt to equity ratios, conditions relating to the borrower's operations to maintain certain working capital, inventory turnover and/or gross margin ratios), or covenants to perform in a certain manner (e.g., not to breach certain security arrangements); and
- **Reporting requirements** (e.g, periodic financial statements, regular submission of accounts receivable listings).

There will usually be certain matters or transactions which the company will have to agree to submit for bank approval (e.g., sale of part of the business, dividends, etc.).

The discussions will generally be held over one or two meetings and then the bank will formally present the term sheet. It is then up to the company to accept or reject it.

Default

Although default is not a desirable outcome for either party, it does occur from time to time, especially during times of an economic downturn. Default may be a minor technical violation of a covenant in a loan agreement, or a more serious indication of financial difficulty.

The default is most serious when the company is not in a position to meet its financial obligations and can no longer make principal and/or interest payments. Alternatively, the bank's security might be impaired if a company makes a large write-down of its inventory/receivables or disposes of a piece of machinery or equipment. The banker will have to analyze this situation (assuming the company will provide the information) or request that a special audit be conducted to determine the bank's position. Sometimes the default is only technical (and thus not immediately serious) as in the case where a company can no longer maintain a certain financial ratio (e.g., working capital ratio of 1.25). In this instance, the bank will probably simply establish a new ratio with which it is comfortable.

Some early signs of future financial difficulty would include a sharp rise in accounts receivable or inventory, increasing bad debts and/or a decreasing gross margin.

The treasurer should keep its bank informed at all times as to the company's financial position and work with it to avoid an act of default. Depending on the type of default, the banker should assess whether the problem is short-term or long-term, whether the problem can be resolved by being more flexible on certain covenants or by extending additional credit to the company or depending upon the nature and condition of its security whether the bank would be advised to act sooner rather than later to protect its interest. Any attempt by the treasurer to avoid or ignore the banker will only precipitate a showdown. The banker may start by tightening up credit lines or asking for additional security. The treasurer should make every effort to work with the bank and attempt to reach a practical solution favourable to both parties.

Other Banks

There are three categories of banks referred to as Schedule I, Schedule II and Schedule III banks, based on the nomenclature in the *Bank Act*.

Schedule I banks are domestic chartered banks. These include the largest five: RBC Financial Group (generally called Royal Bank of Canada), CIBC (Canadian Imperial Bank of Commerce), BMO Financial Group (Bank of Montreal), Scotiabank (Bank of Nova Scotia) and TD Bank Financial Group (Toronto-Dominion Bank). Also included as Schedule I banks are the National Bank of Canada and several smaller banks.

Schedule II banks are subsidiaries of foreign banks. These include most of the larger international banks. Schedule III banks are branches of foreign banks. A list of all banks in Canada is provided as an Appendix to the previous chapter.

It is often productive to discuss banking requirements with banks other than the five largest chartered banks. Many have specialized niches that they try to occupy. The specialization may be by product offered, by industrial sector served, or even by national affinity. The best way to learn about what is available may be by talking to colleagues in the same industry.

Private Lenders

There are a number of private lenders that can provide either term or demand facilities. These include insurance companies, pension funds, or local (or even foreign) private lending funds. These lenders charge significantly higher rates and fees and are generally considered to be lenders of last resort. Nevertheless, the treasurer should consider their availability, in particular when borrowing on a short-term basis.

Factoring

Factoring is a traditional way of trading a company's receivables to a third party for immediate cash. A factoring company (or recently even a bank) will assess the company's receivables in terms of the credit-worthiness of the customers, the anticipated length of time to collect the receivables and the nature of the goods or products sold. The factoring company will discount the receivables (anywhere from 8 per cent to 20 per cent) and give the company immediate cash. Generally speaking, the factoring company will not assume the credit risk of the receivables. The receivables are then collected. As the receivables are converted into cash, the advance from the factoring company is paid down along with an interest rate and/or fees on the advance. The balance is paid to the company.

The treasurer can best take advantage of this arrangement when the cash advance will be relatively high (i.e., 90 per cent of receivables as opposed to 80 per cent) and the credit risk relatively low. Generally, this works for a company in a cyclical industry.

For example, a custom toy manufacturer may ship over 50 per cent of its orders in September and October. It must pay its suppliers and maintain peak production although it will not receive payment from the retail toy or department stores until December. By taking advantage of a factoring arrangement, the company can obtain the cash it needs to continue operation during this peak period. The interest rate charged by the factoring company is higher than a conventional banking facility but represents another alternative source of financing. The treasurer should explore the possibility of setting up a factoring arrangement with a factoring company or integrate it into the existing banking facility.

Letters of Credit

In order to facilitate domestic or international trade, buyers and sellers use letters of credit. A letter of credit (L/C) is an instrument issued by a bank guaranteeing the payment of a customer's drafts up to a stated amount for a specified period.

For example, consider a Canadian exporter that sells computer equipment to South America. As the exporter is not familiar with the purchaser's financial situation, the purchaser must provide a letter of credit before the goods will be shipped. Once the exporter ships the goods, the letter of credit is confirmed and the exporter will receive the funds. This process can be carried out by the two financial institutions or through the use of a trade finance confirming house. In either event the exporter receives payment on a timely basis and avoids credit risk, which is assured by the bank issuing the letter of credit.

Alternatively, a Canadian importer has placed a series of revolving orders with a Mexican parts manufacturer. If the importer gives the manufacturer a documentary letter of credit, the importer's Canadian bank at the same time, will remove the funds from the importer's account. The importer should attempt to have the manufacturer accept a standby letter of credit. In this case, the L/C is funded at the time the manufacturer requires payment (namely, when the goods are shipped). Since this is a recurring order, payments will be spread out over time (as the goods are shipped) rather than paid up front.

Export Development Corporation

In some instances, a Canadian exporter will be selling to a company or government in a country that does not have a developed commercial banking sector. In this case, the traditional trade finance instruments (e.g., letters of credit) are not available. In order to protect the exporter from the risk of non-payment and to facilitate trade, the Export Development Corporation (EDC) was formed.

EDC will protect the exporter from non-payment by providing short-term (up to 180 days) insurance on up to 90 per cent of the value of the exporter's receivables. The premium charged is based on the country/buyer risk and credit terms and range anywhere from 0.4 per cent to 2 per cent. EDC can also provide a longer-term insurance facility (one to five years) on sales of capital goods or capital projects being built by Canadian companies in a foreign country.

The EDC insurance helps the Canadian exporter in another way. For example, consider an exporter selling rail cars to an Asian country. It may require working capital in order to build the cars. Its Canadian financial institutions would be able to advance the funds necessary to build the cars to honour the contract on the strength of the EDC insurance.

In some limited instances, EDC will provide financing of its own in order to assist a Canadian exporter bidding for a foreign contract.

EDC's Web site is *www.edc.ca.*

Business Development Bank of Canada

The Business Development Bank of Canada (BDC) can provide financing to Canadian companies that have been unsuccessful in attempting to borrow funds from the commercial banks or other private sector lenders. BDC can provide loans to support commercial ventures as well as mortgages on a company's real estate assets. BDC criteria and availability of funds have changed from time to time.

BDC's Web site is *www.bdc.ca.*

Other Government Programs

Numerous other government programs are available at both the federal and provincial levels to facilitate funding on commercial activities, or to encourage hiring, investment, or research and development. The treasurer is advised to contact his/her local ministries of trade, industry, science or labour, as well as the Canada Employment Centres.

A good place to start for further information is the Industry Canada Strategis Web site at *www.strategis.ic.gc.ca.*

Appendix 5A

Example of a term sheet for an operating line of credit to a private company

January 2, 2004

Mr. J. Smith
Consolidated Enterprises Inc.
44 River St.
Toronto, Ontario
M1C 4T4

Dear Mr. Smith:

We are pleased to advise that the following credit facility is being offered and has been approved subject to the terms and conditions recited below:

Borrower

Consolidated Enterprises Inc.

Lender

Canadian Dominion Bank ("the Bank")

Amount and Form (and purpose, if necessary)

$500,000 Operating Facility
$100,000 Letters of Credit
$ 5,000 Visa Credit
$100,000 Spot Foreign Exchange

Availability

Operating Facility in Canadian Dollars and may be availed of in any combination of:
— Operating Overdrafts, Acceptances under L/Cs. Letters of Credit available in multiple currencies.

Repayment

On demand.
— Operating Overdrafts are to fluctuate widely with normal receipts and disbursements.
— Letters of credit and other contingent liabilities are to be covered from:
  • the operating facility as they become actual liabilities and/or acceptances.

Interest Rate/Charges

Operating Facility
— Operating overdrafts at prime + 150 basis points per annum, payable monthly in arrears.

Documentary L/C — standard charges

where:

Prime rate means the variable reference interest rate per year as declared by ABC from time to time to be its prime rate for Canadian dollars loans made by ABC in Canada on a 365/366 day year basis.

Fees

Credit Administration Fee — $150 monthly

Structuring Fee: $1,500.

Out of Pocket Review Costs: for periodic realty and PPSA and credit bureau searches, telephone toll charges, on account of the borrower.

Default Charges: $150 late reporting fee per occurrence and made for excesses over lending and/or margin limits.

Security

The entire facility is secured by:

General Assignment of Accounts Receivable registered in appropriate jurisdictions.

Overdraft Lending Agreement $500,000.

Registered General Security Agreement.

Adequate fire and other perils insurance over inventories, equipment, loss payable to the bank.

The operating facility is additionally secured by: Assignment of inventories under Section 178 of the *Bank Act*.

Covenants

The operating facility plus acceptance under L/Cs will not exceed 75 per cent of assigned acceptable accounts receivable (less those over 90 days, other specifically identified accounts, those from associated companies and superpriority payables to include employee deduction payables).

Outstanding L/Cs will not exceed 75 per cent of assigned acceptable inventories.

A minimum current ratio of 1.25:1 will be maintained at all times. To be increased to 1.50:1 effective May 31, 2006.

Total debt to tangible net worth will not exceed 3.5:1 as at January 31, 2004, to reduce to 2.75:1 by May 31, 2005, and 2.25:1 by May 2006. Tangible net worth is defined as paid in capital plus retained earnings plus formally postponed loans from shareholders/associated companies less advances to shareholders/associated companies less intangible assets.

Tangible net worth as defined above of at least $250,000 will be maintained at all times commencing January 2, 2004. To be increased to $300,000 as at May 2005 and an additional $100,000 yearly for year ended May 2006.

The borrower undertakes to:

— advise the Bank of any significant change in its ownership and/or management.

Without the Bank's prior approval, the borrower will not:

— declare and pay cash dividends

— incur capital expenditures in excess of $3,000 per annum

— incur loans from other sources and liabilities with other parties

— acquire businesses, amalgamate with other entities or purchase stocks of other companies

— make (or increase) advances to and repay advances from associated companies, shareholders or officers

— advance drawings and/or salaries in excess of $100,000 annually for each of John Smith and George Smith.

Reporting Requirements

Within 20 days from each month-end, aged listings of accounts receivable, inventory listing, and aged accounts payable.

Within 30 days from each quarter-end, internally prepared interim financial statements appropriately certified by the Chief Financial Officer (or President).

Within 75 days from fiscal year-end, the audited financial statements of the borrower.

Events of Default

Without detracting from the demand nature of this credit facility, the Bank reserves the right to withdraw the foregoing facilities at any time should there be in its opinion:

(a)   any material adverse change in the financial condition and operations of the borrower and guarantors

(b)   any unacceptable change in ownership and management of the company — borrower

(c)   any legal implications or developments detrimental to the affairs of the borrower

(d)   breach of any term or condition contained herein

Please acknowledge your acceptance of the foregoing by signing and returning the enclosed duplicate of this letter.

Yours truly,

Canadian Dominion Bank

Senior Account Manager

_____

Accepted this_____day
of_____2001

By: Consolidated Enterprises Inc.

_____

PART A

PART

B

Corporate
Investment Strategy
and Analysis

It is not unusual for a business to spend more time analyzing a capital expenditure than to decide how to invest excess funds that are 10 — or a 100 — times the size. This section sets out a disciplined and logical approach to making investment decisions.

CHAPTER 6

Investment Strategy

Overview

Investment strategy requires explicit consideration of investment objectives. Investment objectives should flow logically from the mission and strategy of the corporation. The treasurer must know why the company has funds to invest, and when they may be required to be liquidated. This chapter covers investment of idle funds, not long-term strategic investment.

Four investment criteria must be set: the required levels of safety and quality, liquidity parameters, rate of return, and taxation characteristics. This chapter concludes with an investment policy checklist to assist in setting the investment strategy.

Strategic Framework

The first step in investing idle funds is to establish a strategic framework of investment objectives and guidelines. The strategic framework will ensure that goals and objectives are logical, congruent with those of the enterprise, and have been clearly agreed to by senior management. This chapter discusses investment of idle funds, not long-term strategic investment such as business acquisitions.

Setting out an explicit framework will facilitate consideration of other elements of the cash management process. For example, the method of reporting to senior management on the structure of the investment portfolio and the results achieved will implicitly determine the approach used in evaluating the results. That approach depends, in turn, on the company's own objectives. To deal with these issues, reference must be made to the company's goals for the treasury management function, as well as its structure. Is the treasury function a profit centre or a cost centre? Should it maximize return or minimize risk? Is cash and treasury management centralized or decentralized? What scope do operating managers have with respect to treasury issues?

These questions cannot be answered easily or quickly. They require introspection and policy guidance from senior management. As a member of the senior management team, one role of the treasurer is to ensure that appropriate policy guidance is requested and is forthcoming. This will generally take the form of the treasurer proposing a treasury and investment policy for ratification by the executive (and normally by the board of directors as well).

Investment Objectives

Objectives for the investment portfolio should be in writing and should be approved by senior management. There is a large variety of investment vehicles available. The different vehicles have a wide range of characteristics and it is impossible to determine which instruments are appropriate in the absence of explicit (and usually written) objectives.

In larger companies, the portfolio manager and cash manager may be two different people. In those circumstances, written guidelines are essential to ensure that there is effective communication between the parties and that the management of the investment portfolio is consistent with corporate needs. For the same reasons, written objectives ensure that top management is adequately involved in the strategy setting process.

Investment objectives follow directly from the mission and objectives of the corporation. What business is the company in? What goods or services does it sell? What are its markets, its customers and its suppliers?

Other investment objectives result from financial considerations: How is the company's balance sheet structured? How seasonal or cyclical is its cash flow?

Business operations should drive the cash management decision-making process, not vice versa. (That might be one reason for the treasury and cash management process being a cost centre rather than a profit centre.) The company's treasury management policies should enable it to accomplish its strategic objectives. For example, a company in "steady state" in a mature industry with constant sales levels would administer its short-term investment portfolio somewhat differently than a company that required flexibility to engage in an ambitious acquisitions program.

Short-term investment strategies should reflect the corporation's current business plans. These plans set out anticipated cash inflows and outflows over the next fiscal year or two. The uncertainty of those inflows and outflows and the degree of assurance of the level of investment earnings required by the corporation will have a significant effect on the investment portfolio objectives and the appropriate management style.

For example, a business plan anticipating higher levels of inventories and higher levels of receivables in connection with business expansion may require the flexibility to convert significant amounts of short-term investment instruments into cash. The degree of certainty of the asset growth (in other words, the probability of the plan being achieved) will determine the relative need for quick access to the portfolio.

Analysis of the sensitivity of cash flows to changes in revenues, expenses, accounts receivable turnover, and inventory turnover is an important part of this planning process. The relative sensitivity of the need for cash, and the likelihood of that need in light of possible changes in the business operations and the environment, will significantly influence the investment strategy. That is why business operations must drive treasury decisions, not vice versa.

Short-term investment strategy checklist

The short-term investment strategy should consider the following business and financial issues:

- **Corporate Mission**
    (a) What business are we in?
    (b) What is our objective?
    (c) Who are our stakeholders?
    (d) Who are our customers?
    (e) What are our business philosophies and values?
    (f) Who are our suppliers?

- **"Macro" financial issues**

  (a) What are the financial risks in our industry?
  (b) How is our industry perceived by banks and other lenders?
  (c) How is our industry perceived by investors?
  (d) Where are we in the business and economic cycle?

- **"Micro" financial issues**

  (a) What is the structure of our balance sheet? How much leverage do we have? Should it increase or decrease?
  (b) What are our cash needs? How certain are we?
  (c) What are the major financial risks that will affect our cash requirements?
    (i)   bank loans,
    (ii) debt programs,
    (iii) acquisitions or divestitures,
    (iv) lease commitments.
  (d) What are the major operating risks that will affect our cash requirements?
  (e) What are the historic patterns of cash requirements? What will alter those historic trends?
  (f) What contingency plans for cash do we require?
  (g) What are the short-, medium- and long-term forecasts for
    (i)   business expansion or contraction,
    (ii) acquisitions or divestitures,
    (iii) changes to dividend levels.

It is instructive to contrast public and private corporations in considering how business strategy drives the short-term investment strategy. Very often, public corporations have pressure to steadily increase earnings every quarter and very often, consequently, require a short-term approach to investment decisions. Private companies may have the flexibility to take a longer-term approach to management decision making and might accept more risk in their short-term portfolio as a result.

Investment Criteria

Four criteria must be established in setting the short-term investment strategy. They are:

- Safety and quality;
- Liquidity;
- Rate of return;
- Taxation.

If written objectives are not used, the criteria may be implicit rather than explicit. Nonetheless, they are always present. Maintaining written objectives was recommended earlier because management is then forced to address the issues and make the criteria explicit.

Safety and quality

In managing a short-term portfolio on a day-to-day basis, treasurers generally focus on the returns offered. It is normally taken for granted that the principal is secure. It would be more correct to say that the principal is secure within whatever quality parameters have been set: There is always **some** level of risk. Financial risks are reviewed in Chapter 17.

A primary responsibility of cash managers is to prevent the loss of capital. Investments must be analyzed to consider the level of risk of default by the borrower and the possibility that the borrower will not pay the required interest and principal at maturity. Similarly, in the case of marketable securities that may be sold before maturity, consideration must also be given to the risk of a drop in the market value of the security.

Liquidity

Liquidity refers to how quickly the investment can be converted into cash. Marketable securities can often be converted to cash immediately (subject to whatever the normal settlement period is — from half an hour to three business days depending on the security). At the other extreme, other short-term investments may only be converted into cash before the maturity at the option of the issuer such as a bank. In some cases, the investments may not be cashable before maturity.

The liquidity of the portfolio as a whole may be greater than that of the individual investments. To the extent that the portfolio has investments with staggered maturities, the treasurer may be able to deal with unexpected cash requirements simply by not rolling over various instruments as they come due.

The methodology set out in this chapter should ensure that the reasons for a company having or requiring short-term investments are stated explicitly and agreed to by management. Understanding the reasons for needing liquidity in the portfolio for ready access to cash requires an intimate understanding of the financial needs of the company and its business plans. Typical reasons for requiring liquidity, and the ability to invest short-term proceeds quickly are set out below:

- Seasonal sales patterns, and resulting working capital needs;
- Scheduled repayment of bank loans, proceeds from bank loans;
- Sale and leaseback transactions;
- Issuance of bonds or sale of shares;

- Income tax remittances;
- Collection of major contracts;
- Payment of employee bonuses.

Rate of return

The normal measure as to the success of an investment (and the investment portfolio) is its rate of return given the level of risk assumed. The calculation of the return or profit on the investment must take into account all directly related expenses such as commissions to brokers and bank-handling charges.

Although return is often regarded as the most important criterion, there is, of course, a trade off between return and safety. One reason for having written investment objectives is to document the safety/return trade-off that has been selected and ensure approval by senior management and the board of directors.

The rate of return will depend upon the quality of the investment, the issuer, the term to maturity, and any options that exist for early encashment. Modern portfolio theory shows that a blend of investments can offer a higher rate of return with no increase in risk (or the same return with less risk) compared to a few isolated or concentrated investments.

Taxation

Investment instruments differ in their taxation characteristics. Dividends, capital gains and interest income all have different effects for tax purposes. Some investments offer a lower apparent return, but since income from them attracts less income tax, the after-tax return is higher than that of other investments.

Portfolio returns are normally measured on a pre-tax basis. Therefore, if the portfolio includes investment returns taxed at a preferential rate (i.e., dividends on shares, which may be free of tax to a corporation), the return should be adjusted to a tax equivalent basis.

For example, assume that interest is taxed at 35 per cent and that dividends are tax-free. In that case, $1,000 of interest income would result in an after-tax return of $650. $1,000 of dividends would result in an after-tax return of $1,000. Therefore, the dividends are equivalent to interest income of $1,000/0.65 or $1,538. (Note that the factor of 0.65 is equal to one minus the tax rate.)

Therefore, the tax equivalent amount of $1,000 of dividends is $1,538. If the interest and dividends are each earned on an investment with a cost of $20,000, the interest yield is $1,000/$20,000 or 5 per cent, while the dividend yield on a tax equivalent basis is $1,538/$20,000 or 7.7 per cent. This yield of 7.7 per cent is equal to 5 per cent/65 per cent, where 65 per cent is the after-tax yield on interest income.

Management Controls and Reporting

Once the corporation's objectives, cash management strategies and operating guidelines have been determined, it is appropriate to establish the management control and reporting procedures. The objectives of management reporting are for management to monitor compliance with their objectives and guidelines, measure the returns achieved by the portfolio manager, and quickly identify problems as they occur.

Management must receive information quickly. Therefore, the controls and reporting structure put in place should not require an undue amount of preparation time. There is also a cost to prepar-

PART B

ing the information, so that its preparation should be as inexpensive as possible. Reporting procedures that are cumbersome, hence slow and expensive, are unwise. It is far better to focus on the minimum information required, then on how to produce it quickly and cheaply.

There are two internal controls that are easy to establish and yet provide very powerful control. The first internal control technique is *division of duties*. This can manifest itself in several ways. Record keeping should be independent from the investment decision-making process. Reporting and analysis of results should be separate from either record keeping or investment management. In addition, unusual, atypical or large investment decisions should require the approval of at least two individuals. Finally, changes to investment guidelines or operating policies should also require approval by more than one person.

The other internal control technique is that of *management supervision*. A culture of "hands on" management supervision, where managers and executives are familiar with the details of the investment program and effectively supervise the day-to-day routine also has a powerful internal control effect. Of course, management must **manage**, and not get overly involved in the details. Nonetheless, management of the treasury function must be aware of the general activity carried out. (Some high profile losses have occurred where senior management abdicated supervision of their treasury departments. The treasurers were fired — and so were their managers.)

Both of these internal control techniques have the advantage that in addition to ensuring adequate internal controls, they will contribute to a culture of informed and effective management.

Investment Policy Checklist

Having a written investment strategy will facilitate preparation of detailed investment policies to guide day-to-day management of the portfolio. Following are typical investment policies that should be established:

- *Minimum liquidity standards* — For example, the short-term portfolio should have $500,000 available within 10 days and $100,000 available at all times.
- *Prohibited investments* — For example, the short-term portfolio may not include repurchase agreements, reverse repurchase agreements or private placements.
- *Investment quality standards* — For example, all short-term commercial paper must have a rating from an independent rating agency of at least "P-2".
- *Definition of business purpose* — For example, the primary purpose of the short-term investment portfolio is to support the company's day-to-day working capital requirements and its acquisition program.
- *Restrictions on investment strategies* — For example, securities may not be purchased on margin.
- *Expressly permitted investment strategies* — For example, the use of financial derivatives such as options and forward rate agreements is permitted for hedging purposes.
- *Adherence to regulatory requirements* — This will be required by financial institutions, some non-profit entities, and other organizations that are subject to regulatory requirements. (For financial institutions, see Chapters 2 and 3.)

Conclusion

The theme of this chapter has been that investment objectives must be clearly articulated and understood, and agreed to by senior management. The process of investing any portfolio is one of determining the appropriate trade-offs between potential risks and potential rewards. The portfolio manager or treasurer cannot determine this in isolation — it requires participation by senior

PART B

management. Writing out investment objectives and ensuring that they are congruent with the company's business plan is an important step in achieving a rational investment strategy.

A culture that includes a "hands-on" management style, as well as a strong division of duties regarding supervision of the short-term portfolio, will help ensure effective execution of the corporate investment strategy.

7

Financial Statement Analysis

Overview

Financial statement analysis is a study of historic information gleaned from financial statements in order to take action in the future. Different users have differing objectives. Financial statement analysis examines mathematical relationships within the financial statements to assess the business.

Introduction

The primary objective of financial statements (balance sheet, income statement, statement of cash flows, statement of retained earnings, notes to the financial statements) is to provide useful information to interested parties. Different users of financial statements have different needs, but all are concerned about the company's past performance, present condition and future performance to some degree. Current shareholders, who generally are thought of as the primary users, are interested in assessing how management has discharged its fiduciary responsibilities to them as owners of the enterprise. Likewise, management is interested in showing the results of its activities during the year. Prospective shareholders and investment analysts look for information to enable them to predict future income, cash flow, dividends and market price.

Current and prospective creditors have various needs, depending on their relationship with the company. They may be concerned with short-run liquidity, tangible asset backing or the company's long-term financial structure and solvency. They may be interested in whether established debt covenants have been met, or in the level of next year's profits or cash flow.

Government entities such as regulatory and taxing entities may look to financial statements to provide them with information regarding the company's compliance with regulations and legislation.

Financial statement users also need to assess qualitative factors such as the quality of management and its ability to control and utilize resources effectively.

The main use of financial statement analysis is to assist in predicting the future. This is because investors and creditors cannot change what they did in the past. They own shares in the business, or have extended a loan. That has already happened — it is history. The critical question is, What should the users do now — should the loan or invested amount be increased or decreased? The answers to these questions depend on predicting what will happen to the business in the future.

Financial statements do not convey much information on their own; some analysis is required. This analysis requires computations as well as measures to which the results can be compared. Frequently, financial statement analysis entails the use of ratios; however, other techniques are available. Also, it is important to note that financial statements are not the sole source of information for individuals and entities making decisions — other sources commonly are used.

PART B

Limitations of Financial Statement Analysis

There are two fundamental limitations to financial statement analysis. First, a primary goal of analysis is to predict the future. There are many reasons why past statements may be poor predictors. In calculating ratios and deriving statistics, it is important to be alert for qualitative factors that may influence the business in the future, particularly if their effect has yet to be reflected in the analysis. Changes in the competitive environment, the economy, regulation, new product lines, changing demographics, etc. may cause the future to differ materially from that implied in the ratios or percentages calculated.

The second limitation is that financial statement analysis generally is based on financial statements prepared in accordance with Generally Accepted Accounting Principles ("GAAP"). GAAP has many advantages: the information is objective, verifiable and may be somewhat comparable between companies. It also has some constraints which may reduce the usefulness of financial statement analysis in analyzing the past and predicting future results for a company.

GAAP is based on historical transactions. With some exceptions, it conveys limited information about market values or any unrealized gains in values; however, unrealized losses generally are accounted for. Similarly, GAAP does not require future commitments to be recognized (except that any losses must be accounted for or disclosed). Instead, GAAP requires only disclosure of future commitments in the notes to the financial statements.

The limitations of GAAP recall Winston Churchill's comments on democracy: "It has been said that democracy is the worst form of Government except all those other forms that have been tried from time to time." (From a speech in the House of Commons on November 11, 1947.) Despite the limitations of GAAP, it results in information that is objective and can be verified or audited — extremely important attributes.

The user of financial statements should keep these limitations in mind. Where appropriate, other data should be requested. For example, a creditor of a business may require balance sheet information prepared on the basis of liquidation values, or may ask for projections or budgets.

Also, note that internal financial statements that are not necessarily in accordance with GAAP may be used as the basis for financial statement analysis.

Types of Financial Statement Analysis

This section discusses different techniques that users can employ to analyze financial statements. To illustrate the techniques, information from the attached hypothetical financial statements for ABC Limited are used.

Horizontal analysis (trend percentages)

Horizontal analysis examines percentage changes in comparative financial statements. It highlights changes in an item over time. For example, using the income statements of ABC Limited (see page 178), the following percentage changes in net income would be calculated:

20X1 to 20X2	6.7%
20X2 to 20X3	6.0%
20X3 to 20X4	15.7%

Alternatively, trend percentages could be used. A trend is shown by selecting a base period and then dividing it into the comparable ratios for subsequent periods. In the above example, the trend in net income, using 20X1 as a base, would be as follows:

20X1	100.0%
20X2	106.7%
20X3	113.1%
20X4	130.9%

To be most useful, the percentage changes in most financial statement items should be calculated for a number of periods to assess the direction a company's operations are taking.

The usefulness of horizontal analysis and trend percentages is that these methods go beyond comparing absolute changes and clearly highlight changes in items. Although dollar changes are important to consider, the magnitude of a change can often be more informative than simply the amount of the change. However, percentage changes should be evaluated in terms of the items importance to the company as a whole. For example, a 100 per cent increase in a $500 account would obviously be of little concern compared to a 25 per cent increase in a $300,000 account.

147

A trend line is not useful if the base period used is not representative for comparison purposes. Also, trend lines cannot be calculated if the base period is negative.

Vertical analysis (common size analysis)

Vertical analysis reveals the relationship of various components to the total in one particular time period. For example, ABC Limited's 20X4 comparative income statement subjected to vertical analysis looks like the following:

	20X4		20X3	
	000s	% of Sales	000s	% of Sales
Sales	$10,000	100.0%	$8,950	100.0%
Cost of Sales	4,300	43.0%	4,400	49.2%
Gross margin	5,700	57.0%	4,550	50.8%
Operating expenses				
Depreciation	690	6.9%	420	4.7%
Interest expense	340	3.4%	370	4.1%
Other	1,320	13.2%	1,000	11.0%
Operating income	3,350	33.5%	2,760	30.8%
Other revenue	150	1.5%	275	3.1%
Income before taxes	3,500	35.0%	3,035	33.9%
Income tax expense				
Current	800	8.0%	700	7.8%
Deferred	750	7.5%	650	7.3%
Net income	$1,950	19.5%	$1,685	18.8%

Two of the most frequently used results of vertical analysis are the gross profit margin (for ABC Limited, 57.0%) and the profit margin (for ABC Limited, 19.5%). In general, the higher these ratios are, the better. If they are too low, they indicate that either sales are too low or expenses are too high.

Although vertical analysis focuses on one time period, these calculations often are performed for comparative periods. For example, the cost of goods sold as a percent of sales in 20X1 can be compared to the same percentage in 20X2 to assess whether production costs are increasing relative to sale price.

Ratio analysis

Ratio analysis expresses the relationship of one number to another. Horizontal and vertical analysis can be considered categories of ratio analysis.) There is no one right ratio for every company. However, the ratios should be compared against appropriate benchmarks to determine their meaning. In particular, trends within a given company are particularly important.

This section classifies the most commonly used ratios into the following categories:

- Measuring ability to pay current debts (short-run liquidity)
- Measuring the ability to pay long-term liabilities (long-term solvency, efficacy of debt management)
- Measuring the quality of asset management
- Measuring profitability
- Analyzing the company's investment quality (value ratios)

Measuring ability to pay current debts

a. Current (working capital) ratio

This is the most commonly used ratio to assess a company's ability to pay current liabilities (i.e., liquidity). It is calculated as follows:

$$\text{Current ratio} \quad = \quad \frac{\text{Current assets}}{\text{Current liabilities}}$$

For ABC Limited, the ratio would be:

$$20X4 = \frac{\$3,290,000}{\$1,640,000} = \underline{\underline{2.0}}$$

$$20X3 = \frac{\$2,645,000}{\$1,020,000} = \underline{\underline{2.6}}$$

From these calculations, one can determine that ABC Limited's current ratio decreased. However, one cannot conclude whether this is a concern unless other comparison benchmarks are used.

The balance sheet of most companies is divided between current and long-term assets and liabilities. However, for companies with unclassified balance sheets (e.g., real estate companies, utilities), the financial statement user may choose to segregate the balance sheet items between current and long-term or use other, more appropriate ratios.

In general, a higher current ratio indicates that a company has sufficient liquid assets to maintain normal business operations. However, an abnormally high ratio may indicate that management is not maximizing the use of the company's assets or is having sales difficulties. Typically, the ratio should be at least 1.0, preferably at least 1.5. Service companies which don't have inventory may have much lower current ratios.

b. Acid-test (quick) ratio

This ratio assesses a company's ability to pay current liabilities *if all current liabilities came due immediately*. It is a more conservative measure than the current ratio as less liquid assets such as inventories and prepaid expenses are excluded from the calculation. It is calculated as follows:

$$\text{Acid-test ratio} = \frac{\text{Cash} + \text{Short-term investments} + \text{Net accounts receivable}}{\text{Current liabilities}}$$

For ABC Limited, the ratio would be:

$$20X4 = \frac{\$400,000 + 1,290,000}{\$1,640,000} = \underline{\underline{1.0}}$$

$$20X3 = \frac{\$450,000 + 900,000}{\$1,020,000} = \underline{\underline{1.3}}$$

From these calculations, one can determine that ABC Limited's quick ratio decreased. Again, one cannot conclude whether this is a concern unless other comparison benchmarks are considered.

In general, a higher quick ratio indicates that a company has sufficient liquid assets to maintain normal business operations. However, an abnormally high ratio may indicate that management is not maximizing the use of the company's assets or is having sales difficulties. Typically, a ratio of 1.0 would be considered adequate.

Measuring ability to pay long-term debts

a. Debt Ratio

The debt ratio evaluates the proportion of the company's assets that it has financed with debt (i.e., the effect of its debt on its financial position). It is calculated as follows:

$$\text{Debt ratio} = \frac{\text{Total debt}}{\text{Total assets}}$$

The composition of "total debt" may vary. For example, some financial statement users will exclude taxes and other deferred charges because they feel that these items do not represent real liabilities. Some consider deferred taxes to be, in effect, an interest-free loan from the government and, therefore, a component of debt. Still others consider it to be earnings that have not been allowed to flow through to retained earnings and, therefore, a part of shareholders' equity. Also, some may exclude current liabilities other than the hypothecated debt such as the current portion of longterm debt (i.e., bank advances, accounts payable and accrued liabilities, income taxes payable, dividends payable may be excluded).

Excluding deferred taxes, the debt ratio for ABC Limited is as follows:

$$20X4 = \frac{\$5,585,000 - 545,000}{\$11,030,000} = \underline{\underline{0.46}}$$

$$20X3 = \frac{\$5,215,000 - 295,000}{\$9,275,000} = \underline{\underline{0.53}}$$

From these calculations, one can determine that ABC Limited's debt ratio decreased. Again, one cannot conclude how favourable this is unless other comparison benchmarks are utilized.

In general, the lower the debt ratio, the stronger the company's financial position. The higher the ratio, the higher the strain of meeting principal and interest payments and, therefore, the higher the associated financial risk. Accordingly, creditors may be concerned about high debt ratios. They may require a higher interest rate on the debt or include restrictive covenants to reduce the perceived increased risk of loss of their loans. In many industries, the rule of thumb is that the ratio should be no higher than 0.33 to 0.50.

b. Debt-to-equity ratio

A variation of the debt ratio is the debt-to-equity ratio. It also evaluates the proportion of the company's assets that it has financed with debt. It is calculated as follows:

$$\text{Debt-to-equity ratio} = \frac{\text{Total debt}}{\text{Total shareholders' equity}} \quad \text{or} \quad \frac{\text{Total debt}}{\text{Total Shareholders' equity} - \text{Total assets}}$$

The definition of "shareholders' equity" may vary, as noted above.

Excluding deferred taxes, the debt-to-equity ratio for ABC Limited is as follows:

$$20X4 = \frac{\$5,585,000 - 545,000}{\$5,445,000} = \underline{\underline{0.93}}$$

$$20X3 = \frac{\$5,215,000 - 295,000}{\$4,060,000} = \underline{\underline{1.21}}$$

Thus, from 20x3 to 20x4 ABC Limited's debt-to-equity ratio has decreased.

As with the debt ratio, the lower the debt-to-equity ratio, the more favourably the company will be viewed. The higher the ratio, the higher the strain of meeting principal and interest payments and, therefore, the higher the associated financial risk. Accordingly, creditors may be concerned about high debt-to-equity ratios. They may require a higher interest rate on the debt or include restrictive covenants to reduce the perceived increased risk of loss of their loans.

c. Net tangible assets to total debt ratio

This ratio indicates the protection provided by the company's tangible assets after all liabilities have been satisfied. It is calculated as follows:

$$\text{Net tangible assets to total debt ratio} = \frac{\text{Total assets} - \text{Deferred charges} - \text{Intangible assets} - \text{Non-hypothecated current liabilities}^*}{\text{Total debt}}$$

* Current liabilities less short-term hypothecated debt.

PART B

Excluding deferred taxes from the debt calculation, the net tangible assets to total debt ratio for ABC Limited is as follows:

$$20X4 = \frac{\$11,030,000 - 1,300,000 - (1,640,000 - 500,000)}{\$5,585,000 - 545,000} = \underline{1.67}$$

$$20X3 = \frac{\$9,275,000 - 1,500,000 - (1,020,000 - 500,000)}{\$5,215,000 - 295,000} = \underline{1.47}$$

In general, the higher the net tangible assets to debt ratio, the more favourably the company will be viewed. The higher the ratio, the higher the asset value backing every $1 of debt. A common rule of thumb is that this ratio should be $2 for every $1 of debt. Using this rule, a debtor of ABC Limited may have some cause for concern.

d. Cash flow to total debt ratio

This ratio assesses a company's ability to repay borrowed funds. Cash flow is a better indicator of this ability than is net income. It is calculated as follows:

$$\text{Cash flow to total debt} = \frac{\begin{array}{c}\text{Net income + Minority interest in earnings} \\ \text{of subsidiaries + Depreciation + Deferred income} \\ \text{tax expense +/- Other non-cash items (e.g., gains} \\ \text{and losses)}\end{array}}{\text{Total debt}}$$

Excluding deferred taxes from total debt, the cash flow to total debt ratio for ABC Limited is as follows:

$$20X4 = \frac{\$1,950,000 + 690,000 + 750,000}{\$5,585,000 - 545,000} = \underline{0.67}$$

$$20X3 = \frac{\$1,685,000 + 420,000 + 650,000}{\$5,215,000 - 295,000} = \underline{0.55}$$

Thus from 20x3 to 20x4, ABC Limited's cash flow to total debt ratio improved.

In general, the higher the cash flow to total debt ratio, the more favourably the company will be viewed. For many industries, a rule of thumb is that this ratio should be at least 0.30 for each of the preceding five years. Using this rule, a debtor of ABC Limited would be satisfied.

e. Interest coverage (times-interest-earned) ratio

This ratio assesses a company's ability to pay interest expense based on its earnings. It is calculated as follows:

$$\text{Interest coverage ratio} = \frac{\begin{array}{c}\text{Net income} + \text{Minority interest in earnings of}\\ \text{subsidiaries}\\ + \text{Income tax expense} + \text{Total interest expense}\end{array}}{\text{Total interest expense}}$$

Excluding deferred taxes from total debt, the cash flow to total debt ratio for ABC Limited is as follows:

$$20X4 = \frac{\$1,950,000 + 1,550,000 + 340,000}{\$340,000} = \underline{\underline{11.3}}$$

$$20X3 = \frac{\$1,685,000 + 1,350,000 + 370,000}{\$370,000} = \underline{\underline{9.2}}$$

In general, the higher the interest coverage ratio, the more favourably the company will be viewed. A common rule of thumb is that this ratio should be at least 3.0 for each of the preceding five years. Using this rule, ABC Limited's ability to pay interest on its debt would be adequate.

PART B

f. Preferred dividend coverage (times-dividends-earned) ratio

For companies with preferred shares, this ratio is similar to the interest coverage ratio, except that it indicates the margin of safety behind preferred dividends. It is calculated as follows:

$$\text{Preferred dividend coverage ratio} = \frac{\text{Net income + Minority interest in earnings of subsidiaries + Income tax expense + Total interest expense}}{\text{Total interest expense + Preferred dividend payments pre-tax}}$$

To place payments to creditors and preferred shareholders on a consistent basis, the equivalent of preferred dividends on a pre-tax basis (as interest expense is on a pre-tax basis) is used in the calculation. The following formula is used to "gross-up" the preferred dividends to their equivalent pre-tax amount:

$$\frac{\text{Actual preferred dividend payment}}{\text{(i.e., after-tax amount)}} \times \frac{1}{(1 - \text{Income tax rate})}$$

The appropriate income tax rate to use for ABC Limited is calculated as follows:

$$20X4 = \frac{\$800,000 + 750,000}{\$3,500,000} = \underline{44.3\%}$$

$$20X3 = \frac{\$700,000 + 650,000}{\$3,035,000} = \underline{44.5\%}$$

Therefore, the preferred dividend coverage ratio for ABC Limited is as follows:

$$20X4 = \frac{\$1,950,000 + 1,550,000 + 340,000}{\$340,000 + 100,000/(1 - .443)} = \underline{7.4}$$

$$20X3 = \frac{\$1,685,000 + 1,350,000 + 370,000}{\$370,000 + 100,000/(1 - .445)} = \underline{6.2}$$

In general, the higher the preferred dividend coverage ratio, the more favourably the company will be viewed by current and potential preferred shareholders. A common rule of thumb is that this ratio should be at least 3.0 for each of the preceding five years. Using this rule, ABC Limited's ability to pay preferred dividends would be adequate.

Measuring operating efficiency

a. Inventory turnover ratio

For companies that sell goods, the inventory turnover ratio and its counterpart, days-in-inventory, are used frequently. The inventory turnover ratio evaluates the number of times inventory is turned over (i.e., sold) annually. The faster inventory is turned over, the sooner the company creates accounts receivable and ultimately, the sooner it collects cash. Since a large part of many companies' working capital (for manufacturers, wholesalers, and retailers) generally is tied up in inventory, inventory management can have a significant impact on earnings. The inventory turnover ratio is calculated as follows:

$$\text{Inventory turnover ratio} = \frac{\text{Cost of goods sold}}{\text{Average inventory}}$$

If comparative figures are not available, ending inventory balances are substituted for "average inventory". Also, if a company does not disclose its cost of goods sold separately, estimates of the inventory ratio can be garnered from using the Net Sales figure instead.

For companies having very seasonal operations, this ratio may distort reality because it assumes that sales and inventory purchases occur evenly throughout the year. Financial statement users of such companies may want to calculate the ratio on a semi-annually, quarterly or monthly basis.

Therefore, the inventory turnover ratio for ABC Limited is as follows:

$$20X4 = \frac{\$4,300,000}{(\$1,550,000 + 1,250,000)/2} = \underline{3.1}$$

$$20X3 = \frac{\$4,400,000}{\$1,250,000} = \underline{3.5}$$

From these calculations, it appears that ABC Limited's inventory turnover ratio declined. However, without the ending inventory figure for 20X2, this cannot be determined for certain. Also, one cannot conclude whether this is a concern even if the ratio did decline without understanding more about the company.

In general, a higher level of turnover is better. However, the appropriate level will vary by industry. For example, inventories of companies in the fashion, high tech, food production, wholesale or retail industries should turn over faster than for other companies in general.

b. Days-in-inventory (inventory supply)

To express the inventory turnover ratio in terms of the number of days required to sell inventory, the following calculation is used:

$$\text{Days-in-inventory} = \frac{365}{\text{Inventory turnover ratio}}$$

$$\text{or} = \frac{\text{Average inventory} \times 365}{\text{Cost of goods sold}}$$

The days-in-inventory for ABC Limited is as follows:

$$20X4 = \frac{365}{3.1} = \underline{\underline{117.7}}$$

$$20X3 = \frac{365}{3.5} = \underline{\underline{104.3}}$$

In other words, in 20X4, ABC Limited's complete inventory was sold on average every 117.7 days, but was sold every 104.3 days in the previous year.

In general, the lower the figure, the more successful the company is at managing its inventory. A lower figure indicates that the company requires a smaller investment in working capital and therefore, there is less risk of being caught with a large inventory during market declines and the inventory being lost through obsolescence, shrinkage or other factors.

c. Accounts receivable turnover ratio

Most companies offer credit terms to their customers and, therefore, will have accounts receivable outstanding during the year. To measure a company's ability to collect cash from its customers, the accounts receivable turnover ratio and its counterpart, days'-sales-in-receivables, are used frequently. The accounts receivable turnover ratio measures the number of times accounts receivable is turned over (i.e., collected) annually. The faster accounts receivable is turned over, the sooner the company can utilize the cash in earning revenue. A large part of many companies' working capital often is tied up in accounts receivable, therefore, management of receivables can have a significant impact on earnings. The accounts receivable turnover ratio is calculated as follows:

PART B

$$\text{Accounts receivable ratio} = \frac{\text{Net credit sales}}{\text{Average accounts receivable}}$$

If comparative figures are not available, ending accounts receivable balances are substituted for "average accounts receivables". Also, companies generally do not disclose their net credit sales separately. Therefore, the Net Sales figure may be used instead.

For companies having very seasonal operations, this ratio may distort reality because it assumes that credit sales and cash collections occur evenly throughout the year. Financial statement users of such companies may want to calculate the ratio on a semi-annually, quarterly or monthly basis.

The accounts receivable turnover ratio for ABC Limited is as follows:

$$20X4 = \frac{\$10,000,000}{(\$1,290,000 + 900,000)/2} = \underline{\underline{3.9}}$$

$$20X3 = \frac{\$4,400,000}{\$900,000} = \underline{\underline{4.9}}$$

From these calculations, it appears that ABC Limited's accounts receivable turnover ratio declined. However, without the ending accounts receivable figure for 20X2, this cannot be determined for certain.

d. Days-sales-in-receivables

To express the accounts receivable turnover ratio in terms of the number of days required to collect receivables, the following calculation is used:

$$\text{Days-sales-in-receivables} = \frac{365}{\text{Accounts receivable turnover ratio}}$$

A better way to calculate the figure is to count back through monthly credit sales to determine the actual days outstanding, rather than to use averages.

The days-sales-in-receivables for ABC Limited is as follows:

$$20X4 = \frac{365}{3.9} = \underline{93.6}$$

$$20X3 = \frac{365}{4.9} = \underline{74.5}$$

In other words, in 20X4, ABC Limited's complete accounts receivable was collected every 93.6 days, but was collected every 74.5 days in 20X3.

In general, the lower the ratio, the more successful the company is at managing its receivables. A lower ratio indicates that the company requires a smaller investment in working capital and there is less risk of uncollectible accounts receivable occurring.

e. Average days payables ratio

The average days payable calculates the average number of days a company takes to pay suppliers' invoices. It is calculated as follows:

$$\text{Average days payables ratio} = \frac{\text{Average accounts payable balance} \times 365}{\text{Purchases}}$$

If comparative figures are not available, ending accounts payable balances are substituted for "average accounts payable." Also, if

PART B

companies do not disclose their purchases separately, the Cost of Goods Sold figure may be used to estimate average days payable.

Assuming that ABC Limited's purchases in 20X4 were $3,500,000 and $2,900,000 in 20X3, the average days payable ratio is as follows:

$$20X4 = \frac{(\$1,140,000 + 520,000)/2 \times 365}{\$3,500,000} = \underline{86.6}$$

$$20X3 = \frac{\$520,000 \times 365}{\$2,900,000} = \underline{65.4}$$

In other words, in 20X4, ABC Limited took, on average, 86.6 days to pay its suppliers, but took only 65.4 days in 20X3.

In general, the higher the ratio, the more favourable for the company. However, a very high figure may indicate that suppliers are paid too slowly. Ideally, this figure should be greater than average days sales in receivables.

f. Working capital turnover ratio

The working capital turnover, another less commonly used ratio, is calculated as follows:

$$\text{Working capital turnover ratio} = \frac{\text{Net sales}}{\text{Current assets} - \text{Current liabilities}}$$

The working capital turnover ratio for ABC Limited is as follows:

$$20X4 = \frac{\$10,000,000}{\$3,290,000 - 1,640,000} = \underline{6.1}$$

$$20X3 = \frac{\$8,950,000}{\$2,645,000 - 1,020,000} = \underline{5.5}$$

From these calculations, it appears that ABC Limited's working capital turnover ratio declined. However, one cannot conclude whether or not this is a concern even if the ratio did decline unless other comparison benchmarks are utilized.

Measuring profitability

a. Return on sales ratio

The return on sales ratio is calculated as follows:

$$\text{Return on sales ratio} = \frac{\text{Net income}}{\text{Net sales}}$$

The return on sales ratio for ABC Limited is as follows:

$$20X4 = \frac{\$1,950,000}{\$10,000,000} = \underline{19.5\%}$$

$$20X3 = \frac{\$1,685,000}{\$8,950,000} = \underline{18.8\%}$$

From these calculations, ABC Limited's return on sales ratio has improved.

b. Gross margin ratio

The gross margin ratio is calculated as follows:

$$\text{Gross margin ratio} = \frac{\text{Gross margin}}{\text{Sales}}$$

The gross margin ratio for ABC Limited is as follows:

$$20X4 = \frac{5,700,000}{10,000,000} = \underline{57.0\%}$$

$$20X3 = \frac{4,550,000}{8,950,000} = \underline{50.8\%}$$

PART B

The gross margin ratio has improved over the two years, which is a positive trend.

c. Return on assets ratio

The return on assets ratio measures the a company's ability to manage assets to maximize income. It considers the two types of returns that accrue to those financing a company's operations: interest expense for creditors, and net income for common and preferred shareholders (i.e., it reflects the combined effect of both the operating and financing activities of a company). The ratio can be calculated on a pre-tax or an after-tax basis. The after-tax return on assets ratio is calculated as follows:

$$\text{Return on assets ratio} = \frac{\text{Net income} + \text{Interest expense}}{\text{Average total assets}}$$

If comparative figures are not available, the ending total assets figure may be substituted for "average total assets."

The after-tax return on assets ratio for ABC Limited is as follows:

$$20X4 = \frac{\$1,950,000 + 340,000}{(\$11,030,000 + 9,275,000)/2} = \underline{22.6\%}$$

$$20X3 = \frac{\$1,685,000 + 370,000}{\$9,275,000} = \underline{22.2\%}$$

The pre-tax return on assets ratio is calculated as follows:

$$\text{Pre-tax return on assets ratio} = \frac{\text{Net income} + \text{Interest expense} + \text{Income taxes}}{\text{Average total assets}}$$

The pre-tax return on assets ratio for ABC Limited is as follows:

$$20X4 = \frac{\$1,950,000 + 340,000 + 800,000 + 750,000}{(\$11,030,000 + 9,275,000)/2} = 37.8\%$$

$$20X3 = \frac{\$1,685,000 + 370,000 + 700,000 + 650,000}{\$9,275,000} = 36.7\%$$

From these calculations, ABC Limited's pre-tax and after-tax return on assets ratios are fairly consistent in 20X3 and 20X4. However, without the ending total assets figure for 20X2, one cannot conclude this definitively. Also, one cannot conclude whether the ratios are good or bad unless other comparison benchmarks are utilized.

In general, the higher the return on assets ratio, the more favourably the company will be viewed by financial statement users. This is because a higher ratio indicates that the assets of the company have been managed well in earning income.

d. Return on invested capital ratio

The return on invested capital ratio is similar to the return on assets ratio, except that it uses a slightly different denominator. The ratio can be calculated on a pre-tax or an after-tax basis. The after-tax return on invested capital ratio is calculated as follows:

$$\text{Return on invested capital ratio} = \frac{\text{Net income + Interest expense}}{\text{Average short-term hypothecated debt + Average long-term debt + Average shareholders' equity}}$$

If comparative figures are not available, the ending assets figure is substituted for average figures.

The after-tax return on invested capital ratio for ABC Limited is as follows:

PART B

$$20X4 = \frac{\$1,950,000 + 340,000}{(\$500,000 + 500,000 + 3,400,000 + 3,900,000 + 5,445,000 + 4,060,000)/2} = \underline{25.7\%}$$

$$20X3 = \frac{\$1,685,000 + 370,000}{\$500,000 + 3,900,000 + 4,060,000} = \underline{24.3\%}$$

The pre-tax return on invested capital ratio is calculated as follows:

$$\text{Pre-tax return on invested capital ratio} = \frac{\text{Net income + Interest expense + Income taxes}}{\text{Average short-term hypothecated debt + Average long-term debt + Average shareholders' equity}}$$

The pre-tax return on assets ratio for ABC Limited is as follows:

$$20X4 = \frac{\$1,950,000 + 340,000 + 800,000 + 750,000}{(\$500,000 + 500,000 + 3,400,000 + 3,900,000 + 5,445,000 + 4,060,000)/2} = \underline{43.1\%}$$

$$20X3 = \frac{\$1,685,000 + 370,000 + 700,000 + 650,000}{\$500,000 + 3,900,000 + 4,060,000} = \underline{40.2\%}$$

From these calculations, ABC Limited's pre-tax and after-tax return on invested capital ratios have improved slightly. However, without the ending total assets figure for 20X2, one cannot conclude this definitively.

In general, the higher the return on invested capital ratio, the more favourably the company will be viewed by all financial statement users. This is because a higher ratio indicates that the assets of the company have been managed well in earning income.

e. Return on total equity ratio

This ratio reflects the profitability resulting from use of the common and preferred shareholders' capital in the company.

Generally, it is calculated on an after-tax basis only. The return on total equity ratio is calculated as follows:

$$\text{Return on total equity ratio} = \frac{\text{Net income}}{\text{Average total shareholders' equity}}$$

If comparative figures are not available, ending total shareholders' equity may be substituted for "average total shareholders' equity".

The return on total shareholders' equity ratio for ABC Limited is as follows:

$$20X4 = \frac{\$1,950,000}{(\$5,445,000 + 4,060,000)/2} = \underline{41.0\%}$$

$$20X3 = \frac{\$1,685,000}{\$4,060,000} = \underline{41.5\%}$$

From these calculations, ABC Limited's return on total shareholders' equity ratio has remained fairly stable from 20X3 to 20X4. However, without the ending total shareholders' equity figure for 20X2, one cannot conclude this definitively.

In general, the higher the return on total shareholders' equity ratio, the more favourably the company will be viewed by current and potential shareholders. This is because a higher ratio indicates that the assets of the company have been managed well in earning a return in the form of income for all shareholders.

f. Return on common (shareholders') equity ratio

This ratio is a refinement of the return on shareholders' equity and it reflects the profitability resulting from use of the common shareholders' capital in the company. It is calculated on an after-tax basis only. The return on common shareholders' equity ratio is calculated as follows:

$$\text{Return on common equity ratio} = \frac{\text{Net income} - \text{Preferred dividends}}{\text{Average common shareholders' equity}}$$

If comparative figures are not available, ending common shareholders' equity is substituted for "average common shareholders' equity".

The return on common shareholders' equity ratio for ABC Limited is as follows:

$$20X4 = \frac{\$1,950,000 - 100,000}{(\$2,500,000 + 1,500,000 + 1,945,000 + 1,560,000)/2} = \underline{49.3\%}$$

$$20X3 = \frac{\$1,685,000 - 100,0}{\$1,500,000 + 1,560,000} = \underline{51.8\%}$$

From these calculations, ABC Limited's return on common shareholders' equity ratio has declined slightly. However, without the ending common shareholders' equity figure for 20X2, one cannot conclude this definitively.

In general, a higher return on common shareholders' equity is better. This is because a higher ratio indicates that the assets of the company have been managed well in earning a return in the form of income for common shareholders.

g. Financial leverage ratio

Financial leverage calculates the advantage or disadvantage occurring when a company earns a return on total assets that differs from the return on total equity. Positive leverage results when the rate of return on a company's activities exceeds the average interest rate on borrowed funds. Leverage is directly related to the debt ratio —

the higher the debt ratio, the higher the financial leverage ratio. The financial leverage ratio is calculated as follows:

Financial leverage ratio = Return on total equity ratio – Return on assets ratio

The financial leverage ratio for ABC Limited is as follows:

20X4 = 41.0% (from **d** above) – 22.6% (from **b** above) = <u>18.4%</u>

20X3 = 41.5% – 22.2%   = <u>19.3%</u>

From these calculations, ABC Limited's positive financial leverage has declined slightly.

In general, a higher financial leverage ratio is better. However, too much leverage increases the company's financial risk since interest is a fixed cost that must always be paid.

h. Earnings per common share

This ratio is one of the most widely quoted financial statistics for public companies. Under GAAP, companies must disclose the earnings per share ratio (EPS) in their financial statements. EPS permits shareholders to see how profitable their investment in shares of a company has been as well as the likelihood of the company paying out dividends. *"Basic EPS"* is calculated as follows:

$$\text{Earnings per common share} = \frac{\text{Net income} - \text{Preferred dividends}}{\text{Number of common shares outstanding}}$$

Fully diluted EPS is a less commonly used measure of EPS, although GAAP requires disclosure of this figure if it is relevant. Fully diluted EPS is calculated using the same numerator as for basic EPS. However, the denominator includes common stock equivalents such as convertible debentures, convertible preferred shares, stock options, rights, warrants, etc. In other words, fully diluted EPS attempts to calculate the EPS that would accrue to

PART B

common shareholders assuming maximum potential dilution from existing sources.

Basic EPS for ABC Limited is as follows:

$$20X4 \ = \ \frac{\$1,950,000 - 100,000}{2,500,000} \qquad = \quad \underline{\$0.74}$$

$$20X3 \ = \ \frac{\$1,685,000 - 100,000}{1,500,000} \qquad = \quad \underline{\$1.06}$$

From these calculations, ABC Limited's EPS has declined slightly.

Analyzing investment quality

a. Price/earnings ratio

The price/earnings ratio (P/E ratio) is another commonly quoted financial statistic for public companies. The P/E ratio permits comparison of market price with EPS. It is calculated as follows:

$$\text{Price/earnings ratio} = \frac{\text{Current market price of common shares}}{\text{EPS}}$$

Assuming that the current market price of ABC Limited's common stock is $10 per share and was $8 in 20X3, its P/E ratio is as follows:

$$20X4 \ = \ \frac{\$10.00}{\$0.74} \qquad = \quad \underline{13.6}$$

$$20X3 \ = \ \frac{\$8.00}{\$1.06} \qquad = \quad \underline{7.2}$$

From these calculations, ABC Limited's P/E ratio has increased.

The P/E ratio above considers *historical* earnings compared to *current* market prices. However, past earnings are not necessarily indicative of future earnings. The P/E ratio may also be calculated based on forecast earnings for the current fiscal year.

b. Dividend yield

The dividend yield measures the percentage of the market value of a stock that is returned as dividends annually. This ratio assesses the second component of the return to shareholders: the periodic distributions in the form of dividends to shareholders. It is calculated as follows:

$$\text{Dividend yield} = \frac{\text{Dividend per common share}}{\text{Current market price per common share}}$$

ABC Limited's dividend yield ratio is as follows:

$$20X4 = \frac{\$1,465,000/2,500,000}{\$10.00} = \underline{\underline{5.8\%}}$$

$$20X3 = \frac{\$1,000,000/1,500,000}{\$8.00} = \underline{\underline{8.3\%}}$$

From these calculations, ABC Limited's dividend yield has decreased. However, one cannot conclude whether or not this is a concern unless other comparison benchmarks are utilized.

In general, the higher the dividend yield, the more favourably the investing community views the company. However, if the company is attempting to conserve cash in order to make profitable investments, a lower yield may be completely acceptable. A low yield is often evidence of a popular or relatively expensive stock.

PART B

CANADIAN TREASURY MANAGEMENT

c. Book value per share

Book value per share measures the shareholders' equity in terms of each share of stock outstanding. The book value per preferred share ratio is calculated as follows:

$$\text{Book value per share} = \frac{\text{Liquidation (redemption) value of preferred shares} + \text{Cumulative preferred dividends in arrears}}{\text{Preferred shares outstanding}}$$

The book value per preferred share of ABC Limited is as follows:

$$20X4 = \frac{\$1,000,000 + 0}{100,000} = \underline{\$10.00}$$

$$20X3 = \frac{\$1,000,000 + 0}{100,000} = \underline{\$10.00}$$

The book value per common share is calculated as follows:

$$\text{Book value per common share} = \frac{\text{Total shareholders' equity} - \text{Portion allocated to preferred shareholders}}{\text{Common shares outstanding}}$$

The book value per preferred share of ABC Limited is as follows:

$$20X4 = \frac{\$5,445,000 - 1,000,000}{2,500,000} = \underline{\$1.78}$$

$$20X3 = \frac{\$4,060,000 - 1,000,000}{1,500,000} = \underline{\$2.04}$$

From these calculations, the book value of ABC Limited's common shares has declined.

Book value per share ratios are of limited usefulness because they are based upon GAAP historical cost accounting, rather than market values. However, the relationship between book value per share and market price may be of interest, particularly if it has changed significantly from historic norms.

Other ratios

The ratios discussed previously are not the only ratios that may be utilized when analyzing financial statements. Those discussed have the most wide-ranging application. Other ratios may be appropriate, depending on the company being analyzed, such as annual sales per square foot of retail floor area (for retail businesses), leasing revenue per square foot (for companies renting property space), loan loss provisions as a percentage of outstanding loans (for financial institutions), daily revenue per bed (for nursing homes), net cash flow from a property relative to gross income (for real estate companies), etc.

Words of Caution

Financial statement analysis provides clues as to the financial condition of the company, but does not provide final answers. Often, additional investigation is required to determine what the horizontal, vertical or ratio analysis really means. The ratio or percentage may be compared to that of other companies or ratios in the same company but for different time periods. Often, a trend or change in a trend is much more critical than the ratio itself.

The process of financial statement analysis is a repetitive or iterative process. The calculation of a ratio or percentage and comparison of that number to a particular benchmark often raises questions that require further analysis. Those questions are answered by calculating further ratios or obtaining additional information, which raises more questions.

The appropriate ratio for a company depends upon the situation and on many factors such as composition of current assets, type of business activities (industry category), and returns on other investment vehicles with similar and dissimilar risk components. It is important to remember that the significance of a ratio likely will vary between different types of companies and under different economic conditions.

Many ratios are based upon average results for the fiscal year and, therefore, may not uncover concerns within the year. Therefore, it may be useful to calculate certain ratios and perform horizontal and vertical analysis for period of less than one year.

Standards of Comparison

As mentioned above, the appropriate ratio depends on the circumstances. Therefore, in order to evaluate the horizontal, vertical and ratio analysis, one must compare the results to some appropriate benchmark(s). Appropriate benchmarks include the following:

- **Past results of the company** — Comparing the analysis to past results of the company will help assess whether some sort of trend is occurring, be it downward, upward or stable.
- **The company's planned goals and objectives** — A company's goals and objectives are quantified in its budgets, forecasts, and projections.
- **General economic performance** — Some information can be garnered if one compares the company's results to the overall performance of the economy, be it local, national or international.
- **Individual company results** — While it is useful to employ internal and economic comparisons, financial statement

users must be able to assess how one company compares to another.

When comparing results of a company to another, one must ensure that the companies compared are similar. For example, the financial statement user should consider the industry to which the other company belongs, the size of the company, the nature of its operations and its accounting policies. Also, the financial statement user must ensure that the basis used to calculate the ratios are the same. As discussed previously, there are different ways to interpret one particular ratio. For example, if the inventory turnover of one company is computed using cost of goods sold, but net sales for another, the ratios should not be compared.

- **Industry results** — Overall industry results are a common source of comparison. Again, one must ensure that the basis used to calculate the ratios is the same. (See the section "Sources of External Information" below.)

Generally, it is more informative to employ more than one benchmark to evaluate the results of horizontal, vertical and ratio analysis.

Sources of External Information

The best source of additional information is through the Internet. Following are some of the most useful sites for general and statistical information:

Statistics Canada: *www.statcan.ca*. Contains a huge variety of statistical information on the economy, sectors and industries. Most of the in-depth information is available for sale for relatively small fees. "Quarterly Financial Statistics for Enterprises" ($26) contains aggregate financial statements for many industries.

PART B

The Bank of Canada: *www.bankofcanada.ca*. Contains extensive information on Canada's economic indicators. Click on "Research & Publications" and "Rates & Statistics."

For Canadian public companies, *www.sedar.com* contains all regulatory filings including proxy statements, earnings announcements and annual reports. Sites such as *www.stockhouse.ca* and *www.globeinvestor.com* provide links to extensive additional information such as analysts' reports and press releases.

For United States public companies, the Edgar site at *www.sec.gov/edgar.shtml* provides regulatory filings including 10-Ks. Sites such as *www.hoovers.com* and *www.bloomberg.com* provide links to extensive additional information such as analysts' reports and press releases.

Illustrative Financial Statements — ABC Limited

These statements are used in the examples discussed throughout the chapter.

ABC Limited Balance Sheets
As At December 31
(000s)

	20X4	20X3
Assets		
Current Assets		
Cash	$400	$450
Accounts receivable, net	1,290	900
Inventories	1,550	1,250
Prepaid expenses	50	45
Total current assets	3,290	2,645
Long-term investments	190	230
Capital assets, net	6,250	4,900
Goodwill, net	1,300	1,500
Total assets	$11,030	$9,275
Liabilities		
Current Liabilities		
Accounts payable and accrued liabilities	$1,140	$520
Current portion of long-term debt	500	500
Total current liabilities	1,640	1,020
Long-term debt	3,400	3,900
Deferred income taxes	545	295
Total liabilities	5,585	5,215
Shareholders' Equity		
Preferred stock, redeemable at $10 per share (100,000 shares issued and outstanding)	1,000	1,000
Common stock (shares issued and outstanding — 20X4 — 2,500,000; 20X3 — 1,500,000)	2,500	1,500
Retained earnings	1,945	1,560
Total shareholders' equity	5,445	4,060
Total liabilities and shareholders' equity	$11,030	$9,275

ABC Limited
Statements of Income and Retained Earnings
For the Years Ended December 31
(000s)

	20X4	20X3	20X2	20X1
Sales	$10,000	$8,950	$8,050	$7,500
Cost of sales	4,300	4,400	4,100	3,750
Gross margin	5,700	4,550	3,950	3,750
Operating expenses				
Depreciation	690	420	400	350
Interest expense	340	370	310	285
Other	1,320	1,000	800	775
Operating income	3,350	2,760	2,440	2,340
Other revenue	150	275	200	0
Income before taxes	3,500	3,035	2,640	2,240
Income taxes				
Current	800	700	600	500
Deferred	750	650	450	250
Net income	1,950	1,685	1,590	1,490
Retained earnings, January 1	1,560	975	800	570
Less: Dividends paid				
Preferred	(100)	(100)	(100)	(100)
Common	(1,465)	(1,000)	(1,315)	(1,160)
Retained earnings, December 31	$1,945	$1,560	$975	$800

CHAPTER 8

Securities Analysis and Portfolio Management

Overview

The corporate treasurer's objective is to produce the greatest return with an acceptable level of risk. To maximize the return from investment funds while achieving corporate goals, the treasurer must carefully select from a variety of investment instruments. Also, the treasurer continually must analyze the performance of the company's securities relative to other securities in the market, and their ongoing relevance in the portfolio.

Proper portfolio management is important particularly in today's rapidly changing environment where a few hours or days can change the value of a portfolio significantly. Ideally, the corporate treasurer should review a portfolio regularly, such as daily or twice weekly. Portfolio design is an individual matter, driven by each company's risk tolerance and investment objectives.

This chapter provides tools for analyzing securities and for managing a portfolio. The first part of this chapter discusses the structuring of an investment portfolio. The second section addresses monitoring of the portfolio.

Selecting/Structuring a Portfolio

Evaluation of investment objectives, risk tolerance and time horizon

The first and probably most important stage in structuring an investment portfolio is to define the objectives of the portfolio *realistically*. It is important to realize that not all objectives can be maximized. Therefore, the corporate treasurer must rank the investment objectives. The treasurer also must realistically assess the company's risk tolerance as this will have a significant impact on the objectives of the portfolio. For example, if a company has a very low tolerance for assumed risk, selecting maximization of real return as the most important investment objective is not appropriate. However, a portfolio could be designed to maximize the real return *within a given lower level of accepted risk*. Finally, the period of time for which the investment funds are available must be determined. This will direct the term of securities selected for the portfolio.

Risk

In terms of an investment, total risk can be defined as the total variability of the actual returns. Mathematically, total risk of a particular security can be measured by a number of statistical factors:

- **Variance,** which measures the wideness of the distribution of variability. To measure the past variance of a portfolio and/or individual securities, the difference between the returns on individual investments in the portfolio and the average return of the portfolio is reviewed. To measure the future variance of a portfolio, the estimated returns on individual securities are compared to the average expected return of the portfolio (discussed below). It is calculated as follows:

For past returns:

$$\frac{1}{t} \times \left[\sum_{n=1}^{t} (R_n - R_a)^2 \right]$$

$$= \frac{1}{t} \times \left[\left[R_1 - R_a \right]^2 + \left[R_2 - R_a \right]^2 + \left[R_t - R_a \right]^2 \right]$$

For future returns:

$$\sum_{n=1}^{t} \left[P_n (R_n - E)^2 \right]$$

$$= P_1 \left[R_1 - E \right]^2 + P_2 \left[R_2 - E \right]^2 + \ldots + P_t \left[R_t - E \right]^2$$

PART B

where,

t = final time period

R_n = rate of return at period i

R_a = average rate of return of the period i to t

P_x = the probability associated with the xth return

E = expected return

For example, assume a past three-year time period with returns in each year of 10 per cent, 11.5 per cent and 8.5 per cent, respectively. Therefore, the average rate of return for the three-year period is 10 per cent. Variance of these past returns is calculated as follows:

$$\frac{1}{3} \times \left[\left[0.10 - 0.10 \right]^2 + \left[0.115 - 0.10 \right]^2 + \left[0.085 - 0.10 \right]^2 \right] = 0.00015$$

For example, assume a period with anticipated returns of 5 per cent, 10 per cent and 8 per cent, respectively, and an expected return of 9.5 per cent. The probability associated with each forecast return is 50 per cent, 30 per cent and 20 per cent, respectively. Variance of these future returns is calculated as follows:

$$0.5 \, [0.05 - 0.095]^2 + 0.3 \, [0.10 - 0.095]^2 + 0.2 \, [0.08 - 0.095]^2$$
$$= 0.001065$$

- **Standard deviation of returns,** which is the square root of variance. It measures the expected deviation of the actual return to the original expected return. It is the most common measure of risk used in practice.

For example, the standard deviation of the 0.00015 variance calculated for the three-year period above is 0.0326343.

- **Absolute average deviation**, which compares the expected average deviation of the actual return to the original expected return. It is calculated as follows:

$$\sum_{n=1}^{t} \left| P_n (R_n - E) \right|$$

$$= P_1 \left| R_1 - E \right| + P_2 \left| R_2 - E \right| + ... P_t \left| R_t - E \right|$$

Total risk of an *entire portfolio* is quantified as follows:

- **Standard deviation** which is calculated as follows:

$$\sqrt{V_1^2 W_1^2 + V_2^2 W_2^2 + ... + V_n^2 W_n^2 + 2W_1 W_2 V_1 V_2^2 Z_{1,2}^2 + 2W_1 W_n V_1 V_2^2 Z_{1,n}^2 + 2W_2 W_n V_2 V_n^2 Z_{2,n}^2}$$

where,

Vi   =   variance of returns of security i, or the standard deviation of returns associated with security i squared

Wi   =   total value of the portfolio invested in security i (i.e., the weighting of each security)

Zi,j   =   the correlation coefficient between securities i and j. The range of correlation coefficient factors are as follows:

+1.0	—	Perfect positive correlation
+0.5	—	Moderate positive correlation
0	—	No correlation
–0.5	—	Moderate negative correlation
–1.0	—	Perfect negative correlation

Risk tolerance

The major challenge affecting corporate treasurers is balancing investment risk and return. In an ideal world, corporate treasurers would maximize their companies' return without assuming any risk. However, associated with every type of investment is some level of risk, be it credit risk or any other type of risk. In such a situation, capital utilizers would not pay a high rate of return to compensate the corporate treasurer for a risk of potential loss. Therefore, the corporate treasurer must carefully consider his or her company's risk tolerance before designing an investment portfolio or making investment decisions. (See Chapter 9 for a discussion of the various types of risks.)

Return

To assess the effectiveness of investment decisions in light of investment objectives and to determine whether any investment action is needed (such as sale or purchase of certain securities, changing the average term of the portfolio, etc.), the corporate treasurer must evaluate the profitability of individual securities and the entire portfolio on an ongoing basis. The most commonly used measure in this regard is return. The concept of return is discussed in further detail in "Monitoring the Portfolio", starting on page 194, below.

Risk/return trade-off and diversification

Generally, standard deviation (discussed above) is used as a measure of risk. Therefore, the corporate treasurer looks for the most desirable combination of standard deviation and expected returns. Generally, if one or more securities have an equal return, treasurers will select a lower risk (lower standard deviation). Also, given equal risks, corporate treasurers generally prefer a higher return. In fact, the purpose of portfolio management is to find the optimal point between risk minimization and return maximization. Some academic studies have found that securities with high risks tend to have higher average rates of return. However, other studies have not agreed with such findings.

The total risk of an investment can be divided into **undiversifiable** (or **systematic**) **risk** and **diversifiable** (or **unsystematic**) **risk.** Unsystematic risk represents the risk associated with a particular security, while systematic risk is caused by factors that affect the prices of all securities simultaneously. By definition, it is difficult to reduce or control systematic risk through diversification and, therefore, corporate treasurers tend to focus on managing systematic risk. Prices of securities with low systematic risk generally are higher than those with a high systematic risk. Later sections of this chapter discuss models used to evaluate how individuals select their investments (such as the Capital Asset Pricing Model).

The cornerstone of portfolio structuring is diversification. Diversification is the reduction of investment risk by purchasing different securities (e.g., bonds, money market instruments, preferred stock, common stock) in different entities involved in different types of activities (e.g., governments, corporations in different industries, financial institutions) in different locations (e.g., different provinces or countries) and in different maturities (e.g., short-term, medium-term, long-term) for fixed income instruments. The main reason for diversification is to spread the risk to ensure that an unusually large amount of funds are not invested in a particular security(ies) that may default. Since there is no one optimal security for achieving investment criteria, a corporate treasurer should spread his or her risk by investing in a basket of carefully selected securities. (See Chapter 6 for a discussion of investment criteria.)

Effectively, diversification is a form of insurance. For example, while a Government of Canada treasury bill will provide a high level of safety and liquidity, it does not provide the highest rate of return. Take another example. A long-term bond purchased at a premium may provide a high level of regular income but little future potential for capital growth. However, it may not maximize a company's after-tax return.

In general, the higher the diversification and the more that investment risk is lowered, the more portfolio return will be lowered. However, diversification offers additional advantages such as producing a more predictable level of portfolio income. Ensuring that no one holding of securities is so large that it cannot be sold (i.e., marketability) is another reason for diversification. Research studies have indicated that an extensive portfolio size is not needed to provide adequate diversification. For example, one study found that in a portfolio of stocks, 12 to 15 different stocks was adequate. Another study concluded that fewer than 12 or 15 bonds were needed to sufficiently reduce the level of risk in a bond portfolio. In fact, a portfolio with too many holdings can hinder marketability of the investments. Therefore, all holdings of securities ideally should be in tradeable blocks.

It is interesting to note that studies have shown that the longer the investment period, the lower the risk assumed. The standard deviations of annualized returns of individual periods will be lower the longer the investment period employed. In other words, a long investment period will tend to "smooth out" any investment "mistakes" in any particular period.

Diversification alternatives

There are different approaches to diversifying an investment portfolio. One method, called *simple diversification*, simply refers to not putting all investment funds into one asset (i.e., diversifying some-what randomly, diversifying across industries, diversifying across quality of issuers). Studies have found that diversification across industries is no more effective than diversifying randomly. Many industries are highly correlated and this systematic risk cannot be diversified away. Therefore, simple diversification reduces a port-folio's risk to that of the systematic risk in the market.

Harry Markowitz developed a more "scientific" approach to selecting securities. This approach attempts to design portfolios with securities that are not perfectly positively correlated and it sometimes reduces risk below the systematic level without sacrific-ing return. He concluded that the first step in developing a port-folio should be to determine the expected return and risk associat-ed with a variety of different portfolios. From there, the correla-tion between each stock in a portfolio is reviewed.

Markowitz diversification can lower portfolio risk below the systematic level if a portfolio is designed with securities having low correlations. A key problem with using Markowitz's approach is that, historically, few securities have low correlations. Mathematical techniques are used to determine the optimal com-bination of securities.

Selecting the portfolio

In order to select a portfolio, a corporate treasurer must consider both quantitative and qualitative factors. Regarding the former, included are the expected profitability and the risk associated with a portfolio. Therefore, the following factors must be quantified:

- the expected return on each investment component of the portfolio by type of investment (e.g., equity securities, treasury bills, bonds);

- the standard deviation of the expected returns of each investment component;
- the correlations between the various components; and
- the share of the portfolio value invested in each component (i.e., the weighting).

There are numerous qualitative factors that should be reviewed when selecting the portfolio, such as the following:

- Quality of the issuer, which in turn affects the marketability of the securities. For debt issues, treasurers should consider their creditworthiness, the Government of Canada having the highest level of creditworthiness. For all securities, the state of the economy and the relevant industry should be examined as well as factors specific to the issuer such as type of company, quality of management and strength of financial statements over the past history;
- Maturity, if any;
- Coupon rate of interest, if any; and
- Price.

The most common evaluation made by corporate treasurers when deciding how to design their portfolios is the past performance of each investment considered. It is important to bear in mind that historical returns are not good predictors of future returns.

Treasurers should also consider various methods of investment valuation as discussed below.

Duration

Duration of fixed income securities should also be considered when determining whether and how much of an investment portfolio should include fixed income securities. Duration is a measure of the price volatility of a fixed income investment and it considers both maturity and coupon rate. It is the weighted average of the present values of the stream of future receipts. Because different corporate treasurers have different investment horizons, duration is an important consideration. Since duration is an indication of maturity, it can be used to maturity match assets and liabilities. For example, if a treasurer wants to ensure the company's liabilities are matched with assets to prevent liquidity problems, he or she can use the duration of liabilities to design his or her portfolio of fixed income securities.

Duration is calculated as follows:

$$\frac{\left[\displaystyle\sum_{n=1}^{N}\frac{n\times C_n}{(1+R)^n}+\frac{N\times V}{(1+R)^N}\right]}{\left[\displaystyle\sum_{n=1}^{N}\frac{C_n}{(1+R)^n}+\frac{V}{(1+R)^N}\right]}$$

where,

V	=	par value
C	=	semi-annual coupon interest
N	=	number of six-month periods to maturity
R	=	semi-annual rate of return to maturity

A simplified approximation of the above formula is:

$$\left[(1+R)\left(\frac{C}{M\times R^2}\right)\left(1-(1+R)^{-T}\right)\right]-\left[\left(\frac{C\times T}{M\times R}\right)(1+R)^{-T}\right]+\left[\frac{V}{M}\times T\times(1+R)^{-T}\right]$$

where,

$$M \quad = \quad \text{market value; price}$$

For example, assume that a $1,000 three-year 10 per cent bond is priced at $98.50 to yield 12 to maturity. The bond pays interest semi-annually. The approximate duration of the bond would be 5.13 six-month periods, calculated as follows:

$$1.06 \times \left[\frac{50}{985.00 \times 0.06^2} \right] \times \left(1 - 1.06^{-6} \right) - \left[\frac{50 \times 6 \times 1.06}{985.00 \times 0.06^2} \right] + \left(\frac{1}{0.985} \times 6 \times 1.06^{-6} \right)$$

Income tax considerations

Management of a portfolio can be complicated by the tax status of the company. Because the tax effect of portfolio transactions can impact the performance of a portfolio significantly, the income tax situation of the company is important to keep in mind when structuring a portfolio. Consultation with tax specialists should be considered when designing and monitoring an investment portfolio.

Fixed income securities, for example, have both an interest income component and a capital gain or loss component. The interest income is taxable as regular income, at the company's marginal tax rate. A bond with a maturity exceeding one year purchased at a discount will have a capital gain equal to the discount amount. Since only one half of capital gains are taxable, there can be a significant after-tax advantage to purchasing discount bonds. However, this tax advantage often is reflected in the price of a discount bond and, therefore, the discount bond may trade to yield a lower amount. In general, after-tax yield is maximized with the highest possible discount on a security over the shortest possible period. A premium bond, on the other hand, produces a capital loss, of which one half is deductible against any capital gains of the company. The corporate treasurer should evaluate investment yields on an after-tax basis when assessing the portfolio structure and performance.

The tax treatment of non-interest bearing securities such as treasury bills is fairly complex. In general, the return on a non-interest bearing security that is held to maturity is considered to be interest income entirely. However, CCRA deems a holder of a non-interest bearing security to have received taxable income at the end of each year that the security is held based on the yield at purchase. Therefore, a company holding a three-year Government of Canada treasury bill, for example, will have to pay tax in each of years one, two and three, even though the company receives no cash until the end of year three.

If a treasurer sells a non-interest bearing security (or zero-coupon bond) prior to maturity, a capital gain or loss may arise. A capital gain results if the security is sold at a price higher than the price that would be calculated using the original yield at purchase. If the opposite occurs, a capital loss results.

The tax treatment of preferred shares differs significantly from that of other fixed income securities such as bonds and treasury bills. Dividends from a Canadian corporation generally are tax-free to another corporation. Consequently, dividends are correspondingly more valuable than an equal amount of interest income on an after-tax basis.

Sources of information regarding securities

The treasurer should consult a number of sources in developing a portfolio of securities. In addition to keeping informed of current events affecting an issuer through various resources on the World

PART B

Wide Web and regularly reading of business papers and periodicals, the following can be reviewed:

- Investment dealers' research reports on the issuer and other companies in the industry.
- Bond rating services such as Moody's and Standard and Poors'.
- Credit reviews by agencies such as Dun and Bradstreet.

Investment valuation

The purpose of asset valuation models is to determine the present value of the expected future cash flows from the investment. This, in turn, determines the maximum price that a treasurer is willing to pay currently for this investment. The factor used to discount the future cash flows to their present value reflects the required rate of return a particular company demands for investing in a particular security. It is equal to the risk-free rate of return (generally measured by the rate of return on Government of Canada treasury bills) plus a premium to reflect the risk associated with earning the anticipated future cash flows. For example, treasurers likely would demand a higher rate of return (or discount rate) for a common share issue which has paid dividends in only two of the last ten years than for an issue which has paid equal dividends in each of the last ten years.

The *Capital Asset Pricing Model* (CAPM) provides guidance as to the selection of an appropriate required rate of return (discount rate), as follows:

$$D_i = R_r + B_i \times (R_m - R_r)$$

where,

D_i = the required rate of return associated with security i

R_r = the risk-free rate of return, which is generally measured by the return on treasury bills

B_i = the measure of volatility of security i. This factor, also called "beta", is estimated based on a statistical regression analysis between the historical returns of the individual security (or a number of companies within a given industry) and the historical returns of the equity market.

R_m = the average return in the equity market, which is generally measured by the return on the TSE 300

$R_m - R_r$ represents the risk premium relevant for the particular security.

Under the CAPM, the expected return on a particular portfolio is calculated as follows:

$$R_r + B_i \times (E_m - R_r)$$

where,

E_m = the expected market return (such as the TSE 100)

Although theoretically useful, the CAPM has some practical application problems, particularly in Canada. Firstly, because the model relies on data from public stock markets which are not always rational entities, such data may not provide a good indication of values of securities. Secondly, the Canadian stock market is not as broad as in the U.S. and, therefore, conclusions developed from Canadian stock market information may not be reflective of the entire Canadian equity market (which includes numerous other types of securities). Finally, the CAPM is limited to only one factor, the return on the market portfolio and to one parameter, the beta of the security.

The *Arbitrage Pricing Theory* (APT), another securities valuation model, links the expected return on portfolios to five factors. The model quantifies those five factors and establishes the following formula to determine expected return on a portfolio:

$$R_r + \sum_{n=1}^{i} \left(B_n \times f_n \right) = R_r + B_1 \times f_1 + B_2 \times f_2 + \ldots + B_1 \times f_i$$

where,

$$
\begin{array}{rcl}
B_i & = & \text{the sensitivity of the portfolio or security to} \\
    &   & \text{factor i} \\
f_i & = & \text{excess percentage returns relating to factor i}
\end{array}
$$

Studies have concluded that there are probably no more than five factors affecting the returns of each security. Other studies have found that factors affecting securities' return include unanticipated changes in inflation, industrial production, risk premiums and the slope of the term structure of interest rates.

Monitoring the Portfolio

Evaluating portfolio performance

To assess the effectiveness of investment decisions in light of investment objectives and to determine whether any investment action is needed (such as the sale or purchase of certain securities, changing the average term of the portfolio, etc.), the treasurer must evaluate the profitability of individual securities and the entire portfolio on an on-going basis, as well as considering the risk of a portfolio. A change in portfolio structure may be indicated by a change in one or more of the following factors:

- the expected return of a security;
- the risk associated with a security;
- the correlation between one or more securities;
- the risk-free rate of return; and
- features of the client such as risk tolerance and investment horizon.

The treasurer should establish formal guidelines in three areas: the time period between portfolios, changes in the minimum weights before the current portfolio should be restructured, and the review between regular review periods of the portfolio for significant developments. In developing such policies, consideration should be given to the size of a company's portfolio and the transaction costs involved in restructuring the portfolio. Such restructuring costs include not only fees paid to investment dealers, but the cost of the investment manager's time.

The most commonly used measure for evaluating profitability is return. Two returns that should be calculated continually during the portfolio management process are: the expected future return (also called the "ex ante return"), and the actual past return (also called the "ex post" return). The latter helps evaluate the effectiveness of past investment decisions, while the former helps to guide the treasurer in structuring the portfolio for the future. Both the actual return and expected return should be compared to the company's required rate of return in making these determinations. The forecast return may be for a long or a short period, depending on the treasurer's time horizon.

PART B

The rate of return earned should be compared to the expected return on the portfolio, market rates of return and historical portfolio returns. Any variances (which are assured to result) should be explained. For example, a treasurer may have anticipated a 12 per cent before tax return on a particular portfolio. If actual return realized is 9 per cent, an explanation should be sought for the portfolio's under-performance. Was it because market interest rates dropped and a high portion of the portfolio is comprised of short-term instruments? Or was it because of losses from high risk security issuers defaulting?

Once explanations for variances are developed, the treasurer should use the information to assess whether or not changes in the composition of the portfolio are required. Other factors should also be considered, including "macro" factors such as forecast of future interest rates, exchange rates, income tax changes and business cycles, as well as "micro" factors such as expected performance of individual companies and industries. For example, if the return was lower than expected because lower interest rates reduced the expected return on short-term investments, should the portion of fixed rate instruments be increased?

Basis of evaluation

It is important to realize that the original cost of an investment should have a limited impact on portfolio adjustment decisions. For example, assume that a security was purchased for $5,000 and is now worth $4,000. He or she should not simply hold on to the original security because a loss would be realized if an investment with a more appropriate risk/reward premium is available.

Original cost, required for financial statement preparation, should be considered when making portfolio structuring decisions because of the income tax effect on the company. However, a treasurer should not keep securities that would show a loss on sale just to prevent "looking bad" when investing those funds in other securities would be more profitable in the long run. Therefore, a portfolio should be evaluated based on its market value as well its original cost. The treasurer should keep current investment records on a "mark-to-market" basis for making investment decisions.

Calculating return on individual securities or portfolios

As mentioned earlier, there are a number of different performance measures to utilize. The appropriate measure depends on a number of factors, such as the company's financial position and the treasurer's management style. In general, measures employing betas (such as the Treynor Measure discussed below) are appropriate for highly diversified portfolios, while those employing standard deviation of returns as a risk measure are appropriate for less diversified portfolios.

Periodic total return

Return can be stated in terms of a periodic total return. For example, the three-month periodic return on 100 common shares purchased at $10 which have increased to $10.25 and which have paid a $0.50 per share dividend in the period is 7.5 per cent, calculated as follows:

$$7.5\% = \frac{(\$10.25 \times 100) - (\$10 \times 100) + (\$0.50 \times 100)}{(\$10 \times 100)}$$

The general formula for calculating the periodic total return on any security is as follows:

$$R = \frac{P_e - P_b + I}{P_b}$$

where,

R = periodic return

P_e = price of the security at the end of the period

P_b = price of the security at the beginning of the period

I = income received from the security (e.g., dividends, interest)

In calculating return and evaluating a portfolio, it is important to consider the relevant time period and to compare returns stated on the same basis (i.e., using the effective annual return). For example, a $1,000 equity security which increased in value by 10 per cent (to $1,100) during a period when Government of Canada treasury bills yielded 8 per cent appears to have been a good investment. However, this opinion would change if the 10 per cent return was for an 18-month period. The annualized rate of return on this security (assuming no dividends were received) would be 6.56 per cent, calculated as:

$$R_P = \sum_{n=1}^{t}(W_n \times R_n)$$

$$= \left(\frac{1,100}{1,100}\right)^{\frac{12}{18}} - 1 \text{ or } (1+0.10)^{\frac{12}{18}} - 1$$

In order to evaluate the performance of an entire portfolio, the returns on individual securities must be accumulated. The formula for calculating the return on a portfolio is as follows:

$$R_p = (W_1 \times R_1) + (W_2 \times R_2) +...+ (W_t \times R_t)$$

where,

$$R_p \quad = \quad \text{total return on the portfolio}$$
$$W_i \quad = \quad \text{proportion of funds invested in security i}$$
$$R_i \quad = \quad \text{return on security i}$$

Real rate of return

To enhance comparison of different periods' returns, the treasurer could also eliminate the effect of inflation which varies from year to year. For example, a 15 per cent rate of return in a year of 3 per cent inflation differs significantly from a 15 per cent return when inflation is 12 per cent. The formula for adjusting nominal rates (those including inflation) to a real rate of return (excluding inflation) is as follows:

$$R_a = \left[\sum_{n=1}^{t} (1 + R_n) \right]^{\frac{1}{n}} - 1 =$$

$$(1 + Rr) = \frac{(1 + R_n)}{(1 + R_i)}$$

where,

$$Rr \quad = \quad \text{the real rate of return}$$
$$Rn \quad = \quad \text{the nominal rate of return}$$
$$Ri \quad = \quad \text{the rate of inflation}$$

For example, when the nominal (stated) return rate is 15 per cent and inflation is 12 per cent, the real return rate is 2.67 per cent:

$$1 + Rr = \frac{1.15}{1.12}$$

The arithmetic and geometric averages returns (in dollars or percentage) on individual securities should also be calculated when evaluating the portfolio. The arithmetic average is simply the sum of the returns each period divided by the number of periods summed. The geometric average is calculated as follows:

$$R_a = \left[(1 + R_1) \times (1 + R_2) \times \dots \times (1 + R_t) \right]^{\frac{1}{n}} - 1$$

For example, the geometric average return of a security that earned a return of 5 per cent in year 1, 9 per cent in year 2 and 6 per cent in year 3 would be 3.94 per cent calculated as follows:

$$\left[(1.05) \times (1.09) \times (1.06_5) \right]^1 - 1$$

Risk-adjusted performance measures

The *Sharpe Measure* evaluates the excess return for each unit of standard deviation. The higher the measure, the better the security or portfolio performed. It is calculated as follows:

$$\frac{R_i - R_r}{SD_i}$$

where,

R_i =   historical average return of security or portfolio i

R_r =   historical average risk-free rate of return

$$SD_i \quad = \quad \text{standard deviation of security or portfolio i}$$

For example, a portfolio with a standard deviation of 1.25 that earned an average return of 16.5 per cent when the average yield on Government of Canada treasury bills was 10.5 per cent would have a Sharpe measure of 4.8 per cent:

$$\frac{16.5 - 10.5}{1.25} \quad = \quad 4.8\%$$

The *Treynor Measure* is similar to the Sharpe measure, except that it uses the beta of the portfolio as a measure of risk rather than standard deviation. It is a more appropriate measure for companies having more than one type of security in its portfolio. The formula is as follows:

$$\frac{R_i - R_r}{Bi}$$

The *Adjusted Jensen Measure* is often calculated instead of other risk-adjusted measures because it reflects the diversifiable risk. It is calculated as follows:

$$\frac{R_i - R_r + B_p \times (R_m - R_r)}{SD_i}$$

Portfolios with foreign securities

If a portfolio contains foreign securities, rates of return must be converted to Canadian dollars before their performance can be compared with that of other securities. For the most accurate results, any return actually received on the investment (such as dividends or interest) should be converted using the exchange rate

PART B

at the date of receipt. The beginning security price should be converted at the beginning exchange rate, and the ending price should be converted using the ending exchange rate.

The rate of return on foreign securities is comprised of two components: the periodic return in the foreign country (the total of income and capital gains), and any appreciation or depreciation of the foreign currency against the Canadian dollar (C$). The periodic return is calculated using the formula mentioned above with figures in foreign currency (i.e., not converted to C$). The change in the foreign currency against the C$ is calculated as follows:

$$Rf = \frac{X_e - X_b}{X_b}$$

where,

R_f = the change in the foreign currency against the C$

X_e = the foreign exchange rate (stated in terms of C$) at the end of the period

X_b = the foreign exchange rate (stated in terms of C$) at the beginning of the period

Note: if a stock held by the company is split or receives a stock dividend during the period, historical information should be adjusted to ensure it is comparable with current data.

Expected return

The treasurer may need to estimate the expected return to be achieved from individual securities and the portfolio in total.

These rates would be used as budgets against which actual returns will be compared. Formally, expected return represents the sum of the products of possible return rates times their probabilities of occurring. For example, a security considered to have a 5 per cent probability of yielding 7 per cent, a 25 per cent chance of yielding 5 per cent and a 70 per cent chance of yielding 9 per cent next year has an expected return of 7.9 per cent, calculated as follows:

$$(0.05 \times 0.07) + (0.25 \times 0.05) + (0.70 \times 0.09)$$

Although this formula appears "cut and dried", a significant amount of judgment is required to develop the probability factors and the possible rates of return. Although it is tempting to rely on past returns as a guide to develop expectations about future rates of return, historical returns are not good predictors of future returns. They serve as a good starting point, but should not be considered in isolation. More important factors to consider include expectations about the economy, the industry and the firm in particular. However, it is very hard to predict these types of factors.

Calculating expected return on a portfolio

As with total return on a portfolio, the expected returns on individual securities must be accumulated to calculate expected return on a portfolio. The formula for calculating the expected return on a portfolio is as follows:

$$E_p = (W_1 \times E_1) + (W_2 \times E_2) + ... + (W_t \times E_t)$$

where,

R_p	=	total return on the portfolio
W_i	=	proportion of funds invested in security i
R_i	=	return on security

PART B

C H A P T E R 9

Short-Term Investments

Overview

Treasurers may find that their company has an excess of cash, either temporarily or on a more long-term basis. The receipt of excess funds may be known reasonably well in advance through careful cash flow forecasting, or it may come as a surprise. Certain companies have seasonal operations creating excess funds for part of the year, but a deficiency for the remainder. Unusual circumstances also can result in an excess of funds such as a sale of capital assets or a subsidiary. In any event, reality will never coincide exactly with forecasts, no matter how much effort is put into forecasting cash flow. Whatever the cause of the excess cash, the key concern is utilizing the excess funds to help achieve a company's goals.

This chapter and the next discuss the alternative investments available in terms of their nature, relative return, flexibility, ease of access to the underlying funds and safety. This chapter focuses on short-term (or temporary) investments, defined as those maturing or expected to be liquidated within a company's operating cycle, which generally is considered to be one year. Chapter 10 addresses investments used for investing funds on a longer-term basis.

Canadian Money Market

"Canadian Money Market" refers to the market for short-term, non-equity, fixed income financial instruments such as treasury bills, government bonds, negotiable bank paper, finance company paper, and commercial paper from non-financial corporations. "Paper" refers to legally issued promises to pay.

This market originally consisted of the initial issuance of the securities, or the primary market, as well as secondary trading of the instruments. The market then developed into one in which short-term funds are lent and borrowed using the negotiable money market instruments as security. Participants in the market include purchasers of the investments (corporations and money market investment dealers), issuers of the securities (the Bank of Canada; chartered banks; foreign banks; non-bank financial institutions such as sales finance or acceptance companies, trust companies and mortgage loan companies; all levels of government; Canadian and foreign corporations), and agents of purchasers and issuers (i.e., money market dealers).

Money market instruments are issued only by entities with strong credit ratings. Generally, maturities are 90 days or less. The money market also includes securities with terms to three years, those being most commonly Government of Canada bonds. In addition, longer term issues are traded on the money market when their terms shorten as they approach maturity.

The money market in Canada is quite broad and deep and, therefore, can often absorb a large volume of transactions with little effect on price. However, it is sensitive to significant changes in the supply of and demand for funds, which can occur frequently. It allows fast, low cost trading in a range of volumes and instrument types.

Companies have the choice of fully paying for short-term investments when purchased through an investment dealer. Alternatively, certain instruments can be purchased "on margin"; that is, the investments are purchased on credit against specified collateral. The Investment Dealers Association of Canada and the stock exchanges of Canada have established a schedule of margin rates for various instruments with which investment dealers must comply.

Canadian Money Market Instruments

Money market instruments generally are issued in various denominations or multiples thereof. The denomination amount varies depending on the specific instrument type and may be as low as $1,000 or as high as $1 million. Most are issued and sold on a discounted basis. However, some are interest bearing. Interest rates and yields are quoted based on a 365-day basis, unlike foreign money market instruments. Each type of security has a stated maturity although commercial paper issuers may permit flexibility as to the term. The instruments can be resold before maturity or may be occasionally repurchased or extended by the issuer.

Settlement (delivery and payment) procedures and systems are well established and prompt. Treasury bills settle the business day following the sale transaction date and Government of Canada bonds maturing within three years settle two business days following the sale. In the case of some notes, settlement may be negotiated, but it generally takes place the following business day.

Government paper

Government of Canada treasury bills

Treasury bills are issued and traded in very high volume, and T-bills are the shortest term instruments issued by the federal government. Generally, they are issued with terms to maturity of 98 days, 168 or 182 days, and 350 or 364 days. There is also a fairly active market in treasury bills prior to their weekly issuance, called "when-issueds".

Treasury bills are free of credit risk and, therefore, are acceptable to all investors. They are highly liquid because large volumes can be bought and sold without significant change to market prices. Return on treasury bills is lower than on higher credit risk instruments such as commercial paper, bankers' acceptances and deposits with financial institutions (all discussed below). New treasury bills are auctioned to money market dealers and chartered banks every Tuesday. A company cannot purchase treasury bills directly from the federal government; instead, it must contact a money market dealer or a chartered bank.

The results of the weekly treasury bill auction significantly affect general interest rates since they are used by the Bank of Canada to set the Bank Rate. The Bank Rate is the minimum rate at which the Bank of Canada will make advances to the chartered banks. It is set at 1/4 of 1 per cent, or 25 basis points, above the weekly average tender of 91-day treasury bills. A change in weekly yields influences the market's expectations about the general level of interest rates.

Government of Canada treasury bills are sold at a discount and mature at par (100.00). Their market value fluctuates with changes in a number of factors such as interest rates and market liquidity. The difference between the bills' maturity value and the price paid is the total return to the purchaser. This difference is treated as income rather than capital gains for income taxation purposes. Because of the high safety and liquidity of these instruments, the return typically is the lowest of all short-term investments.

On April 2, 2003, there was $105 billion of treasury bills outstanding.

Provincial and municipal short-term paper

Trading volumes in the provincial and municipal short-term instrument market are much lower than that for Government of Canada treasury bills and bonds. (The market for municipal paper is thinner than that for provincial paper.) Provinces issue their own short-term paper and also authorize their crown corporations and agencies to do so. Provinces more commonly issue 91-day treasury bills (on a discounted basis), but also issue short-term bonds (on an interest bearing basis) on an infrequent basis. They make much higher use of the medium- and long-term bond market (see Chapter 10), but these bonds become part of the money market as they approach maturity.

Larger municipalities most commonly issue short-term debt with terms less than 90 days on a discounted basis. As with provincial paper, medium- and long-term municipal bonds (issued on an interest bearing basis) may start to be more actively traded in the money market as they approach maturity.

Generally, this paper earns a higher rate of return than Government of Canada paper. Because the marketability of provincial and municipal short-term paper is lower, and credit risk is higher (and varies among provinces and municipalities), the credit standing of these issues generally is higher than financial institution and corporate paper. Such paper may be in either registered or bearer form. It is sold either to investment dealers on an auction bid basis, or through negotiation with or without an investment dealer.

On April 2, 2003, provincial governments and their enterprises had $20.2 billion of short-term paper outstanding, while municipal governments had $140 million outstanding.

Chartered bank paper

A variety of deposit instruments are issued by Canadian chartered banks. They are an important factor in the Canadian money market. Deposit instruments may or may not be transferable and they may be sold on either a discount or an interest bearing basis. Usually, they are sold directly to the bank's customers rather than through money market/investment dealers.

This paper typically earns a higher rate of return than government paper since the marketability of chartered bank short-term paper generally is lower than government paper, and credit risk is higher (and varies among the banks). The credit standing of these issues generally is higher than other financial institution and corporate paper.

Three examples of chartered bank paper are discussed below. Other types are discussed below in the section "Foreign currency money market instruments."

Bearer deposit notes

Bearer deposit notes are secured by the general credit (standing) of the issuing bank and are issued at a discount in minimum amounts of $100,000. The term of these instruments ranges between 30 days and one year.

Term notes, certificates of deposit, guaranteed investment certificates and term deposits

The term of these instruments varies between one day and five to seven years. They bear fixed interest rates and are issued in very low minimum amounts (usually $500 to $1,000). Therefore, these investments are more flexible and more appropriate for small amounts of funds available for investment. However, their rate of return typically is lower than Government of Canada treasury bills. They are issued in registered form and may be transferable or non-transferable. (Certificates of deposit are negotiable and transferable; term deposits are both; guaranteed investment certificates are neither.) Interest may be payable on a monthly, semi-annual, annual basis or on maturity.

Other demand deposits

Chartered banks, as well as other financial institutions, offer a variety of savings and/or chequing deposit accounts. Although ease of access to funds is a primary advantage of placing excess funds in demand deposits, interest rates are much lower than those available for other relatively safe investments.

In general, the yield earned on fixed term deposits is lower than that earned on bankers' acceptances and commercial paper. However, it may be lower or higher than that earned on treasury bills.

PART B

Finance and consumer loan company paper

Finance companies issue short-term promissory notes, which may be secured or unsecured, usually on a discounted basis. (However, discount finance paper differs from a discounted instrument such as treasury bills — see the section "Calculating Price and Yield on Short-Term Investments" below.) The notes are negotiable and transferable. Terms range from demand to 365 days, and can be arranged to fit the investor's needs. These notes may be in bearer or registered form, and are sold either directly to investors or through money market dealers (the latter being more common). Denominations vary from a minimum of $50,000 to $5 million.

Trust and mortgage company deposit receipts

Trust and mortgage companies offer a variety of interest bearing demand and term deposits and certificates similar to those offered by chartered banks. Trust company deposits are non-transferable and therefore, do not trade in the secondary markets. Deposit terms vary from one to five years, and certificate terms vary from 24 hours to one year. Minimum invested amounts also vary by institution, for example $500 to $25,000. Frequently, interest rates are higher on trust company deposits than on chartered bank deposits.

Investments in other financial institutions

In addition to chartered banks, finance and consumer loan, and trust and mortgage companies, other financial institutions such as credit unions and caisses populaires offer various types of short-term investments. (For a discussion of the various financial institutions in Canada, refer to Chapter 2.)

Repurchase agreements or "buy-backs"

In repurchase agreements (or "repos"), a company agrees to buy certain securities from a money market dealer and to resell them to the dealer (and the dealer agrees to repurchase them) at a future date. In effect, these agreements provide a source of inventory financing for money market dealers, and a rate of return for the investor. The securities act as collateral for the transaction. Repurchase agreements are quite safe investments because the securities generally are of high quality (government, corporate or finance company securities). Denominations are usually multiples of $100,000. Terms are negotiated between the dealer and the company and are classified as either call or fixed-term agreements. Overnight agreements are the most common, are very liquid and typically have a lower rate of return than the latter. The return to the investing company is the difference between the amount the dealer pays to buy back the securities and the amount paid by the investing company. The investor often does not take possession of the securities; instead, they are held at another financial institution or by the dealer on behalf of the company.

A *reverse repurchase agreement* (or "reverse repo") is the opposite of a repurchase agreement. The company holding the securities agrees to sell and repurchase them at a later date. The treasurer might decide to use reverse repurchase agreements as an alternative financing means.

Bankers' acceptances

Bankers' acceptances (BAs) are commercial drafts that have been "accepted" by the borrowing corporation's bank. It is similar to commercial paper but is guaranteed by a bank. Banks charge a *stamping fee* for providing this guarantee. The fee generally ranges from 1/2 per cent to 1 per cent depending on the borrower's credit

PART B

quality. *Accepted* means that the payment of interest and principal is guaranteed by the bank. Acceptances are treated by banks as their own liabilities (offset by an equivalent asset), but the issuer must make the funds available to the bank on maturity. Acceptances are backed by the credit of the issuer's bank as well as that of the issuer. Therefore, they are very safe instruments, even though they bear credit risk related to the corporation and the bank. As a result, the yield on BAs usually is lower than that on commercial paper but higher than that on treasury bills. The BA secondary market is very liquid.

Bankers' acceptances are issued at a discount to face value through money market dealers. Terms range from 30 days to one year generally, and denominations vary from $100,000 to $1 million.

On April 2, 2003, there was a total of $41 billion of bankers' acceptances outstanding.

Commercial paper

Commercial paper refers to short-term, unsecured promissory notes issued by a variety of non-financial corporations with solid reputations. Terms range from overnight to one year; however, the most common maturities are 30, 60 and 90 days. The minimum investment generally is $100,000 and the instruments are purchased at par with interest payable at maturity. The market usually is limited to well-known, strong companies. Commercial paper often is backed by the general credit of the issuer, but also may be backed by an unused line of credit at the issuer's bank and/or a guarantee from the issuer's parent company or an affiliate. As a result, the yield on commercial paper generally is close to that of the 30-day finance paper rate, and is higher than treasury bill yields.

Commercial paper is sold both on a discounted basis (like treasury bills) and on an interest bearing basis, the latter being the most common. However, the yield on commercial paper is quoted on a discount basis regardless of the method on which it is sold. (See the section "Calculating Price and Yield on Short-Term Investments" below for example yield calculations.)

A secondary market exists for commercial paper, but it is not as actively traded as other money market instruments such as treasury bills. Until the early 1990s, commercial paper was considered a very safe investment. However, the Olympia & York downfall made many investors realize that a risk of loss still exists. The company could not renew its commercial paper facility (on which it relied heavily for short-term financing) because of the market's concerns about its repayment ability.

On April 2, 2003, total commercial paper outstanding was $117 billion. Of that, $11.6 billion was denominated in United States dollars.

Foreign currency money market instruments

Among the various sources of short-term investments issued in Canada in currencies other than the Canadian dollar, the following are the most common:

- Canadian chartered banks;
- Canadian subsidiaries of foreign banks;
- Foreign companies; and
- Other financial institutions such as trust and mortgage companies.

Such investments may be preferable for a company which has operations generating and requiring cash flows in foreign curren-

PART B

cies. Treasurers having a strong view on the future direction of certain currencies may also invest in them (that is, they offer a speculative opportunity).

Foreign currency deposits

Chartered banks offer demand and term deposits in a number of currencies, the most common being the U.S. dollar. Some trust and mortgage companies also offer U.S. dollar demand and term deposits in competition with the chartered banks. Terms of such instruments can be one day to one year and are interest bearing. Minimum amounts vary by currency, although most banks have no minimum amounts for U.S. dollar deposits.

These deposits involve foreign exchange risk due to possible future exchange rate fluctuations in the value of the foreign currency relative to the Canadian dollar.

Swap deposits and split swap deposits

Chartered banks offer swap deposits which are Canadian dollar deposits converted into the foreign currency selected by the investor (usually U.S. dollars) on the deposit date, and converted back to Canadian dollars at the end of the term of the deposit. However, no exchange risk results as a forward contract is entered into *on the date of deposit* (and converted to the foreign currency) to convert the foreign currency back to Canadian dollars. There is a cost of hedging the foreign currency amount which is reflected in the interest rate otherwise earned. (A forward swap differential arises from differences between the two countries' interest rates. It is added to, or deducted from, the spot exchange rate to calculate the exchange rate on forward contracts. The "all-in yield" quoted includes both the cost of the hedge and the interest rate earned.

Split swap deposits effectively are the same as swap deposits, except that the foreign exchange hedge is arranged with a financial institution other than that holding the deposit. The minimum denomination on swap and split swap deposits is $100,000 and terms of deposits are flexible.

The Money Market in Other Countries

In addition to, or rather than, investing short-term funds in Canadian money market instruments, an investing company may decide to invest in short-term instruments in other countries. A company having significant foreign operations may do this to off-set (or hedge) foreign currency obligations. A company also may elect to invest in foreign currencies if management assesses that a higher overall return (including the interest rate and effect of exchange) can be achieved. To reduce the risk of adverse foreign exchange rate fluctuations, a company may decide to enter into transactions to hedge its foreign currency exposure.

Although there are numerous foreign money markets in which to invest, the two most commonly used by Canadian investors are discussed below. Other markets offer comparable products.

U.S. money market investment vehicles

Because of the strength of the U.S. as a world financial power and its proximity to Canada, Canadians will more commonly invest in U.S. instruments than in investments of other countries. The U.S. money market is comprised of instruments similar to the Canadian money market such as:

- U.S. Government treasury bills; (Interest yields on these instruments are calculated on a 364-day basis.)
- negotiable certificates of deposit;

- commercial paper; and
- longer-term U.S. government bond issues.

Interest rates and yields on most U.S. instruments (except U.S. Government treasury bills) are stated on a 360-day basis as is euro-currency instruments. To compare the yields on U.S. and Canadian instruments, the yields must be restated to the same basis. The appropriate formulas are as follows.

To convert the yield on a U.S. (or euro-currency) instrument from a 360-day basis to the equivalent Canadian yield:

$$\text{U.S. yield} \quad \times \quad \frac{365}{360} \quad = \text{Canadian yield}$$

$$\text{Canadian yield} \quad \times \quad \frac{360}{365} \quad = \text{U.S. yield}$$

For example, a 90-day U.S. money market instrument yielding 10.50 per cent yields 10.64 per cent on a Canadian basis:

$$10.50\% \quad \times \quad \frac{365}{360} \quad = 10.64\%$$

Interest earned on foreign currency deposits *with Canadian institutions* are not subject to withholding tax. Interest earned on foreign currency deposits with *foreign institutions* generally will be subject to the foreign country's withholding tax. However, certain U.S.-denominated instruments issued by U.S. corporations, such as actively traded commercial paper and bank term deposits, are not subject to withholding tax. Any withholding tax paid by Canadian residents can be applied against Canadian income tax on U.S. source income which prevents income being taxed at more than the higher of the two countries' income tax rates.

Euro-currency investments outside North America

A "euro-currency" instrument is an investment denominated in a currency of a country other than that of the issuer of the instrument. Canadian dollars deposited with a German bank would constitute a euro-currency deposit. The deposit does not have to be with a European issuer even though the phrase "euro-currency" implies it. For example, Japanese yen deposited in an Australian bank would be a euro-deposit. The most common currencies include U.S. dollars, Euro and sterling. Interest is calculated on a 360-day basis. (See the section "U.S. money market investment vehicles" above for interest conversion formula.)

The euro-currency market is a large, unrestricted international market. Euro-currency investments generally are purchased through investment dealers. There is an active secondary market in euro-currency issues.

Types of euro-currency investments include the following:

(a) **Term euro-currency deposits** — These deposits have characteristics similar to term deposits placed with financial institutions, but are placed with a non-resident bank. They are registered, non-negotiable, generally non-redeemable and have terms of one day to ten years. There are no set minimum deposit amounts, and various interest payment options are available.

(b) **Euro-currency certificates of deposit** — These instruments are similar to euro-currency deposits, but because they are negotiable, they are more marketable. Terms vary from one month to five years, but terms may be negotiable in the medium range. Minimum deposit amounts vary by term, but range between US$10,000 to US$25,000.

PART B

(c) **Euro-commercial paper** — Similar to Canadian commercial paper, these unsecured, negotiable promissory notes are issued by financially strong corporations. They are issued on a discount basis in bearer form. Terms range from seven days to one year, and the minimum investment is higher than euro-deposits at US$50,000. (U.S. issuers are restricted to 183-day maturities.) Interest rates are higher than that on euro-currency deposits and certificates of deposit. However, "euro-CP" is less liquid and less secure.

(d) **Euronotes** — These are notes issued in maturities of 30, 60, 90 and 180 days together with a standby credit facility committed for three to five years. They generally are interest bearing, although some euronotes are sold on a discount basis. The euronote market is relatively liquid.

Calculating Price and Yield of Short-Term Investments

As mentioned earlier, different money market instruments are sold on different bases. Some earn a return on a discounted basis (e.g., treasury bills, finance company paper and some commercial paper), and some are interest bearing (e.g., Government of Canada, provincial and municipal government bonds, chartered bank paper, trust and mortgage company deposit receipts, some commercial paper). When evaluating various alternative investments, a key consideration is relative yield rates. The yield on **interest bearing instruments** sold at par is easy to determine — it is the same as the stated interest rate. Total return is calculated as follows:

$$\text{Return} = \text{price} \times \text{yield (stated interest rate)} \times \frac{\text{term in days}}{365 \text{ or } 360^*}$$

The price of an interest bearing instrument issued at other than par is the present value of all future cash flows, being interest and the principal repayment, discounted at a rate based on market rates of return.

To calculate the yield on interest bearing instruments, the accrued interest at the time of purchase must be considered:

$$\text{Yield} = \left[\frac{1 + \left(I \times \dfrac{DI}{365} \right)}{P} \right] - \left(1 + \frac{365}{DS} \right)$$

where:
- I = coupon rate of interest
- DS = number of days from settlement to maturity
- DI = number of days from issue to maturity
- P = price

Calculating the yield on **discount instruments** (such as government-issued treasury bills, finance company paper, etc.) is a little more complex. For such instruments, the difference between the discount and the par at maturity represents the income. Investors do not put up 100 per cent of the par. The formulae for calculating the yield on and price of treasury bills are:

$$\text{Yield } \% = \frac{100 - \text{price}^{**}}{\text{price}^{**}} \times \frac{365 \text{ or } 360 \text{ days}^*}{\text{term to maturity}}$$

---

* For Canadian interest bearing and discount instruments, the quoted rate of return is based on a 365-day year. For U.S. and euro-dollar instruments, the return is based on a 360-day basis.

PART B

$$Price^{**} = \frac{100}{100 + \frac{(yield \times term\ to\ maturity)}{365\ days}} \times 100$$

For example, if the price for a Canadian treasury bill is 98.515 and the term to maturity is 91 days, the yield is 6.05 per cent:

$$Yield\ \% = \frac{100 - 98.515}{98.515} \times \frac{365}{91} \times 100$$

The yield on **discount finance company paper** is higher than the quoted (or commercial discount) rate. This is because an investor effectively is given prepaid interest; the investor does not pay 100 per cent of par value. The formulae for calculating the yield on and price of discount finance company paper is:

$$Yield\ \% = \frac{quoted\ rate \times 100}{price \times 100}$$

$$Price = 100 - \frac{quoted\ rate \times 100 \times term\ to\ maturity}{365\ days}$$

For example, if the quoted rate for an issue of 90-day discount finance company paper is 10 per cent, the price is 97.534:

$$Price = 100 - \frac{10\% \times 100 \times 90}{365}$$

The yield is 10.253 per cent:

$$Yield = \frac{10\% \times 100 \times 100}{97.534}$$

---

* For Canadian interest bearing and discount instruments, the quoted rate of return is based on a 365-day year. For U.S. and euro-dollar instruments, the return is based on a 360-day basis.

** Price is in terms of a base of 100 and represents what per cent of the full face (or maturity) value is paid by the investor.

The yield on **swap deposits** is a combination of the yield on the foreign currency deposit and the profit or loss on the foreign exchange transaction.

CHAPTER 10

Long-Term Investments

Overview

Treasurers may find that their company has an excess of cash, either temporarily or on a more long-term basis. Whatever the cause of the excess cash, the key concern is utilizing the excess funds to help achieve a company's goals. When funds are available on a long-term basis, (expected to be required later than a company's operating cycle, which generally is considered to be one year), managers have a number of choices for investment.

Developing a long-term investment portfolio can require more effort and creativity than a short-term portfolio. The relative risks and rewards are both increased.

This chapter discusses alternative longer term investments available in terms of nature, relative return, flexibility, ease of access to the underlying funds and safety. Some of the instruments discussed in Chapter 9 can be used for investing long-term funds. There are also many instruments specific to long-term investing.

Investment Risk

The treasurer must understand the risks associated with various investments before being able to evaluate the various alternative long-term investments and design the company's portfolio. The components of **investment risk** are discussed in Chapter 17 and subsequent chapters. The significance of the risk components differs between short-term and long-term investments. Specifically, credit, investment and securities price risks are higher because of the increased time the instruments are outstanding and the increased likelihood of an issue declining in value. On the other hand, liquidity risk may be less of a concern since the intention is to hold the investment on a long-term basis, possibly to its maturity.

Money Market Instruments

Certain Canadian and foreign money market instruments discussed in Chapter 9 can be included in a company's long-term investment portfolio.

Government of Canada bonds due in more than one year

Government of Canada bonds are free of credit risk, but their liquidity is somewhat lower than Government of Canada treasury bills. In typical market conditions with long-term interest rates exceeding short-term rates (a normal interest rate yield curve), the return on Government of Canada bonds due in more than one year is higher because of their longer term to maturity. However, an "inverted yield curve" (which occurred in Canada during the mid-1980s), results in short-term instruments earning a higher yield than a comparable longer term instrument. Government of Canada bonds are interest bearing. Interest is paid semi-annually and may be in either bearer form or fully registered. Terms vary to 30 years. Maturities are varied because government bonds are issued at irregular intervals.

On April 2, 2003, $274 billion of Government of Canada bonds were outstanding.

Chartered bank paper due in more than one year

This category includes instruments such as term notes, certificates of deposits, guaranteed investment certificates and term deposits. The term of these instruments varies between one day and five years. These are interest bearing and are issued in very low minimum amounts (usually $1,000). Therefore, these investments are more flexible and more appropriate for small amounts of funds available for investment. They are issued in registered form and are generally non-transferable. Interest may be payable on various bases such as monthly, semi-annually, annually or on maturity.

Long-term U.S. government bonds

Maturities on long-term U.S. government bonds range from three to 30 years.

Longer-term Euro-currency deposits

These deposits have characteristics similar to term deposits placed with financial institutions, but are placed with a non-resident bank. These are registered, non-negotiable, generally non-redeemable and have terms of one day to 10 years. There are no set minimum deposit amounts, and various interest payment options are available.

Euro-currency certificates of deposit due in more than one year

These instruments are similar to euro-currency deposits, but because they are negotiable, they are more marketable. Terms vary from one month to five years; however, terms may be negotiable in the medium range. Minimum deposit amounts vary by term, but range between US$10,000 to US$25,000.

The Canadian Bond Market

The term *Canadian Bond Market* represents a variety of long-term debt instruments issued by various Canadian corporations, financial institutions and levels of government. While provincial and municipal governments and related entities issue medium- and long-term bonds and debentures and may issue such debt two or more times per year, corporations issue the highest volume and largest selection of long-term debt. Purchase and sales transactions occur by negotiation rather than auction as many money market instruments do. The bond market is very large and well developed. As a result, bond instruments are relatively liquid in general. However, the specific characteristics of a bond issue will define its liquidity relative to other issues.

Yields on corporate bonds typically exceed those on government bonds. Yields vary widely among various corporate bonds due to differing credit risks and the wide variety of features that can be attached to different bond issues.

Investors have the choice of fully paying for long-term investments when purchased through an investment dealer. Alternatively, certain instruments can be purchased *on margin*, which is equivalent to saying that the investments are purchased on credit against specified collateral. The Investment Dealers Association of Canada and the stock exchanges of Canada have established a schedule of margin rates for various instruments with which investment dealers must comply. Corporations would not generally purchase securities on margin. In any event, it is generally not advisable to use margin accounts to purchase bonds for a long-term investment portfolio. The carrying cost of the margin account can easily offset the yield earned on the investment. Instead, the long-term investment portfolio should be designed using excess cash.

Canadian Bond Market Instruments

Introduction

Bond market instruments may be secured or unsecured, in bearer or registered form. Bearer form bonds have interest coupons attached that must be clipped and cashed. Registered bonds may be fully registered or registered as to principal only. Terms may be from one to 30 years or longer, and stated interest rates may be fixed or floating. The wide variety of issuers allows investors to tailor their portfolios to an acceptable level of credit risk. There is an active and deep secondary bond market, which increases the marketability of bonds. Bonds generally trade in multiples of $1,000 and prices are quoted in terms of a base of 100. For example, a bond quoted at 102 1/2 means that the 102.5 per cent of its par value must be paid (i.e., a premium of 2.5 per cent must be paid) plus accrued interest. Interest generally is paid semi-annually, with the specific interest payment dates varying by issue.

Bond market instruments vary by the type of security backing them, as discussed below.

Unsecured debt (debentures)

A debenture represents an issuer's unsecured promise to repay the borrowed funds, and generally ranks behind all other long-term debt of the issuer. Some instruments may contain a floating charge on assets to provide some level of collateral. For example, finance companies commonly issue *collateral trust notes*, which are secured by discounted notes of customers of finance companies (e.g., automobile, furniture and appliance dealers).

Debentures typically are issued by financially strong corporations, financial institutions and government entities because they are unsecured. Rates of return generally are higher than secured debt instruments and vary depending on the quality of the issuer, hence the risk assumed by the investor. For example, the credit risk associated with municipal debentures is considered to be higher than provincial debentures, but lower than most corporate debentures. In turn, the yield on municipal debentures is higher than provincial debentures but lower than most corporate debentures. The marketability of debentures varies by issuer.

Debentures may have fixed or floating interest rates. (The latter are called *floating rate debentures* or *floating rate notes*). Floating rate debentures reduce the risk associated with investing in long-term instruments, particularly in times of volatile interest rates. As a result, they generally are issued at lower rates. (See the section "Floating interest rates", page 287 below.)

Secured debt

Mortgage bonds

Mortgage bonds are secured by claims on certain assets of the issuer. These bonds have less credit risk associated with them than unsecured debt instruments because failure by an issuer to meet interest or principal payments will result in ownership of the capital assets being transferred to investors. However, liquidating the assets may not net the amount originally invested. The quality of both the security and the issuer affects the credit risk associated with mortgage bonds.

There are a number of different types of mortgage bonds:

(i)   *First mortgage bonds* represent a first charge on the issuer's capital assets (generally land and buildings) and earnings and, therefore, are less risky than other long-term investments. As a result, return from first mortgage bonds generally is lower than other investments.

(ii) *Collateral trust bonds* are backed by securities such as common shares and debentures owned the issuer. The risk associated with collateral trust bonds varies directly with both the quality of the issuer and the quality of the securities collateralized.

(iii) Other mortgage bond securities such as second mortgage bonds, equipment trust certificates and prior lien bonds.

Mortgage-backed securities

Mortgage-backed securities ("MBSs") are packages of residential mortgages which permit investors to share in the principal and interest flows of the underlying mortgages. These are very safe instruments as they are guaranteed by the Canada Mortgage and Housing Corporation (CMHC), a federal crown corporation. The term of MBSs is five years. The rate of return on MBSs is higher than that of Government of Canada bonds, and is comparable to guaranteed investment certificates and term deposits (discussed in Chapter 9). The investor receives monthly cash flows comprised of a combination of principal and interest. However, some uncertainty is associated with future cash flows as the mortgagers may prepay some of the underlying principal.

Other asset-backed securities

There are also securities backed by high quality assets other than government-guaranteed residential mortgages. Mortgage lenders market bundles of residential mortgages (in packages of $1 million, for example) that are not secured by the federal government. Other securities are backed by leases or receivables. The market is less liquid than for MBSs and other bonds, and the rate of return is higher than for MBSs.

Subordinated debt

Subordinated bonds provide a low level of security since claims of bondholders rank below claims of other debtholders of the company. As a result, such bonds generally will earn a yield higher than secured bonds.

Other Features of Long-Term Debt Instruments

Bonds and other long-term instruments are issued with a variety of characteristics. The combination of features for a particular issue is extensive. These characteristics can significantly impact the risks associated with the instruments and their pricing, often as much as the quality of the issuer does. Therefore, in compiling the long-term investment portfolio, the treasury manager must evaluate carefully the relative features of various issues.

Sinking funds and purchase funds

When a long-term debt instrument contains a *sinking fund* feature, the issuer has undertaken to regularly set aside funds with a trustee to retire some or all of the debt. Sinking funds generally start operating after a specified period, possibly two to five years following issue date. The sinking fund may either repurchase the instruments in the market (a "market" fund), or may repurchase instruments from each holder relative to their holdings (a "pro rata" fund). A sinking fund may be either specific to the issue, or used to retire any of a number of debt issues of the company. Some issues permit the issuer to accelerate retirement based on its earnings for a period.

This commonly used feature increases the liquidity and marketability of an instrument, particularly if the feature is specific to the issue rather than being a general fund. As the issuer retires debt and is relieved of future principal and interest payments, the overall quality of the issue generally increases. Also, the value of sinking fund bonds is improved because of increased demand in the market for them. As a result, the return (yield to maturity) on sinking fund debt trading at par or at a discount generally is lower than comparable long-term debt issues without this feature. Sinking fund debt trading at a premium often will trade at a high yield to maturity because of the possibility of calling the debt for retirement below the premium price. In times of expected decreasing bond prices, the sinking fund feature provides a cushion against losses.

A *purchase fund* is similar to a sinking fund. However, funds set aside for purchase funds are used to retire part of an issue **only** when the market price is below a certain level, usually issue price.

It is a non-cumulative feature and results in a significant fluctuation in the amount of debt repurchased by the issuer from year to year. This feature also increases the liquidity and marketability of an issue, but is preferable for investors as it does not force investors to sell debt trading at a premium. As a result, the return (yield to maturity) on purchase fund debt usually is lower than that of sinking fund debt.

Serial (instalment) debt

Serial bonds and debentures are similar to "pro rata" sinking fund bonds in that a specified amount of bond principal is retired each year. This feature is no longer common in the market; instead, sinking fund issues are used more frequently. However, municipal debentures commonly are issued in instalment form.

Callable (redeemable) debt

Callable (redeemable) debt permits the borrower to repurchase and cancel part or all of the debt issue prior to maturity at a specified "call price" plus accrued interest. The call price is generally above par, and is designed to compensate investors for potential loss of yield and the disadvantage of having a long-term investment eliminated. Generally, callable debt trades at a higher yield to maturity than non-callable debt. The call price may be one amount, may vary by year the issue is outstanding or may fluctuate according to a specified benchmark yield based on, for example, Government of Canada bonds. An issuer may not be able to call a debt issue for a certain period such as the first 75 per cent of its term, or may be able to call the issue under certain circumstances. Sinking fund requirements usually are callable at 100 (that is, 100 per cent of their face value).

While Government of Canada bonds are never callable, most non-federal government issues contain a call feature. Corporate issuers by far are the most frequent users of call features. Because the total yield of callable debt is uncertain, issuers either must increase the coupon rate of interest on callable debt or otherwise make the issue more attractive to investors. Callable debt appeals to investors desiring a higher rate of return who are not concerned about losing a particular instrument to the call. However, when a callable bond is purchased at a premium, the investor should consider the yield to the possible call dates as well as yield to maturity. Frequently, the former is lower than the latter.

A variation on this is "fixed/floating" debt often issued by banks. While it has a long-term maturity its interest rate is reset on earlier dates and callable by the issuer on those earlier dates.

Extendible debt

Extendible debt is issued with a relatively short term (e.g., five years), but can be extended at the *investor's option* within a specified election period. To encourage the investor to extend the term of the debt, a higher coupon rate frequently is offered for the second term. Such issues are termed **split-coupon extendibles**. As a result, stated interest rates on extendible debt generally are lower, while marketability and prices in the secondary bond market are higher and yields to maturity are lower. Extendible debt is more common in periods of rising inflation when investors generally reduce the extent of long-term investments. Various levels of government as well as corporations have issued debt with extendible features.

Extendibles will be attractive for investors wanting the flexibility to increase their portfolio's return in ways other than straight buying and selling transactions. To evaluate extendible debt, the investor should compare an extendible issue to other extendible debt, as well as to individual medium- and long-term issues. Shifts in interest rates can cause an extendible bond to take on characteristics of a long- or short-term instrument. For example, an 8 per cent, five-year extendible bond that is trading in a 5 per cent interest rate environment will be priced more as a long-term instrument than as a five-year instrument.

Retractable debt

Retractable debt is the opposite of extendible debt. It is issued with a long term to maturity (e.g., 10 years), but the investor can force the issuer to repurchase its holdings at par, at a specified earlier date. As with extendible debt, debt with retractable features is usually issued with a lower coupon rate, while marketability and yield in the secondary bond market are higher.

Convertible debt

Convertible debt has characteristics similar to both debt and equity. It carries a fixed coupon rate and has a specified maturity date. Because convertible debt permits the investor, *at its option*, to convert the debt into common stock of the issuing company at a specified "conversion price", convertible debt offers a capital appreciation potential in addition to a stream of future interest payments. The "conversion privilege" lasts for a specified period of time. Most convertible bonds and debentures are callable and have a sinking fund. Some contain "forced conversion" clauses which permit companies to call the debt at a specified price if the underlying common shares have traded at a specified level for a specified period of time. The call price will be lower than the common shares' market price and therefore, investors effectively are forced to convert their debt to common shares.

Convertible debt generally carries a lower coupon rate. Their market prices are more affected by equity-related factors such as the quality of the issuer and the price of the underlying common stock. When the conversion price is below the market price of the common, the price of the debenture rises. However, when the conversion price is far above the market price or when stock markets are very depressed, the market prices the convertibles as debt instruments.

Floating interest rates

Floating rate notes are issued for a specified term (i.e., three to five years) but the interest on them is reset at regular intervals, such as semi-annually. The coupon rate is based on a market rate such as the commercial paper rate, bankers acceptance rate, or bank prime. A minimum rate of interest may be guaranteed to investors.

In principle, between reset dates a floating rate note would be valued like a bond, since the return for the current period is known. However, there is considerable liquidity risk, especially if the credit quality of the issuer is perceived to have deteriorated. For that reason, the market in Canada for floating rate notes is quite illiquid.

The floating rate increases the investor's exposure to changing levels of interest income, but decreases the risk of loss (or gain) of principal due to market price changes. Floating rate notes are one example of instruments that separate the credit risk term from interest rate risk. In other words, the investor may have six-month interest rate risk, and five-year credit exposure. In that respect, floating rate notes are reminiscent of some of the more exotic interest rate derivative products.

There has been limited experimentation in Canada with inflation-indexed bonds. The Government of Canada issued $700 million 30-year bonds in 1991. They yield a real (after inflation) return of 4 1/2 per cent. The principal is adjusted for inflation. Unfortunately (for the promoters of the bonds), ordinary government bonds have yielded a real return higher than 4 1/2 per cent. The issue has not been popular, and the market is consequently not very liquid.

Zero-coupon bonds

Zero-coupon (or strip) bonds result from physical separation of the interest flows (called strips or bearer coupons) and the principal repayment (called residual or bond residue). The coupons and bond residue are sold separately at a discount. The return to the investor is the difference between the purchase price and the redemption value. Once the components of a bond are separated, they cannot be registered. Therefore, careful safekeeping is important.

Occasionally, zero-coupon bonds are actually issued. These pay no interest until maturity. (Note that many short-term money market instruments such as commercial paper and treasury bills are zero-coupon instruments. In fact, any instrument sold at a discount — that is, not bearing an interest payment — is inherently a zero-coupon. This discussion refers to longer-term bonds that do not pay interest.) No such issues have occurred in Canada; a few have been issued in the United States.

Much more common is the creation of synthetic zero-coupon bonds or bond strips. These result from the separation of interest cash flows from the principal repayment ("residue"). The coupons and bond residue are sold separately, on a discounted basis. Note that the coupons are then non-interest bearing instruments.

For example, a $1 million 10-year Government of Canada bond, paying a 6 per cent coupon rate (semi-annually) would be stripped into 21 separate instruments. There would be 20 coupons of $30,000 each (0.06 × 1/2 × $1,000,000), and a principal repayment of $1 million. Each coupon would be individually priced at market rates. If the market price for a five-year government bond were 5 per cent, then the five-year coupon would be priced at about 78, or $23,400. ($1/(1.025)^{10}$ × $30,000 = 0.78 × $30,000 = $23,400.)

The longer the term of the zero-coupon bond is, the higher its discount will be. The duration of a zero-coupon bond is equal to its term, thus its price is particularly volatile. This can result in deep discount factors for longer maturities. For example, a 25-year strip would be priced at 15 to yield 8 per cent, or at 12 to yield 9 per cent to maturity. (And it can be seen that an increase in interest rates by one percentage point reduces the market price by 20 per cent.)

Investment dealers sell individual strip bonds, or a portion of a pool of strip bonds. While the market is not particularly active, strips are popular for tax deferral plans such as RRSPs. Because they are taxable, strip bonds make an excellent investment for RRSPs. Otherwise, they are not generally desirable, since interest must be accrued annually for tax purposes, although it is only received when the strip matures.

Other features

Long-term debt with less common characteristics are also issued from time to time. For example, **income debentures** do not pay interest unless an issuer earns a certain level of income. The interest may or may not be cumulative. Due to income tax rules which

239

treat income from income bonds and debentures as dividends, these instruments are rarely issued.

Exchangeable debentures are similar to convertible bonds and debentures, except the debt can be exchanged for shares of companies other than the issuer. The shares of the companies permitted for exchange are owned by the issuer. Exchangeable debentures are issued very infrequently.

Negative pledge debt prohibits new debt to be issued that would create bondholders ranking ahead of existing bondholders. It is more secure than debentures and, therefore, bonds with this feature usually will provide a lower yield to the investor.

Long-term debt may be issued along with warrants or other securities such as common shares to increase the saleability of the debt issue in the primary bond market.

Foreign Currency and Foreign Entity Bond Issues

An investor may invest in instruments in other countries, or instruments issued in Canada in other currencies. This may be advantageous for a company having significant foreign operations. A company also may decide to invest in foreign currencies if management assesses that a higher overall return (including the interest rate and effect of exchange rates) can be achieved. To reduce the risk of adverse foreign exchange rate fluctuations, a company may decide to enter into transactions to hedge its foreign currency exposure. Evaluating foreign debt for investment requires consideration of the same factors as for Canadian debt. However, certain factors such as the political and economic stability of the relevant country play a more important role.

A "euro-currency" instrument is an investment denominated in a currency of a country other than that of the instrument's issuer. For example, a U.S. dollar bond issued in Germany is a euro-bond. The debt instrument does not have to be issued by a European borrower even though the phrase "euro-currency" implies it. The most common currencies include U.S. dollars, Euros and U.K. sterling. The euro-currency market is a large, unrestricted international market. Euro-currency investments generally are purchased through investment dealers. There is an active secondary market in euro-currency issues and, subject to certain conditions, withholding tax is not applicable.

Types of euro-currency investments include the following:

(i) **Euro-bonds and euro-debentures** — interest bearing, bearer form instruments having terms of five to 30 years. They usually are unsecured due to the high quality of the issuers, and listed on a stock exchange. These are often issued in small denominations such as $1,000.

(ii) **Floating rate notes** — These notes generally are higher yielding than other foreign long-term debt because they are unsecured. FRNs are long-dated instruments whose interest rates are linked to short-term money market indices. There are numerous variations of FRNs.

The floating rate note market currently is very limited which reduces the liquidity of FRNs and increases their volatility.

Beware of so-called "Prime Bank Notes" offering high interest rates. There is no such thing as a prime bank note, but there are various scams around.

PART B

Selecting the Portfolio Term

It is commonly thought that the term of the investment should be matched with the requirement for funds. For example, an excess of cash for a period of two years should be used to invest in instruments with a remaining term to maturity of two years. The major concern would be that funds may be "locked in" for a period and could not be liquidated readily as needed. Also, by investing for shorter terms, the investment yield would fluctuate and may not be maximized. This approach is appropriate for short-term investments as well. However, investors may decide to maximize the objectives for a long-term portfolio based on their view on future interest rate movements.

Long-term debt instruments are subject to significantly more market price volatility than short-term investments. The investor should be able to design a long-term portfolio using any of the available maturities, after subjecting the instruments to a market evaluation. For example, when interest rate declines are anticipated (and bond prices are expected to increase), the investor should increase the term of the bond portfolio to achieve the maximum increase in value. The opposite is also true: If interest rates are expected to increase (and bond prices to fall), the term should be shortened. Historically, medium-term bonds (i.e., those with terms of five to 10 years) historically have tended to provide better returns than long-term instruments in rising interest rate conditions. Generally, they offer the same or higher rate of return as well as much less risk of price decline than long-term bonds.

Quantitative Analysis of Debt Instruments

Accrued interest

Bond prices are quoted excluding accrued interest (i.e., they are quoted "clean"). Depending on the particular bond market, there are different ways to calculate the number of days between the last coupon date and the value/settlement date:

(i) the actual number of days (the **actual basis**). This is used in Canada and the United Kingdom.

(ii) using 30-day months (the **30-day basis**). This is used in the U.S. and the euro-market.

There are also different ways to calculate the number of days in one year:

(i) using an actual year, which is 365 or 366 days (the **365-day basis**). This is used in Canada and the United Kingdom.

(ii) using a 360-day year (the **360-day basis**). This is used in the U.S. and the euro-market.

(iii) the number of days in the current coupon period (which generally is semi-annual) multiplied by two (the **actual basis**). Since a semi-annual period can range from 181 to 184 days, the year calculated under this method can be from 362 to 368 days.

Canadian bonds are quoted on an actual/365 basis, while U.S. and eurobond issues are quoted on a 30/360 day basis. Quoting in other countries' markets varies.

For example, assume a 6 per cent Canadian corporate bond maturing on June 30, 2011, is purchased at 105 on March 22, 2003. Since the last interest payment date would have been December

31, 2002, the purchaser must pay for the interest accrued from January 1 to March 27 as well as the purchase price. (The *settlement date*, not the *transaction date*, is relevant for calculating accrued interest. The settlement date varies by country, from one to seven days. For example, eurobond issues settle in seven days. However, in Canada, it is generally two to five days after the transaction date.) Therefore, the purchaser would pay $1,073.56, calculated as follows:

Purchase price	105/100 × $1,000	$1,050.00
Accrued interest	86* days/365 × $1,000 × 6%	14.14
		$1,064.14

Fixed rate debt

Pricing of bonds

A number of factors affect bond prices: quality of the issuer, maturity of the issue and the stated interest rate on the bond relative to current and expected future interest rates. Bond prices and interest rates are inversely related. As actual and expected interest rates increase, the price of a bond decreases and vice versa.

The total return on bonds includes income (from the regular flow of interest and reinvestment of these amounts) and fluctuations in market value (which can increase or decrease the return). Because the return on long-term debt instructments is, by definition, realized over a number of years, the time value of money must be considered in pricing these instruments. Pricing bonds and other long-term instruments involves calculating the **present value** of the total cash flows (interest, principal, call premium, etc.) realized from purchasing the instrument. The general formula for pricing bonds is:

$$P = \sum_{i=1}^{t^{*}n} \frac{Ci}{(1 + r/n)} i + \frac{Ft^{*}n}{(1 + r/n)^{t^{*}n}}$$

$$= \frac{C_1}{(1 + r/n)^1} + \frac{C_2}{(1 + r/n)^2} + \ldots + \frac{C_t}{(1 + r/n)^{t^{*}n}} + \frac{F_{t^{*}n}}{(1 + r/n)^{t^{*}n)}}$$

where:

P = price of bond

C = interest to be received each compounding period

r = required (or risk-adjusted) rate of return per year

n = number of compounding periods per year (note that most bonds compound semi-annually)

t = number of years (term) to maturity

F = par value received at maturity

For practical purposes, this calculation can be done using a business calculator, present value tables or a computer program.

The required rate of return may vary by investor and is affected by changing market conditions. Its two components are the risk-free rate of return (often indicated by comparable risk-free instruments such as Government of Canada treasury bills) and the premium required to compensate the investor for the potential for default.

The price of a **fixed rate** bond changes over time because of changes in the required rate of return since future cash flows are known. However, the price of a **floating rate** bond will fluctuate also because of fluctuating coupon rates.

Calculating bond yields

Current yield — Current yield is a simple way of estimating the return on a bond. It is calculated as follows:

$$\text{Current yield} = \frac{\text{annual coupon}}{\text{bond price}}$$

The current yield is a very rough way of estimating the return on a bond as it does not consider any future capital increase or decrease. It should be supplemented with other analyses.

Yield to maturity — Yield to maturity refers to the return earned on a bond at a given price if held to maturity. Total yield on a debt instrument is a function of the annual interest flows and any capital gain or loss resulting from purchasing an instrument at other than par value. (A capital gain results when an investment is purchased at a discount; a capital loss arises when it is purchased at a premium.) The yield to maturity on bonds discounts all future payments of interest and principal to the current market price of the bond. It can also be called the internal rate of return. The yield to maturity is calculated using the same formula as for pricing bonds. However, the unknown is "r" (yield to maturity) rather than "P".

Again, this calculation can be done using a business calculator, present value tables or a computer program.

An *estimate* of yield to maturity may be obtained by using the following formula:

$$\text{Yield} = \frac{\text{annual interest per \$100 of par} + (\text{par value} - \text{price})/\text{term to maturity}}{(\text{par value} + \text{Price})/2}$$

For example, a $10,000 5 per cent bond maturing in 5 years that was purchased at 98 would yield approximately:

$$5.45\% = \frac{500/100 + (100 - 98)/5}{(100 + 98)/2}$$

Yield to maturity is not an entirely accurate reflection of return for the following reasons:

- It excludes the effect of compounding of the amount invested other than annually.

- It assumes that all interest payments can be reinvested at "i", which is the initial purchase yield rate. However, if the company can reinvest the interest flows at higher than "i", the effective yield will be higher for a debt instrument with a higher coupon rate.

For callable bonds called at a premium, the yield to maturity is calculated using bond yield tables, a calculator or a computer after the coupon rate and price are adjusted as follows:

$$\text{Adjusted coupon rate} = \frac{\text{stated coupon}}{\text{call price}}$$

$$\text{Adjusted price} = \frac{\text{price}}{\text{call price}}$$

Bond yields are quoted in terms of *basis points*, one basis point being 1/100 of 1 per cent. Therefore, a bond yielding 6.75 per cent is said to be yielding 25 basis points more than a bond yielding 6.50 per cent.

Floating rate debt

Determining the price of a floating rate instrument is more complex than a fixed rate instrument because coupon flows are not known. Other things being equal, the value of a floating rate issue immediately before and after an interest reset/refix date should be close to par (or 100), and should be par at the reset date. However, this assumes that the final redemption will be at par and that the spread of the coupon rate over the index rate is adequate compensation for risk assumed by the investor. *Between reset dates*, the price of the debt will have to provide a market rate of return to the investor. To compare floating rate instruments with other types of instruments, the following formula for determining the return on floating rate issues between reset dates can be used:

$$R = \frac{F + (i - d/N) - (P + A)}{P + A} \times \frac{N}{T} \times 100$$

where:

F = principal at maturity (however, if the value of a floating rate instrument does not return to par at a reset date because of the market's concerns about the creditworthiness of the issuer, R will become an estimate of price at maturity)

i = current coupon rate

d = total number of days in current coupon period

N = number of days in year basis

A = accrued interest on settlement date

T = number of days to next reset date

For example, a $100,000 7 per cent Canadian financial institution floating rate bond that pays interest semi-annually on June 30 and December 31 is purchased at 99 on June 30. Therefore, no accrued interest is paid. Assume that interest rates are reset quarterly on March 31, June 30, September 30 and December 31. Further assume that the price of the bond returns to par at reset dates. The return to reset date would be:

$$4.1\% = \frac{100 + (0.07 \times 184/365) - (99 + 0)}{99 + 0} \times \frac{365}{92} \times 100$$

To compare floating rate instruments whose coupons are based on the same index, the following formula can be used. The "margin" includes the spread of the coupon rate over the index as well as the increase of capital.

$$\text{Margin} = \frac{(R - P) + \frac{S}{t}}{P/100} \times 100$$

where:

R = redemption price

P = current price

t = number of years to redemption

S = spread of coupon over interest rate index

Other Types of Long-Term Investments

Preferred shares

Certain types of preferred shares are very similar to bonds and other interest-bearing long-term investments. However, a preferred shareholder ranks after bondholders and other creditors in realizing on principal on liquidation of a company. If preferred shares are cumulative, their dividends are similar to interest since they must be paid before common shareholders receive any return. However, there is no legal obligation for companies to pay dividends, whether they are cumulative or not, until they are declared by the company. Therefore, a higher level of risk is associated with preferred shares than with bonds, and with non-cumulative preferred shares over cumulative shares. Some preferred shares have purchase or sinking funds. Investors holding retractable (or term) preferred shares can be redeemed at the holder's option for a specified period at a specified price.

Preferred shares are unsecured (as are debentures), but rank below debtholders in the case of liquidation. As a result, the yield from preferred shares typically is lower than long-term debt issues with comparable stated interest rates to the preferred's dividend rate.

A key difference between long-term debt instruments and preferred shares is the treatment of the return for tax purposes. Interest is fully taxable; dividends earned from Canadian corporations are only partly taxable. (For example, refundable tax is payable by private companies on dividends received on equity holdings of less than 10 per cent. This tax is refunded when the company pays dividends itself. Intercompany dividends in public corporations are generally tax-free. However, in some cases, preferred dividends may be taxable.) The investor should compare the after-tax return from preferred shares to the after-tax return from other investments. In addition, other factors such as credit quality of the issuers should be considered.

Issuers of preferred shares attach other features to issues equivalent to those often found in long-term debt issues. Preferred shares may be convertible, callable and/or floating rate (variable rate). They may be issued with warrants, or issued in foreign currencies. They may be participating, which means they may earn dividends beyond the stated rate if the issuer earns adequate income.

As with long-term debt instruments, the investment quality of preferred shares is affected significantly by the quality of the issuer (measured in terms of financial strength, financial results, etc.). A second key consideration is the issuer's past dividend-paying record since the preferred shareholder has no legal claim to the issuer's underlying assets. These factors, in addition to market rates of return, economic conditions and similar factors affect the market prices of preferred shares. Preferred shares trade on established equity markets, rather than over-the-counter as long-term debt instruments do.

Calculating the yield on preferred shares

The yield on most preferred shares, including retractable shares having a market price **above** their retraction price and callable preferreds having a market price **above** their call price, is calculated as:

$$\text{Yield} = \frac{\text{annual preferred dividend}}{\text{market price of the share}}$$

The yield on retractable shares having a market price **at or below** the retraction price and on callable preferreds having a market price **above** their call price, is calculated as a yield to maturity with the maturity date being the earliest retraction date and call date, respectively. (See the section "Calculating bond yields" above for a discussion of yield to maturity.)

Common shares

Common shares significantly vary in the level of security, capital gains potential, dividend return and other factors. They are usually considered to be riskier than debt instruments. However, common stock of "blue chip" companies can provide a safer investment than debt instruments of certain companies. For example, in hindsight, the relatively stable return from Canadian bank stocks would have been preferable to purchasing bonds of Canadian airlines.

Other

Various off-balance sheet products may also be used to refine the risk profile of a portfolio. See Part D for a discussion of the use of derivatives.

PART B

C

Financial and Cash Management

Strong controls, effective budgeting, and tight credit and collection practices will all improve the management of cash and help the finance function add value to the business. This section sets out best practices in financial and cash management.

CHAPTER 11

Financial Strategy

Overview

In theory, the objective of the business enterprise is to maximize shareholder wealth. In practice, however, the relationship between management decisions and changes in shareholder wealth are often unclear. This chapter suggests that the use of clear goals and objectives will result in an improved financial performance and a higher value for the business.

Corporate Mission and Financial Objectives

Every business organization has a mission that indicates why it exists. There may be a formal mission statement, clearly laid out and widely understood by shareholders and employees. The mission of the enterprise may be obvious and implicit. Or, as is more often the case, the mission may be unclear. In the latter case, if pressed, management might suggest that the mission of the business is to survive, to achieve ever increasing levels of profitability, or some meaningless aphorism. But every business does have a mission, whether clear or cloudy, useful or pointless.

Business objectives should be set by senior management as a means of fulfilling the mission of the enterprise. At the level of the overall business, the objectives should be broad and clear and also permit assessment as to when and how they are achieved. Objectives commonly will relate to various functional areas. For example, there may be objectives relating to marketing and sales, customer service, production, human resources, and shareholder relations. There may be specific financial objectives to guide the enterprise in the short-, medium- or long-term.

Regardless of objectives otherwise determined, every business enterprise has a fundamental financial objective — the maximization of shareholders' wealth. Absent that as a financial objective, the corporation may be focused excessively on perpetuating management rather than benefitting shareholders. Since shareholders have the ultimate ownership interest in the corporation, the focus on their well-being is appropriate. In financial terms, well-being equates to maximizing wealth.

The notion of risk and return is often implied in a company's strategy. High returns are associated with risky strategies, moderate returns with less risky strategies. Similarly, returns may be more or less volatile, depending upon the strategy followed.

Shareholder Wealth

Shareholder wealth is increased by maximizing the amount of cash flow ultimately accruing to the shareholders. This cash flow originates from two sources: dividends paid out by the corporation, and increases in the market value of the corporation (that is, an increase in the value of common shares). Cash flow in the business can be distributed to investors through dividends or the repurchase of shares, or it can be retained in the business to generate sales and income growth, thus presumably increasing share values in the long run. Income, as measured by generally accepted accounting principles, is the normal measure of cash flows actually earned by the business.

In public corporations, as well as other corporations where management is separate from share ownership, the managers are agents of the shareholders. That is, they work for and on behalf of shareholders. If the shareholders were polled, it is unlikely that they could agree upon any overall corporate objective other than that of shareholder wealth maximization. Secondary objectives such as being a good corporate citizen or minimizing pollution can only endure if the business itself is profitable and thriving.

Literature on management often refers to *stakeholders* to describe the various parties with an interest in a business enterprise. Stakeholders include shareholders, employees, creditors, customers, suppliers, governments, and even the public. It is unlikely that all of these stakeholders would agree on corporate objectives. Since the owners of the business probably would agree on the financial objective of maximizing their wealth, this focus appears defensible.

While the financial objective of generating shareholder wealth is simple to state, it is not in itself terribly useful as a plan for action. The relationship between management decisions and changes in shareholder wealth is generally uncertain and unpredictable. Nonetheless, attention to shareholder wealth provides a useful focus for evaluating financial strategies and policies.

Planning and Maximizing Share Price

An increase in share price is one element of maximizing shareholder wealth. (The other is dividends.) In addition to benefitting shareholders directly, appreciating share prices have other beneficial effects on the business enterprise:

- Improving access to capital;
- Facilitating the acquisition process;
- Improving the ability to resist being acquired;
- Management retention and compensation;
- Relations with creditors; and
- Relations with shareholders.

Therefore, corporate financial strategy should be designed to have a positive impact on the share price. In the case of private corporations, increases in the market value and marketability of the corporation overall have the same effect as an increase in the share price of a publicly traded corporation.

The simplest measure of share price is the market to book ratio. This is the ratio of share price to book value per share, or the ratio of the market value of the entire company to its book value. In either case, book value refers to shareholders' equity accruing to the common shareholders: that is, common share capital, paid in capital and other surplus, and retained earnings.

In theory, a market to book ratio of greater than 1.0 suggests that every dollar put up by the equity holders has been transformed by management into a market value of more than a dollar.

Similarly, a market to book ratio of less than 1.0 indicates that management has destroyed value.

The use of differing accounting policies will significantly influence market to book ratios. Even different accounting practices within a policy have significant effect. For example, fixed assets might be depreciated over 10 years or 30 years. While such variations in practice should be based upon differing factual situations, that is not always the case.

Another difficulty with the market to book ratio is that financial accounting does not track fair values, rather it simply records actual dollars expended. The impact of inflation or changes in purchasing power is not taken into account.

A related problem is that analysis of the process of creating value or destroying value must be done based on incremental effects. For example, a company may have a low market to book ratio as a result of poor management decisions historically. The relevant measure is the impact of the current management decisions on improving the market to book ratio. When evaluating a real company, it can be difficult to disentangle the impact of old and new decisions upon the market to book ratio.

The market to book ratio is a measure for evaluating how cheap or expensive the shares or market price of a company will be. The market value itself is ultimately based upon future cash flows and it can be instructive to analyze those cash flows themselves.

The market price of a company is based upon the future income stream (cash flows) expected to accrue to shareholders. Those cash flows must be discounted at an appropriate interest rate to determine their present value. As a practical matter, cash flows and discount rate are very difficult to determine, although their theoretical components can readily be analyzed.

PART C

Expected income stream or cash flows depends upon projected profitability and growth. The appropriate discount rate to discount the stream is based upon risk considerations as well as overall economic outlook. Putting those factors together, it can be seen that share prices can be enhanced by altering numerous factors:

- Expected sales growth rate;
- Expected operating profit growth;
- Expected investment in working capital and capital assets (fixed assets);
- Current interest rates and cost of capital; and
- General economic outlook.

Some of these cannot be influenced by the company itself. Nonetheless, they are important considerations in arriving at a strategic plan. Other factors should form part of the overall corporate objectives and then help drive the strategic plan itself.

The Central Role of Financial Objectives

For better or worse, accounting provides the language and primary means of evaluation in the modern business environment. Facts, transactions and items are recorded in terms of money. That is, things that are purchased and tangible are accounted for. Events are ignored if they don't have immediate monetary impact. Assets or liabilities not acquired from outsiders, that are not tangible and paid for, or that represent future commitments ("executory contracts") are not effectively measured and recorded by the accounting system. Therefore, most companies have relatively poor information on such items as internally developed goodwill, environmental damage or liabilities.

Financial accounting measures are nonetheless useful in setting clear and unambiguous objectives and in permitting their evaluation.

Using Financial Goals

An example of the implementation of financial policy, and its useful-ness in setting quantifiable goals, is set out below. A useful summary measure of the effectiveness of an enterprise is return on capital employed ("ROCE"). ROCE is net income divided by capital employed. It is often derived by considering two related measures, profit on sales and capital turnover:

$$\text{ROCE} = \% \text{ profit on sales} \times \text{capital turnover ratio}$$

$$= \frac{\text{net income}}{\text{sales}} \times \frac{\text{sales}}{\text{capital employed}}$$

$$= \frac{\text{net income}}{\text{capital employed}}$$

ROCE is normally examined by considering its trend over time, comparing it to what should be theoretically possible or desirable given the nature of the enterprise, and by comparing it to plan. The equations above can be used to break it into components:

- *Net income*, which depends upon gross margin on sales, the relationship between gross margin (total contribution) and fixed costs, and taxation; and
- *Capital employed*, which is net working capital (current assets less current liabilities) plus non-current assets (in general, primarily fixed assets).

The profit on sales ratio measures the amount of net income generated by each dollar of revenue. Capital turnover indicates the level of sales that $1 of capital employed will support.

Thus, ROCE could be increased by any or all of the following strategies:

PART C

- Increase sales volumes (keeping fixed costs the same);
- Increase the gross margin on sales (keeping sales volumes constant);
- Reduce the level of capital employed (while keeping sales constant);
- Increase sales volumes (by keeping capital employed constant); or
- Reduce income taxes (assuming no change to income before taxes).

Sales volume is the domain of marketing policy. Margins, cost structures, and productivity are influenced by operations management. The level of capital employed may be influenced by operations management (for example, inventory control). However, the primary determinant of the amount of capital employed is financial policy. Thus, financial policy itself will directly affect ROCE. The level and use of capital in business enterprises are discussed in more detail below.

The ratio of net income to sales may be further analyzed using various measures. A particularly interesting one is to relate it to measures based on the number of employees. For example:

$$\frac{\text{Net income}}{\text{Sales}} = \frac{\text{net income}}{\text{headcount}} \; / \; \frac{\text{sales}}{\text{headcount}}$$

Headcount can be measured as "full time equivalent" (FTE) staff, or any other measure that tracks the level of employment.

This approach tracks net income per employee — a powerful measure of the overall effectiveness of the organization — and also tracks sales per employee, a good measure of efficiency. This is particularly interesting when comparing the results of different business units within the same organization. In addition, sudden or unexpected changes in these measures may be leading indicators of problems.

Cost of Capital and Rate Of Return

The minimum acceptable return from a project is the rate of interest that the firm is paying for the capital invested in it. A firm draws capital from various sources and each has a different cost. The objective should be to develop a financing structure that minimizes the firm's weighted average cost of capital.

The cost of capital in capital budgeting processes is the hurdle against which investment alternatives are judged.

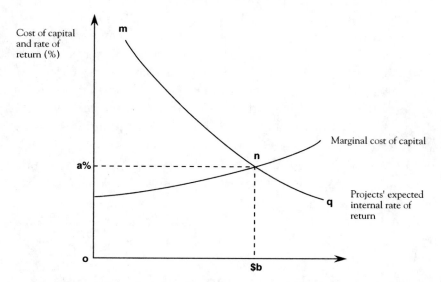

Projects falling on the curve m – n would be undertaken, as their forecasted return exceeds the cost of capital a%. The capital budget needed to finance is $b. Projects falling on the curve n – q would be rejected, as their return would not cover cost of capital of a%.

Capital budgeting and the financial structure of the firm (the mix between equity and debt) cannot be viewed in isolation from each other. Changes in financial structure will affect cost of capital calculations, and vice versa. As the proportion of debt increases relative to equity, there is a greater probability that earnings per share and return to equity will vary from one year to another. The more debt there is to service, the less profit there is to distribute to shareholders. The result may be an increase in the rate of return required by holders of equity, or the lowering of share prices.

At the same time, the cost of debt may rise at an increasing rate as the leverage ratio increases. This may in part be due to the need to use a variety of debt sources, some of which may charge different interest rates. It will also be due to risk assessments made by sources of loan finance who may consider that the more debt the firm has, the higher the interest requirements, and the higher the interest charges, the greater the probability that earnings will not always be sufficient to meet these charges. Risk premiums may be the result. We can describe this dilemma in terms of cash-flow ability to service debt. When considering the appropriate capital structure, it is important to analyze the cash flow (capacity) of the firm to service fixed charges. The greater and more stable the expected future cash flows of the firm, the greater the debt capacity of the firm.

Control of Working Capital and Cash Flow

The maintenance of satisfactory cash flows is always an important objective. Working capital is the ratio of current assets to current liabilities. The acid test ratio is:

$$\frac{\text{current assets minus inventories and prepaids}}{\text{current liabilities}} = \frac{\text{liquid assets}}{\text{current liabilities}}$$

The control of working capital is the key to the maintenance of cash flows which are positive (i.e., net inflows) at the time they are needed. Such control may be obtained under three headings:

- *Sufficient working capital* such that the business can cope with volume and inflationary increases in the cost of its inputs. A situation of negative cash flow (i.e., net outflows) will lead to an increase in current liabilities, a situation which trade creditors and the bank will eventually restrict in their own interest. This risk can only be offset by having positive incoming cash flows with which to offset any imbalance between current assets and the current liabilities, preferably at least to a point where the acid test ratio shows a balance between liquid assets and current liabilities plus imminent outgoings, such as for payments of interest on longer-term loans.
- *Working capital turnover* — The flow of working capital, particularly cash, is summarized below. The speed of the flow is important. The faster it goes, the greater the output that may be obtained from expensive fixed assets, and the smaller the investment in working capital needed to obtain this output. At the same time, the business must seek to prevent the unnecessary build up of working capital within the cycle, by monitoring stock levels and debtors.

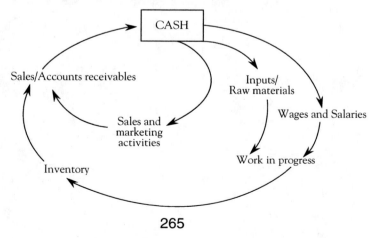

PART C

- Product life cycle — Analysis of the product mix relative to positions on product life cycle may show which products should be producing positive cash flows and which are not, especially when there is a heavy demand for cash to finance new product development.

12

Controls, Systems and Budgets

Overview

The purpose of controls and systems is to ensure that performance is optimized. The control system is not an end in itself — a truism that sometimes is forgotten.

The discussion in this chapter relates primarily to feedback controls and the use of the control system to enhance performance in real time.

Management controls — regardless of their type — seek to ensure that performance conforms to plans. This entails an iterative process of evaluating performance and taking corrective measures when performance differs from plans. There are three phases to the management control process:

- establishing standards;
- measuring performance against standards; and
- correcting deviations from standards.

The Control Process

Controls can be classified according to function and timing:

- *Feedback controls* detect deviations from the standard and provide for corrective measures to be taken before the operation is completed.
- *Approval procedures* require that approval be obtained before a next step can be taken.
- *After-the-fact controls* measure results after the operation is completed.

Establishing standards

The control process begins with plans. In the planning process, there is a continuous narrowing of detail from specific tactical plans to broad strategies. The tactical plans establish goals, targets, and standards to guide the fulfilment of strategic plans.

Managerial decision is important at this point in choosing and defining specific standards to guide action. The key to determining what standards will be set is the answer to the question: what is it that management wishes to measure? Standards cannot be set for everything so choices must be made about those key activities that managers wish to monitor continuously.

The "80/20" rule can be an important guideline. In 1906, an Italian economist Vilfredo Pareto described the unequal distribution of wealth in Italy, and noted that 20 per cent of the people owned 80 per cent of the wealth. Since then, this observation has been applied (somewhat illogically) to many other areas, and it stands for the proposition that 20 per cent of something may be responsible for 80 per cent of the results. So, 20 per cent of customers yield 80 per cent of the profits, 20 per cent of inventory takes up 80 per cent of warehouse space, 20 per cent of employees account for 80 per cent of absences, and so on. The 80/20 rule is not an immutable law; rather, it is a reminder that a few things will account for most of the results. The converse also applies: 80 per cent of something will account for only 20 per cent of the results.

Measuring performance against standards

There are many important facets to the measurement of performance. First, how much variation will constitute a reason for taking corrective action? Second, managers must be on the alert to determine whether standards should be altered. As changes in the environment take place, it may be necessary to correct standards before looking at performance. Variable budgets are designed to do precisely this. Third, management must develop the proper type of reporting and information system to appraise, compare, and correct performance. This aspect of control opens up a vast subject because it concerns not only control but all other aspects of management as well. As far as control is concerned, the management information system must identify those points in a manager's area of responsibility, the surveillance of which will permit the manager to exercise the appropriate control over employee performance in achieving the targets for which the manager is responsible. This is a complex design problem because it must be responsive to a manager's needs, knowledge, preferred methods to get and use information, the standard under review, and so on. The less con-

PART C

crete the standard against which performance is measured, the more difficult the information system design problem.

Control reports will vary at different levels in the organization. The chief executive officer, for instance, will want reports concerned with whether the missions and objectives of the company are still adequate, whether critical parts of the strategic plan are being implemented (for example, acquisitions, divestitures, new product development, and progress of new facility construction), and whether current operations are satisfactory. The executive vice-president will want more penetrating details about the operations of the enterprise, and the focus of lower level managers will be narrower.

Reports that compare actual results with desired results may be useful for certain types of information but inadequate for others. When managers are appraising the overall performance of other managers, a comparison of financial results of their area of operation with predetermined objectives is a needed base for evaluation. For many other types of activities, however, what is required is advance warning, or predictors of results. This is future-oriented, feedforward, control. Managers do not want to find out that sales last month were 10 per cent under what was desired. They want to know today that sales next month may be 10 per cent under standard unless some action is taken to counter the trend. Really effective control requires accurate prediction.

Ingenuity is needed to find useful predictors. Forecasts provide one type of forewarning. A sales manager may use a composite of field visits, customer inquiries, complaints, returned merchandise, and so on, to foresee future deviations from plans.

Evaluating performance and taking corrective action

Measurements of past performances and predictions of things to come alert management to what is going on or likely to happen but do not determine what should be done. There are two phases to this activity. The first concerns the evaluation of the warning signals, and the second relates to managerial decision about any remedies for correcting deviations for standards.

Proper evaluation of signals is important. Some methods to predict future events may not be entirely reliable and considerable judgment may be required to prevent precipitous action. For example, a sudden increase in the sale of a product may indicate a fad and not a long-lived increase in consumer demand. To take action on the current jump in sales could lead to excessive overcapacity, rising costs per unit, and declining profits.

Once a manager decides that corrective action is required, the issue then joins the entire process of management. A revision of plans may be required. New standards may be needed. Better motivation of employees may be desired, and so on. Although control may be identified as a key function of managers, it cannot be performed without simultaneous actions among other functions.

Effective Budget Systems

Designing and implementing an effective system of controls is complex — more so in larger enterprises. Some guidelines and factors that improve the likelihood of installing a successful and effective budgetary system are set out below.

- There should be support by top management. No control and budget system can be successful without the unqualified support of senior management.

PART C

- There should be a clear organizational structure. For the budget process to be effective, managers must understand their accountabilities and authority. They need to have clearly defined roles in the organization and fully understand their relationships with peers, subordinates, and superiors in the organization. This is necessary to ensure that the budget covers precisely the responsibilities of each manager.

- The budget system should form part of an effective, company-wide, planning program. It is an integral part of the planning process. The challenge (and duty) of senior management is to convert long-range strategic plans into quantitative budgetary objectives for each business area.

- Responsibility for the budgetary system must be clearly laid out and understood. Although the ultimate responsibility rests with top management, in all but the smallest firms, the task is delegated to someone else, often a comptroller or planning manager. The work of preparing the budget becomes one of collecting, disseminating, organizing, and evaluating information. In larger companies, the precise duties may be set out in a detailed procedural manual.

- Budgets should not dominate the decision-making process. They do not replace the need for judgment by managers. Common sense must be used in day-to-day decision-making. For example, managers should feel comfortable in deviating from budgets if they have valid business reasons. Similarly, the budget should not be used as a reason to be uncooperative with another department. As the environment changes, flexibility may be necessary. The budget should be administered firmly, but also flexibly, when appropriate.

- Keep it simple and easy to understand. Avoid accounting jargon, esoteric language, and arcane criteria.

- Do not let the budget process become overly complex or cumbersome. The budgetary process is a mechanism to delegate authority. If there are detailed restrictions, too much detail, or a confining process, the managers will become frustrated. This will lead to resentment and, probably, bureaucratic inertia. The budget is a tool for management: it is not to be confused with management itself.

- State measurement criteria clearly. The budget process will work better if budgets have clearly defined standards to measure performance. The advantage of clear standards is that exceptions can be reported objectively, and appropriate follow-up measures can be taken. Alternatively, superior performance can be noted objectively, and appropriate action can be taken. All of this will result in the process being perceived as fair, which will improve buy-in to the process by managers and staff.

- There must be adequate understanding of the purpose and limitations of the budget throughout the enterprise. Budgets are tools to help the company achieve its objectives. They are not meant to frustrate or annoy, as lower-level managers in some companies feel. Budgets should not be used to pressure unduly or to goad employees to higher levels of performance.

- Discourage game-playing with budgets. For example, extra spending at the end of the fiscal year to ensure a higher base for the following year's budget should be discouraged. There are two general ways to do this. One is by having a corporate culture in which such games are simply not considered appropriate. The other (related) technique is to follow the guidelines laid down here. If the budgetary

PART C

process is perceived as being fair and equitable, then there will be buy-in and it will be used effectively by both managers and employees.

- There should be widespread participation in the development of the budget. People generally do not like budgets, since they do not like to be controlled. By involving as many as possible in the development of the budget, the constraints resulting from it become more palatable. Another subtle benefit often results: as more people understand the overall organizational objectives and constraints, they can better appreciate the reasons for their own budgetary goals.

- The budgetary system should be economical. It should be cheap to operate with the minimum number of controls and reports, yet still be effective. The system should be kept as simple as possible. The cost of a control or report versus the benefits resulting therefrom should be a major consideration.

- Budgets should be meaningful. Budgets should be established only for the important things that management wishes to measure, monitor, and understand. This is closely related to the accounting concept of "materiality". Something is material if it can influence the action taken by a decision-maker. If an item is not material, the budget should ignore it. Note that materiality depends not only on the absolute dollar amount, but also the nature of the item. An increase of $10,000 in total salary costs may be immaterial to the budget, whereas the same increase in promotional expense may be material. The operational consideration is whether the decision-maker may take action based upon the item. (Materiality is not a number that is *set*, rather it is *discovered*, based upon the behaviour of people.)

- The budgetary system must be tailored to the enterprise. There is no one ideal budgeting, suitable for all organizations. The unique characteristics of a company, including ownership, management style, size, problems, purpose, and environment all enter into the design.

- It will often be beneficial to have both a budget, which is fixed for the year, and a rolling estimate of what results are likely to be.

Company Size

There are significant differences in control systems between large and small companies. In very small companies, relatively few budgets and tactical plans are required because managers are in constant contact with each other and their employees. The production process, marketing considerations, cash flow analysis, etc., tend to be much simpler than in a larger enterprise. Therefore, it is easier to manage and monitor the company without an elaborate reporting system.

In larger organizations, communication problems between managers at all levels become more difficult to resolve. It becomes more difficult to co-ordinate activities. As a result, the budgetary system frequently plays a major role in operating the business and assisting communications between managers. Larger organizations are also subject to more external threats and require a wider network of scanning techniques to anticipate the threats. As a result, control systems in larger companies are more complex.

275

Cost of Management Information

Time

The value of any piece of information is related to time. The most simplistic view taken is that the value of the information reduces as time passes. This implies, however, acceptance of one of the myths of information — that the quicker the information is available the greater its value. The true relationship of time to information is more complex than this. This relationship depends upon the type of decision to be taken. There are three categories: decisions that are improved by the speed of information flow, those that are unaffected by it, and those that are actually hindered.

The simple relationship, where the value of information is corelated to time, applies to the first type of decision — for example, control information. Even in this case, however, it would be pertinent to analyze the cost of not having the information, which increases as time increases. Strictly speaking, this will be the case when the process is not in control. When the process is in control, the value of the control information is limited, but the purpose of control information is to monitor.

In a complex decision, there may be a series of sub-decisions, each of which involves gathering of information. Some information may be used to determine further information requirements. Information for this type of decision could have a value time relationship. This cannot be considered a general pattern as the value may fall between the two decisions or it may increase for the second decision or it may decrease. It will become more complicated as more decisions are involved with the piece of information.

A decision may be hindered by timely data if the data is highly variable. Highly variable data requires the passage of time to determine the extent of the variability.

An example of this is found in process control. The output of a production process is monitored to ensure that items produced are acceptable. Some process control systems have fixed time interval sampling of the process, others have a variable time interval sampling. With the variable time interval sampling, the sampling will be carried out at a fixed time interval until it is thought the process is going out of control. The time interval will then be reduced to check on the process. If it is out of control then this will be rectified, and if a false alarm has occurred then the fixed time interval sampling will be resumed. With examples of this type, the timing of the information becomes more important when there are indications the process is out of control.

Knowledge

Knowledge can be defined as the body of facts relating to the principles and practices of management and any related facts necessary for the successful management of an organization. It would be foolish to consider that every manager would personally know all of this knowledge, but it would not seem unreasonable to suggest that a manager should be able to have access to this knowledge through the management team of an organization and through management education.

Knowledge determines the extent to which the information approaches its true value. It does not add to the true value of the information, but a lack of it does not allow the true value to be achieved. An individual's perception of his state of knowledge is not necessarily reliable. Individuals may have a pessimistic or an optimistic view of their state of knowledge.

The factor of knowledge is extremely important when talking in terms of information needs because there is no point in providing information if the knowledge as to how to use it is absent. It would therefore seem reasonable that the information analyst should provide access to the knowledge as well as the information.

Prior information

In determining the value of a piece of information, all the other information connected with it must be considered — for example, a company must decide whether or not to carry out a market survey into the sales of a commodity. The value of the information produced will be affected by the information already available. If the product is new, and no other sales information is available, the value of such a survey in most cases will be more than if the product is an established one with past sales figures which can be used to forecast. The factor that could reverse this relationship could be termed the surprise factor. The larger the surprise factor of a piece of information the greater the value of that piece of information.

Accuracy

The greater the accuracy of a piece of information the greater its value; however, the law of diminishing returns applies. There are a number of cases where accuracy is of great importance, especially at the operational level. There are also quite a number of cases where absolute accuracy is both unnecessary and possibly misleading.

Accuracy is also related to time and cost. As a general principle, the greater the accuracy required the more time and/or cost will be incurred. If information is being prepared for a time-dependent decision, the level of accuracy and/or cost could well be forced on the manager by the time constraint.

Quantity

The amount of information can affect its value. If the quantity of information is so large as to overload the manager, the value may be reduced. All managers suffer under a time constraint; therefore, there is a chance that some of the value of a large amount of information may be lost because of insufficient time to study it. If a large number of pieces of information are provided for a particular decision or series of decisions there can be a similar effect.

Power

Managers will use some information to create uncertainty rather than to reduce it. Information may not be the only source of a manager's power in the organization, but it is certainly an effective one. The power may be exercised by information being released selectively, slowly, or not at all.

Using Management Information Systems Effectively

The budget and control system is an integral part of management information systems. Computers are almost invariably used in this process. The degree of sophistication used in practice is enormous. At one end of the spectrum, a spreadsheet summarizing budget versus actual results may be prepared, using manual input, by a clerk. At the other extreme, a thousand-person systems department may generate hundreds of thousands of pages of data monthly to help in the management process. It is a supreme irony of this information age that many managers in the latter case might have been better served by a one-page spreadsheet, which they do indeed sometimes produce themselves by keying in data manually.

PART C

Much has been written about how to control management information systems. Several recurring themes are set out below:

- *Focus constantly on profits, otherwise you won't get them* — Sometimes, the system overwhelms the managers. Many computer systems conversions of the 60s and 70s failed because the technology became an end in itself, rather than a means to improve operations and, consequently, profitability.

- *Any activity managed on the basis of technical criteria will be unprofitable* — The easiest mistake made in managing systems is to treat the function differently from any other. Certainly, the systems function is an unusual blend of development and production, all too often with a bit of research thrown in, but it presents no new problems to the experienced manager. Developing computer systems involves complex design decisions and trade-offs, in which many of the parameters are uncertain. The technology involved is developing so rapidly that even full-time systems people have to restrict their view in order to cope with the range of options. When executives become unhappy at the cost of or poor contribution of the systems department, it is easy to be lured into discussing technical alternatives and specific application problems. Once that happens they are lost. The executives may understand enough, or believe they do, to become advocates of one solution or another. They may, on the other hand, find the detail and its complexity hopelessly confusing. Either way, the technology is fascinating, and they will have joined the alligator-fighters. The swamp will remain undrained. The management role in systems is the same as anywhere else: set the right objectives, monitor performance, and insist on results. Above all, management should demand that solutions to problems be stated in non-technical terms.

- *Any organization, system or procedure left undisturbed for three years will become inefficient* — The scope for improving performance in each area of an organization's activities would normally be identified as the first step in a full information strategy study. This would be followed by an assessment of the quality of the existing systems and the preparation of a future systems plan. The effectiveness of current technology and development techniques would be audited, and a cost, benefit and risk analysis prepared. The conduct of an information strategy study has many other aspects and benefits; however, it is possible to form a quick assessment of the health of a company's systems using only three criteria.

(a) *Effectiveness* — Are systems having a visible and significant effect on the largest costs, or promoting the biggest revenue earners? Are they doing more than saving heads and automating paperwork? Do managers rely on them for monitoring and control? Are they giving the company an edge over its competition? If the answer to these questions is generally "No", opportunities are being missed.

(b) *Economy* — Has the systems budget formed an increasing percentage of turnover in each of the last three years? Is more than 20 per cent of the budget spent on keeping systems running, rather than on new work? Are developments measuredin years rather than months? If so, resources may well be being wasted through poor techniques or inadequate use of packaged systems.

(c) *Obsolescence* — Is any development work done by the users of systems for themselves, with English-like languages or other simple tools? Are data processing and

281

office technology part of a single co-ordinated approach? Do micro-computers outnumber non-intelligent terminals? If not, the systems approach may be dated and will prove increasingly expensive each year until it is changed.

- *Left to themselves, people will make their work more complex rather than simpler* — Everybody knows that, however conscientious an employee, the daily pressures on him or her are more personal, more complex, and more trivial than making a profit. Systems staff may be more highly trained than many, but are no different. Therefore, unless their view of their role is suitably shaped by their objectives, the priorities they adopt may be incompatible with those of senior management.

Systems people are mainly motivated to provide a service to their users. They take a professional pride in satisfying as fully as possible the requests of the accountants, buyers, inventory managers, and the occasional executives with whom they deal. Such requests are rarely couched in terms of profit, and if they are, will be overwhelmed by others related to automating paperwork, providing reports, and other secondary activities.

Frequently, the users make greater demands than they realize on the development skills and technology of the systems department, which rises to the challenge. Systems people are something of an elite. Their career prospects and personal esteem can depend on the technical merit, not to say pioneering nature, of the solutions which they produce. The more elaborate, automated and integrated their system, the greater their market value in a highly mobile profession.

- *No justification study will bear any resemblance to the costs and features of the final solution* — Balancing the potential benefits of a system against the dangers of over-complication is something not often attempted. Most often, senior management plays a passive role, with middle-level systems staff and their users agreeing on a need and a solution and submitting a justification of the expenditure for approval. Such justifications can be weak, but they are rarely challenged, because everyone concerned wants to believe in them, or at least to see them accepted.

Common weaknesses in justification studies are:

(a) Only one alternative solution is properly estimated. Second and third choices are either dismissed in a couple of lines or costed very superficially.

(b) An all-or-nothing proposal. The costs and benefits of discrete elements in the solution should be given, so that management can choose to omit an expensive feature.

(c) There is a single cost and often a single benefit figure. Each of these should be ranges, with estimates of the probability of achieving the extremes as well as the middle of the range.

(d) There is no risk analysis. Threats of increased costs or lower benefits should be identified, with actions planned to minimize the risk.

(e) There is no impetus to achieve the benefits. These may be described as "intangible", or expressed in terms which cannot later be used to enforce their achievement. Proposed new staffing or inventory levels, for example, should be related to the level of sales so that changes in the business environment can be suitably compensated for.

PART C

283

Even when a proper justification study has been submitted and approved, often no attempt is made to limit the development to that described in the study. All manner of changes in scope or sophistication are allowed to influence the costs adversely, without any measurable effect on the benefits.

- *Nine-tenths of resources will be spent on tasks which have a minimal impact on profitability* — Setting the right objectives is more important to systems profitability than any other factor, including investment. Asking a systems department to "develop a management information system" (or an inventory system, bonds system, etc.) is like saying to an architect, "build a house". Other "objectives" may be added, such as "make it integrated", "do it by the start of the next fiscal year", or "do it for $20,000". This is like telling the architect, "make it a big house, don't give the foundations time to dry out, and make sure it looks nice". Such objectives determine the type of system produced, but do not specify the type of system required.

Senior executives have more information about the performance of the business than anyone in the systems department. They should state the costs to be attacked, the improvements to be gained, and the market or product directions to be supported, in quantified terms.

Useful objectives might be: (1) Increase inventory turnover by 1.5 times per annum; (2) Shorten production lead-times by five working days; (3) Develop point-of-sales systems to support a 50 per cent increase in volume with no increase in costs; and/or (4) Improve the accounts receivable to sales ratio by two weeks.

The objective should be set jointly for the systems department and the user department most affected, with the latter managing the project. By setting quantified objectives, senior management can concentrate attention on the essentials and can indicate what will be regarded as acceptable performance from the development team.

- *Optional extras will double the costs and the time-scale for development* — Even if all other factors have been handled correctly, it is still possible to push a project from profit to loss through poor implementation. Poor planning, organization and control techniques at this stage can double the cost of a system, extend time-scales by years and create a system which does not meet the original objectives.

Good control begins before the development project is even launched, by obtaining satisfactory answers to the following questions:

(a) Is it the right project (in scope, objectives, priority, etc.) at the right time?
(b) Is it achievable or overly ambitious?
(c) Are the risks identified and minimized?
(d) Are the resources available and justified?
(e) Does everyone understand and accept their role in it?
(f) Is the technology being properly handled?
(g) Are the milestones clearly defined and realistic?
(h) Is the project structured to give results as early as possible?
(i) Have any organizational implications been allowed for?

Once launched, a project can acquire a direction and momentum which makes it difficult to steer if the planning has not been reasonably well done. If the scope, objectives and milestones are clearly defined, it is possible to control against these. Most people, however, make the mistake of only controlling against the milestones. This may tell them that the project is late, but not why.

PART C

By identifying and justifying every departure from the original scope and objectives as the development proceeds, two things are achieved. First, the new scope, and therefore the new time-scales, are defined, allowing cost and progress to be controlled against them. Second, the overall viability of the project is kept in view, and it becomes apparent early if the cost or impracticality of what is being developed means that its new scope should be reviewed.

Developing profitable systems is always harder than most people expect. It need not be as difficult as many people make it.

C H A P T E R **13**

Managing Cash

Overview

Cash provides a focal point when analyzing the financial health of a company because of its central role in all business activity.

Traditional cash management comprises managing deposits and disbursements while ensuring adequate control and generating appropriate information. In a broader sense, however, optimizing the use of cash ensures that the business as a whole is operating efficiently. For example, ensuring that the billing cycle is operating quickly to minimize the level of accounts receivable will also improve customer service. Minimizing inventories to conserve cor-

287

porate cash may have far-reaching effects on the production process.

This chapter presents an overview of cash management from both viewpoints. Other sections of this book present more information on specific aspects of cash management:

Investing surplus cash — Chapters 6–10

Cash forecasting and budgeting — Chapter 16

E-Commerce and E-Payments — Chapter 14

Credit and collection — Chapter 15

Banking services and relations — Chapters 4–5

Objectives

Cash management has four primary objectives:

1. To have sufficient cash on hand to pay bills and other obligations as they come due.
2. To have extra cash available if required for emergencies or unusual needs.
3. To minimize the amount of cash tied up in the business (primarily in inventory and accounts receivable).
4. To invest surplus cash safely and profitably.

The corporate cash management process consists of:

*   planning cash flows;
*   forecasting cash flows;
*   handling day-to-day cash receipts and disbursements;

- arranging for short-term cash;
- investing surplus cash effectively; and
- dealing with issues related to international cash management, such as foreign exchange.

Cash on Hand

Cash may be held for five primary reasons:

1. *Transactions* — Cash balances are held to conduct day-to-day business activity. Payments are made in cash, receipts are in cash and are deposited in the company's bank account. Cash balances held in connection with day-to-day activity are referred to as *transaction balances*.

2. *Precaution* — The inflow and outflow of cash is not predictable, although the degree of uncertainty depends upon the particular industry. Just as companies require safety stocks of inventories, they also need some cash in reserve to deal with fluctuations in the inflow and outflow of cash. These reserves are referred to as *precautionary balances*. To the extent that the company is able to borrow on short notice, it requires lower (or no) precautionary balances. As a practical matter, most companies would hold precautionary balances as liquid marketable securities or similar instruments to maximize their income.

3. *Opportunity* — Particularly when economic times are tough, "cash is king". A firm with ready access to cash may be able to take advantage of opportunities as they arise. As with precautionary balances, access to borrowing power, as well as holdings of marketable securities, or other very liquid assets, are alternatives to holding cash.

PART C

4. *Finance* — Funds may be accumulated to acquire assets or to retire debt.

5. *Compensating balances* — Depending on the banking arrangements, companies may be required to keep bank balances to provide compensation to their bank for providing services. With the trend towards separating the components of bank service charges, this has become less common. The *Bank Act* provides that compensating balances may not be required under a loan agreement, unless the borrower concurs.

What is Cash?

Most corporate cash is represented by demand deposits at chartered banks, rather than notes or coins. The deposits may have resulted from cheques or cash being deposited, or because the company was granted a loan: the key point is that the corporate cash balance is that against which the company can write cheques.

Marketable securities or other very liquid assets refer to "near cash" or "cash equivalents". *Marketable* means that the securities can be readily sold without disrupting business operations. Other very liquid assets may be redeemable by the holder (for example, mutual funds and some term deposits) even though they are not, strictly speaking, marketable, since they cannot be sold to a third party.

Cash Flow Cycle

Cash is an integral part of most business activity. Inventory is purchased, and eventually paid for in cash. Inventory is combined with goods and services purchased with cash (including employees' salaries and wages), and is converted to something that is sold. For service industries, the inventory may be intangible, but it still results in sales. Those sales create receivables that are eventually converted into cash. Along the way, cash resources may come into the firm by way of loans, other financing, or equity infusions. Cash is disbursed for taxes, interest, and dividends. The notion of a *cash flow cycle* is a powerful and familiar one — with good reason.

The time that it takes cash to flow through the working capital accounts can actually be measured, and the length of the cash flow cycle thereby determined.

The cash flow cycle is defined as the average age of accounts receivable *plus* the average age of inventory *less* the average age of accounts payable.

An important element of the corporate cash manager's job is to control the length of time taken by the cycle. A short cycle is better.

Managing Corporate Cash

Many elements of managing cash involve the same considerations as managing a business. Healthy liquidity is generally the sign of a well-run enterprise. Effective management of day-to-day operating activities both *results* in effective management of cash and banking relationships, and is itself a cause of good cash management.

A successful cash action plan benefits the enterprise in many ways. First, there is renewed emphasis on cash retention. This reduces the costs of obtaining short-term cash, and improves corporate liquidity by establishing a cash cushion. Second, there is a heightened sensitivity to the need for cash and the working capital position. Cash flow and working capital requirements are better understood and eventually used as management tools. Third, there is also an increased focus on the immediate cash consequences of the daily activities of the enterprise. As a result, management will

PART C

consider the effects on cash and working capital of business decisions. Fourth, the activities of every employee may be related to specific effects on cash. Thus, specific accountabilities and responsibilities may be assigned: measurement of effects on cash and cash flow provide objective quantitative measures. Fifth, the cash action plan provides a common goal for all employees to work towards. Management textbooks emphasize the necessity of enterprises having simple goals on which all staff can focus. The cash action plan broadcasts the notion that all actions can be measured by their effect on cash.

An action plan to manage corporate cash could comprise seven steps:

1. Determine the level of cash.
2. Examine the cash flow cycle.
3. Determine the length of the cycle.
4. Find the bottlenecks that exist in the cash flow cycle.
5. Develop specific action plans to eliminate those bottlenecks.
6. Implement the action plan. Be sure to give individuals very specific responsibility for taking action.
7. Evaluate the results of the action plan (and go back to step 1 or 4).

Cash inflows

The cash action plan starts by looking at the beginning cash balance.

A major goal is to accelerate receipt of cash. Various banking services can be used to this end, depending upon the nature of the business. For example, payments from customers may be accepted directly at bank branches, rather than mailed. This may result in immediate or, depending upon the arrangements, at least, faster credit to the company's account. Occurrences such as mail strikes would thereby have a less disruptive effect. Other bank services such as lock boxes, cash concentration accounts, and mirror accounts all have the effect of making cash receipts available to the enterprise sooner. Talk to your banker.

The process of speeding up on cash inflows requires analyzing cash receipts. Where are payments coming from, and how might they be accelerated to be accessible at one centralized collection point? Centralizing information as to available bank account balances is often the first step in altering the corporate culture to focus more on cash and achieve the advantages set out above.

Numerous techniques are available to better control disbursements. Again, centralized control, or at the very least, centralized information, is often appropriate. Disbursements should be delayed and controlled. If possible, the time that cheques spend in transit should be maximized to increase the "float". Use company credit cards rather than cash advances for travel and entertainment expenses. (Note that the same controls over travel and entertainment expenses, as well as the expense reporting process, should still be required.)

Information Systems

It is essential to have a system with proper financial and management controls. Reports designed to facilitate financial reporting (for example, for the year-end financial statements or for income tax purposes) may be inappropriate for management reporting purposes. Financial reporting is backward-looking. It gives historical information and is often highly summarized. Management reporting is forward-looking and designed to encourage action. It may be quite detailed and specific.

PART C

Information must be relevant, otherwise it is useless. To manage cash flows, the enterprise's information systems must generate a cash flow statement. Actually, the "information system" may be manual or manually keyed into a spreadsheet: the important point is to actually report the cash flow information in some way.

Often, management uses the reports that are available, rather than the reports it really needs. A symptom of this is lack of understanding of the reports that are prepared. Consultants often hear: "What does this report mean? What is this information? I don't know how to use it, so why are they sending it to me? Nobody has ever asked what information I need to control cash."

The solution is to ensure that the users are involved in the development of the reports. Often they will learn a lot as well. The format and content of the reports should depend upon how the information is to be used, by whom, and how often. Simply providing "information" is not enough. It may not be relevant, which means that it is not information, it is data.

Budgets

A budget is a financial projection: it is forward-looking and, therefore, an important management planning and control tool. Often, companies have both short- and long-term budgets. The short-term budget is an aid to monitoring and assessing the performance of the business in the current or following fiscal year. Long-term budgets are used to direct the strategy of the enterprise over three to five years.

Comparison of actual to budgeted results provides the management control mechanism. Such performance reports, if prepared promptly, are a powerful management tool — both for the writer and for the recipient. This analysis can be the trigger to carefully consider and resolve problems and opportunities on a timely basis.

The review of cash flows and cash positions should be an integral part of the budgetary process. If cash flows can be anticipated, then management is addressing causality, which is the way to properly take control of cash. The budgetary process is also iterative: interrelationships are studied, factors and assumptions modified, the results examined, and further changes made as necessary. The same process is also appropriate for studying cash flows, again, because of their intimate relationship with all elements of the activity of the enterprise.

The budgetary process also helps ensure accountability as it facilitates reporting by direct responsibility. The effects of individual action can be measured and assessed.

Operations Management

Operations management incorporates the decision-making required for the production of goods and services. "Production" has traditionally been associated with manufacture of goods, using inputs of labour, materials, and overhead. However, service industries also "manufacture" their output, similarly using labour, materials, and overhead. Although their output may not be tangible, principles of sound operations management also apply.

The bulk of the activity of most enterprises is in operations (or production), rather than, for example, marketing or finance.

PART C

Therefore, the results of operations and improvements to the production process will have the most significant effects on cash and cash flow.

Management of logistics, the flow of goods, and the physical distribution network can free up significant amounts of cash and capital. For example, consider warehousing. Should the product be shipped directly to the retailer, should warehouses across the country be maintained, or should public warehouses be used? In the case of a service, analogous questions apply. How should the service be provided or distributed to the consumer?

Effective management of inventory has been the classic example of freeing up cash while simultaneously forcing the enterprise to focus on its operational efficiency. By eliminating buffer stocks, companies are forced to correct the causes of inefficiencies in their production process.

Working Capital

All cash managers know that their objective is to collect receivables quickly, and pay disbursements slowly. However, there are some relatively subtle ways to do this without irritating customers or suppliers. For example, speeding up all phases of the ordering and billing cycle will not only free up cash, but improve customer service. How long do orders wait before being filled? Why? How long is it before shipments are billed? Why? Is the customer contacted after shipment to ensure that all is satisfactory? If payment is not received, is the customer contacted to see if there is a problem?

In the case of accounts payable, a similar focus on the inventory control, purchase order, and receiving and disbursements function can also be beneficial. Is inventory ordered when it is really needed, or "just in case"? Why? Is the supplier notified promptly of quality, quantity, or damaged inventory problems? Is the receiving process efficient so that shipments received are quickly available for use?

Sundry Cash Disbursements

Fixed assets, income taxes, and similar payments often represent major cash disbursements. Effective control over these payments is ancillary to, and will result from, a well-run business operation.

The timing of major fixed assets purchases should be integrated into the firm's long-term business plans. It is important to separate *operational* decisions (when and what to buy) from *financial* considerations (lease or purchase, how to finance).

Income taxes are a significant component of cash payments. Effective tax planning may defer or reduce tax payments. This may include taking advantage of government assistance schemes and similar incentives. In addition to federal and provincial tax instalments and payments, other disbursements include employee withholding taxes, employment insurance, Canada/Quebec Pension Plan, Goods and Services Tax, other excise taxes, provincial retail sales tax, employer health taxes, capital taxes, workers' compensation premiums, pension plans, and other benefits. Any cash flow budget must consider these often significant and quite "lumpy" payments.

PART C

Summary

This chapter presents an overview of considerations that pertain to corporate cash management in Canada. Managing corporate cash is a vital part of ensuring a healthy and viable enterprise.

The broad approach of an action plan is presented, along with typical key concerns, which are developed in more detail in later chapters. This chapter concludes with financial and operations checklists to help evaluate cash management procedures and processes.

Financial Checklist

This cash management checklist covers collections, disbursements, control, and investment. All "No" answers should be followed up, and the "Comments" column should be used for areas that require additional explanation or clarification.

Collections	Yes	No	N/A	Comments
1. Are deposits made on a regular basis, at least daily?				
2. Are deposits made late in the day to include receipts received in that day's mail?				
3. Does the bank provide credit for deposits on the date the deposit is made?				

Collections	Yes	No	N/A	Comments
4. Do employees avoid bank line-ups by dealing electronically or as preferred customers at the branch?				
5. Is mail received throughout the day?				
6. Are appropriate procedures in place to handle remittances from outside Canada?				
7. Are cheques received in the mail deposited the same day?				
8. Do salespeople who pick up cheques turn them in for deposit on the same day?				
9. Are cheques received segregated and deposited immediately, rather than accompany the paper flowing through the accounts receivable department?				
10. Are billings to major customers handled on a priority basis, rather than included with other billings?				

PART C

Collections	Yes	No	N/A	Comments
11. Are penalties imposed, or is other appropriate action taken, for customers that do not pay pursuant to billing terms?				
12. Are discount terms not overly generous?				
13. Are invoices processed regularly during the month rather than being held up for month-end?				
14. Are invoices issued within a day of the goods or services being delivered?				
15. Are electronic funds transfer systems being used where appropriate?				
16. Are pre-authorized payments used where appropriate?				

Disbursements	Yes	No	N/A	Comments
1. Are bank accounts consolidated to improve control over costs?				

Disbursements	Yes	No	N/A	Comments
2. Is "positive pay" or are other fraud prevention techniques used to monitor disbursements?				
3. Are disbursement accounts zero-balanced daily to avoid leaving idle balances?				
4. Are bank accounts monitored daily to prevent fraud and monitor disbursements?				
5. Are payments made no earlier than their due date?				
6. Are government remittances, employee deductions, sales deductions, sales tax, etc., being forwarded no earlier than their due date?				
7. Are there special procedures in place for large disbursements to ensure that they are not paid too early?				
8. Are late payment charges avoided by paying invoices on time?				

PART C

Disbursements	Yes	No	N/A	Comments
9. Are excessive courier and delivery charges avoided by mailing cheques on time?				
10. Is re-keying of data from bank statements avoided?				
11. Do you know the value of your cheque float?				

Control	Yes	No	N/A	Comments
1. Is the company advised of all cash inflows on the day of receipt?				
2. Are cash receipt reports reviewed on date of receipt?				
3. Does the bank automatically reduce borrowings with funds deposited?				
4. Are daily disbursement reports obtained to allow management to monitor activity and fund as required?				
5. Are daily bank balance reports received and acted on?				

Control	Yes	No	N/A	Comments
6. Do bank reports include all loan and deposit accounts?				
7. Are bank reconciliations prepared at least monthly and reviewed independently of the accounts payable area.				
8. Are cash flow projections updated regularly?				

Investment	Yes	No	N/A	Comments
1. Is the bank service contract negotiated by senior management?				
2. Have bank charges been compared to outside surveys?				
3. Are account balances maintained at appropriate levels given the interest payable on positive balances?				
4. Is there a diary system for maturing investments?				
5. Are automatic note roll-overs in place?				
6. Are maturities matched to cash requirements?				
7. Are cash policies set centrally?				

PART C

E-Commerce and E-Payments

Overview

Electronic payments began in Canada as *Electronic Funds Transfer*, or EFT, a means to support automated crediting to or debiting directly from bank accounts for direct credit of payroll, or to collect payments such as insurance premiums and other regular payments. The term *e-commerce* emerged into popular use in the late 1980s, initially to refer to business-to-business electronic transactions. As the Internet has become the ubiquitous mode of communication, much e-commerce is now transacted through the Internet, sometimes using the World Wide Web, sometimes using other modalities.

This chapter reviews various ways of transferring funds other than by the traditional paper-based methods. The Canadian payments system is also reviewed.

Origins of Electronic Payment Transactions

Beginning in the 1960s, financial institutions around the world began to develop the means to convey paperless transactions. In most cases, the intent of these electronic systems was to provide banks the ability to lower operating and infrastructure costs to themselves while offering clients a new service, Electronic Funds Transfer, or EFT.

EFT began in Canada as a means to support electronic crediting to or debiting directly from bank accounts, in support of either direct credit of payroll or to collect for things such as insurance premiums and other regular forms of collections. At the time, many banking organizations were starting to develop relationships with payroll service companies or the payroll departments of larger employers, and saw the opportunity to generate greater margins though an EFT-based service.

The first iteration of the EFT payment systems was based on the exchange of fixed length transactions by tape transported between banks along with the physical cheque exchanges. This tape-based exchange evolved the creation of the CPA005 standard for electronic credits and debits, and was used for nearly 30 years with minor modifications.

Also beginning its primitive existence in the late 60s, the Automated Teller Machine (ATM) or Automated Banking Machine (ABM) came into being, first in the U.S. and then in Canada. These first generation machines were more mechanical than electronic in their operation, but they introduced the idea that money could be conveyed in a manner other than cash or cheque (although they output cash). Credit cards were also emerging in this time frame, and although they were largely paper-based systems, they reinforced again the idea of value transfer through a device or system, namely the plastic card.

None of these new or emerging electronic payment schemes came into being as a stand-alone concept. They resulted from a new service or business approach that demanded a payment process that was more sophisticated than the traditional paper-based schemes of the past. Whether to provide a faster payment, or to lower costs, or to provide a more efficient delivery system or for other reasons, electronic payments evolved from a need that was founded in the changing dynamics of business overall.

Electronic Processes for Business

The term e-commerce emerged into popular use in the late 1980s initially to refer to business-to-business electronic transactions. Since the mid 70s, companies have been developing electronic links with one another to support the purchasing, transporting and invoicing for the supply chain. Many of the larger manufacturers, especially in the automotive sector, had been struggling to lower costs and improve quality to compete on a global scare.

The concept of just-in-time (JIT) logistics was introduced, refined and re-refined to reduce the costs and risks of excessive inventory. At the same time, many JIT companies found that rather than reduce costs, they shifted their costs from the warehouse to the road. Essentially, they had created a logistics management challenge that could only be solved by ensuring as many of the suppliers were using the same JIT techniques as the big manufacturers.

Most of the technical efforts used to provide electronic linkages and management infrastructures were termed Electronic Data

Interchange, or EDI. EDI provided a set of standards, business processes and technologies that allowed companies to link to one another.

In the early days, most of these initiatives were aimed at reducing inventory and accelerating the supply chain, but as these electronic procurement systems and relationships evolved, it became necessary to introduce an electronic payment mechanism to support these initiatives. Suppliers that were JIT for the supply chain wanted to be JIT for payment too. Paper cheques that were paid 60 to 90 days after goods were delivered became a substantial problem for these supply chain participants, many of whom were much smaller and cash flow-challenged.

EDI started with General Motors in 1984 that proclaimed that any of its electronically-linked JIT suppliers could join its EDI-based payment process and receive a guaranteed electronic business payment on a 33-day billing cycle. This initiative, spearheaded by Charles Golden, Corporate Treasurer at the time, was intended to provide a strong incentive to suppliers to become involved with both JIT and its related electronic supply chain improvements.

Electronic commerce (EC) defined

Although the term e-commerce or EC has its roots in the EDI implementations of the late 1980s, the popularization of the Internet has shifted the perception of what the term means. While beginning as a business-to-business reference, with the advent of companies like Amazon.com and eBay, not to mention the impact of the dot-com era, the term has shifted from the idea of corporate exchanges to consumer-oriented processes, that is, online buying of goods and services through Web sites.

This has served only to create confusion and misunderstanding of the meaning of electronic commerce, and resulted in confusion regarding the idea behind e-commerce. Just as the term "food" can mean anything from mealworms to pizza to steak, so too can the term e-commerce cover a lot of different, but equally relevant, meanings.

In its most simple form, e-commerce is about electronically-facilitated transactions. However, it is also about relationships. It is these relationships that define the types of interactions that make up EC. Some relationships are complex and highly interactive involving integration of many organizations and their systems, while others are quite simple and straightforward, like requesting a product of service via a fax or e-mail.

EC involves the application of a number of electronic technologies in combination. Exchanges can be defined on three levels: peer-to-peer, interactive and EDI, or direct data exchange. These are all part of the EC matrix. The distinguishing attributes are:

PART C

- Peer-to-peer — Whether using traditional e-mail or real-time exchanges like MSN or AIM, this component of the EC relationship involves interaction between two or more individuals, using computers and telecommunications to create some kind of business activity. The key feature is that humans are involved at both ends of the activity, and are needed to invoke the transaction at one level or another.
- Interactive applications — This set of relationships involves a human at one end of the transaction interacting with a computer or device in a patterned dialogue at the other end. An example of this interaction would be an Automated Banking Machine or Point of Sale terminal, which is completely mechanized in its response, but requires a series of inputs or choices by a human in order to

function. Similarly, a Web site that is set up to take orders and provide automated but intelligent responses would be part of this definition.

- EDI, or other forms of direct data exchange — Electronic Data Interchange (EDI) is the direct, computer-to-computer interchange of structured business documents in a standardized, electronic fashion. This definition can be refined to direct application-to-application exchanges of business transactions. EDI consists of computers from two different organizations sharing and exchanging data with one another, with no human intervention required. This could involve traditional standards for data construction like the ANSI standards, or more modern methodologies such as XML.

Figure 1 — E-Commerce relationships

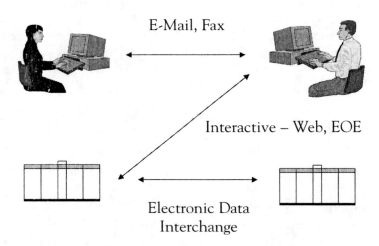

E-Mail, Fax

Interactive – Web, EOE

Electronic Data Interchange

EDI payments process

The use of EDI, and in fact all forms of electronic commerce, is based on a clear intent to accomplish a business objective such as reducing inventory, lowering personnel costs, speeding up access to information, or reducing errors. EDI-based payments are intended to communicate relevant remittance data along with the value transfer, satisfying the recipient's need for reconciling information for the payment. In essence, EDI payments are the equivalent of the cheque and the stub traveling through the payments system in an integrated fashion.

Implementing EDI payments can cause a major change to the culture of any organization — often more than the impact on its systems. Therefore, the factors affecting its use and implementation are often directed towards the minimization or control of the human aspects of the process.

To fully appreciate the business and cultural impacts, the technical process and flows need to be understood.

There are four technology elements to the EDI payments schema:

- Communications facility — either a commercial network provider, bank or Internet;
- A mailbox or similar information storage and forward/retrieval facility (usually part of the communications facility);
- A message structure translator; and
- Applications interface to link the internal system with the outside world.

The Canadian Payments Association (CPA) created rules and standards for the processing of financial EDI transactions in late 1992 under CPA rules E3 and H6. This created a new payment sys-

PART C

tem designed for business-to-business transactions. Under it, all relevant remittance detail can be transferred through the banking system, and it satisfies the needs of both the payment originator and receiver.

Organizations that need to facilitate payments without remittance information can continue to use the EFT system, based on the CPA-005 standard.

The Canadian Payments Environment

The Canadian Payments Association (CPA) is a not-for-profit association that was created in 1980 by an Act of Parliament. The CPA's role, as amended through the *Canadian Payments Act* in 2001, is to:

- establish and operate national systems for the clearing and settlement of payments;
- to facilitate the interaction of its clearing and settlement systems and related arrangements with other systems or arrangements involved in the clearing or settlement of payments; and
- to facilitate the development of new payment methods and technologies.

The CPA is also mandated to address public policy objectives. This requires the Association to promote the efficiency, safety and soundness of the clearing and settlement systems, and to take into account the interests of users and other stakeholders.

There are a number of committees of the CPA to help develop and implement rules that apply to the clearing and settlement of different types of payments between its member financial institutions, ensuring that the system is safe and that payments are exchanged efficiently.

The association also monitors payment system developments and related issues in a global context to ensure the framework for clearing and settlement continues to be relevant and serves the needs of all constituents.

One of the key systems that helps the Canadian payments environment operate in an efficient manner is the Automated Clearing Settlement System.

ACSS overview

The Automated Clearing Settlement System (ACSS), introduced in 1984, is a system that facilitates the accounting and settlement of the majority of payment items in Canada. In 2002, more than 17 million items were exchanged between banks on an average business day's clearing totals.

The term "clearing" refers to a process of exchanging and reconciling individual payment items that result in a transfer of funds between members of the payment system.

The term "settlement" relates to the process of adjusting the different financial positions of each clearing financial institution to reflect the net amounts due to them and from them as a result of the inter-member exchange of payment items. Each direct clearer financial institution in Canada handles the exchange of individual items, but the Bank of Canada is responsible for managing the actual settlement between them.

As of 2003, there are 11 direct clearers in the Canadian payments system, plus the Bank of Canada, making a total of 12 participants. In order to qualify as a direct clearer and gain access to the clearing and settlement system, a financial institution must process at least one half of 1 per cent of the total annual clearing

PART C

volume (in 2003, this would be 22 million items annually). Direct clearers handle the clearing and settlement of payment items for their own customers, as well as customers that maintain accounts at other financial institutions (known as indirect clearers).

The ACSS is a computer-based information system that tracks both the volume and value of payment items exchanged between direct clearing members of the CPA, and determines the balances due to and from participants. ACSS rules and standards detail the procedures that apply to the exchange, clearing and settlement of items cleared through this system.

The ACSS is used for both paper-based payment items such as cheques and electronic items, including Automated Funds Transfer debits (e.g., pre-authorized debits) and credits (e.g., direct deposits). As of 2002, three-quarters of all payment items exchanged in Canada are electronic-based payments, including EFT, EDI, LVTS, as well as Interac-based shared ATM or Point-of-Sale networks.

How it works

When payment items are exchanged between direct clearers, data is entered into the ACSS to track the total volume and value of items in the particular stream. The direct clearer that is owed money makes these entries. In other words, the delivering direct clearer enters the data for debit streams, and the receiving direct clearer enters the information for credit streams. At the end of the daily exchange process, these entries are used to determine the net positions of the direct clearers.

Direct clearers maintain settlement positions in accounts held at the Bank of Canada. In the morning of each business day, the Bank of Canada adjusts the financial positions of the individual direct clearers by transferring funds among their accounts to reflect the net balances of the previous day's ACSS clearing. In turn, indirect clearers settle the same day with their respective direct clearers through special accounts they maintain with them.

Clearing of electronic payments

The clearing process for electronic payments is more efficient than that of cheques and other paper-based payment items, as there is no requirement to deliver a physical payment item. All processes for the exchange and clearing of electronic payments are fully electronic, although in this situation the ACSS entries reflect national totals rather than regional data.

There are some variations in the procedures and schedules that apply to the various streams of electronic payments, and these are outlined in the CPA's ACSS rules. Within this framework, there may also be some variation in the details of how each direct clearer processes these transactions.

Direct clearers sort and categorize electronic payments by stream and by the direct clearer (and/or indirect clearer) to which they are to be sent. Examples of streams are Automated Funds Transfer (AFT) debits, primarily pre-authorized debits; AFT credits, mainly direct deposits; Electronic Funds Transfer/Point-of-Sale transactions, which track debit card transactions; and bill payments. Most electronic payments are exchanged in bulk between direct clearers over a frame-relay network.

Each direct clearer enters into the ACSS the total volume and value of transactions for which it is owed funds. That is, the direct clearer delivering the transactions will enter the data for debit streams, while the receiving direct clearer will enter the totals for credit streams, such as bill payment remittances. These figures are combined with the totals for all other paper-based payment items to determine the net balances due to and from each direct clearer.

The Bank of Canada then completes the settlement process for each participant's records on the following business morning.

Although the vast majority of the daily transaction volume is cleared through the ACSS (approximately 99 per cent), these transactions represent only about 15 per cent of the total value cleared. A substantial proportion of the total value is cleared via the Large Value Transfer System (LVTS).

Large Value Transaction System (LVTS)

LVTS is the updated electronic wire system introduced by the CPA in February 1999 to facilitate the transfer of irrevocable payments in Canadian dollars across the country in real time. Through LVTS, funds can be transferred between participating financial institutions virtually instantaneously, and the money can thus be credited to the recipient's account on a timely basis. As all LVTS payments are immediately final and irrevocable, the recipient may withdraw the money, invest it or use it to make another payment in full confidence that the incoming payment will not be reversed for any reason.

Any individual payments made in Canada for sums greater than $25 million must be processed via the LVTS, which replaces cheques and any other forms of payment. This means that cash managers and accounts payable commitments will need to consider the implications of forwarding these large value payments through their bank's electronic LVTS-based payment service.

LVTS is unique among payment systems because it is a blend of the two main models used around the world for modern payment systems. It achieves this status because it provides a payment finality that is usually part of a Real Time Gross Settlement (RTGS)

316

system, with the added benefit of lower collateral costs associated with a netting system.

Each payment is final and settlement is assured immediately upon the completion of the individual transaction, even though the actual settlement occurs at the end of the day on the books of the Bank of Canada. The purpose of this approach is to lower the overall (systemic) risk in the payment system. Systemic risk occurs when the inability of one financial institution to meet its settlement obligations could cause other institutions to fail in a domino effect.

In 2002, LVTS was used to clear and settle about $115 billion in Canadian dollar payments each business day, or approximately 85 per cent of the total value moving through the Canadian payments system. Approximately 14,000 LVTS payments are processed each day, with the average value of a transaction in the range of $8 million. LVTS is also particularly suitable for time-sensitive payments of any value.

CPA members that establish and maintain an LVTS settlement account at the Bank of Canada, and provide an acceptable system interface, may participate directly. There are no minimum payment value or volume requirements, although LVTS transactions tend to be for larger amounts.

The Bank of Canada is responsible for monitoring the flow of payments through LVTS, ensuring that participating financial institutions maintain adequate levels of collateral. The CPA administers the daily operations of LVTS, as well as the LVTS rules.

All LVTS payments are final and irrevocable. This means that once a payment is sent, the payer or the financial institution that sent it cannot reverse it. For the recipient, risk is completely elim-

PART C

317

inated because the payment cannot be withdrawn due to stop payment orders, insufficient funds or forged endorsements. Financial institutions are assured of same-day settlement for LVTS transactions, even in the unlikely event that a participating institution were to fail. This certainty of settlement eliminates systemic risk that could cause a cascade of defaulting financial institutions.

The LVTS has four elements to control and minimize risk:

- The multilateral net debit position of each participant is continually updated based on every payment made in real time by the LVTS system.
- The participants' net debit positions are continuously reviewed against pre-determined ceilings or limits.
- All participants have pledged collateral to the Bank of Canada to cover largest permitted exposure. This ensures settlement for the participants, even if one of them were to default.
- Because of continuous monitoring of exposure, the Bank of Canada can guarantee settlement in the extremely unlikely event that more than one LVTS participant were to fail on the same day during LVTS operating hours.

EDI payment transactions

The transaction format most common for Canadian financial EDI is the ANSI 820. This format permits sufficient detail so that the recipient may reconcile the payment to their accounts receivable records.

This transaction structure, which originated under the American National Standards Institute (ANSI) Accredited Standards Committee (ASC) X12, is incorporated into the CPA regulations as rules E3 and H6.

Transaction flows

To ensure certainty in completing the transaction, multiple acknowledgments are used.

The first acknowledgment (referred to as ANSI designation 997) is a Functional Acknowledgment that may be positive or negative. A positive 997 allows the transaction to proceed to more detailed levels of checking. A negative 997 means that there was something structurally wrong with the message and further action by the originator is required.

If a positive 997 is generated, then an ANSI 824 Application Level Acknowledgment is created — again positive or negative. A negative 824 means that critical data fields are missing or incomplete, or that funds or credit limits are not available. This is somewhat like an electronic NSF notification, albeit before the event has occurred. A positive 824 is an acceptance of the transaction.

Figure 2 — Financial EDI flows

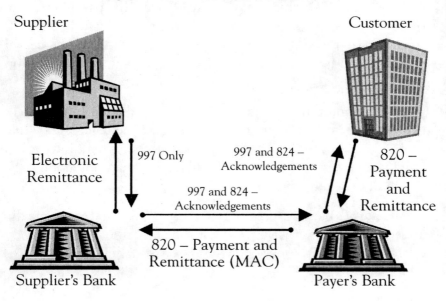

Supplier

Customer

Electronic
Remittance

997 Only

997 and 824 –
Acknowledgements

997 and 824 –
Acknowledgements

820 –
Payment
and
Remittance

820 – Payment and
Remittance (MAC)

Supplier's Bank

Payer's Bank

PART C

Finally, the 824 is acknowledged by a 997, ensuring that the 824 acknowledgment message arrived back to the originator. This same transfer of acknowledgments is also exchanged between banks if the receiver used a different bank than the originator.

Why use the EDI payment instead of EFT?

Electronic payments from an accounts payable application would ideally provide direct input into an accounts receivable application of another firm. This does not occur with EFT or Wire/LVTS-based transactions because these types of transactions do not convey remittance information in a form that an accounts receivable system can use. If electronic payments do not need to communicate remittance detail, for example, for periodic payments, the use of EFT or LVTS would be appropriate. In other cases, an EDI payment would be preferred.

Accounts payable applications

A payments file is created by the payer's accounts payable system. An EDIT translation program must convert it into an ANSO 820 format. Once it is in that format, it can be encrypted and processed through a security module or process that creates an authentication code.

At this point the transaction is sent and, after the correct acknowledgments are returned, may be considered complete. While there is the possibility that the payee's account may have been closed in the interim, which could still require the transaction to be unwound, this would be very unusual.

The payer's bank will check that the payer is valid, decrypts the transaction if necessary, verifies that the authentication is correct, and confirms that the payee or the payee's financial institution is recognized.

Accounts receivable applications

The seller's accounts receivable contains all the details concerning open invoices. The remittance information must include sufficient detail so that the correct items may be noted as paid. Some applications use mathematical formulae to match the payment to some combination of outstanding invoices to that client.

Other cash application systems require more detail as to each invoice paid and related activities such as adjustments and corrections. EDI is then the best method as it can convey all the necessary information. To process an EDIT payment, a translation program will be required to convert the information to a format recognized by the accounts receivable system.

This may in fact be the same translator used to originate transactions, or it may be a stand-alone translator that automatically dials out to the mailbox on a daily basis, receives the file, sends the necessary acknowledgments, and translates the EDI file into the internal accounts payable format. There is generally no MAC or encryption at this stage because the actual funds transfer has already been handled by the bank.

At this point, the information can be directly applied to the outstanding receivable, marking any of the unpaid items for an "exception report" so that further collection follow-up can be applied. It is more straightforward to receive EDI payments than to send them. The greater amount of effort is by the originator.

EFT

The Canadian EFT transaction standard that is used between banks is commonly referred to as the CPA-005 format. These EFT transactions can be issued in both credit or debit forms and are governed by specific rules for each.

PART C

A typical Canadian EFT transaction flows as follows:

- The initiating company creates the payment record in a bank proprietary version of the interbank CPA-005 format. This will include such information as destination, bank and account number, name, amount, value date and a brief description.
- The information is then forwarded to the company's bank (via direct transmission or in smaller volume situations through the bank's cash management service). This is usually done 18 hours or more days prior to the value date to ensure that all end points equal value dating.
- The payer bank will convert the proprietary EFT message into the CPA-005 standard and forward it during the appropriate business day to the receiving bank via transmission though the Automated Funds Transfer system.

Figure 3 — Canadian EFT flows

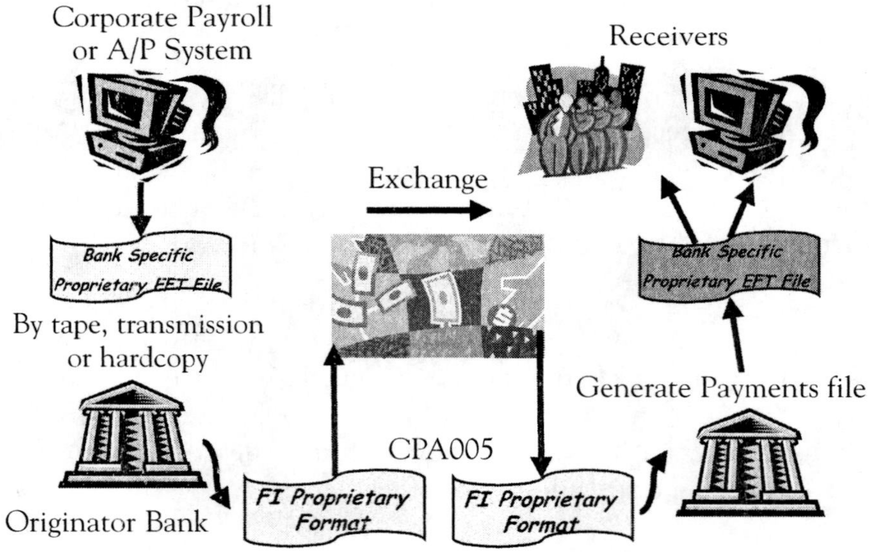

Corporate Payroll or A/P System

Receivers

Exchange

Bank Specific Proprietary EFT File

By tape, transmission or hardcopy

Bank Specific Proprietary EFT File

Generate Payments file

Originator Bank

CPA005

FI Proprietary Format

FI Proprietary Format

- On the value date, all credits or debits are posted and settlement via the ACSS occurs. No acknowledgements for individual events are received.
- The destination client is updated either through a cash management inquiry or via a printed statement of the account.

Emerging Technologies for E-Payments

Smartcards

Smartcards, or stored value cards, are what might be termed "token" cards.

A financial institution will remove money from an account, upon request by the client, and place an equivalent "token" of value on the card. The "real" money remains in the possession of the financial institution until the token is redeemed when the card is used at a later date. In the past, the analogy to this would be the traveler's check.

Smartcard technology has been used in the financial industry for nearly 20 years. Several banks have also experimented with Smartcards for security access application, storing encrypted access codes, and use at the point-of-sale in a stored value application under the brand name of Mondex.

Mondex

Mondex is a specific brand of Smartcard or Stored Value card developed by the National Westminster Bank in the U.K. Its rights were initially sold to Royal Bank in the mid 1990s. The Royal Bank subsequently expanded the participation and ownership rights for the Mondex system to all the major Canadian financial

323

institutions in 1996, and Mondex became the de facto Smartcards standard for Canada. Since that time, the Mondex brand and over-all technology ownership has been purchased by MasterCard International.

Some of the important attributes of the Mondex technology approach are:

- High-grade encryption technology;
- The ability to transfer payments anonymously and directly between individuals as well as with merchants;
- A global brand name.

A pilot project was established in Guelph, Ontario, in early 1997 to determine consumer acceptance of the concept. At its peak, 12,000 Mondex Smartcards were issued and several hundred mer-chants participated, ranging from parking lots to retail outlets. At the same time, banks in the U.K. were experimenting with their version of Mondex in the city of Swindon.

Both pilot locations have ended. While the banks involved declared that both pilots were successful as a "proof of concept," there have been no further roll-outs or tests.

Debit card

Debit card systems in Canada are now all integrated under the Interac brand. The Canadian debit card concept, which was envi-sioned as part of the original design of the Interac concept in 1985, began with a pilot project started by the Quebec-based Caisse Desjardins in early 1986, the same year that Interac-shared bank-ing machines services began.

From a technology viewpoint, debit cards are more or less banking machine access cards simply used with a different access device, that is, a swipe device at the point-of-sale. The growth of debit card transactions in Canada has been astonishing, and since 1998, debit cards have become the dominant form of payment next to cash itself. Clearly, consumers are looking at the debit card as their electronic chequebook.

Much of its success is due to cooperation between the major financial institutions and the fact that our financial institutions are national in scope. Part of the reason the United States has not been quite as successful is because they still have regional banking.

The current methodology is that although the merchant has a terminal that connects with the Interac environment through a financial institution, it really has no access to the data. All it gets is an approval or decline. The financial institution then credits the positive responses to the merchant's account at the end of the day.

There are stringent cryptographic requirements to protect the Personal Identification number right at the button level of the keypad. There is also high-grade cryptography applied in the transaction stream to ensure that client card information is protected.

Telephone banking

There have been telephone-based financial service offerings in the United States since the late 70s. They began to be used in experimental form in Canada in the mid 80s, mainly by the credit union movement.

In the early 90s, Interactive Voice Response (IVR) technologies became more affordable and viable, and telephone-based banking services began to grow into the larger Schedule I banks. This has now turned into a popular service for most Canadian financial institutions.

PART C

Most financial institutions now operate their telephone banking front-end, meaning the actual client interface that manages the customer data base and interaction in-house. But many have outsourced the "back-end," which is the data output to the corporate payee. In many cases, this is handled either as a paper output or in the CPA EDI format defined under rule H-6.

Due to its commoditized nature, few banks are looking at telephone banking service and related IVR support systems as a long-term technology platform for the future.

Internet/PC banking services

Although cautious at first, all Canadian financial institutions have now embraced the Internet, especially the Web, as a primary channel for delivering services in the future. Canadian financial institutions were initially concerned about security issues and exposure of client information. However, these concerns have faded as technology has become more robust. The use of Secure Socket Layer (SSL) security, coupled with the prospect of additional layers of security, has mitigated the security concern.

Consumers can now access a full range of banking services through the Web. Businesses now have access to most cash management systems through Web browsers as well.

Electronic bill presentment

There has been a great deal of technology effort expended in the financial community in the area of Electronic Bill Presentment (EBP). The concept behind EBP is to provide a facility for electronic billing distribution for companies like utilities and retailers, or anyone who has to mail out a statement of account.

The motivation for developing this approach is the rapid consumer uptake in PC/Internet/ Telephone banking. Financial institutions believed that consumers who bank electronically would be willing to receive their monthly bills electronically as well. This is supported by the statistic that the growth in pre-authorized debits (direct debits) has grown at the average rate of 16.6 per cent per year for the past four years. POS or debit card transactions have grown at the average rate of 120 per cent per year for the same period.

The counterargument is that consumers do not like to initiate receiving their bills electronically. They prefer to receive them (passively) in the mail. Doubtless, there will be a technological solution to this eventually.

Electronic money

There many emerging schemes that fall into the category of e-money. All of these are focused on the facilitation of payments over the Internet. They all work from the point of view of a "token" of value sent from one computer to another, somewhat like the smart card. The main difference is that rather than loading the tokens of value onto a card device, the value is loaded and stored on a computer hard drive.

No successful e-money programs have emerged yet from this approach. In the short to medium term, credit cards will continue to be dominant for facilitating electronic or Web-based payments.

Micro-payments and mini-payments

Micropayments are extremely low value payments. The basis for this concept is where Web consumers may wish to purchase a single article from an electronic newspaper and pay the component value for this item, perhaps 1/10 of a cent. The reality is that while this is possible, bookkeeping for these types of events is more onerous than the revenue/profit opportunity justifies.

PART C

Credit card companies are developing strategies for mini-payments instead, that is, individual items in the unit price range of $0.25 or so. The likely solution will be that minimum accounts balances will be required by the service provider, not by the bank, so one would have to put a $5.00 or $10.00 amount in reserve with the company and draw down on it.

E-payment proxy-based services

Paypal is the most well-known of several e-payment services that have evolved. PayPal acts as a payment intermediary, but is not currently regulated as a financial institution. It provides a service that allows any business or consumer with an e-mail address to send and receive payments online. It uses a secure and fast computer-aided methodology to transport payments through national payment systems of different countries.

Paypal has made arrangements to receive and send payments using the domestic payments infrastructure of each country's banking system. Users must register with Paypal to send money. However, if the recipient has an e-mail address, there does not need to be any pre-registration by receivers. The service is free for payment senders, as all fees and charges are paid by the receivers.

Paypal is an example of the creation of new payment intermediaries that the e-payment process requires. It is different from a token-based payment because it does not purport to provide a transportable, cross-system payment item; rather it takes part of the payment risk and acts as a true intermediary.

Electronic cash management/treasury services

In the late 70s, most of the banks that provided corporate account services developed electronic cash management tools to aid their business banking clients with managing their money better. In doing this, the goal was to generate additional fee revenue, as well as to increase the velocity of cash movement through the system.

All the banks initially developed some form of PC- or terminal-based proprietary system for their business clients to use. Over the past several years, all these proprietary systems have converted to Web-based versions.

E-Payment Standards

Standards are critical for the success of any community with a common interest. They help each participant understand the needs of the others, and provide clarity and objectivity for resolving process issues. Message standards remove any ambiguity in allowing different organizations exchange transactions.

Until 1980 in the Canadian payments environment, most standards were developed by the commercial banks through the Canadian Bankers Association (CBA). Since 1980, with the creation of the CPA, payment system standards have been created and maintained as a common industry group, including banks, Trust Companies, Credit Unions and Caisse Populaires.

There are currently three main groups of standards that are used for Canadian e-payments:

EFT Standards — These are proprietary to the banking system and are created, developed and administrated through the Canadian Payments Association. Standards for EFT (CPA-005) and for other Canadian specific applications have evolved through committee development within the banking community. Most recently, the development of the LVTS standard was undertaken as a specific project, and delivered as a completely new set of transaction standards and processes in 1999.

329

There are also international standards such as SWIFT (Society for Interbank Financial Telecommunications) that are used by Canadian banks.

EDI Standards — Although adopted into Canadian CPA standards (E3 and H6), the foundation of Canadian EDI Payments standards are based on the ANSI X12 cross-industry standards. The transactions that are facilitated by the EDI structure are as follows:

Figure 4 — EDI transactions

820 - Payment Order (Value and non-value)
821 - Financial Reports
822 - Account Analysis
823 - Lockbox
824 - Application Acknowledgment
827 - Financial Return
829 - Cancel Payment
997 - Functional Acknowledgment

Not all of these standards are ensconced in the CPA rulebook. Many of them are provided as part of the informational services that banks offer and are therefore applied on a proprietary basis by each bank.

In order to use the ANSI X12-based EDI standards, there is generally an interpretive exercise referred to as an Implementation Guide that provides the rules and data descriptions needed to establish an exchange relationship. In many cases, the banks have already developed a template or pro-forma to help this process along. However, the major challenge of establishing an EDI payments program is obtaining the participation of the client or supplier.

New or Emerging Standards — This includes the use of the eXtensible Mark-up Language standard XML. The XML standard is a type of EDI standard, but it differs from the older and more established ANSI approach by providing a methodology to carry both the data and the decoding book in the message. The simplest definition of XML is self-defining documents.

The perceived benefit of XML is that many newer applications carry the XML coding capability as part of their design. The issue or problem is that it still takes quite a bit of set-up, defining and negotiation with a trading partner to establish real connectivity. At present, the use of XML in the payments system is virtually non-existent.

Float Implications for Electronic Payments

"Bank-induced float" occurs when there is a delay between the time a payment is deposited into an account and when value is applied to the account by the bank to the depositor's credit. In the U.S., for instance, it is quite common for a deposit made on the west coast, drawn on a financial institution on the east coast, to have a three- or four-day delay before real value or "good funds" can be applied.

In Canada, there is no bank-induced float under any payment method, be it cheque, EFT or EDI. Instead, in Canada, value is applied immediately. However, from an accounts receivable perspective, the receiving organization still does not know what the funds are for. This is where an EDI transaction can provide value, as the funds and the remittance detail are both delivered together.

There is, however, a mail float in Canada. This term refers to the period of time from when the stamped envelope is put into the postal system to the time the recipient opens the envelope and deposits the payment item.

In the past, payment terms tended to be based upon when a cheque was posted. It is becoming more common to specify when payment must be received, which creates a motivation to use more effective payment instruments such as EDI. In the event, EFT and EDI payments can offset the costs of mail float and missed discounts by facilitating quicker transactions.

Ironically, the LVTS system may induce a one day float, depending on the timing of the transaction. Because the originating bank has to provide collateral to offset the transaction risk, transactions may be held overnight before final processing to the recipient.

Procurement cards

The procurement card is a relatively recent phenomenon that uses a consumer-based credit card and its support infrastructure, but focuses on supporting business-purchasing activities. Procurement cards work best for low-dollar, high-volume activities, like buying office supplies.

In many organizations, low-value, high-volume purchases can account for as much as 70 per cent of total transaction volumes, but less than 10 per cent of total money spent. Often, the administration costs of these activities can exceed the prices of the actual purchases. In these cases, traditional business purchasing techniques such as EDI do not fit well because of the effort needed to administer the ordering process and enroll the supplier. By charging the items to a procurement card, many costly manual procedures disappear or are streamlined.

The key values of such a card are to:

- Increase efficiency by reducing the paperwork required to manage small value transactions;
- Reduce inventory and space requirements by acquiring low value commodity products as they are needed;
- Lower the overall cost per transaction;
- Exercise more control over purchasing and payables through improved tracking of the financial activity;
- Improve supplier relations by using a tool which has almost immediate payment (as opposed to the supplier waiting 30 plus days for an invoicing cycle);
- Obtain supplier discounts where volume can be established.

All major credit card issuers offer procurement card programs and have significant success in marketing them to medium- to large-sized firms. Small enterprises are not as likely to use the procurement card because of their inherently low overhead costs.

Balance and transaction reporting

As organizations become increasingly global in their operations, there is a need to understand their balance sheet on a total company basis. Even in countries such as Canada that have national banking systems, there can be significant complexities in arranging for consolidated transaction and balance reporting.

ANSI standard 821 can accommodate balance and transaction reporting, and supply detail in a standardized format. This means that a company can receive the information from two or more banks in the same format. This then permits the company to organize the information from a variety of banks and compare it in a meaningful way.

PART C

Generally, if an organization uses only one or perhaps two banks, it is usually more effective to use the cash management service their bank offers. If an organization deals with multiple banks, or is consolidating information from banks in the United States, Canada and elsewhere, then there may be merit in using the 821.

E-Payments Outside of Canada

The United States

While U.S. cheques can be drawn on Canadian banks, many Canadian firms operate accounts at a U.S.-based bank to overcome float delays and ease the management of foreign exchange. As well, in many cases, cross-border electronic payments can be facilitated through SWIFT-based transfers or bilateral arrangements between a U.S. and Canadian bank. Typically, however, cross-border electronic payments are awkward, difficult and often expensive for both the payer and the receiver.

There has been a great deal of work over the past decade to develop a more compatible exchange process between Canada and the U.S., leading to the creation of the Cross Border Payment (CBP) transaction in the U.S. This transaction provides for the insertion of an EFT or single-remittance segment EDI into or out of the U.S. Automated Clearing House (ACH) system.

Alternatively, many of the larger Canadian commercial banks have established full-blown EDI relationships with a partner bank in the U.S. to facilitate a cross-border transaction via a correspondent relationship. This does not resolve the issue of the multitude of banks in the U.S. that still remain unable to receive or distribute remittance details, and are forced to send an EFT and transport the remittance detail to the receiver in another fashion.

Conclusion

E-payments are now the dominant form of exchange in Canada — whether using EFT, EDI, LVTS methods. To maximize the value obtained from using e-payments, organizations need to focus on automating the integration between the banking system and their accounting systems. Successful organizations have integrated and automated links to minimize manual intervention. This improves the speed, accuracy and efficiency of their receipts and payment processes.

PART C

C H A P T E R **15**

Credit and Collection

Overview

Managing working capital is one of the most important responsibilities of the financial manager. Outflows of cash are often relatively well controlled. Cash inflows — such as bank borrowings and collection of accounts receivable — are inherently less controllable. Nonetheless, accounts receivable is usually a major component of working capital, so there can be significant financial benefits if it is well controlled. In addition, a thorough understanding of accounts receivable can lead to improvements in marketing, customer service, and other areas.

Basis for Credit

When credit is granted, two fundamental assumptions are made: *confidence* and *futurity*.

The party that extends the credit must have *confidence* that the other party will be both willing and able to repay the obligation when it comes due. **Willingness** depends upon the character of the debtor. **Ability** to pay depends upon the financial strength and capability of the debtor. This may be influenced by external factors such as the state of the economy, the business environment, and so on.

Futurity refers to the notion that the future is never certain. (Some people find it hard enough to predict the past.) Consequently, every potential credit transaction requires an answer to the question: is this transaction worth the risk of possible loss? In contemporary corporate finance terms, the question would be whether there is a sufficiently high reward to risk ratio to make the transaction worthwhile.

Credit as a Strategic Tool

Credit policy can be used positively, as a strategic tool. A significant example of this is the use of credit to promote sales: credit may be as important as delivery dates, price or quality in securing an order. Examples of credit policy used strategically are:

- *Marketing* — Credit can be a mechanism to expand into new territories, new product lines, or otherwise endeavour to obtain a competitive edge.
- *Seasonality* — Credit can help smooth out what would otherwise be seasonal variations in sales, for example, in the farm equipment or fashion industries.

- *Improves purchasing power* — The availability of credit may improve the ability of the purchaser to buy goods and services (although, perhaps only temporarily).

Abuse of Credit

Credit can be abused. This can occur in many different ways, and may involve the following:

- *Extravagance* — It may be too tempting to improve the lifestyle of a business — or consumer — if someone else's money is involved.
- *Speculation* — The temptation to take an undue amount of risk may be too strong.
- *Overexpansion* — Credit extended unwisely and taken inappropriately has led to the collapse of many businesses.
- *Overtrading* — From the perspective of the credit grantor, too much capital tied up in accounts receivable can result in excessive interest expense or even bad debt write-offs.
- *Fraud* — Despite rapid communications, good information availability, and state-of-the-art computerization, it can be relatively easy to defraud an unsuspecting grantor of credit.

Credit Policy

Credit has a central role in the profitability and solvency of an organization. Credit is also a major marketing tool and affects many other corporate functions. Consequently, every enterprise should have a credit policy.

PART C

339

Creating a credit policy

There are three steps to be taken in formulating a credit policy:

Objectives of company in areas of sales, profits, marketing strategy and product development must be determined and integrated with the objectives of the credit function.

The second step is to assess the *internal and external influences.* Some of the influencing factors would be industry conditions, competitive influences, the company's capital and financial condition and the compatibility factor with other departments. Minor influences might include availability of credit information and industry terms of sale.

The third factor is *tactics*, which involves deciding what courses of action will result in the achievement of the goals within the constraints of the industry conditions and general economic factors.

Credit policies may be classified as *lenient* or *restrictive*. Degrees of each will often exist within company divisions or units, depending upon profit margins and competitive conditions.

A lenient policy may accept larger risks or permit larger amounts of credit. A lenient policy is common in heavy competition, highly profitable industries or in new territory selling situations. Little or no credit investigation is made into well-known or well-rated concerns and marginal accounts receive only a cursory investigation, perhaps a simple reference check or bank report.

A restrictive policy may be called for if there is little or no competition, a low profit margin, low sales volume, if the product is custom-made or if the company has a poor cash position. As well, if demand for the product or service is high, selective culling of accounts may build profits.

A restrictive credit policy may be offset with a more lenient collection policy. The reverse is also true. A lenient credit policy can be countered with an aggressive collection policy. This is what happens in industries such as trucking, or the courier business. Unfortunately, too many companies have lenient credit and lenient collection policies, the results of which can be disastrous in terms of bad debts.

Developing and communicating a credit policy

In most companies, the responsibility for establishing the parameters of a credit and collection policy rest with the Chief Operating Officer or the Chief Financial Officer. The responsibility for administering the policy will rest with the Credit Manager. The policy is different from the procedures used to carry out the policy. A policy will apply to general, common situations that extend over long periods of time. In a sense, the credit policy is the link between the goals and the specific directives used to achieve the goals. In this respect, a policy may contain the actual credit department goals in areas such as assistance to other departments, for example, sales. Safeguarding major investments and goals of marketing may also be included. A sample of a generic credit policy follows this section.

Once formulated, the credit policy should be communicated to all areas of the company: accounting, sales, production and marketing departments. A précis of the policy may be provided to all customers in the form of a "welcome" letter to new accounts and follow-up letters to existing accounts.

PART C

Example of a credit policy

Credit Policy

Subject Accounts Receivable — Credit & Collections.

Objective To establish guidelines for the extension of credit, recognizing the importance of the credit function in protecting the Company's investment in receivables while, at the same time, not hindering the development of profitable sales.

Applicability Applies to all divisions and subsidiary companies of _____ .

Responsibility The General Manager responsible for each operating unit is responsible for the effective utilization of the credit and collection function.

Every company division is responsible for its own written accounts receivable *procedures* which must conform to this policy. Where extraordinary circumstances warrant deviation, these must be specifically covered by the company in writing and approved by the Corporate Vice-President, Finance.

General Policies All credit granting and collection procedures will be approved by the Credit Manager.

Credit Approval Existing customers as well as prospective customer with whom we anticipate doing busi-

---

ness, must be investigated for the purpose of establishing, reconfirming, modifying and monitoring their credit standing and limitations. The degree of investigation will be dictated by the anticipated value of the order or account, risk involved, and profitability of the sale. For any open lines of credit in excess of $50,000, a financial statement of the customer must be obtained.

The Division Credit Manager is responsible for keeping the Sales Department informed of receivable balances and credit limits for each customer, usually through monthly agings and advice on selected accounts. A copy of all credit department correspondence will be routed to the General Sales Manager.

A credit application will be completed for every new customer. As well, a customer update request will be sent to every customer at least once per year to ensure that information on ownership and financial results are current.

Credit Verification — Many sources of credit information are available such as credit reference books, credit reporting agencies, banks, other vendors. The Credit Manager shall implement a program using the most appropriate sources available, maximizing outside services and information to the fullest degree. Credit limits should be established for both new and existing customers. Systems must

PART C

also be in place to ensure complete and up-to-date information on existing customers.

Terms of Sale   The Company's terms of sale are net 30 days. Other terms require prior approval from the General Credit Manager. Alternatives to open accounts such as deposits will be used for those customers unable to meet our standards. The responsibility for informing the customers of the terms and conditions of sale rests primarily with the sales department.

Collections   One of the prime requisites for effective collection effort is prompt and accurate billing. Controls shall be established and enforced by the Credit/Financial Manager to ensure compliance. The invoice is the first line of collection. Terms and conditions of sale will be prominently displayed on all invoices.

Complaints regarding billing must be acknowledged promptly and resolved within a reasonable time. Many customers will withhold payment of an entire invoice pending receipt of an adjustment, which may represent only a fraction of the invoice.

Collection effort, to be effective, must be consistent, usually through the use of letters, telephone contacts, sales department contacts and personal visits, depending on the circumstances and amount of the billing involved. Appropriate procedures may vary from division to division, the General Credit Manager will have the responsibility to ensure that proper training and procedures are in effect.

When the situation warrants, and after other collection efforts have been exhausted, uncollected accounts should be referred to the appropriate collection agency, generally when the account reaches 75 days past due.

Although operating management with the aid of salespeople, may be consulted and used to assist in the collection effort, the primary responsibility for collections rests with the Division Credit Manager.

Accounts Receivable

1. *Records and Agings.* Individual records for each customer will be maintained. The monthly aging of receivables information should reflect the following:

(a) Name of account;

(b) Total amount due;

(c) Aged balances:

> Current
> 31 – 60
> 61 – 90
> 91 – 120
> 121 – 1 year
> Over 1 year;

2. *Comments — Past Due Accounts.* Accompanying the aging should be reports providing comments and additional data on

PART C

specific accounts over $10,000 over 60 days old, including specific actions that have been and will be taken and the probability of collection.

3. *Uncollectables.* Accounts that are uncollectable should be written off when reasonable collection means have been exhausted. The Credit Manager must ensure that all write-offs are approved by the appropriate operating manager. Although charged to the appropriate Reserve For Uncollectable Accounts, active collection must be continued until the account is collected or determined to be uncollectable owing to bankruptcy, out of business without further recourse, or similar reason. Proof of uncollectability, usually a collection agency report, or bankruptcy proceedings should be obtained and maintained in the customer file to support such write-offs.

4. *Recoveries.* Any recovery of accounts previously written off must be credited to the same reserve account charged with the uncollectable.

Insolvency

A copy of all correspondence regarding matters of insolvency or business failure will be routed to the General Credit Manager, who will be responsible for directing the measures appropriate to assuring the Company's continuing involvement in all meetings relating to our position as a creditor.

Opening Credit Accounts

Applications and forms

Building a credit system is based upon sound principles, first and foremost of which is a strong information system. This usually begins with the *credit application.*

The credit application should be designed to encompass credit policies and objectives, as well as industry practices. Beginning with the legal name of the business, any trade styles used, physical address, names of owners/principals/officers, the home addresses of the principals and so on, the application becomes a verifiable document. Verification will depend upon the time needed to make the analysis, amount of the credit line, and degree of difficulty obtaining information.

The application should be completely filled out and signed by an appropriate person within the prospective company.

Role of the sales representative

The sales representative is usually the first contact with a new customer can be of immense aid in ensuring that the customer gets started on the right foot. Many companies use a Sales Report so that any information the representative may have about the account will be included in the analysis. This information might include:

- Names of other suppliers;
- Type of products manufactured/wholesaled or service performed;
- Opinion of facilities, general condition of plant;
- Opinion of management;

PART C

347

- In new businesses, an opinion as to the qualifications of principals; and
- Economic conditions in the sales territory.

The amount of information and degree of completeness will, of course, be commensurate with both the risks and the opportunities for future business. If the sale is a one-time purchase, the long-term solvency of the account is secondary to the short-term liquidity. In any case, it is important to take advantage of the knowledge gathered by the sales representative and to involve them in the data collection process.

Updating information

Once accounts are opened, most companies rely only on hearsay or rumours to keep up-to-date on changes within existing customers. Unfortunately, the bankruptcy files are full of out-of-business companies that paid their bills promptly right up to the date of filing. Even though an account has been on the books for years, the vigilant credit professional keeps a close watch to note even apparently small changes such as a minor change in the name of the customer.

Other companies send credit update requests to customers on a regular basis. In most instances, only basic information is requested, for example, change of management, bank, etc. If the name of the party responsible for the account was not on the original application, this is a good time to request that person's name. This is a key collection requirement.

Extending Credit

Information requirements

The extension of credit will be guided by several factors, including amount and frequency of orders, industry conditions and external factors in such areas as marketing strategies.

The credit information to be collected, in addition to the credit application, can be varied and possibly time-consuming. Company sales personnel, interviews with customers by telephone or in person, banks and other financial institutions, trade references, public records, and credit agencies such as Dun & Bradstreet are the most common. On the basis of the evaluation, credit lines or limits can be established in accordance with pre-set guidelines. Alternatives to regular open-account terms should also be in place. If, for instance, 30-day terms appear to be unacceptable for a particular account, would an advance deposit make the order more acceptable?

The analysis, following the credit investigation, will again be varied according to the company conditions, but generally will follow these areas:

- Organization of business;
- Length of time in business;
- History of business;
- History of principals;
- Operation of business;
- Financial information;
- Payment history;
- Banking sources and relationships; and
- Industry and economic conditions.

Organization of business

The three major types of businesses in Canada must be understood in order to identify the extent of responsibility of the owners or shareholders.

1. *Sole Proprietorship* — The sole proprietorship is a business owned by one person. This type of operation is common in the smaller business and is easily formed. The owner of such a business has both personal and business assets at stake and is personally liable for all indebtedness.

   There are significant disadvantages to dealing with proprietorships. As the business failure statistics indicate, one person often cannot conduct efficiently all important facets of a complex business as it grows. In the event of death or illness, a creditor may have to wait long periods for payment of bills. Heirs seldom run the business as successfully as the founder. Finally, the most important reason is simply control. A sole owner has no one to answer to and can divert funds for any purpose.

2. *Partnerships* — A partnership is an association of two or more persons to carry on as co-owners, much the same as a proprietorship. The legal status of partnerships is based upon common law and statute which pictures the organization as an aggregate of individuals who can be sued, for instance, in the names of the partners. In a *general partnership,* each partner has unlimited liability to creditors. In a *limited partnership,* limited partners are liable only to the extent of their investment, but there must be one or more general partners. A partnership composed of active businesspeople will tend toward a more flexible and competent management than a proprietorship, if the partners have diversified abilities and experience. The disadvantages of dealing with this type of business from a creditor's point of view lie

mainly in the control and stability areas. Dissension and friction among the partners often seriously retard business progress. The stability and continuity of a partnership is uncertain, for instance, upon a partner's death, insolvency, lunacy or withdrawal. For these reasons, financing is often difficult to obtain in large amounts.

3. *Corporations* — A corporation is an artificial body created by law which empowers the organization to act in many respects as an individual. A corporation stands on its own and has a perpetual life so that the death or withdrawal of a shareholder does not affect the business stability or continuity. Unlike proprietorships and partnerships, shareholders and managers of a corporation are not liable for its debts. The shareholders may lose whatever investment was made in the shares of the company, but they will not be called upon to meet the debts in the event of the assets becoming insufficient. Because of the limited liability, this has become the most common type of ownership in Canada for all but the smallest business.

Other forms of business ownership such as cooperative and joint ventures are less frequent but should be recognized during the credit analysis.

Cooperatives are found in the farming, marketing and financial (credit unions or caisses populaires) industries. In many respects, they are similar to corporations, the capital being supplied by members who buy shares. Surplus earnings may be distributed to members by way of dividends or immediate savings on purchases.

Joint ventures are associations of two or more business organizations formed to carry out a single business transaction. The construction field frequently has these types of entities. The legal responsibility is generally similar to a partnership.

PART C

351

In assessing the creditworthiness of a customer or prospective customer, the type of business ownership is a key factor. When possible, every effort should also be made to determine if there is a parent-subsidiary relationship, or affiliated companies involved in the day-to-day affairs of the customer.

Length of time in business

The length of time in business, from a credit standpoint, refers to the length of time the owner has been in control of the business. The first six years of a business' life is a critical period. The testing of the company's management, marketing and personnel occurs during this period. Interestingly, the first year of a business is very low in failures, probably because the company has not devoured its capital, nor run out of available suppliers. Some companies will not deal with businesses which have been in existence for one year or less, although such a policy is normally too restrictive.

New businesses

The assessment of a new business should fully cover two important areas:

1. Amount of starting capital;
2. Source of the starting capital —
   The usual sources of capital include:
   - Savings;
   - Loans from relatives or banks;
   - Inheritance;
   - Sale of another business; and
   - Sale or mortgage of property.

The source and amount of starting capital is an excellent indicator of the owner's commitment level, as well as providing financial information.

Nature and operation of business

What a company does, how it does it, and who it competes against are the basic ingredients of a credit analysis. In analyzing a company's financial condition, the line of business determines, for example, whether an accounts receivable figure is too high, too low or about average for the industry. Does management have experience in the line of business? It is difficult to say without knowing the line.

The line of business can often be determined by knowing the company's name, however, this can easily be wrong or misleading. The line of business can commonly be determined from the credit application or salesperson's report. Commercial credit reports also provide the SIC (Standard Industrial Classification).

Retailers

- Most retail lines are very competitive. Some lines are dominated by large chains that control pricing.
- The buying process is most important. Management must be experienced or employ experienced personnel.
- Gross profits are higher than wholesalers.
- In the grocery business and certain other retail businesses, the stores control the allocation of shelf space so that manufacturers have relatively little power.

Wholesalers

- Profit margins are usually low.
- Competition is not that great in most lines and few industries are dominated by large firms.
- There is usually only a small investment in fixed assets.

Manufacturers

- As principal costs are labour and materials, working capital is a key influencer in the credit decision.
- Long-term debt may be high to finance working capital and fixed assets.
- Extent of competition varies widely; influences are difficult to determine.

Transportation

- Profits are very low and the industry is highly competitive.
- Labour and fuel are the major costs.
- Very little inventory carried.

Seasonality

Many lines are more affected by seasonal characteristics, for example, farm equipment, fashion industries and department stores. It is important to determine what the major selling season is and what effect it has on cash position. In the fashion industry, for instance, inventory build-up in the spring for the fall lines will mean low cash positions and very often operating losses for the period. The nature of the product and the diversity of products within a company's lines should also be assessed.

Types of customers and number of accounts

The quality and number of accounts a prospective customer has are important. A company's fate may be in the hands of one or two major customers, the loss of which may cause a rapid deterioration and eventual failure. Alternatively, selling to a large number of clients may cause a load on the staff, facilities and systems to handle the volume.

Credit information

Bank references

Checking bank references is a common practice in Canada. The two means of obtaining banking reference information are to use your own bank or to deal directly with the prospective customer's bank. Your customer's banking relations are in many cases his or her most important financial relationship. Banks are intimately involved with the activities of their accounts when financing is involved. A simple switch in banking source is a major change in most cases, important enough that several companies' procedures call for immediate reassessment of a customer's credit lines when a bank is changed. The credit manager must realize, however, that the banker's relationship is different from the unsecured creditor and there may be instances, particularly when the collateral may be *your goods*, that the bank's interests may be at odds with these suppliers.

When banking sources are checked, it is important that the information be as factual as possible. Whether the banking relationship is described as "satisfactory for normal commitments" or "considered satisfactory for requirements" is less important than factual information that supports the whole story of the business.

PART C

Generally, the information requested should consist of all or part of the following:

- How long the bank has had the account;
- Borrowing or non-borrowing account;
- Security on loans;
- Fluctuations in loans; and
- Fluctuations in cash balances.

Credit agencies

Reports from credit agencies can be a useful source of information. In Canada, reports are available from D&B Canada (*www.dnb.ca*), Equifax Canada Inc.(*www.equifax.com/EFX_Canada*) and Canadian Credit Reporting Ltd (*www.canadiancredit.com*).

All agencies provide payment history for various suppliers, in addition to financial information, and other useful information such as claims, banking information and existing credit granted. The credit agencies also provide a record of recent enquiries, as well as a proprietary credit score to rate creditworthiness of the account.

Some industries and associations also provide credit reports to members, consisting mainly of trade information and varying amounts of other information. The quality and scope of the information varies, but the dates can be useful since it is industry-specific.

Public record and corporate information

If an outside agency is not used as a source of information, the credit investigation should also include the means to check sources of corporate information. A great deal of information is in the public records. Writs, judgments, real estate transactions, registered debt, financing statements and mortgages are all available. The following is a list of sources for provincial and federal corporations. This information will include incorporation details, correct legal name, and names of shareholders of record. The same offices in Ontario also house all registrations under the *Personal Property Security Act,* an invaluable source for investigating a company's registered debt. Fees vary by jurisdiction.

Federal:	Corporations Canada 9th Floor, Jean Edmonds Towers South 365 Laurier Avenue West Ottawa, Ontario K1A 0C8 Tel: (866) 333-5556 *www.strategis.ic.gc.ca*
Alberta:	Corporate Registry, Companies Branch 8th Floor North, 10365 97th Street Edmonton, Alberta T5J 3W7 Tel: (403) 427-2311 *www.gov.ab.ca/gs/services/cpns/index.cfm*
British Columbia:	Registrar of Companies 940 Blanshard Street Victoria, British Columbia V8W 3E6 Tel: (604) 387-4471
Manitoba:	Corporations Branch 405 Broadway, 10th Floor, Woodsworth Bldg. Winnipeg, Manitoba R3C 2L6 Tel: (204) 994-2500 *www.gov.mb.ca*

PART C

New Brunswick:	Department of Justice, Corporate Services Division P.O. Box 6000 Fredericton, New Brunswick E3B 5H1 Tel: (506) 453-2703
Newfoundland:	Department of Consumer and Commercial Affairs Atlantic Place, 5th Floor, Water St. St. John's, Newfoundland A1C 5T7 Tel: (709) 737-2781 *www.gov.nf.ca/gsl/cca*
Nova Scotia:	Department of the Attorney General Registryof Joint Stock Companies P.O. Box 1529 Halifax, Nova Scotia B3J 2Y4 Tel: (902) 424-7770 *www.gov.ns.ca/snsmr/rjsc*
Ontario:	Minister of Consumer & Business Services Companies Branch 393 University Avenue Toronto, Ontario M7A 2H6 Tel: (416) 963-0552 *www.cbs.gov.on.ca*
P.E.I.:	Department of Justice Corporations Division P.O. Box 2000 Charlottetown, Prince Edward Island C1A 7N8 Tel: (902) 643-5253

Quebec:	Inspecteur General des Institutions Financieres Companies Service 800, Place d'Youville Quebec, Quebec G1R 4Y5 Tel: (418) 643-3625 *www.revenu.gouv.gc.ca*
Saskatchewan:	Registrar of Companies 2121 Saskatchewan Drive, 3rd Floor Regina, Saskatchewan S4P 3V7 Tel: (306) 565-2962

Internet

Many companies have a Web site setting out their history, management, business and other information. Often they provide links to press releases and financial statements. Spending a few minutes browsing through sites can be a valuable source of information.

Use a reliable search engine to look for other references to the company on the internet. This can provide information such as positive or negative press reports and lawsuits.

Direct dealings with customer

Although common sense suggests the desirability of direct contact with the customer, this is often only done at the end of the collection process. Personal calls to customers eliminate any confusion that correspondence might cause. Personal calls build customer goodwill, make it easier to request financial information directly, and give the credit manager the opportunity to see the facilities and the condition of the equipment.

PART C

Credit department records

Beginning with credit applications, the professional credit department maintains credit files on each customer. Depending on the complexity of the credit operation, the variations can range from computerized files on each account, tickler or accordion files. Standardized forms are helpful for credit applications, sales department information, shipping records, payment history (particularly if the information on payment history is not permanently stored in a computer system). Other forms should be prepared in advance, such as personal guarantee forms. It has been said that documentation is the heart and soul of collection work, the same can be said for credit files.

Management history

Analyzing the character and management capacity of the principals is important, but often neglected. While current financial information is difficult to gather, it is reasonably easy to analyze. Historical information, on the other hand, is both difficult to obtain *and* difficult to analyze; however, there may be no better prediction of the future than the lessons of the past.

Character

Willingness and ability is shown by the past record. The credit analyst should look for the following:

- Past history of lawsuits or bankruptcy/business failure;
- Past experience in line of business;
- Management experience;
- Age;
- General reputation in community; and
- Other business interests.

Financial statement analysis

Financial statements are not readily supplied by private companies in Canada. In the last decade, however, more and more credit policies include a requirement for financial statement information at some level of credit exposure. A financial institution rarely provides credit lines of any significance without complete and full disclosure. The professional credit department should be guided by the same principles.

The various ratios used in financial statement analysis are discussed in Chapter 7. In addition to horizontal, vertical and ratio analysis, the credit analyst should be particularly attentive to working capital.

Working capital analysis

Working capital, the excess of current assets over current liabilities, is used to finance the current operations of a business. The amount of working capital a company has and the consituents of its assets and liabilities, relates directly to the company's ability to pay its bills. Insufficient working capital is a major cause of failure.

Working capital analysis reveals what funds are available from one period to the next and what application has been made of the funds; for example, a dividend policy may deplete the working funds or permit a healthy increase in net worth if earnings are retained.

Other questions that arise are:

- Has new financing been used to strengthen working capital or finance an expansion of fixed assets?
- Have earnings been sufficient to provide for growth and increased sales volume?

PART C

Credit assessment without financial information

While financial information is one of the best ways to evaluate a company's creditworthiness, only rarely will a supplier have such a restrictive credit policy that a lack of financial information prevents opening an open account. Credit strength is easily demonstrated without providing a financial statement (a major reason why managers decline to provide them). If a business' payment record is prompt, if it doesn't borrow or have registered debt, if management seems experienced, a financial statement may not be required.

Many times, it is fairly easy to gauge a company's size from the sales levels or number of employees. Combined with a representative trade supplier survey and a good factual bank reference, a good estimate of financial position can be made.

Setting Credit Limits

The credit limit is the maximum amount of credit a company will extend to a customer. Further shipments will be stopped when the limit is exceeded until payments are made. The disadvantages of using credit limits are:

- If the method of setting the limit is faulty, too much credit can be extended.
- The alternative is also true: business could be turned away unnecessarily.

The advantages of credit limits lie in the speed of order processing. Orders can be approved automatically, saving time and paper work. Orders are shipped faster and often costs are decreased.

Methods

There are several methods of setting credit limits. Depending upon the classification system utilized, the most common of which are the following or some derivation of the following:

- *Requirements limit,* that is, no limit— applicable to the largest clients or government accounts.
- *Usual requirements limit* — normal requirements are determined by past experience or normal industry practices.
- *Size of order* — an order limit can be established easily beyond which approval is required. This might not be desirable in a multi-branch ordering situation as credit exposure can increase quickly.

Setting monetary limits is a source of difficulty for many credit professionals. Various formulas have been devised, including the following:

- *Financial statement method* — based on the results of an analysis of financial statements, a credit limit of 5 per cent to 10 per cent of net worth or working capital can be set. Other factors such as economic conditions, marketing strategy can enter into the decision. This method would be used with a long-term customer or upon entering a relationship of more than a single order.
- *Credit agency ratings* — a simple method that sets limits on the basis of a credit rating. For example, a poor rating could receive a limit of $3,000, while a AAA or government could receive a requirements limit. While the credit rating system is based upon careful and totally objective investigation, the absence of ratings in many cases will require that a "manual" system of setting limits on the ratings be also set up.

PART C

Whatever the method, its use must be tempered by practical considerations. What the competition does often has the greatest influence. If a competitor is extending credit up to $50,000, comparable limits may have to be set to avoid losing a customer. Obviously, the size and financial situation of your company has a great influence. A financially strong company can use this strength to great advantage. When combined with good collection policies, the risk is reduced; however, the reverse is also true.

Collection Practices

Some credit departments mistakenly separate the functions of credit from collection. There is no doubt that collection practices need to conform to the overall credit policies and circumstances. Collection approaches need to recognize product and customer characteristics, competitive factors, profit margins as well as economic conditions that exist, and yet the vast majority of Canadian companies treat the collection function haphazardly and without a strategy. Simply using a variety of collection techniques without thought to the ramifications may collect the accounts, but with the loss of the customer.

A working collection policy is the key to improving the efficiency of the function. The primary responsibility of the credit manager is to manage the risk, thus increasing sales. The second responsibility is to administer the systematic, steady progression of collection steps, which can only be accomplished with well-defined policies and procedures.

Past due charges

Many sellers charge — or attempt to levy — customers a past due charge. This rate is usually set by industry standards, when in fact the charge should be set to exceed the approximate cost of capital.

In the real world, however, there are problems with past due charges. The primary difficulty is the legal collectability of the charges. Should the account become uncollectable, the past due charges may not be collectable since most credit applications are not contracts. Another difficulty is that the customer may not accept the change and simply refuse to pay.

Collection responsibilities

While the vast majority of companies use the same personnel who made the credit decision for the collection process, there is an increasing number of companies using sales staff to make the collection. This can be of value if the sales staff call frequently, such as the food industry, soft drink manufacturers or auto parts wholesalers. If commissioned salespeople are employed, it may be desirable to withhold commissions until the accounts are collected. This has an immediate effect on the collections. On the other hand, industry practice may not permit this.

When to start collection efforts

The collection effort starts when the account is opened. With large new accounts, a call should be made five to 10 days *before* the account is due to "welcome" the customer and ensure that the customer received the invoice, that the documentation is in order and that a cheque will be processed. This is not only excellent customer relations but trains the customer as well (aside from getting the cheque on time).

The normal collection process is part of the policy decisions that need to be made, for example, profit margins, industry practices, staffing needs, etc. Each of these areas will need to be analyzed. In some industries, a grace period of ten to fifteen days passes before a letter is sent, in others, a telephone call is made first, then letters.

PART C

Properly training the staff to make effective calls, and recognize danger signals, prepare rebuttals for excuses from customers, know the language of the courts (writ of execution, petition in bankruptcy, etc.) pays immense dividends. Most experienced collectors can sense when a customer is not going to pay. If the collection call has been done properly, whether this occurs when the account is one hour past due or 60 days, the collector knows that it is time for the next step in the process — a final letter, placing for collection or calling the company lawyer. All of this should be determined in advance.

Reminder

Notification of past due balances is the second step and can be referred to as the *reminder stage*. While the telephone is the most useful tool, most companies lack the staff to call all accounts which are one to ten days past due. For some reason, the staff is always available to call accounts that are 120 days past due but not the current ones. In any event, the reminder stage can be accomplished with stickers or requests printed on statements. Reminders shuld not offend, and encouragement should be gentle but at the same time professional. The main point is to convey the concern of the seller to the buyer. The next routine reminder, either by telephone or by written notification should be sent no later than five days after the preliminary reminder. However, because of the inconsistency of mail delivery, ten days may be a better choice.

The objective of reminder notices is not only to collect the money but also to test the customer's intentions. Creditors tend to be placed into three categories:

1. Those that demand and expect to get paid on time;
2. Those that will let us be a little slow from time to time; and
3. Those that don't seem to care.

366

Discussion

When reminders do not produce an appropriate response, that is, a cheque, it is time for discussion. This stage is a transition from the impersonal to a personal appeal for payment of the account. Collection letters have generally now been replaced by e-mail and phone calls. The use of "sales techniques" to collect produces the best results. A sales technique is the ability to come up with a reason why the customer, who is now a debtor, should pay today. This can be an appeal based on the credit rating (your credit rating is a valuable asset), or an appeal to reputation (you can still restore your credit reputation by paying your debt immediately) or a softer appeal to fair play (pointing out that the relationship has been like a partnership over many years).

Creating a script for a telephone call requires planning, an objective and prepared response for whatever the customer/debtor answers.

An example — "Mr. Smith, this is Janet Brown from Excelsior Plastics. I'm calling about the $4,414.67 that is now overdue. Mr. Smith, will you have a cheque ready for me to pick up this afternoon?"

Now, list all the common reasons why the bill hasn't been paid: no money, no cheques, can't collect own receivables, computer is broken, sales are down, and I'm expecting a big cheque next week. The list is endless, including the favourite — the cheque is in the mail.

The professional credit department will have researched all of the common excuses and have prepared rebuttals so that the collection call ends in a definite "yes" or a definite "no". It is necessary to test the intentions of the customer and be alert to danger signals. Suppose a customer says "I can't pay because I'm just changing banks", how does the collector respond? Should the account be sent to a lawyer or collection agency, even though it is not that old? The answer is that a professional collector will, at the end of the call, either have a promise of payment, a payment plan or the collector should proceed to the next step in the policy, whether it is collection or a lawsuit.

If letters are used, the letters should become forceful and give a date when further action will be taken. If the letter says ten days, then ten days is all that should pass, not 11 or 15. The customer/debtor has to understand that "we are a professional organization". Here are some examples:

Example 1

Unfortunately your account is at a point where it can no longer be tolerated. Therefore, should payment in full not be received in this office by November 20, your account will be assigned to our solicitors for collection. In so doing, your credit reputation will be irreparably harmed.

Example 2

We hereby issue a formal demand for payment of the following invoices:

Date	Invoice Number	Amount

Total amount outstanding: _____

If we do not receive payment in full or make acceptable arrangements with you by November 20, we will take whatever action we deem necessary to enforce collection.

This is our formal demand for payment, govern yourselves accordingly.

> ## Example 3
>
> Unfortunately you have left just one course open to us and that is, to take the necessary legal action to enforce payment. This is a great expense for both of us. Your cheque for $500 by November 20 will settle the matter.

If the effort exerted during the *discussion stage* fails to produce a satisfactory result, either a cheque or a payment plan, there is no choice left but to take drastic action. Restraint no longer needs to be practised, as the sole objective is to recover as much of the debt as possible. However, punitive action should only be taken if there is evidence that moneys or assets are available to satisfy the debt. A new credit investigation is often called for (but rarely done). It may be more desirable to write off the account than to pursue it if there is in fact no money available. Vengeance may be sweet but the potential expense is often not worth the effort.

Recovery

The discussion stage may end with arrangements for payment, post-dated cheques, promissory notes, securing the transaction, or even full payment.

If all efforts fail to successfully arrange for payment of the account, the last stage of the process occurs. The credit manager no longer has to practise good customer relations or restraint in his efforts, although as mentioned earlier, it may be more desirable to write off the account than proceed with punitive action. If, however, there is evidence that a portion or all of the account is recoverable, the following steps may be of help.

PART C

Collection Agencies

The use of collection agencies is common in Canada. Agencies range in size from small local firms dealing with companies whose accounts are confined to the local area to large national/international agencies who can collect accounts around the world. All agencies operate on the same basis, charging a fee on amounts collected. These fees vary according to the amount collected. The major agencies offer a free demand service of approximately ten days. A free demand service incorporates a final demand letter on the agency letterhead. If payment is made within the demand period, there is no fee. If payment is not received, further collection is commenced under normal fees.

Some agencies also offer demand letter services, utilizing word-processing to give every letter the "custom" look. These services may be purchased in a series of letters.

Some of the areas to be considered during the selection:

- Does the agency conform to the overall philosophy of the credit policies of your company? Agencies collect with different means. Some are softer in approach and are more capable of setting payment plans. Others are of the "knee-breaking" type, resorting to tactics such as feigning anger with the creditor and throwing the telephone into a nearby wastepaper basket for effect.
- Will the agency provide regular (at least once per month) reports on *all* accounts? This is very important. Some agencies are very neglectful in this area.
- How will collected funds be remitted? Once per month or less frequently?
- Does the agency provide Small Claims Court services?
- Can the agency collect in your entire trading area? Some smaller agencies forward accounts to other agencies or lawyers.

- How effective are they in collecting? Some are very proficient at selling their services, but collection skills are very weak.

Once again, overlapping your credit policies and philosophy can pay dividends when using a collection agency. In most cases, the cost of collection does not exceed the marginal revenue from the sale, and of course, the costs of bad debts greatly exceeds that of an agency.

When to use an agency or lawyer

Here are a few guidelines for placing with an agency or lawyer:

- When an NSF cheque is received and not made good within a few days.
- After three (or even two) broken promises for payment.
- When the customer/debtor appears to be avoiding any contact. Messages are not returned, decision maker is never in, etc.
- If time and effort being expended on collecting accounts could be put to better use, such as "training" every new customer.
- Finally, when your well-trained collector has resorted to all available in-house means.

Note that none of the above have anything to do with the age of the account. That is because an agency should be receiving accounts at any time that in-house means come to a standstill which could be at 31 days, or 180 days. The agency is another step in your process, not a dumping ground.

The final suggestion regarding collection agencies is to document your requirements and put them out to tender with a number of agencies. Rely on strategy rather than salesmanship.

PART C

371

Some creditors prefer to use the services of lawyers to effect their collection recovery. While many lawyers can be effective in sending letters on their letterhead, lawyers who are specialists in other means of collection are not found that frequently. Lawyers will usually charge a fee whether or not the account is collected.

Court Action

With the exception of Small Claims Court procedures, the issuance of a writ or statement of claim to effect payment will be carried out by a lawyer. It is important to realize that obtaining judgment does not automatically result in payment of the debt. If the company has little or no means to satisfy the obligation, it may be years before the claim can be settled. Bringing suit against a debtor produces adverse publicity for the defendant, which can also cause other creditors, particularly their banking sources, to review the existing lines of credit. The resulting reviews can cause an avalanche of other claims.

It is important, then, for the credit manager to do some homework before bringing suit. Does the debtor have assets or means to pay? Is the business a proprietorship or partnership, so that the personal assets can be attached? Are all proofs of delivery or documents proving the services were provided still available? Was a promissory note ever signed?

Small Claims Courts

Small Claims Courts are a useful avenue to collect smaller amounts. In most jurisdictions, the courts are "user friendly" and the use of lawyers is discouraged. The forms are easily filled out and for a nominal amount a Writ or Summons will be issued by the Court.

Maximum amounts collectable in small claims courts in canada

Alberta	$4,000
British Columbia	$10,000
Manitoba	$5,000
New Brunswick	$3,000
Newfoundland	$3,000
Northwest Territories	$5,000
Nova Scotia	$5,000
Ontario	$6,000
Prince Edward Island	$5,000
Quebec	$3,000
Saskatchewan	$5,000
Yukon	$5,000

There are differences in Small Claims Courts in each jurisdiction (as well as all other court procedures). In British Columbia, for example, it is possible to issue a Garnishing Order before judgment.

Some of the larger collection agencies dealing nationally have Small Claims Court Departments and the facilities to handle out-of-province claims.

PART C

Appendix 15A

Example application for credit

Legal name of company	Trade name (if any)
Street address	Postal code
City and province	Telephone
Nature of business (please specify)	
Date business started	Monthly credit requirements $
Building owned ( ) Rented ( )	Are you a subsidiary? If so name parent company
Full names of directors or partners 1	Address
2	
3	
4	
Full names of officers and shareholders if a corporation (attach details)	Address
President	
Vice-president	
Secretary	
Treasurer	Branch and account number
Name of bank	
Name of bank manager	Telephone
Trade references and address 1	
2	
3	
Please attach set of financial statements	

TERMS OF CREDIT (30 days net)

All merchandise must be paid for in full within 30 days of date of each invoice, failing which an interest charge will be levied at the rate of 2% per month on all overdue accounts.

PURCHASER'S SIGNATURE
ACCEPTED BY_____

on_____

VENDOR'S SIGNATURE

Appendix 15B

Internal procedures checklist

Credit Approval	Yes	No	N/A	Comments
1. Is a written application required?				
2. Is there a standard form for credit applications?				
3. Are applicants checked out with a credit bureau?				
4. Does the evaluation consider bank credit history?				
5. Does the evaluation consider bank references?				

Invoices	Yes	No	N/A	Comments
1. Are invoices sent out promptly, not just at month-end?				
2. Is the invoice always accurate?				
3. Are payment terms clearly stated on the invoices?				
4. Are customers' special instructions followed carefully?				

PART C

Terms of Sale	Yes	No	N/A	Comments
1. Are the terms of payment clearly shown?				
2. Is the late payment penalty clearly shown?				

Statements	Yes	No	N/A	Comments
1. Are monthly statements submitted to all open accounts?				
2. Are statements prompt and accurate?				

Problem Identification	Yes	No	N/A	Comments
1. Is the average collection period calculated on a regular basis?				
2. Is the collection period compared with industry averages?				
3. Are changes to the collection period followed up?				
4. Is the collection period compared with payment terms?				
5. Is there a monthly aging of all outstanding accounts receivable?				
6. When a problem is identified, is corrective action prompt and firm?				

Follow-up	Yes	No	N/A	Comments
1. Is there a systematic procedure for follow-up on slow accounts?				
2. Is the telephone used to contact delinquent accounts?				
3. Is the telephone technique effective?				
4. Are there special procedures for collecting past-due accounts?				
5. Is there a late-payment penalty?				
6. Is an advance deposit required for seriously past due accounts?				

PART C

CHAPTER 16

Cash Forecasting and Budgeting

Overview

Every company, no matter what size or industry, must carefully monitor its cash flow. Not paying attention to cash flow can result, at best, in lost opportunities for maximizing interest revenue or minimizing interest expense. At worst, it could result in illiquidity and, ultimately, insolvency.

Two basic tools for managing cash flow are cash forecasts and cash budgets, which are the subject of this chapter.

Cash Forecasts and Cash Budgets

A **cash forecast** is a schedule representing the most likely prediction of the sources and uses of cash for a particular period. It is usually prepared in blocks of time of one year initially, and then broken into shorter time periods. It shows details of the change in beginning to ending cash balance. Thus, it indicates reasons for expected fluctuations in the cash balance for the period under consideration. The net excess (deficiency) estimated after preparation of the forecast represents the increase (decrease) to the cash balance for the period.

A cash forecast plays an important role in carrying out the company's financial policy. For example, consideration must be given to dealing with excess cash. Should it be invested in short-term instruments such as treasury bills, used to reduce existing debt, or used for other purposes such as increased management bonuses? On the other hand, if the cash forecast indicates a deficit, then the deficit must be funded through, for example, increasing operational cash inflows, borrowing funds or issuing equity securities.

Because cash forecasts comprise a "best guess" as to cash flow activity and, in turn, affect investing and financing activity, they should not remain static. As information comes to light that renders the earlier cash flow assumptions incorrect, then the forecasts should be updated.

The purpose of a **cash budget** is to communicate the company's goals to employees and to motivate them to work towards meeting those goals. It does **not** represent what management believes is most likely to occur. The format and components of cash budgets will be the same as cash forecasts. However, the latter represents an ideal state of affairs, not necessarily the most likely scenario.

Both cash forecasts and budgets are often broken into daily, weekly, monthly, quarterly or semi-annual periods. More detailed forecasts and budgets for very short periods frequently are the most useful.

Importance of Forecasts and Budgets

Cash forecasts and budgets are important tools for financial managers in attaining the proper balance between safety (or liquidity) and profitability. They are necessitated by the objective of ensuring that adequate cash resources for day-to-day operations are maintained and excess resources are placed in adequately liquid investments earning some return. *The cash forecast and cash budget form part of the master budgeting and forecasting process that summarizes the company's plans and expectations for the upcoming period(s).*

Cash forecasts and cash budgets should play an integral role in helping to manage all of the company because:

- They ensure management, employees and the company are **focused**. It is an important step towards having all areas of the company (e.g., departments, divisions, etc.) work towards the same goals and to ensure management sets realistic goals.
- They help ensure business activities are **run effectively.** Cash forecasts predict whether cash will be required in various future periods to fund a shortfall in cash in advance of when those funds are needed. The treasurer can then negotiate to borrow funds or issue equity from a position of strength rather than under undue pressure. This, in turn, permits flexibility in searching for sources of funds and will lower the cost of financing operations. If the cash forecast indicates excess funds, you will have sufficient time to assess the most suitable sources in which to invest and,

PART C

therefore, earn a return. In addition, cash planning helps to coordinate the activities of the entire company.

- Cash budgets help **motivate employees** to meet established goals. If goals are realistic and employees are involved in the planning stage, they are more likely to work towards meeting goals.

- They provide a **measure of control** for performance evaluation purposes. Actual performance should be measured against cash budgets at selected intervals. The nature of discrepancies needs to be investigated and corrective action taken if thought necessary. This measure of control is necessary for all levels of the entity (e.g., divisions, projects, etc.).

- They often are **required by lenders before funds can be obtained.** For example, banks and other financial institutions will want to know how the company plans to repay a loan before funds are committed and advanced. Similarly, before issuing securities to the public, a prospectus, approved by the appropriate provincial securities commission(s), must be produced and distributed. Depending on the requirements of the relevant securities commission, this prospectus may have to include a multi-year projected income statement and balance sheet (for which the cash position must be forecast). In addition, supplemental schedules of forecast cash flow often are included.

Thus, one objective is to show potential creditors or investors that your company has a viable, well-thought out plan for putting funds requested to profitable use. Another objective is to indicate that orderly repayment (in case of debt) is feasible, or reasonable returns in the form of dividends or other items (in the case of other securities) is likely.

Because most companies use accrual-based accounting and reporting systems, it is important to ensure that goals, activities and evaluations relevant to the cash forecasts and budgets are consistent with those used in the accrual-based reporting system.

Preparing Cash Forecasts

In general, past results (actual or estimated actual, if actual is not yet available) are the starting point for preparing cash forecasts. However, you should recognize that past results are not necessarily and not usually indicative of what will happen in the future. Therefore, consideration must be given to existing and anticipated environmental factors (e.g., economy, industry, etc.).

Preparing forecasts and budgets for several years or periods can be extremely time-consuming. Either general spreadsheet programs or specialized software may be used. The latter can perform the forecast and budget calculations as well as scenario analysis once the assumptions and relationships among data are specified. Such programs may permit faster preparation of forecasts and budgets, more extensive scenario analysis and the ability to react quickly to unexpected situations as they develop.

It is important that various levels of knowledgeable personnel be involved in the cash forecasting and budgeting processes. Senior management, which often has a significant amount of experience in the industry and sees the "big picture", should have input into the preparation of the forecasts and budgets.

The steps required to prepare a cash forecast are set out below and illustrated in a comprehensive example that starts on page 397.

PART C

383

1. Forecast revenue schedule

The first step is to forecast revenue on an accrual basis and prepare the forecast revenue schedule. This is the most important step as other items affecting the cash forecast generally are derived based on revenue figures. For example, revenue estimates will have a significant effect on planned purchases, estimated cost of revenue budget, accounts receivable figures, etc.

Different approaches to preparing the revenue forecast include the following:

(a) An *internal approach* relies on the knowledge base within the company to forecast revenues. Sales/marketing personnel prepare forecasts based on their area of product specialization. The marketing/sales manager reviews these estimates. The general starting point for these employees is consideration of prior years' revenue.

(b) The *external approach* begins with a consideration of general economic conditions and the condition of the particular industry under consideration. Total industry revenue is first projected. Your company's market share then is estimated by considering such factors as historical market shares, new companies entering into the industry, planned competitive strategies, etc. Finally, the forecast is broken into product lines.

(c) The preferable approach is a combination of the internal and external approaches. A single approach should never be used since the business environment is too dynamic. Instead, revenue forecasts can be prepared under each approach and differences then reconciled.

In preparing revenue forecasts, factors such as the following should be considered:

- *General and industry economic conditions* — For example, in a recession, industries manufacturing and selling necessities such as food perform well. However, companies involved in producing and marketing luxury items such as cars, appliances and real estate-related products do not.
- The *amount and pattern of past revenue* (e.g., by product line, geographic area, salesperson).
- *Predictions of marketing personnel.*
- *Existing marketing campaign plans.*
- *Competitors* — What are the strengths and weaknesses of competitors compared to your company? What effect have they had on recent results of your company? What are their plans?
- *Expected price changes* — Anticipated price increases and decreases should be reflected in the forecast. The effect of unit price changes on unit sales needs to be assessed as well. For example, a 10 per cent increase in sales prices may result in a 20 per cent decline in unit sales. In this case, revenue would be lower than the prior year.
- *Product line plans for the company* — For example, are new products planned to come on-line during the forecast period? Is production of certain current products expected to be stopped?
- *Revenue budgets,* if already prepared.

It is important to ensure that all assumptions used to develop the revenue forecast are consistent with an accrual basis of accounting, not a cash basis. (Step 3 converts accrual-based figures to the cash basis.)

PART C

A revenue forecast should be prepared for both number of units and dollar volume of revenue. You should prepare the forecast under various "what if" scenarios since projections of any kind are purely judgemental and not all factors affecting revenue can be accurately predicted.

"What if" or scenario analysis is very useful in assessing the effect of changes in different variables affecting revenue (as well as other items). Preparing and analyzing the effect of various possible revenue figures helps ensure the corporation is equipped to react to actual results. Such analysis can indicate potential areas of concern as well as areas of opportunity.

Detailed month-by-month revenue forecasts, rather than summarized or annual forecasts, should be prepared. This will aid in preparing month-by-month detailed cash forecasts. This is particularly important for seasonal operations (e.g., the retail industry).

Information for forecasts of any kind should be prepared by, or with significant input from, the most knowledgeable individuals in the company. Therefore, in producing revenue forecasts, the marketing department should be involved in the departments. If an employee knowledgeable in economics exists in your company, he or she will be an invaluable reference point. If not, external sources should be consulted. For example, economic predictions such as interest rates and housing starts should be obtained. Such information is available from large financial institutions that have economic research departments as well as from investment dealers. Statistics Canada has a vast array of historical information available which may be useful in the process. Other sources of information include industry associations and the general media (e.g., newspapers and periodicals).

Once the revenue forecast is prepared, consideration must be given as to whether the figures are realistic. For example, if expected revenue looks too low, consideration should be given to various methods of increasing revenue as well as the likelihood of the company undertaking such plans. If such plans are likely, the revenue forecast should be revised.

2. Detailed cost schedules

The second step is to estimate various costs/expenses on an accrual basis and prepare detailed schedules for each category of items. Some cost-revenue relationships may be linear and therefore, easy to predict based on past experience. For example, if a company has no plans for expansion or cost-cutting measures, personnel costs may be calculated based on expected revenue levels (per Step 1 above). However, more often than not, relationships among revenue and cost items will not be that apparent. In addition, historical references should not be simply accepted before understanding why those relationships existed and whether they are still applicable. For example, the company's strategic plan, changing regulations, changing industry structure and competitiveness and economic conditions should be considered.

It is important to ensure that all assumptions used to develop the revenue forecast must be consistent with an accrual basis of accounting, not a cash basis. (Step 3 converts accrual-based figures to the cash basis.)

Regression analysis and other statistical tools may be useful in developing past relationships among financial statement items. However, the ultimate caveat regarding forecasts must be kept in mind: past relationships may not, and are not likely to, continue in the future.

PART C

Past relationships of cost of revenue to revenue often can be used to establish a reasonable estimate for forecasting purposes. However, many companies with complex cost structures will need to analyze in detail each component of the cost of revenue (e.g., direct labour, direct material, overhead items such as indirect labour, supplies, rent, depreciation). As well, cost of revenue in the case of companies that produce goods will have to be allocated between ending inventory and cost of revenue.

There may be a direct and well understood relationship between selling/marketing expense and revenue. However, the company's marketing thrust and the competitive environment must be considered to determine if this relationship is still applicable.

A company with fixed interest rates on its debt (e.g., bonds, certain bank financing) can easily forecast interest expense. However, due to recent experience with significantly fluctuating interest rates, many lenders will not, or generally do not, lend fixed rate funds. (There are, however, financial instruments such as interest rate swaps that permit fixing of interest rates on debt for a certain cost.) Therefore, it is important to research anticipated interest rates to project interest expense. Scenario analysis is especially useful because of the good possibility of changes (and possibly wide swings) in interest rates. (For managing interest rate risk, see Chapter 18.)

A company with foreign operations (e.g., subsidiaries, distribution centres, purchases) will have to consider expected exchange rates. Again, scenario analysis will be very useful. There are instruments that permit fixing exposure to foreign exchange fluctuations such as forward rate agreements and futures. If a company uses these, forecasting cash flows will be easier than otherwise. (For managing foreign exchange risk, see Chapter 19.)

Consideration of future tax rates (both federal and provincial), level of investment in fixed assets (which affects the amount of capital cost allowance permitted to reduce taxable income), anticipated revisions to tax legislation, and other factors needs to be made to estimate the amount of income taxes to be paid.

At the end of this step, various schedules will be prepared such as schedules of purchases, production, inventories, operating expenses, selling/marketing, and general and administrative. Again, it is important to recognize the significant increase in quality of forecast cost figures if knowledgeable individuals are involved in the forecasting process.

The starting point for both steps 1 and 2 is usually past operating results from a company's accrual-based reporting system. These results are then adjusted to reflect management's expectations for future operations.

3. Turning revenues and costs into cash flow equivalents

Revenue and expenses (as reflected on the income statement) rarely equal cash inflows and outflows. This is because customers often do not pay for goods and services immediately, and companies do not pay funds for goods and services used as the costs are recognized for accounting purposes. For example, employees earn their wages as the time clock ticks. However, they may only receive a paycheque biweekly. *Step 3 changes estimates of revenue and expenses on an accounting basis to the cash basis.* Modifying accrual-based estimates to the cash basis will likely require a reasonable amount of effort.

Completion of this step produces several schedules. Specifically, schedules of cash collections from customers, of cash

PART C

389

disbursements for purchases, and of cash disbursements for operating expenses must be prepared.

The first stage in the process is to eliminate non-cash items that are shown as revenues, gains, expenses or losses on forecast schedules. Typical items include depreciation, amortization, gains and losses on the sale of capital assets and deferred income taxes.

Cash flow from operating activities should be calculated first. This will tell you how much cash is available for investing and financing purposes. If a shortage of cash from operations is indicated, available sources of cash (e.g., borrow from financial institutions, issue debt or equity securities, sell unnecessary capital assets, sell investment assets, sale/leaseback of capital assets, sell a division or subsidiary) must be considered.

The company's history of collections and payments should be assessed, as well as the likelihood of this experience continuing in the future. To begin, terms of credit should be reviewed and it should be determined through discussion with appropriate personnel whether changes are anticipated. For example, if credit terms are net 30, and customers typically pay their accounts within 35 days but a significant decline in economic conditions is expected, using a 35-day collection period for cash forecasts may not be reasonable. However, if collection efforts will likely increase (which would likely increase costs — this should be reflected on the cash forecast), the 35-day period may be appropriate.

If substantial revenue growth is expected, asset accounts are generally increased by a reasonable amount (e.g., inventory and accounts receivable). If real revenue growth is expected to continue, investment in capital assets (such as land, building, equipment) as well as employees will be necessary. Anticipated growth may be the result of increased physical volume revenues as well as inflationary price level increases. High inflation tends to force firms into the financial markets for funding; however, funding costs in a highly inflationary economy are expensive due to high interest rates.

The balance in various account categories such as accounts receivable and accounts payable must be estimated to support expected revenues. A linear or proportional relationship between revenues and accounts receivable likely will hold true if credit terms and economic conditions are expected to stay the same; however, past relationships must be reconsidered during each forecasting session.

4. Sources other than operating activities

Cash inflows and outflows related to sources other than operating activities must be estimated in this step. Cash flows can be affected significantly by activities other than the regular operations of the company. For example, cash inflows may arise during a particular year from the sale of subsidiaries, divisions or capital assets. Proceeds from insurance policies (cash inflows) may or may not adequately cover the expenditures necessitated by some disaster such as a fire or flood.

5. Investing cash flows (including capital expenditures)

The next step is to consider and analyze investing cash flow items. This step requires forecasting the extent of capital additions and disposals in the upcoming period(s). Forecasting of capital asset transactions is very important due to the high dollar value of cash receipts or payments that can result. In addition, capital asset transactions are often more discretionary than operations.

PART C

During this step, it must be considered whether or not certain investments must or should be made even if cash is not available. For example, certain equipment may need to be replaced to continue operating your business effectively no matter what the source of the funds is. If so, a decision about the likely mode of financing these investments is required in step 6.

Special consideration will have to be paid to expenditures which will be capitalized (i.e., recorded as an asset rather than as an expense). If, for example, interest and wage payments will be capitalized during the construction of a building, these cash outflows should be included in the cash forecast.

An estimate of dividends to be paid is required. The best starting point is past dividend payment policies. Then, expected cash flow from operations should be examined. If cash flow is estimated to be "tight", the desirability of paying dividends should be reconsidered and senior management consulted as to its views.

6. Excess or deficiency of cash before financings

The next step is to calculate the excess or deficiency of cash before financing activities. This calculation estimates what your company's financing needs are. If a deficiency is identified, consideration must be given to the most appropriate action (e.g., increase revenues, decrease payments). For example, management may decide that while expenditures are in line, there is room to increase revenue through enhancing marketing strategies.

If excess cash is anticipated, any revenues from investment of those funds will have to be calculated and included on the cash forecast.

7. Planned financing activities

The next step is to adjust the results to reflect planned financing activities. Possibilities include:

- *Borrowing funds* from a bank or other financial institution, or from the investing public (through an issue of debentures or bonds, for example). Important factors to include in the evaluation are the cost of borrowing, whether or not there are sources willing to lend money to the company, and the extent of current borrowings. If current borrowings are too high, increasing existing debt levels may put the successful future of your company in jeopardy.
- *Postponing payments* to creditors (e.g., trade accounts payable, bank loan). A key consideration here is the likelihood of upsetting important creditors and damaging future relationships.
- *Reducing discretionary expenses* such as advertising and management bonuses, and reducing staffing levels.
- *Reducing customers' credit terms or otherwise accelerating customer payments* to reduce accounts receivable collection time. This may not increase the turnover of accounts in recessionary times if customers are in tight cash positions themselves.
- *Postponing or accelerating planned capital expenditures.*
- *Postponing or increasing dividend payments.*
- Entering into *sale/leaseback transactions* to increase cash inflows.

Another item of consideration is whether a minimum cash balance is required as a measure of security. If so, this amount should be included when calculating the level of financing required (i.e., reduce forecast cash surplus or increase cash deficit).

PART C

Cash outflows in the cash forecast will have to be adjusted for estimated interest costs, principal repayments and dividend payments based on the selected financing method(s).

Steps 1 through 7 should be repeated for different key assumptions until the desired plan is obtained. Performing adequate scenario analysis is very important since it is impossible to predict the future exactly or even fairly closely for most companies. (**Scenario analysis** is applying different "what if" possibilities to different key variables/assumptions affecting the cash forecast.) Therefore, you need to think through various alternatives that may transpire.

8. Compile the cash forecast

This step is simply a summary of steps 1 through 7. The objective is to summarize the information prepared in the previous seven steps for distribution to interested parties in your company.

9. Revise the cash forecast for new information

The process of forecasting cash flow is iterative and requires much thought and effort. Because no one can predict the exact combination of events that will occur in the future, forecasts will not be met. Therefore, they should be modified as new information becomes available; cash forecasting and budgeting should be considered a continuous process. To illustrate, if revenue for a given month was below expectations, management should reconsider whether the forecast for remaining months is appropriate or should be adjusted. Of course, there is a tradeoff between the benefits from more accurate forecasts, and the costs involved.

Preparing Cash Budgets

Once the cash forecast has been prepared, it should be modified as necessary to prepare the cash budget. During this process, the effect of various budget figures on the company must be considered. For example, budgets that obviously are not attainable may have a negative impact on employees instead of encouraging them to work harder to achieve the high standards. On the other hand, an easily attainable budget may result in employees not reaching their full potential, only that envisaged in the budget. Therefore, care must be taken to select the highest motivating budget.

The budget may be equal to the forecast at the start of the year. The budget would be fixed, whereas the forecast will be adjusted to reflect estimated actual figures.

After the budget has been prepared and communicated to various levels of the company, the next phase is to assess performance, analyze discrepancies and take any necessary corrective action. This phase involves comparing actual results to the cash budget. It serves as the control mechanism. Unless discrepancies are analyzed and corrective action implemented, a significant benefit of the cash budgeting process is lost.

You must assess the degree to which employees' compensation should be based on achieving budgeted results. In general, the more directly their remuneration is based on meeting budgets, the harder they will work towards meeting them. However, the extent to which employees are remunerated based on meeting their budgets should be determined by considering the achievability of the budgets.

PART C

Improving the Accuracy of Cash Forecasts and Budgets

The following suggestions will help to enhance the cash forecast and budget process:

- An *adequate amount of time* should be dedicated to the process. Also, the process should be started sufficiently early to permit appropriate consideration of all key variables.
- The forecast and budget should be *prepared by knowledgeable, experienced personnel.* Sound judgment plays an important role in the process. Input from those directly involved in line activities should be obtained.
- The forecast should be *broken down into very detailed components.* Analysis of assumptions at this level is necessary. For a cash forecast to be relatively accurate, the assumptions used to prepare the forecast must be of high quality.
- *Various scenarios should be applied.* The more scenarios used, the more likely the forecast and budget will be well-thought out plans that are useful to your company. Preparing cash forecasts and budgets is an iterative process. The results of one scenario often raises questions which need to be answered to fine-tune the forecast or budget.
- *Use spreadsheets or specialized software.* They permit quicker preparation of cash forecasts and budgets, and make additional scenario analysis more feasible. Software packages are available which permit the integration of an accrual-based reporting system with a cash forecasting and budgeting system.
- *Regression analysis* may be useful for developing relationships among variables and key accounts. Regression analysis is a statistical model that measures the average amount of change in a dependent variable that is associated with a unit change in the amount of one or more cost drivers.

There are various off-the-shelf software programs available to assist in performing regression analysis.

Summary

Preparing cash forecasts and budgets are a necessary and integral part of managing a company. The more time spent on developing forecasts and budgets, the more prepared a company will be for dealing with its dynamic environment.

Example

The following example illustrates the steps involved in preparing a cash budget as discussed above. It sets out a monthly forecast for a six-month period.

Step 1. Forecast revenue schedule

A company may forecast its revenue using the following format:

	Jan.	Feb.	March	April	May	June	Total
(in $000s)							
Cash revenue	$100	$150	$200	$100	$300	$250	$1,100
Credit revenue[1]	400	450	600	300	300	700	2,750
Total	$500	$600	$800	$400	$600	$950	$3,850

Major assumptions:

[1] On average, customers pay 50 per cent of the amount due within 30 days and the remainder within 60 days. Insignificant bad debts are expected. Credit revenue in December was $800.

Step 2. Forecast cost schedules

Once forecast revenue schedules are prepared, schedules detailing purchases and operating expenses can be prepared.

Purchases and Cost of Revenue:

	Jan.	Feb.	March	April	May	June	Total
(in $000s)							
Cost of revenue[1]	$300	$360	$480	$240	$360	$570	$2,310
Add: Desired ending inventory[2]	180	240	120	180	285	450	450
Less: Beginning inventory[3]	(200)	(180)	(240)	(120)	(180)	(285)	(200)
Purchases	280	420	360	300	465	735	2,560
GST	20	29	25	21	33	51	179
	$300	$449	$385	$321	$498	$786	$2,739

Major assumptions:

[1] Cost of revenue is 60 per cent of revenue. Excludes GST.
[2] Desired ending inventory is 50 per cent of cost of revenue for the next month. Cost of sales for July is expected to be $900.
[3] Beginning inventory for January is $200.

Operating Expenses:

(in $000s)	Jan.	Feb.	March	April	May	June	Total
Salaries, wages and benefits	$30	$30	$30	$30	$30	$30	$180
Commissions[1]	50	60	80	40	60	95	385
Personnel costs	80	90	110	70	90	125	565
Rent[2]	80	80	80	80	80	80	480
Depreciation	40	40	40	40	40	40	240
Insurance[3]	10	10	10	10	10	10	60
Miscellaneous	10	10	20	10	10	20	80
Total	$220	$230	$260	$210	$230	$275	$1,425

Major assumptions:

[1] Commissions paid to salespersons are 10 per cent of sales.
[2] Rent is paid in the month following its incurrence. December rent expense was $50.
[3] Insurance is paid in January for the entire year — $120.

Step 3. Turning forecasts into cash flow equivalents

A number of adjustments must be made to turn accounting-basis revenue and cost amounts to their cash flow equivalents.

Cash Collections from Customers:

	Jan.	Feb.	March	April	May	June	Total
(in $000s)							
Cash revenue[1]	$100	$150	$200	$100	$300	$250	$1,100
50% of current month's credit revenue[1]	200	225	300	150	150	350	1,375
50% of prior month's credit revenue[1]	400	200	225	300	150	150	1,425
	700	575	725	550	600	750	3,900
GST and provincial sales tax collected	75	105	85	105	80	90	540
Total	$775	$680	$810	$655	$680	$840	$4,440

Notes:

[1]   From Step 1.

Operating Expenditures:

(in $000s)	Jan.	Feb.	March	April	May	June	Total
Expenses[3]	$220	$230	$260	$210	$230	$275	$1,425
Adjustments							
Depreciation[3]	(40)	(40)	(40)	(40)	(40)	(40)	(240)
Rent[1]	(30)						(30)
Insurance[2]	110	(10)	(10)	(10)	(10)	(10)	60
Income tax instalments	50	50	50	50	50	50	300
	310	230	260	210	230	275	1,515
GST paid to suppliers	30	25	25	30	30	50	190
Total	$340	$255	$285	$240	$260	$325	$1,705

Major assumptions:

[1]   Rent is paid in the month following. December rent expense was $50.

[2]   Insurance is paid in January for the entire year — $120.

Notes:

[3]   From Step 2.

Steps 4 – 6. Estimate cash gains and losses; analyze investing cash flow items; calculate excess/deficiency of cash before financing

Before considering financing activities, the information from steps 1, 2 and 3 must be compiled, and other items affecting cash considered.

(in $000s)	Jan.	Feb.	March	April	May	June
Beginning cash balance[1]	$50	$100	$99	$102	$100	$97
Cash receipts:						
Customers[3]	775	680	810	655	680	840
Sale of land[3]					950	
Cash available **A**	825	780	909	757	1,730	937
Cash payments						
Purchases[2]	500	280	420	360	300	465
Operating costs before GST[3]	310	230	260	210	230	275
GST and provincial sales tax paid to suppliers[4]	50	54	50	51	63	101
GST remitted or refunded[5]	40	25	51	35	54	17
Dividends	50					
Capital acquisitions					100	
Total **B**	950	589	781	656	747	858
Minimum cash balance desired	100	100	100	100	100	100
Total cash needs	1,050	689	881	756	847	958
Net cash excess (deficiency) before financing	$(225)	$91	$28	$1	$883	$(21)

Major assumptions:

1   January 1 cash balance was $50.
2   Credit terms from suppliers are n/30. The company does not pay suppliers before the due date. December purchases were $500.

Notes:

3   From Step 3. Includes GST.
4   From Steps 2 and 3.
5   Difference between GST and PST collected from customers and GST paid to suppliers (per Steps 2 and 3 schedules). Net GST and PST owed to (from) the government is remitted (received) one month following the month of collection. At the beginning of January, $40 was owed for these taxes.

PART C

Step 7. Reflect planned financing

A company may have decided it requires financing prior to the cash forecasting exercise. However, through forecasting its cash flows, a company may find it needs financing to achieve its future goals.

(in $000s)	Jan.	Feb.	March	April	May	June
Financing[1]						
Borrowings[2]	$225	$0	$0	$0	$0	$0
Principal payments[3]	0	(90)	(25)	0	(110)	0
Interest payments[2]	0	(2)	(1)	(1)	(1)	0
Net financing effect	$225	$(92)	$(26)	$(1)	$(111)	$0
Investing[4]						
Deposit excess cash	$0	$0	$0	$0	$(775)	$0
Interest earned	0	0	0	0	0	6
Liquidate investments	0	0	0	0	0	15
Net investing effect	$0	$0	$0	$0	$(775)	$21
Net cash excess (deficiency) before financing A–B	$(125)	$191	$128	$101	$983	$79
Net financing effect	$225	(92)	(26)	(1)	(111)	0
Net investing effect	0	0	0	0	(775)	21
Cash balance, end of month	$100	$99	$102	$100	$97	$100

Major assumptions:

[1] The company does not need to borrow until month-end.

[2] The company has arranged a $250,000 line of credit at 12 per cent before or during January that requires only interest payments to be made during the first year. Borrowings must be in $5,000 blocks. Interest is rounded to the nearest $1,000.

[3] Repayments to be made at month-end, and must be in $5,000 blocks.

[4] An interest rate of 9 per cent could be earned in short-term investments that are cashable every 30 day period. Deposits are made at month-end, interest is receivable monthly at the end of the following month and investments can only be made in $5,000 blocks.

Step 8. Compilation of the cash flow forecast

Following is the result of the previous steps in a presentable format:

(in $000s)	Jan.	Feb.	March	April	May	June
Cash receipts:						
Customers[1]	$700	$575	$725	$550	$600	$750
GST and PST collected[1]	75	105	85	105	80	90
Sale of land[2]					950	
Borrowings[3]	225	0	0	0	0	0
Interest on short-term investments[3]	0	0	0	0	0	6
Liquidate investments[3]	0	0	0	0	0	15
Total cash receipts	1,000	680	810	655	1,630	861
Cash payments:						
Purchases[2]	500	280	420	360	300	465
Personnel costs[5]	80	90	110	70	90	125
Rent[5]	50	80	80	80	80	80
Insurance[5]	120					
Miscellaneous[5]	10	10	20	10	10	20
Income tax instalments[1]	50	50	50	50	50	50
GST paid to suppliers[5]	50	54	50	51	63	101
GST and PST remitted to the government[2]	40	25	51	35	54	17
Dividends[2]	50					
Principal repayments[3]		90	25		110	
Interest payments[3]		2	1	1	1	
Acquire investments[3]					775	
Capital aquisitions[3]	0	0	0	0	100	0
Total cash payments	950	681	807	657	1,633	858
Net cash inflow (outflow)	50	(1)	3	(2)	(3)	3
Beginning cash balance	50	100	99	102	100	97
Ending cash balance	$100	$99	$102	$100	$97	$100

Notes:

[1] From Step 3.
[2] From Steps 4 – 6.
[3] From Step 7.
[4] From Step 2.
[5] From Steps 2 and 3.

D

Treasury, Risk Management and Derivatives

The first step in managing financial risk is to understand it. This section provides a guide to the products, techniques and issues involved in managing financial risk in Canada.

407

CHAPTER 17

Financial Risk Management

Overview

The trade-offs between risk and reward drive every business decision. The risk management process requires that management understand the risks and ensure that appropriate strategies are in place to deal with them. Recent business failures remind us that the responsibility for understanding and controlling risk rests at all levels in the organization, from the Board of Directors down.

This chapter discusses how to analyze and manage risks, with a particular focus of financial markets risk, the traditional purview of the treasurer.

Framework for Managing Risk

Categories of risk and reward

The process of risk management cuts across organizational boundaries within a business organization. In recent years, it has become possible to apply more sophisticated tools to analyzing and quantifying risks.

Risks may be classified into four broad categories:

- Financial markets risk;
- Credit risk;
- Business risk;
- Operational risk.

Financial markets risk is the risk of "losing money in the market," that is, losses resulting from changes in market values such as interest rates, foreign exchange rates, equity prices or commodity prices. Previously, this was the area focused upon when a treasurer referred to "risk management."

Credit risk is the risk of a debtor "breaking its promise," that is, not fulfilling its obligations. This is the risk of the debtor being unable, unwilling or otherwise less likely to repay its debts.

Business risk is the risk where "the plans are wrong," that is, the assumptions underlying a business plan fail to reflect what actually happens. This includes risks that can be quantified such as a change in demand for a product due to economic changes or a competitor's behavior. It also includes risks that cannot be quantified such as a new technology or changes in consumer behavior due to government fiscal measures.

Operational risk is the risk of "something going wrong," that is, loss due to human error, processing mistakes, theft or fraud, technical failures or physical catastrophe. This is the risk upon which traditional insurance products focus.

While different tools are employed for dealing with each type of risk, there are common elements and principles. In larger organizations, these different risks are dealt with in different areas, although in the final analysis there is usually a "Chief Worry Officer," such as the CEO or CFO who is concerned about all of these categories. A recent development initiated by financial institutions but now being imitated by a few large manufacturing companies is the concept of a "Chief Risk Officer" to formally assess and monitor risks across the organization.

The key principle underlying any analysis of **risk** is that of **reward**: the reason for assuming any risk is the hope of achieving a commensurate reward. Risk and reward are key elements of any business decision. It is impossible to eliminate risk, but it is possible to assess it qualitatively and quantitatively and ensure that the possible benefits make sense. Nor would we want to eliminate risk, since that would reduce the prospective rewards.

In the past, the notion of a trade-off between risk and reward was applied primarily to **financial risk** management. It is now evident that this concept is also a powerful tool in analyzing the other categories of risk as well: **business risk, operational risk and credit risk**. In financial markets it has been well-established that non-systematic risks can be diversified away by investing in a portfolio of securities. Similarly, other categories of risk may also be diversified away by holding a variety of investments, selling into different markets, or carrying out different business activities.

PART D

411

Steps to manage risk

The process of managing any risk can be divided into four steps. These steps provide a framework around the process of risk management. They do not provide concrete guidance as to the specific strategies to be followed.

- Identify the risk;
- Quantify the exposure, if possible;
- Determine the effect of the exposure on business strategies;
- Select a strategy for dealing with the risk.

These steps are elaborated on below with particular reference to managing financial markets risk.

Corporate policy and risk management

Fundamental to the risk management process is that financial objectives and strategies for the enterprise as a whole and its individual business units must be clearly understood. For that to occur, corporate strategies and objectives must be clearly set out and used as the starting point for determining financial strategies.

Recent business failures remind us that responsibility for understanding and controlling risk rests at all levels — from the Board of Directors down. At a policy level, risk management should be approved by the Board. Effective management control of financial risks requires that senior management understand the nature of the enterprise's financial risks and clearly articulate a strategy for dealing with those risks. This requires effective lines of communication to ensure that the use of financial instruments occurs in a way that is consistent with corporate objectives.

Financial risk management can be complex because it cuts across the organizational hierarchy so that risk positions can be consolidated and evaluated. The basic design of a risk management system depends upon fundamental matters such as the level of centralization or decentralization in the organization. Should divisions or departments be responsible for financial risks resulting from their business activity? Or should such risks be controlled centrally, normally through the corporate treasury? Such considerations form the basis for the design of the risk management process.

Risk management systems should be an integral part of the management information system and the information flowing through the organization. The combination of corporate policies and the risk management system must be able to:

- identify the different financial risks;
- enforce common standards for risk taking and measurement of risk; and
- be decision-oriented and produce information useful for making specific decisions.

Financial risk management is often assumed to be more an art than a science. However, the process lends itself to quantification and consequently a considerable degree of rigor is possible. Unlike many other business risks, it is possible to quantify the amount of risk being taken and compare that to the organization's appetite for financial risk.

Financial Market Risk

Market risk refers to the risk of loss arising from changes in the market value of a financial instrument. This could also be expressed as the risk of loss arising due to volatility in the market. Market risk can be classified by its nature:

PART D

- *General market risk* — the risk of loss arising from an adverse market movement unrelated to the specific financial instrument involved.
- *Specific market risk* — the risk of loss caused by an adverse price movement in the particular financial instrument.
- *Systemic market risk* — the risk that a disruption in a particular segment of the financial market may cause widespread difficulties in other areas.
- *Liquidity risk* — risk that a party may not be able to liquidate or close out a position in financial instruments at close to its apparent market value. Note that liquidity risk from the perspective of many regulators and financial institutions is sufficiently significant that it is treated as a risk separate from general market risk. However, for our purposes, we can treat liquidity risk as simply adding to the uncertainty of market valuation.

Market risk can be analyzed by considering the fundamental elements that influence the price of a financial instrument in the market. These are as follows:

- *Price or rate or delta risk* — this is the exposure to a change in the value of a financial instrument that corresponds to a particular change in the price of an underlying asset.
- *Convexity or gamma risk* — this is the exposure to changes in delta risk as market levels move. For example, if interest rates change, the delta risk may change even though no other changes have occurred.
- *Basis or correlation risk* — this is the risk of a difference arising between the price performance of two different financial instruments. For example, an exposure to interest rate risk (a "long" position) might be hedged with an opposite (or "short") exposure in another interest rate risk instrument. To the extent that the two instruments do not move togeth-

er, the result will be basis risk. Basis risk is also frequently used in a narrower sense: the difference between the pricing of an exchange traded future and the underlying instrument upon which it is based.

- *Discount rate or rho risk* — this is the risk of a change in the value of a financial instrument due to a change in the rate used for discounting future cash flows.

- *Volatility or vega risk* — this represents the exposure to a change in the value of a financial instrument resulting from a change in the expected volatility of the price of an underlying asset. This type of risk only pertains to options because only in the case of options is volatility expressly included in the determination of the market value.

- *Time decay or theta risk* — this represents the exposure to a change in the value of a financial instrument due to the passage of time. An example of this might be the present value of a zero-coupon bond increasing steadily over time due solely to the passage of time, assuming that interest rates remain unchanged. Another example is in the case of an option which will lose value as time goes by if all else remains equal.

To the extent that there is a lack of liquidity in the financial markets, uncertainty arises with respect to the amount at which particular financial instruments may be reversed or unwound.

Many financial instruments are inherently quite illiquid. For example, over the counter transactions with financial institutions, purchases of shares of relatively small capitalizations, and debt contracts between financial institutions and borrowers are by their very nature not liquid. Nonetheless, various techniques have arisen for enhancing their liquidity.

Market risk is controlled by updating the market value of the portfolio frequently and by understanding the effect on portfolio value of market value changes. Modelling the impact of market movements can range from a simple "what if?" analysis on a spreadsheet to a complex Monte Carlo simulation, depending upon the size and structure of the financial risks being taken. The key is that management understand the nature and amount of the market risks being taken.

Underlying most analyses of market price risk is the assumption that market prices vary continuously from one trade to the next. This assumption has been proven wrong during numerous market shocks of the last two decades. In fact, the methodology for quantifying risk has been thrown into question. This is discussed further towards the end of this chapter.

The process of managing financial markets risk can be divided into four steps. These steps are:

- Identify the risk;
- Quantify the exposure;
- Determine the effect of the exposure on business strategies;
- Select risk management products.

Identify the risk

The first step in managing financial markets risk is to ensure a clear understanding of the nature of the risk. What are the underlying economic and business factors that create the exposure? It is important to be very clear on the direction of the exposure. If the Canadian dollar becomes weaker relative to the U.S. dollar, does that have a positive or negative impact? For a company that purchases source materials or supplies outside of Canada payable in another currency or that sells its finished goods in the export market, the effect of foreign exchange fluctuations can be very significant.

Another factor to consider in assessing the source of exposure to financial risk is contingent exposure. Future exposure to foreign exchange, for example, may be contingent upon increasing sales or winning a particular contract. Exposure that is contingent may require a different approach to risk management compared to exposure that is absolute or not contingent.

It may be beneficial to actually write out a paper discussing the sources of risk and creating simple cash flow projections or even diagrams to identify the precise nature of the risk. All four general classes of financial risk should be considered — interest rate risk, currency risk, commodity price risk and equity risk.

Quantify the exposure

Quantifying financial risk is generally done by measuring the effect on income of the risk. A conceptually straightforward, yet powerful way to do this is to perform a sensitivity analysis of net income as the sources of risk, such as interest rates or foreign exchange rates are varied. This can be done by modelling future cash flows of the company and then considering the effect on income and cash as the financial parameters are varied. For example, quantification of interest rate exposure would be done by reviewing mismatches of assets and liabilities and considering the impact on interest expense if refinancing occurs at market rates.

Similarly, the impact of foreign exchange exposure can be assessed by preparing cash flow forecasts for flows in different foreign currencies and reviewing the impact in Canadian dollars under different assumptions as to future exchange rates. This sort of analysis is often based upon simplifying assumptions that later must be re-examined. Nonetheless, there is considerable merit in taking a "big picture" perspective at the outset and later narrowing the focus.

PART D

Effect of exposure on strategies

There is no reward without commensurate risk. A degree of introspection is required to assess whether a particular risk *should* be managed and why. The critical question is to consider how the risk management process will enhance shareholder value. An extreme case of this might be a gold mine which could completely eliminate its commodity price risk by selling its future production in the forward markets. However, investors in the company probably expect that the market value of their investment will vary in the same direction as the market price of gold. Consequently, hedging that risk may not enhance shareholder value. However, in other cases, assumption of financial risk could represent a distraction or at least an inappropriate outcome for a company. In that case, it would be appropriate to hedge the exposure.

A sensible risk management program should follow logically from the company's overall corporate strategy. In fact, financial risk management should be an integral part of the company's overall business and financial strategy. As noted above, overall corporate policies provide a framework and foundation for assessing the appropriate level of financial risk.

Select risk management products

The range of products available to risk managers range from the relatively mundane, such as bonds and fixed income products, to arcane and exotic instruments. An initial decision must be made as to the products and markets that the company will use as part of its risk management program.

It can be useful to visualize the financial markets as existing along several different dimensions or axes.

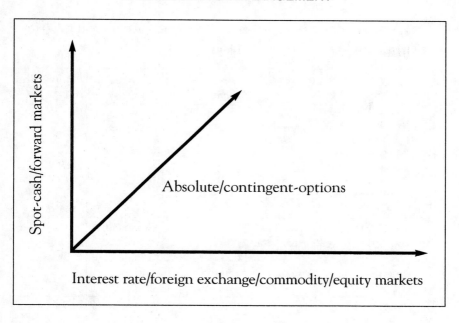

The first dimension is the type of risk being managed: *interest rate risk, foreign exchange risk, commodity price risk,* or *equity price risk*. For each of these markets, products are available in the *spot* or *cash market* or in the *forward markets*. Another dimension to consider is "*absolute*" products that have symmetrical or bilateral outcomes, versus *option* or *contingent* products that have asymmetrical or single-sided pay-offs. Finally, yet another (fourth) dimension to consider is *over-the-counter products* that are obtained as customized solutions from banks and investment dealers versus *exchange traded* products which are also available through banks and investment dealers but represent products traded on a public exchange with standardized terms and conditions.

PART D

Specific financial instruments represent various combinations of products along the dimensions:

		Interest rate risk	Foreign exchange risk	Commodity price risk	Equity price risk
Spot/cash	OTC*	Bonds Treasury bill	Foreign exchange spot	Commodity sales	Private placements
	Exchange*				Common shares Preferred shares
Forward-Absolute	OTC	Forward rate agreements Interest rate swaps	Foreign exchange Cross-currency swaps	Commodity forwards Commodity swaps	Equity swaps
	Exchange	BA futures Eurodollar futures	Foreign exchange futures	Commodity futures	Index futures
Forward-Option	OTC	Interest rate options — caps, floors, collars Swaptions	Foreign currency options — puts, calls, collars Currency swaptions	Commodity options — puts, calls, collars Commodity swaptions	Stock options puts, calls Share swaptions
	Exchange	BA options Bond options Eurodollar options	Currency options	Commodity options	Share options Warrants

* OTC = Over the counter
* Exchange = Exchange traded

The characteristics of various financial products are discussed in the next two chapters. The following is a brief summary of the advantages and disadvantages of different types of products:

Type of product	Advantages	Disadvantages
Spot or cash products	Simple to use and understand	May be cumbersome since investment properties cannot be isolated
Forward products — over-the-counter	Flexible — can be completely customized to suit user's needs	Potentially illiquid Need to establish credit line with bank
Forward products — exchange traded	Liquidity and transparent and efficient pricing	Lack of flexibility May have basis risk Bookkeeping and monitoring required due to margin requirements

PART D

Credit risk

Credit risk, also called default risk or counterparty risk, is the risk of a loss being incurred if a counterparty defaults on a financial instrument. The loss due to a default is the cost of replacing the financial instrument, less any recovery. Thus, for there to be any credit risk, the financial instrument must have a positive market value (that is the financial instrument is "in the money") *and* the counterparty must default. Corporate treasurers need to consider credit risk from two perspectives: the risk that their company will lose if their counterparty (usually a bank) defaults, and the risk that *their* company represents to the bank.

A related type of risk is *settlement risk* which occurs when an exchange of payments is made, for example in the case of foreign exchange forwards or cross currency swaps. This is the risk that the counterparty will fail to meet its obligations for the contract and not remit funds in exchange for funds that have been disbursed.

The amount of credit risk varies depending upon the attributes of the particular financial instrument. The following are some of the factors that will lead to a change in the amount of credit risk:

- The *time to maturity* of the financial instrument — the greater the time remaining until maturity, the greater the risk of a decline in the credit quality of the counterparty;
- The *volatility of the market* — changes in the market price of the financial instrument directly influenced the amount of credit exposure, and
- *Exchanges of principal* amounts which result in *settlement risk* — settlement risk will often be many times greater than the credit exposure that otherwise arises in the case of a financial instrument.

The unusual aspect of credit risk involved in most financial instruments is that the amount is uncertain because it depends upon market price movements. The loss due to a default in the case of a financial instrument is the cost of replacing the instrument less any recovery. Thus a loss can occur only if there is a default **and** the derivatives contract has a positive mark-to-market value (is "in the money") to the non-defaulting party. Unless both conditions occur, there can be no credit loss. The replacement cost equals the net present value, at the time of the default, of the expected future cash flows.

The underlying *principles* involved in managing and measuring credit risk in derivatives transactions are essentially the same as those for other financial instruments such as accounts receivable or bank loans. The same principles of sound credit management for other items on a balance sheet also apply to derivatives. However the amount at risk is not the face value or principal amount of the instrument, so that *measurement* of the risk can be complex.

In the case of off-balance sheet financial instruments, credit risk should be measured in two ways:

- *Current exposure,* which is the replacement cost or market value of outstanding contracts. As noted above, replacement cost equals the net present value, at the time of the default, of the expected future cash flows. If the market value is negative, there is no current credit exposure.
- *Potential future exposure,* which is an estimate of the maximum likely future replacement cost of the derivatives contract. It is determined based upon probability analysis of likely movements in market rates over the term of the contract. The analysis should be based upon predetermined parameters, that is, how "likely" (or how probable) a movement in market rates should be considered.

Credit risk fluctuates over time with the variables that determine the value of the derivative contract. In the case of an interest rate swap, the variable is interest rates. For a cross currency swap, the variable would be exchange rates.

For example, consider a company that has entered into a five-year floating-to-fixed interest rate swap with a bank. The agreement provides that the company receives fixed interest payments semi-annually at 7 per cent per annum, and pays floating interest payments semi-annually at bankers' acceptance rates (BA) + 1 per cent. Since entering into the swap, fixed rates have declined to 5.5

PART D

per cent, so that the net present value of the remaining cash flows is $100,000 — this represents the amount that the swap is "in-the-money" for the company. In this example, we assume that floating rates of BA + 1 per cent represent the company's normal cost of floating funds, so as interest rates change there will be no gain or loss on the floating side. (In analysing the effect of fixed interest rate changes, it is useful to consider that the company is in a similar position as if it held a bond — as interest rates decline, the market value of the bond increases.) Therefore, the current credit exposure is $100,000, which represents the amount of credit risk that the company has now with its bank. (In this example, the bank has no credit risk with the company, since the swap is out-of-the-money to the bank.)

The company has undertaken an analysis of market interest rates over the remaining life of the swap, and concluded that the present interest rates of 5.5 per cent are unlikely to rise or fall by more than 2.0 per cent. A rise of 2.0 per cent, to 7.5 per cent would represent a loss of $150,000; a fall of 2.0 per cent, to 3.5 per cent, a further gain of $150,000.

This can be summarized as follows:

	Interest rates		
	3.5%	5.5%	7.5%
Current exposure	$100,000	$100,000	$100,000
Possible change	150,000		(150,000)
Total	$250,000	$100,000	$ (50,000)
Possible exposure	$250,000	$100,000	$ nil

Thus, over the life of the swap, possible future exposure may range from $250,000 to zero; present credit risk is $100,000.

The actual methodologies for calculating possible credit exposure can be quite complex, and for many corporations probably not necessary. This does not mean that credit risk should be ignored, rather that a precise calculation would not be very useful. It is necessary to have an understanding of the magnitude of current exposure, and how exposure may change as the market moves.

An ironic aspect of credit exposure is that it only exists if the derivative value changes to the company's benefit. There is no current credit exposure in the case of a contract that is a loser ("out-of-the-money").

Various types of credit enhancement are available to reduce credit risk on financial instruments. Several U.S. derivatives houses have set up special purpose derivatives subsidiaries that have been structured so that they receive a AAA credit rating from credit ratings agencies.

Credit risk can also be reduced through proper documentation provisions such as ensuring that credit exposure on derivatives ranks equally with other obligations of an issuer (*pari passu* clauses). In addition, provisions to put up collateral or to renegotiate the financial instrument at various intervals by paying out any market value also serve to substantially reduce credit exposure. Bilateral and multilateral netting are becoming more popular as techniques to reduce credit exposure, although these are primarily used between large financial institutions. It is likely that over time such provisions will become more common between large corporations and their banks.

The best way to reduce credit risk from dealings in financial derivatives is to comply with the normal principles of prudent

PART D

credit management. It is important to "know your customer" and to keep apprised of any changes in its financial situation or management. Many well run companies have effective procedures for monitoring the credit of their customers. Similar procedures should also be in place to monitor the credit capacity of their financial institution counterparties.

Business risk

Uncertainties underlie the business planning process. Business risk is the risk where "the plans are wrong," that is, the assumptions underlying a business plan fail to reflect what actually happens. This includes risks that can be quantified such as a change in demand for a product due to economic changes or a competitor's behavior. It also includes risks that cannot be quantified such as a new technology or changes in consumer behavior due to government fiscal measures.

With the constant change in the business environment, business risk is the most dangerous as well as the least understood category of risk facing corporations. It is most often evidenced by a company executing a strategy that in hindsight turns out to have been ill-advised.

An example of a shifting environment creating a high level of business risk is the story of Confederation Life Insurance Company, the fourth largest life insurance company in Canada, in 1993. Confederation Life was shut down and liquidated in 1994, with losses of $1.3 billion, because it concentrated its energies and assets in real estate at a time when prices were at an all-time high. This became a classic example of using incorrect assumptions to drive a strategic plan.

Confederation Life is a good example of business risk because it shows how it can be difficult to distinguish business risk from other risk categories. After all, it was falling real estate prices (arguably, financial markets risk) and losses on loans (credit risk), as well as poor management oversight (operational risk) that led to its demise. But in this case, it was errors in that company's strategy that ultimately created the problems. The profound lesson is that had there been adequate analysis and monitoring of those other risks, earlier warning would have been provided and corrective action could have been taken.

A specific category of business risk is worthy of separate discussion: legal and regulatory risk. This refers to uncertainties or incorrect assumptions as to the legal and regulatory environment in which the business operates. As a result, the environment may change in an unexpected manner.

The enforceability of financial instrument contracts is a risk that participants face in complex financial transactions. This was highlighted in the *Hammersmith and Fulham* case decided in 1991. The U.K. House of Lords concurred with the judgment of lower courts and ruled that local authorities (municipal governments) in the U.K. that had been active participants in the market for interest rate swaps in the mid 1980s, lacked the legal capacity to enter into those transactions. Therefore, the derivative transactions entered into were void. The effect of this judgment was to nullify agreements between 130 municipal councils in the United Kingdom and about 80 banks. The resulting losses to swap dealers came to about US$150 million.

Any corporation incorporated under a corporations statute (such as the *Canada Business Corporations Act* or the *Ontario Business Corporations Act*) has the rights and responsibilities of a natural person. Therefore, such a corporation can enter into any

PART D

contract that could be entered into by a natural person. However, special purpose corporations that are incorporated under a special statute, letters patent, or some other method, may only have such rights and responsibilities as are specified in their corporate charter. Therefore, it is important for anyone dealing with any entity, other than a business corporation incorporated under a corporations act or a financial institution, to ensure that the counterparty has the legal authority to enter into the transaction. Some potential legal risks have been reduced through legislation subsequent to the *Hammersmith and Fulham* case. Nonetheless, a prudent corporation would consult legal counsel before dealing with a counterparty other than a financial institution or business corporation.

Operational risk

Operational risk is the risk of "something going wrong," that is, loss due to breakdown in administrative controls, procedures or operational routines. It encompasses losses due to human error, processing mistakes, theft or fraud, technical failures or physical catastrophe. This is the risk upon which traditional insurance products focus.

Operational disasters and catastrophes may have a remote chance of occurring, but when they do happen, the results can be, well, catastrophic. Contingency planning, back-up procedures, as well as comprehensive insurance cover are all techniques used to deal with this risk.

In addition to risks affecting any area of the company, operation risk in treasury operations can be subdivided into procedural risk, systems risk and management risk.

Procedural risk is the risk of errors occurring due to breakdowns in the processing routine or internal controls. These risks can be limited by a clearly defined organization structure specifying the division of duties between the treasury officers who enter into the transactions and accounting staff who record it. Procedural risk is also reduced by a clearly defined mandate of the organization and a well understood strategy for entering into financial instrument transactions.

In larger treasury operations, various computer systems and computerized spreadsheets may be required for valuation, position, and risk analysis. *Systems risk* is the risk of systems — both manual and automated — not producing accurate and reliable information. This may result in inaccurate credit risk measurement, market risk measurement, misstatement of income or errors in reporting transactions. Systems risk is minimized by having a well-established procedure in place to control the consummation of new transactions, testing procedures in place for new models, and effective oversight by management over the treasury operation.

A related risk is that a company's management does not understand or adequately control its exposure to the financial markets. This risk, sometimes called *management risk*, increases as the complexity of financial instruments increases. Management risk can be reduced by:

- clearly articulated and predefined strategies to ensure that a company's financial instruments transactions fall within pre-established risk parameters;
- the oversight of informed and involved management and executive management;
- clearly laid out policies and procedures that set out mechanisms such as credit controls and appropriate management reports;
- an accounting and administration support area that is independent of those who enter into treasury transactions and

PART D

429

that has technology appropriate to monitor and control the financial instruments portfolio, and

- an appropriate level of education of staff and management.

In larger treasury operations the following additional controls are appropriate:

- an independent internal audit function to verify that the control process is operating in a satisfactory manner and that transactions are complete and recorded correctly, and
- the establishment of an independent risk management function that monitors day-to-day activity independently of the accounting support area and the treasury dealers.

Other risks

Virtually all risks faced by a business organization can be placed into one of the four categories discussed above. Some analyses identify additional major categories, such as liquidity risk, which we included in financial markets risk.

There are additional types of risk that do not neatly fit into the framework set out here. Rather than force them into the framework, we list them separately.

Tax risk is the situation where the determination of income for tax purposes is at variance with the economic substance of the transaction. Consequently, there may be tax exposure in an unexpected or surprising manner. In Canada, many transactions are tax neutral because the tax accounting should follow the financial accounting principles. Nonetheless, there is often some uncertainty as to the tax effect of a particular transaction.

Accounting risk has received considerable press in American publications because sometimes desirable risk management practices produce anomalous results for accounting purposes. In Canada, in general, financial accounting should be consistent with the economic substance of the transaction so that accounting risk is minimal. However, anomalous results do arise from time to time particularly with instruments that are on the leading edge of financial risk management. Financial reporting and accounting is discussed in more detail in Chapter 2. Unfortunately, in recent cases, accounting risk has come to refer to accounting or audit failure — the risk of intense control breakdowns that result in incorrect financial reporting.

Systemic risk refers to the risk that a disruption at a particular firm, in a market segment, in the settlement system, or in some other area in the financial system will cause widespread difficulties in financial markets. This risk is of great concern to regulators and governments. There is not a great deal that an individual corporation can do about systemic risk other than to comply with the prudent practices of financial risk management set out above.

Other risks include risks that cannot be anticipated or identified. For example, before the *Hammersmith and Fulham* case, enforceability of contracts was considered to be of limited concern. Market discontinuities such as the market fall in October 1987, the early 1990s and 2000-2002 suggest that there may be market risks that are not properly captured by the standard statistical models that are used. There is not much that can be done to control a risk that is not known to exist — except to emphasize the importance of controlling those risks that have been identified.

Quantifying Risk

Using the risk category framework in this chapter, financial market risk and credit risk can be readily quantified, whereas business risk and operational risk cannot really be quantified — at least, not very easily (although, of course, insurance companies must able to

PART D

quantify the risks for which they provide coverage.) Risks that cannot be quantified should still be analyzed and managed.

Most assets or liabilities subject to financial market risk or credit risk are financial instruments.

All financial instruments can be analyzed as one or more cash flows. These cash flows may be absolute (that is, they are certain to occur), or they may be contingent (that is they may or may not occur) as in the case of options and option-type financial instruments.

The market value of a financial instrument is, by definition, the same as the discounted present value of those future cash flows. In the case of absolute cash flows the formula is relatively straightforward, although the discount rate may be subject to some debate or uncertainty.

There are numerous mathematical approaches to analyzing financial markets risk and return. Two fundamental techniques are used.

One method is to estimate the maximum likely loss that a portfolio is subject to, based upon estimates as to the volatility and the liquidity of the market. "Value at Risk" and similar methods use simulation or analysis to estimate the maximum loss that can occur, say, 95 per cent or 99 per cent of the time. One difficulty has been that despite all the theory, losses have occurred that vastly exceed the estimates. This is due to discontinuities, lack of liquidity, and other problems that happen during times of significant adverse market movements. There are also theoretical problems in assessing very unlikely events.

Another approach is to produce a "risk adjusted rate of return" that takes into account the risk assumed (based upon expected or historic volatility). Popular measures include RAROC (Risk-Adjusted Return On Capital), EVA (Economic Value Added) and even NPV (Net Present Value). With EVA, the cost of capital is subtracted from the return. NPV is essentially a form of EVA that covers more than one year.

Internal controls

Good control practices

Management of financial risk can be a very simple or a very complex activity depending upon the nature of the financial portfolio. However, even where a corporation has a straightforward inventory or position of financial instruments, it can generate information that is of interest to many different areas within the corporation and to many different levels of management.

A risk management system is an integral part of the corporation's management information system. It must be able to identify financial risks, set common standards for risk taking and measurement, and be oriented to facilitating decisions.

The *Group of Thirty*, a Washington-based organization, released an authoritative summary of good control practices over derivatives and financial instruments. They recommended that corporate treasurers should follow some of the same disciplines appropriate for dealers:

> As appropriate to the nature, size, and complexity of their derivative activities, end users should adopt the same valuation and market risk management practices that are recommended for dealers. Specifically, they should consider regularly marking-to-market their derivative transactions for risk management purposes; periodically forecasting the cash investing and funding requirements arising

PART D

433

from their derivative transactions; and establishing a clearly independent and authoritative function to design and assure adherence to prudent risk limits.

The first specific technique mentioned was to *track the market value* of the instruments. Even if derivatives are used to hedge a risk, there is always the possibility that the hedge may be less effective than planned. It is good practice to know the market value of financial instruments used as a full or partial hedge and compare that to gains or losses on the position being hedged. This is particularly important when a hedge is put on in anticipation of future transactions: in general, proper accounting treatment will require that hedge gains or losses be used to adjust the book value of the future transaction.

The second management practice recommended was to *periodically forecast the cash investing and funding requirements arising from derivatives transactions.* The frequency and precision of cash flow forecasts would depend upon the level of complexity of the portfolio of financial instruments. At the very least, the company's regular cash flow forecast should incorporate funding needs related to the use of derivatives.

A simple example of a cash flow forecast might be taking into account the effect of a floating-to-fixed interest rate swap in changing effective interest expense. In other cases, forward foreign exchange contracts, forward rate agreements, futures and options might have cash flow effects that differ significantly from their income statement impacts. For more complex portfolios, funding forecasts would take into account payment mismatches.

Forecasts should also examine the potential impact of special credit provisions that might require (or produce) cash. These include contractual provisions to unwind (pay out the market value of) financial instruments if credit covenants are breached, and agreements to pay out additional collateral.

The third recommendation was to *establish a clearly independent and authoritative function to design and assure adherence to prudent risk limits.* This may not appear to be a practical requirement, particularly for smaller treasury operations. However, as the volume of activity increases it becomes important for there to be a degree of independent oversight. It is corporate end users who are most likely to suffer unexpected losses resulting from breakdown in their internal control and management systems: a premise supported by periodic press reports. Financial institutions may have a greater level of risk, but they also have control systems in place, including independent risk management functions.

Speculative activity

The Appendix sets out an internal control checklist that is appropriate for both investment portfolios and speculative or trading activity. However, in the case of active trading of financial instruments, certain additional controls are appropriate. For the controls listed above, daily reporting — or reporting on some more frequent basis — is appropriate. In addition, there should be a separate area in the organization that independently monitors risk assumed by the trading process. In an active trading operation, the risk limits by portfolio need to be controlled using state-of-the-art simulation or modelling techniques. The next two chapters review management of interest rate risk and foreign exchange risk.

Microcomputers

Many financial risk management operations are controlled using microcomputers. The microcomputer environment is inherently difficult to control because the machines are designed to facilitate ease of use. Nonetheless, it is possible to install adequate controls by ensuring that new programs are tested and documented, back up procedures are in place, and that input is reconciled to output where feasible.

PART D

Appendix 17A

Internal controls checklist

The following checklist is designed to assess internal controls over the financial risk management process. Not all controls will be appropriate in all cases since materiality, risk and cost need to be taken into account.

	Yes	No	N/A	Comments
1. Have risk management policies been approved by the Board of Directors?				
2. Is the mandate and the objective of the financial management process clearly specified?				
3. Is there effective management supervision over financial risk? (a) Are reports useful and do they cover an appropriate level of detail? (b) Do reports appear at an appropriate frequency?				
4. Is there a process for requiring approvals and authorizations in place? (a) Does a second independent individual approve the transaction? (b) Is the second approval acquired where appropriate? (c) Are there clear rules about who can bind the company?				
5. Is management knowledgeable as to financial risk management and the products available?				

FINANCIAL RISK MANAGEMENT

	Yes	No	N/A	Comments
6. Are market values calculated frequently?				
7. Are there position limits for every portfolio? (a) Are there sub-limits by maturity period? (b) Is value at risk measured and limited?				
8. Are there concentration limits in place to ensure that an excessive position is not accumulated with any one counter party or in any particular market?				
9. Are liquidity limits in place? (a) Is liquidity measured and controlled?				
10. Are credit limits in place and are position (a) For off balance sheet instruments, is exposure measured as both current exposure and potential exposure?				
11. Is accounting and financial reporting separate from trade execution? (a) Are bank accounts reconciled independently? (b) Are statements from brokers reconciled independently? (c) Are confirmations from financial institutions reviewed independently and promptly?				
12. Are market values obtained independently of the trade execution area?				

	Yes	No	N/A	Comments
13. Are there adequate controls over computers and computer systems? (a) Is the process of developing computer systems properly controlled? (b) Are computer reports automatically distributed to the appropriate parties? (c) Are operating and processing controls in place? (d) Are there adequate procedures to ensure back up and recovery?				

CHAPTER 18

Managing Interest Rate Risk and Derivatives

Overview

Interest rate risk is the risk that a movement in interest rates will adversely affect the cash flow or profitability of the enterprise. Management of interest rate risk is a core responsibility of the corporate treasurer.

This chapter discusses techniques for identifying and measuring exposure to interest rate risk, as well as the derivatives and other instruments available for its management.

PART D

Interest Rate Risk

Interest rate exposure arises because assets and liabilities are both sensitive to changes in interest rates. In cases where the interest paid or received is fixed for a period of time, there is still exposure to changes in the value of the asset or liability due to market interest rate changes.

The risk can be demonstrated with an example. Consider a 10-year, $10 million corporate bond, issued at par, with a coupon of 6 per cent, payable semi-annually, when market rates are 6 per cent (payable semi-annually). Assume that one year later, market rates are 7 per cent. The corporation has an economic gain since the present value of its debt repayments, discounted at market rates, will now be less than $10 million. The lender has an economic loss, for the same reason.

This risk is not captured by an accounting system that follows the "historical cost convention" but will manifest itself in unusually high or low returns over some later period of time. In the example above, at 6 per cent interest, the corporation pays $600,000 per annum for the use of a loan of $10 million. If it were to borrow that amount when interest rates are 7 per cent, it would have had to pay $700,000 per annum. The economic gain of $100,000 per annum may show up in the company's results, but it will be hidden as a reduction in interest costs from what they otherwise would have been. (Firms that *trade* financial instruments, including financial institutions, would generally report market gains and losses as they occur.)

This risk is not just of theoretical concern. Interest rate yields on Canadian three-month treasury bills have ranged from over 21 per cent in 1981, 6.5 per cent in 1987, 14 per cent in 1990 and less than 2 per cent in 2000. Changes in long-term rates have not been as dramatic, but there has, nonetheless, been considerable fluctuation. This has had a significant effect on the financial welfare of lenders and borrowers.

Traditional methods of managing interest rate exposure sufficed for most corporations until about three decades ago. Until that time, there was limited volatility in rates and issuing long-term corporate bonds involved significant costs and delays. It was normal for bond issues to require three to six months to go from the prospectus stage to being issued. There was little chance of the corporation being seriously hurt by fluctuations in interest rates. This era came to an abrupt end in the late 60s and early 70s, when the effects of inflation and a breakdown of international fixed exchange rates had significant effects around the world. The present environment is of volatility in interest rates as well as foreign exchange rates.

Debt issues are no longer brought to market with three month delays. "Bought" deals may be transacted in a matter of hours — or less. Today, the treasurer must make quick decisions to take advantage of windows of opportunity in the debt markets. The change in the volatility of interest rate movements has resulted in an increasing number of debt products becoming available to the corporation to assist in managing interest rate risk.

Balance Sheet Mismatches

To discuss interest rate risk management, it is necessary to agree on what is meant by "interest rate risk". At first blush, it would appear rather simple: A borrower is at risk of having to pay more interest if rates increase, and an investor or lender is at risk of receiving less interest if rates decline. In fact, interest rate risk is a little more subtle.

Interest rate risk results from timing mismatches or gaps between the setting of rates on a borrower's liabilities and the rates of return earned on the assets. This is easy to see in the case of a financial institution or other enterprises whose assets are primarily financial. It may be harder to relate this concept of risk to typical corporations, where any assets other than working capital consist primarily of capital assets: buildings, land, equipment and capitalized leases, which generate relatively stable long-term rates of return. When such an enterprise fixes its cost of funds for a shorter-term horizon than the expected life of the asset (which is often the case), it is in exactly the same position as a financial institution which borrows short-term funds to purchase long-term assets. Both the corporation and the financial institution would then have exposed themselves to financial risk if interest rates increased.

Conversely, a corporation or financial institution that borrowed long-term fixed rate funds to finance assets of which rates of return vary frequently, would be exposed to potential losses due to lower interest rates as the assets yield lower returns in the current market. Of course, a decline in interest rates would result in a gain since the assets would then yield more than the level of interest that was expected.

Two borrowers that appear very similar — and have similar balance sheet structures — can have quite different interest rate risk exposures. *In some industries, interest rate exposure stems more from instability of the rate of return on their assets than from the maturity structure of their liabilities.*

Managing Interest Rate Risk

One conclusion from the discussion above might be that the treasurer should endeavour to eliminate maturity gaps in the structure of the balance sheet of the corporation. That is, the term structure of the enterprise's assets and liabilities should be matched. This, however, ignores the fundamental nature of business activity: the acceptance of a calculated risk in return for the prospect of profit.

In fact, many viable hedging proposals are rejected because the elimination of risk invariably reduces the potential rewards. Often senior management will prefer to tolerate existing risks rather than reduce potential returns.

An example of this could be seen in the mining and extraction industries. Gold mines can generally predict their level of costs fairly accurately but cannot predict the selling price of gold: that depends upon the market at the time of sale. There is a well developed forward market that permits selling future production now for delivery at a future date at an agreed-upon price. It would be quite feasible for a company to sell forward 100 per cent of its gold production and lock in a guaranteed selling price. Many do not, however, because fixing a guaranteed selling price eliminates any prospect of selling for more than that price. As hedging has become accepted practice, it no longer provides a competitive advantage.

Thus, the key to risk management is not merely eliminating risk but rather selecting and structuring a risk reward profile that fits the goals and objectives of the corporation. In fact, because the definition of risk can be so broad, risk will never actually be *eliminated*. Rather, the treasurer may *alter* the risk reward profile of the enterprise.

Off Balance Sheet Products and Derivatives

Many instruments designed to assist in managing interest rate risk are "off balance sheet" products. This is because they represent the exchange of promises to do something in the future. This is in contrast to normal business activity, which is based on a transaction that has already occurred. Assume for example, that a corporation borrows from a bank in exchange for agreeing to repay interest and principal at future dates. This transaction results in the

PART D

immediate recognition on the corporation's balance sheet of an increase in cash and an increase in the liability to repay the cash. Conventional financial reporting is designed to properly reflect this sort of agreement.

In the case of an off balance sheet transaction, there is generally no immediate transaction at all, rather it represents an "executory" contract. For example, an interest rate swap is an agreement to exchange the net amount of two different interest rate calculations, at a future date. Financial reporting has difficulty determining how to record a contract that represents an agreement to do something in the future. The contract may be recorded in the notes to the financial statements, but will not be shown in the balance sheet since it results in changes to neither assets nor liabilities, but rather is a commitment (accounting issues are discussed further in Chapter 20).

Off balance sheet products are also called "derivatives" because their value is derived from a financial metric (such as interest rates).

Thus, the risk management instrument is separate from the security or financial instrument that is on the balance sheet. A floating rate borrower who wishes to limit the risk of floating rates increasing, does not enter into negotiations with his present creditor. Rather, an interest rate swap may be entered into, or a "cap" may be purchased, in either case from a third party. A combination of the two positions — the floating rate debt and the additional financial instrument — will then provide the risk reward profile that the treasurer seeks.

The separation of risk management instruments from underlying securities gives the treasurer flexibility to manage interest rate risk in a volatile environment. The different hedging vehicles permit the treasurer to change the company's risk reward profile as required, without disturbing the pattern of existing assets and liabilities.

Identifying Interest Rate Exposure

In order to identify interest rate exposure, it is necessary to analyze for each borrowing or investment, the following information:

- Is the interest rate fixed or floating?
- What is the actual interest rate, for fixed rate borrowings or investments? What is the interest basis for floating rate items?
- What is the currency of the borrowing or investment? Transactions must be grouped according to currency as movements and interest rates will be different for each. In the case of a transnational enterprise, interest rate risk in different currencies may be handled by different treasury centres.
- What is the maturity date or the period to maturity? This information is required in order to produce a profile of exposure showing the sensitivity to interest rate fluctuations in different time periods. This is also called a gapping report.

The simplest way to analyze information once the data above is available is to do some "what if" analysis on the extent and acceptability of exposure to interest rate changes. Typical questions (which can easily be answered on simple spreadsheet models) may be as follows:

- What will be the impact on the company's profitability if interest rates change as predicted by current forecasts?
- What will the effect on profit be of a 1 per cent increase or a 1 per cent decrease in interest rates? What about a 2 per cent increase or decrease? 4 per cent?
- By how much do interest rates need to move to significantly affect the level of profitability? What is the likelihood of such a movement taking place?

PART D

These questions could be considered on a quarterly, annual or other basis depending on the materiality of the results and the pattern of exposure of the company.

Information Requirements

As noted above, it is not usually meaningful to refer to eliminating risk. Rather the risk profile of the company may be altered in a way that better suits its appetite for risks or rewards. To identify interest rate exposure and to establish an interest rate strategy, the treasurer must consider internal and external forecast information. The internal forecast required is an accurate cash flow forecast (see Chapter 16). It will be necessary to identify the relative degree of certainty of the flows, and forecast items which are particularly uncertain should be appropriately identified. For example, if the treasurer expects interest rates to rise and is certain of a future borrowing requirement, then the full amount of the borrowing may be hedged to lock in a lower interest rate. The hedging instrument to be used would then depend upon the degree of certainty of the borrowing taking place and of the timing of the flow of funds resulting from the borrowing, as well as expectations as to future interest rate movements.

The external information that the treasurer requires is a forecast of interest rates. Interest rates are affected by numerous economic factors including fluctuations in foreign exchange rates and interest rates in other countries. Fiscal and (to a greater extent) monetary policy will also have a significant impact on interest rate changes.

Interest rate forecasts are available from many sources including media reports, economics departments of banks and investment dealers, industry journals and trade associations. From the external forecasts, the corporate treasurer should determine a view of future interest rates. While the amount will change from time to time, it is desirable to publicize it within the enterprise because of the pervasive impact it will have on the company's treasury policy.

Strategies and Policies

Chapter 6 lays out the importance of an investment strategy. Chapters 11 to 13 set out the importance of corporate strategies in general. The appetite of the company to potential gains or losses from assuming interest rate risk must be set by senior management. (In practice, it would be proposed by the treasurer — in writing — and ratified by senior management.) In determining an appropriate level of risk, it is important to have a reasonable amount of sensitivity analysis to determine the likely risks and rewards as market interest rates change. From time to time, there are reports of company treasury departments incurring substantial losses due to unanticipated market movements. It is important that the magnitude of interest rate exposure taken by the company is appropriate to the size of its resources and its appetite for risk.

Characteristics of Interest Rate Management Products

Custom or generic

Financial instruments may be divided between *over the counter* and *exchange traded*.

Over the counter products are generally purchased from banks. They are custom products and contain terms and conditions, amounts, dates and other details as agreed to between the customer and the bank. As a result, there is complete flexibility as to the terms of the contract. However, the corporation may (depending

PART D

on the instrument) require credit approval from the bank, and may be precluded from undertaking contracts for relatively small amounts. An interest rate swap is an over the counter product. While it may be drawn up under the provisions of a "boilerplate" master agreement, its specific conditions will be tailored to the needs of the corporate customer.

Exchange traded instruments are traded on a public exchange. Corporations can purchase and sell exchange traded instruments through brokers. The exchange acts as a clearing house and ensures an orderly market. The corporate customer will be required to put up margin (which often may be in the form of an interest bearing instrument such as a treasury bill) to ensure that the exchange had no credit risk from its activity. The market value of the customer's position will be reviewed daily and compared to the margin posted. Any deficiency will require that the customer produce additional margin. Excess over the required margin may be repaid to the customer upon its request. Interest rate futures trading on various exchanges are examples of exchange traded interest rate risk management products.

Certainty or insurance

Some risk management products represent binding contracts to both parties. In other words, a corporate customer irrevocably reduces its risk profile — in both directions. While exposure to an adverse movement is eliminated, the benefit from a favourable movement is also eliminated. Forward rate agreements, financial futures and interest rate swaps are examples of risk management instruments with this characteristic.

A fundamentally different type of instrument offers *insurance*. These instruments are called options. The purchaser of such an instrument, at its option, decides whether to exercise its rights under the agreement. The protection provided is analogous to that of a conventional insurance policy: the corporation is protected from adverse movements but will still benefit from favourable movements in interest rates. As is the case with conventional insurance, a premium is charged for this protection. Interest rate options including caps, floors, and collars, as well as more exotic products such as swaptions are examples of interest rate management products that offer insurance.

Fixed or floating rates

The choice between fixed and floating rates for financing or investments is a basic dimension available to the treasurer managing exposure to interest rate risk. Once that fundamental decision has been made, a range of financial instruments may be used to modify the risk. The choice of fixed or floating rates is based upon several factors:

- What is the maturity profile of the assets being financed? As noted earlier, even fixed assets eventually "mature".
- What is the gapping position of the corporation's balance sheet overall?
- Is the corporation risk adverse or a risk taker?
- What is the view of future interest rates?
- What access does the corporation have to fixed and floating rate markets? The corporation may have access to fixed funds only at unattractive rates or for reasons of balance sheet structure may not have any access at all.

PART D

Short-term or long-term products

Different financial instruments traditionally have different terms to maturity. Thus, consideration of which instrument is appropriate will depend upon the time frame that is of interest.

Several derivative products have the odd effect of separating their term to maturity from the term structure of interest rates. For example, interest rate swaps and floating rate notes have interest rate risk exposure that differs from the term of the instrument. A conventional five-year bond will be priced at the market interest rate for five year exposure. However, a five-year interest rate swap that pays floating rates will have a legal term of five years but carry short-term interest rate risk. (This assumes that the fixed interest amounts payable by the corporation offset fixed interest rate amounts received by it — see the discussion of interest rate swaps below.)

Types of Interest Rate Management Products

Interest rate futures

An interest rate *future* is a specific type of futures contract. A futures contract is an agreement on an exchange to buy or sell a standard amount of a specified financial instrument, currency or commodity at a fixed price at a particular future date.

The other interest rate risk management instruments discussed in this chapter are "over the counter". These *forwards* represent specific agreements between a company and a financial institution (usually a bank) with customized contractual terms. By contrast, an exchange traded future will have standardized contract terms and trading is conducted on and regulated by a futures exchange. The standardized contract terms will address the number of dollars represented by a contract, the dates on which the contract settlement price is determined, the last date on which the contract can be traded, the minimum price movement and the mechanics for delivery of the amount of the contract upon its expiry.

Selling an interest rate future subjects the seller to the same risk as if, for example, it had borrowed by issuing a bankers acceptance or selling short a bond. Similarly, purchasing a futures contract is the equivalent to placing a deposit (or buying a Guaranteed Investment Certificate at a financial institution), or buying a bond.

To hedge against a decline in interest rates, an investor would buy futures, which is known as a long hedge. To protect against rising interest rates, the investor would sell futures, a short hedge.

Forward rate agreements

A forward rate agreement is often referred to as an FRA. FRAs are used to "fix" or lock in interest rates for periods up to 24 months. The buyer or purchaser of an FRA is protected against increases in interest rates. The seller of an FRA is protected against the decrease in interest rates.

Forward rate agreements are based upon the pricing for three-month bankers' acceptances (BAs) in Canada. For example, an investor might buy a "3 x 6" ("three by six") FRA. This sets today the rate on a 90-day bankers' acceptance in three months. A "4 x 7" FRA sets today the rate on a 90-day bankers' acceptance in four months. Since FRAs are sold "over the counter", they can be structured with terms to meet a customer's needs exactly.

Under the FRA, the seller agrees to pay the purchaser if the market bankers' acceptance rate, on the settlement date, is greater than that specified in the FRA agreement. The cash payment occurs at the beginning of the period specified in the contract (the settlement date). The amount is determined by multiplying the difference between the settlement and contract rate by the amount of the contract and its term. That amount is then discounted back to the settlement date using the settlement rate.

The forward rate agreement does not involve buying or selling the actual underlying bankers' acceptance. Rather, it is a contract between the buyer and seller to compensate each other if the market rate should be higher or lower than the contract rate. Both parties have obligations. If the market rate is higher than the contract rate then the seller must pay the buyer. If the market rate is lower than the contract rate then the buyer must compensate the seller.

A forward rate agreement is similar to an interest rate swap in the effect that it has on managing exposure to interest rate risks. With an FRA, as with a swap, floating rate debt may be converted to fixed rate. If circumstances should change, that effect can be eliminated by unwinding the position through an offsetting transaction.

Interest rate options

Interest rate options are sold under different names depending upon the needs of the purchaser. The most common interest rate options sold are caps, floors, and collars.

Interest rate caps

An interest rate cap places a limit on exposure to floating interest rates. For a fee (option price), the customer (usually a borrower) selects a term to maturity and a maximum interest rate level. The vendor sells an option that provides that the interest expense incurred by the purchaser will not exceed the indicated cap rate. The fee will vary depending upon the maturity, market price and cap rate as well as market conditions at the time the cap is sold.

Interest rate floors

An interest rate floor places a limit on exposure to floating interest rates. For a fee (option price), the customer (generally an investor) selects a term to maturity and a minimum interest rate level. The vendor sells an option that provides that the interest income earned by the purchaser will not be less than the indicated floor rate. The fee will vary depending upon the maturity, market price and floor rate as well as market conditions at the time the floor is sold.

Interest rate collars

An interest rate collar places upper and lower limits on the floating rate of interest. A collar is essentially the purchase of a cap and the sale of a floor at the same time but with different strike rates. With this structure, the purchaser is protected from interest rates above the indicated cap rate while giving up any potential downside gain, if short-term rates are below the indicated floor rate. In effect, the purchaser of a collar is guaranteed that interest rates may float only between the cap rate and the floor rate. The cost of the collar is based upon the difference between the premiums paid to purchase the cap and the premiums received from selling the interest rate floor. Of course, collars may be structured for investors or borrowers.

PART D

Interest rate swaps

An interest rate swap is an agreement between two parties to pay each other a certain rate of interest for a specific period of time. As with the other instruments discussed in this section, interest rate swaps are distinct from the underlying financial instruments that they are based upon.

Vanilla interest rate swaps

Straightforward interest rate swaps are commonly referred to as "vanilla" or plain interest rate swaps. The simplest interest rate swap converts a floating rate of interest into a fixed rate (or vice versa). One party agrees to pay the counterparty a fixed rate of interest. In return, the counterparty agrees to pay the party a floating rate.

In Canada, the fixed rate is set as a spread over the yield on a Government of Canada bond for a similar term. The floating rate is most often based upon the rate of interest paid on Bankers' Acceptances.

Under the interest rate swap agreement, the counterparties agree on how often they will exchange interest flows. Then, on every settlement date, generally semi-annually, the interest owed by each party to the other is calculated and the net amount is exchanged. This continues until the swap matures.

The effect of an interest rate swap is that a borrower or investor that has exposure to floating rates is able to convert the interest income or expense to a fixed rate (or vice versa). This enables it to manage its exposure to movements in interest rates.

Example

The following is an example of how a corporate borrower would use an interest rate swap to convert floating rate interest rate exposure to fixed rate debt.

In this example, assume that the borrower has $20 million of floating rate debt outstanding in the form of three-month bankers' acceptances. The three-month bankers' acceptances currently cost 6 per cent per annum in interest expense. In addition, the company pays a stamping fee to its banker on its bankers' acceptance borrowing of 0.75 per cent. Although the company has borrowed through bankers' acceptances, it is primarily financing fixed assets. Consequently, it would prefer not to have exposure to short-term interest rates but to fix its interest rate expense for the next three years. The current market rate for a three-year swap is 7 per cent.

Example of simple ("vanilla") interest rate swap

Multicorp has financed its fixed assets with floating rate debt. This interest rate swap enables it to convert its floating rate interest obligation to a fixed rate obligation. The underlying debt remains unchanged.

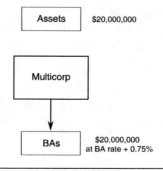

PART D

Current bankers' acceptance rates are 6 per cent, for an all-in cost of 6.75 per cent per annum. The BA rate is reset every quarter, as Multicorp reissues its bankers' acceptances at prevailing market rates.

At present, every three months the company issues $20 million of bankers' acceptances at the prevailing market interest rate. If interest rates go down, the company benefits. If rates go up, the company incurs higher interest expense.

Multicorp has financed its fixed assets with floating rate debt. This interest rate swap enables it to convert its floating rate interest obligation to a fixed rate obligation. The underlying debt remains unchanged.

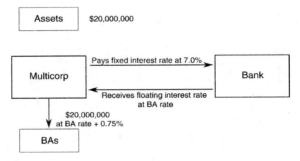

The company now enters into a three-year interest rate swap with a bank. The company agrees to pay the bank a fixed rate of interest of 7 per cent, every six months. The bank agrees to pay the company at the rate on three-month bankers' acceptances compounded quarterly and paid every six months. (Note that there are two floating rate bankers' acceptance settings on the three-month bankers' acceptances during each six-month period.) As set out below, the company has now fixed its interest rate exposure at 7.75 per cent.

The company is paying on its bankers' acceptances at the current bankers' acceptance rate plus the stamping fee of 0.75 per cent.Under the interest rate swap, (a completely separate transaction from the bankers' acceptances themselves), the company receives a floating rate interest flow also determined by bankers' acceptance rate. The net cost is 0.75 per cent. In addition, under the interest rate swap, the company is paying out a fixed rate of 7 per cent. Therefore, the company's total interest expense is 7.75 per cent.

In summary:

Pays on bankers' acceptances issued:	(3-month BA rate) + 0.75%
Receives on interest rate swap:	– (3-month BA rate)
Pays on interest rate swap:	7.0%
Net cost of financing:	(BA rate) + 0.75% – (BA rate) + 7.0% = 7.75%

Thus, Multicorp has converted the floating rate bankers' acceptances into fixed rate debt. The debt will cost 7.75 per cent per annum for three years, regardless of what happens to 3-month BA rates during that time.

Asset swaps

In the example of a vanilla interest rate swap above, the customer uses an interest rate swap to alter the interest expense incurred on its debt (a liability). An asset swap works in the same way as such a liability swap except it is used to convert an asset from one interest rate basis to another. For example, an investor might wish to convert a floating rate asset to a fixed rate asset without selling the original asset. The mechanics of the swap itself are identical.

Delayed start swap

A delayed start swap is a swap in which the fixed rate of interest to be exchanged is determined on the contract date, but the swap itself does not start until an agreed upon future date. The calcula-

PART D

tion of interest flows does not begin until that future date. In the example above, if the 7 per cent rate were agreed today but the swap were not to begin for one year, that would constitute a delayed start swap. Delayed start swaps are used to lock in a future borrowing cost.

Other variations

Interest rate swaps may be customized to the requirements of the customer. As a result, there are many variations, limited only by the imagination of the customer and the banker.

An accreting swap is the swap in which the notional principal on which the interest flows are calculated increases over the term of the swap. An amortizing swap is a swap in which the notional principal decreases over the term of the swap. Swaps can also have up front fees from the bank, offset by higher interest payments over the term of the swap. Swaps can be structured to match any pattern of debt, issuance, and repayment.

CHAPTER **19**

Managing Foreign Exchange Risk and Derivatives

Overview

Foreign exchange risk is the risk that movements in exchange rates will adversely affect the financial position, cash flow or profitability of the enterprise. Management of foreign exchange risk is normally the responsibility of the treasurer.

This chapter discusses techniques for identifying and measuring exposure to foreign exchange risk, as well as the derivatives and other instruments available for its management.

PART D

Foreign Exchange Markets

The size, liquidity and sophistication of global foreign exchange markets parallel the depth, complexity and pervasiveness of international trade. Global foreign change trading volumes were approximately US$1.2 trillion per day in 2001. (This represents a reduction from 1998 volumes of over US$1.4 trillion per day, due in part to the Euro replacing several European currencies and corporate merger and acquisition activity reducing the number of very large companies.)

Only about 14 per cent of transactions have a non-financial customer on one side of the transaction. The trade flows underlying foreign exchange transactions constitute perhaps 5 per cent of the total volume. The balance is financial trading to hedge commitments, or for speculative purposes.

Foreign exchange markets do not consist of physical locations in the sense that the Toronto Stock Exchange has an address. Rather, foreign exchange markets are a global web of banks, other dealers and clients. They are connected to a variety of communications and information sources.

There are three major geographic regions where currencies are traded, covering off different time zones during their hours of highest activity:

- North America — the major centre is New York, but also Chicago, San Francisco and Toronto, as well as other cities.
- Europe — the major centres are London, Frankfurt, Zurich, Amsterdam and Paris.
- Asia — the primary centres are Tokyo, Hong Kong and Singapore, but also Sydney and other cities.

The primary currencies involved in the global foreign exchange markets are the U.S. dollar (90 per cent of all transactions), Euro (38 per cent), Japanese yen (23 per cent), British pound (13 per cent) and the Swiss franc (6 per cent). (Total volumes will add to 200 per cent since each transaction involves two currencies.) U.S. dollar/Euro transactions account for 30 per cent of all trades, the next-largest volume being U.S. dollar/yen at about 20 per cent. Transactions involving the Canadian dollar (almost all of which have the U.S. dollar on the other side) account for about 2 per cent of global volumes.

Central banks play a major role in foreign exchange markets. They are the issuers of currency in each country and are responsible for implementing monetary policy by manipulating (they would say "managing") supply and demand. Some central banks participate actively, others simply try to keep abreast of developments in the market. Their motives differ from those of the other players in that they are concerned with long-term consequences of foreign exchange rates rather than shorter-term speculation.

Brokers are an important element of the foreign exchange market. They bring together buyers and sellers by serving as intermediaries. Brokers are never party to a deal — that is, they do not normally act as principals; rather, they connect the two parties who then deal directly with each other. The brokers have a major impact in improving market liquidity by presenting opportunities to both buyers and sellers.

The terms *clients* or *customers* are used to refer to foreign exchange market participants who are not dealers or brokers, but are end users of foreign exchange. Clients vary from individuals to global organizations. Many larger corporations have their own dealing rooms and in some cases deal quite aggressively. Even smaller corporations often have access to information services so that they are not solely reliant on their banks for market information.

PART D

461

Spot and Forward Transactions

A foreign exchange contract is an agreement to *exchange* foreign currencies at a predetermined date and for predetermined amounts.

A spot transaction is an agreement to exchange currencies immediately, which generally means within two business days or less. (In some cases, transactions that are five days or less in the future are treated as spot transactions.) Normal spot settlement for Canadian dollars and Mexican pesos is the next business day. Normal spot settlement for other currencies is two business days later. Nonetheless, other settlement dates may be established by mutual agreement.

A forward transaction is an agreement to exchange currencies at a future date, where the number of days in the future is greater than that that would count as spot settlement.

The forward exchange rate normally differs from the spot rate. The difference between the two rates is either a discount or a premium. The difference is a discount when the forward rate is cheaper than the spot rate. The difference is a premium when the forward rate is more expensive than the spot rate.

As shown in below, the difference between the forward and spot rates represents the effect of an interest rate differential between local interest rates in the two currencies involved. It does *not* depend directly upon expectations as to future exchange rates.

Interest rate differential

The difference between spot foreign exchange rates and forward foreign exchange rates is referred to as the *forward points*. In the example below, the spot rate for Canada/US$ is 1.5000, while the forward points for a 30-day forward are 25. The forward rate is, therefore, 1.5025.

The forward points are based entirely on the interest rate differential between the two currencies. In this example, 30-day interest rates are 5.0 per cent (per annum) in Canadian dollars, and 3.0 per cent in U.S. dollars.

If an investor starts with Canadian dollars, and wishes to have U.S. dollars available at the end of 30 days, he or she has two choices: convert the U.S. dollars immediately and invest at U.S. interest rates, or invest at Canadian interest rates and buy a foreign exchange forward to fix the Canada/US$ exchange rate in 30 days' time. Due to arbitrage, both will yield approximately the same result.

Invest in Canadian Dollars

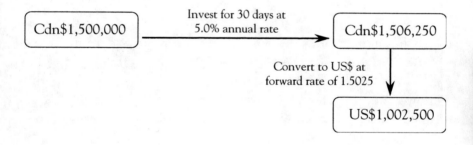

PART D

Alternative

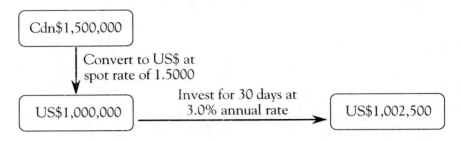

What is Foreign Exchange Risk?

In broad terms, foreign exchange risk can be defined as exposure to future movements in exchange rates. The exposure can be direct, that is, resulting from an underlying transaction in a foreign currency. Alternatively, the exposure may be indirect, such as that which results from a foreign currency asset or liability on the balance sheet.

A foreign currency denominated asset implies that future cash inflows deriving from the asset will be in a foreign currency (thus becoming a direct exposure). Similarly, an obligation or liability denominated in a foreign currency indicates that eventually cash flows must be disbursed in that currency to settle the obligation.

Foreign currency risk is generally analyzed under three categories:

- Trading or transaction exposure;
- Translation or balance sheet exposure; and
- Economic or operational exposure.

Transaction or trading exposure

An entity is exposed to transaction or trading exposure when it enters into a transaction involving a currency other that in which its primary operations are conducted. This can vary from the purchase of hotel rooms and meals in another country in the course of a trip, to the sale of merchandise to a customer in another country where payment is exigible in the local currency, to complex long-term business relationships involving cash flows in a foreign currency.

Transaction or trading exposure arises whenever a company is entitled to receipts or must make payments in a foreign currency. Examples of this exposure are set out below:

- The purchase or sale of inventory where payment is made in foreign currency.
- Any pricing policy where a product is priced in one currency but invoiced in another.
- Accounts receivable collections accepted in a foreign currency. This may result from the sales being invoiced in a foreign currency or because practice has been to accept payment in a currency other than that invoiced.
- Payment of royalties or licence fees in a foreign currency.
- Repayment of loans or other debt denominated in a foreign currency.
- Disposal of assets where the proceeds are received in a foreign currency.

Transaction exposures relate to future cash flows of any sort denominated in a foreign currency. The flows may be related to daily business operations or to investments or financing.

The operations of a subsidiary or branch operating in another country represent a particular type or transaction exposure. Rather than treat every inflow and outflow of the local currency as constituting foreign currency exposure, it is more practical to look at the entire local operations and consider the net impact of all of the activity on the parent's foreign currency risk profile. In the case of branch operations, where the activities are reasonably integrated with those of the parent, translation exposure (discussed below) will result from the net effect on the parent's balance sheet. Transaction exposure will result from individual transactions although it is more useful to look at the net impact of all foreign currency cash flows rather than review it transaction by transaction.

In cases where the foreign denominated operations are relatively self-contained, the net impact on the parent will result from translation exposure of the net balance sheet position, as well as economic exposure stemming from the operations occurring locally in the foreign currency. These are discussed below.

Translation or balance sheet exposure

Traditionally, translation exposure has resulted from the application of accounting techniques. Translation gains or losses result where assets, liabilities and operating results are converted into the primary reporting currency for the purposes of financial reporting. Translation exposure in the accounting sense arises wherever the foreign currency denominated assets and foreign currency denominated liabilities are not equal.

Translation exposure does also represent a true economic risk to the enterprise. Net assets or liabilities denominated in a foreign currency cannot be conclusively expressed in terms of the base currency until conversion actually occurs.

Even if foreign assets and liabilities are matched, some translation exposure may still occur for activities involving foreign currency receipts or disbursements.

For example, a Canadian-based company may be precisely matched with respect to its obligations and assets. If it has a U.S. dollar obligation due to be settled in 30 days, it may well decide to fund its U.S. dollar bank account whenever it is convenient in order to have the funds available to pay off the obligation.

Assume that the company orders inventory for US$100,000 on January 10. The material is delivered on February 10. The purchaser funds its U.S. dollar bank account and builds up a balance of US$100,000 in it on March 10, which is the date on which it receives an invoice. A cheque is then issued to the U.S. supplier on April 10. If the company had no foreign currency exposure (in this case U.S. dollar exposure) on January 9, then on January 10 it now has an obligation that cannot be translated for certainty into Canadian dollars until it is discharged. Any difference in the timing between when the inventory is valued in Canadian dollars and when the accounts payable is paid results in exposure to the company in the event of fluctuation of the Canadian dollar/U.S. dollar exchange rate. Interesting accounting issues arise depending upon the timing of the recognition of the U.S. dollar obligation. Notwithstanding the accounting treatment, the company has a U.S. dollar liability, and has exposure to exchange rate changes until it has built up the balance in its U.S. dollar bank account.

PART D

Economic or strategic exposure

Economic exposure is sometimes used to refer to what is better called translation exposure. True economic exposure captures "true" economic risk, not subject to arbitrary accounting assumptions. The impact of foreign currency denominated asset and liability mismatches will have an affect on the economic risk to the business: hence economic exposure.

Economic or strategic exposure has an even broader meaning. It refers to the results of the interaction between the company's business and the effect of foreign exchange rates in general. For example, a Canadian company with a factory in the United States will realize various consequences if the Canadian dollar declines relative to the U.S. dollar. In other words, if U.S. dollar denominated items become relatively more expensive in Canadian dollar terms:

- Net investment in U.S. operations (that earn U.S. dollar cash flows) will increase in Canadian dollar terms.
- Revenues earned by the U.S. operations (billed in U.S. dollars) will increase in Canadian dollar terms.
- Expenses incurred by the U.S. operation (denominated in U.S. dollars) will have the effect of reducing net income measured in Canadian dollars.
- Debt in U.S. dollars to fund the U.S. operation will be worth more in Canadian dollars. This will require more Canadian dollars to discharge the debt resulting in an eventual loss to the company.
- Imports into Canada of the output of the U.S. plant will now be worse off because their cost (in Canadian dollars) will be higher.

This list could go on. The impact of economic exposure is never simple to evaluate, but can have important effects on the economic well being of the company.

In fact, a *Canadian* company selling *only within Canada* can incur economic exposure to foreign exchange rate fluctuations. In the example above, if the U.S. currency has strengthened relative to the Canadian dollar, a Canadian-based manufacturer selling only in Canada may now have a price advantage against a U.S. exporter selling into the Canadian company's market. The United States originated goods would now cost more in Canadian funds if their U.S. dollar price is kept constant. Thus in this case, the domestic manufacturer has benefitted from the strengthening of the U.S. dollar. If the Canadian dollar had strengthened, the domestic manufacturer would have been at a disadvantage.

Derivatives and Off Balance Sheet Products

Foreign exchange forward and future contracts used to manage foreign exchange risk are generally derivatives (the value of which *derives* from exchange rates) and represent "off balance sheet" products. This is because they represent the exchange of promises to do something in the future. This differs from normal business activity, which is based on a transaction that has occurred. For example, in the case of a $100,000 purchase of inventory from a United States supplier, discussed above, once the purchase has been made accounting convention will result in the recognition of an asset — inventory and liability in U.S. dollars to pay for the inventory. The balance sheet of the corporation will thus reflect an increase in inventory and an increase in accounts payable, denominated in United States dollars. Conventional financial reporting is quite successful in correctly reflecting this sort of transaction.

The corporation may then decide to enter into a foreign exchange forward contract with a bank in order to fix the Canadian dollar cost of discharging the U.S. dollar account payable. The foreign exchange forward contract will provide that at a particular date in the future, the corporation will pay a bank a certain amount of Canadian dollars and in return the bank will pay the Canadian company a certain amount of U.S. dollars (presumably $100,000 dollars in order to repay the U.S. dollar account

PART D

payable). That foreign exchange forward agreement represents an exchange of promises or an "executory" contract. It does not require that either party do anything at the time that the agreement is entered into.

Conventional financial reporting has difficulty recording a contract that represents an agreement to do something in the future. The contract may be treated as a "hedge" of the transaction, thus effectively eliminating foreign currency risk. Alternatively, (or in addition) the forward exchange forward contract may be noted as a commitment in the notes to the financial statements. In any case, the foreign exchange forward contract may not be recorded on the balance sheet itself since it results in changes neither in assets or liabilities but rather is a commitment. (Accounting issues are discussed further in Chapter 20.)

The separation of the foreign exchange forward — an *instrument* to manage foreign exchange risk — from the underlying risk itself (the foreign currency exposure), gives the treasurer flexibility to manage foreign exchange exposure in a volatile environment. The treasurer is able to alter the company's foreign exchange risk profile without disturbing the underlying foreign currency assets and obligations.

Foreign Exchange Exposure Models

We discussed above three different types of exposure to foreign exchange movements. There are also different foreign exchange exposure models. The models represent differing viewpoints as to the effect of changes in exchange rates on corporate performance. It is important that the treasurer ensure that the exposure being managed corresponds to the appropriate definition in light of the companies' objectives.

The exposure models are as follows:

- Accounting exposure;
- Cash flow exposure;
- Strategic exposure; and
- Market value of equity exposure.

Accounting exposure

Accounting exposure measures the sensitivity of shareholders' equity and net income to fluctuations in exchange rates. It focuses on accounting measurements of exposure of financial assets and liabilities and fluctuations in the current year's reported financial performance. It is based upon accounting reporting rather than underlying economic exposure.

To the extent that the performance of a corporation is measured in accounting terms it would be appropriate for the treasurer to manage accounting exposure.

Cash flow exposure

Cash flow exposure measures the sensitivity of cash flows to fluctuations in foreign exchange rates. It is premised on the basis that cash flows are more accurate indicators of corporate welfare than reported accounting results. In a sense, cash flow exposure is more objective since cash flows are not influenced by accounting deferrals and accounting policies.

A corporation that measures its success by the stability (or growth) of cash flows would require its treasurer to manage cash flow exposure.

PART D

Strategic exposure

Strategic exposure measures the ability of the corporation to optimize its strategic options despite fluctuations in exchange rates. It looks beyond recognition of only financial and contractual assets and liabilities. It recognizes the significance of economic exposure to the company so that the objective is to manage foreign exchange risk to optimize the company's strategic choices.

Management of strategic exposure normally requires the ability to also manage accounting exposure and cash flow exposure since those views of foreign exchange risk are incorporated into the strategic exposure model.

Market value of equity exposure

Exposure to the market value of shareholders' equity measures the sensitivity of changes to the company's value as foreign exchange rates vary. Market value of shareholders' equity is (by definition) equal to the present value of future cash flows accruing to the company (and its shareholders) in the future. This viewpoint is consistent with modern portfolio theory and the capital asset pricing model. It is assumed that the markets reflect all information so that a corporation's shares always reflect their "fair" value. There are a number of practical difficulties with actually implementing this exposure model, but it forms a useful framework around which to evaluate other measures of foreign exchange exposure.

Corporate objectives and systems

The purpose of this discussion has been to emphasize that the manner in which foreign currency exposure is managed will depend upon corporate objectives. (In some cases objectives may not be specified with sufficient clarity to allow this as a guide.)

472

Placing some degree of rigour on the definition of the foreign exchange exposure being managed can have the beneficial effect of forcing a more in-depth look at the company's strategic planning process.

The data required to measure accounting exposure is readily produced by accounting systems. That required to assess cash flow, strategic or equity exposure is generally not provided by corporate information systems. Those approaches require information on pricing, costs, strategic options, markets and the environment that is also very important to implementing and evaluating strategic plans.

Identifying Exposure

Foreign exchange exposure is normally viewed as resulting from a position that may be held in a foreign currency. The currency position arises from a difference between assets and liabilities denominated in the foreign currency. A position may also arise where there is a mismatch between future anticipated cash flows in that foreign currency.

There is a significant difference between the overall net position in a particular foreign currency and the gap created by the mismatch between future anticipated cash flows. The net currency position measures the extent to which the company is exposed to future fluctuations in exchange rates between Canadian dollars and that foreign currency. As a practical matter, most companies would define their net position as either the net of all transactions already entered into involving foreign currencies, or that number as well as transactions expected to be entered into over some predetermined period of time (say a year).

PART D

473

The open position is the net of foreign currency assets, liabilities and any future foreign currency cash flows. It takes no account of mismatches in the timing of those cash flows. Therefore, a "gap" will result where there is a projected timing mismatch in the future cash flows. For example, the company may have a "flat" net foreign currency position — that is a zero or negligible net open position. Nonetheless, it could have very large offsetting gap positions in particular future time periods. An open position can be specified in terms of the absolute amount of the foreign currency. A gap position must be defined both as an amount and within a time frame.

A spot position is generally defined as the net of a company's foreign currency assets and liabilities at the indicated date as well as projected cash flows in that currency over the next few days. "Few" may be defined as two days, to correspond to the market definition of spot foreign exchange. Other companies treat cash flows over the next five or seven days as being part of the spot position.

The value of any foreign currency position can be determined by calculating what it would cost to eliminate the exposure. A gap may be eliminated by entering into foreign exchange forward contracts.

For example, assume that on January 1, a company has a flat overall U.S. dollar position. That is, it has no U.S. dollar assets or liabilities on that date. On February 1, it is expecting receipt of a U.S. dollar cheque for $1 million. On March 1, it must pay out US$ 1 million. Thus, it has a gap from February 1 to March 1, where it is "long" in U.S. dollars. This gap may be eliminated by a foreign currency swap, in effect, two back to back transactions (see *Forward foreign exchange contracts*, below). The swap will eliminate the gap by converting U.S. to Canadian dollars on February 1, and converting Canadian to U.S. dollars on March 1.

Hedging

Following is an example of using foreign exchange forwards to hedge an exposure.

Example: Hedging foreign exchange — a case study

Electric Teddybears Inc. (ETI) imports toys from the U.S. On February 1, 2004, it ordered merchandise totalling US$200,000, payment due March 1, 2004. All of ETI's sales are in Canada. ETI is exposed to fluctuations in the Canada/U.S. dollar exchange rate until it acquires US$200,000, or otherwise freezes what that amount will cost it in Canadian funds.

Assume that on February 1, 2004, the spot Canada/U.S. rate is 1.2500, and the 30-day forward rate is 1.2525. ETI could therefore acquire U.S. funds immediately (spot) for a cost of 1.2500 2 200,000 = Cdn$250,000. However, ETI doesn't need the U.S. funds on February 1 — it will need them on March 1. Therefore, ETI could instead enter into a forward foreign exchange contract, for settlement March 1, at a rate of 1.2525. Under that contract, on March 1, ETI will pay its bank 1.2525 $200,000 = Cdn$250,500. The bank will pay ETI US$200,000.

As the discussion of interest rate differential, on page 462 indicates, the forward contract did not "cost" ETI $500 ($250,500 – $250,000). Rather, the $500 represents the difference between investing idle funds at Canadian interest rates rather than U.S. interest rates. ETI has eliminated its exposure to the movement in foreign exchange rates by purchasing the forward contract. It could have eliminated its exposure by purchasing at a spot rate instead, if it wanted to have the U.S. funds on February 1 rather than March 1.

PART D

Assume now that on March 1 the actual spot rate were still 1.2400. ETI could then purchase US$200,000 for $200,000 1.24 = Cdn$248,000, or $2,000 *less* than the spot rate on March 1 (and $2,500 less than the forward rate on that date). If the actual spot rate on March 1 were 1.2600, then the U.S. funds would cost ETI $252,000, or $2,000 *more* than the spot rate on February 1. By purchasing the forward contract, ETI has eliminated risk — both the risk of loss and the "risk" of gain.

If ETI wanted to receive the benefit of a strengthening Canadian dollar, but wanted to eliminate its exposure to a weakening Canadian dollar, it could buy an option. In this case, an option to buy US$200,000 at a rate of 1.2500 on March 1, might cost $1,000 on February 1. This would give ETI the right (but not the obligation) to buy the U.S. dollars at 1.25. If the rate were below 1.2500 on March 1, ETI would let the option expire, worthless. If the rate were above 1.2500, ETI would exercise the option. If the Canadian dollar strengthens, ETI will receive the benefit, less the cost of the option.

In the example above, a foreign currency swap is used to *hedge* an exposure — in that case, a gap or timing mismatch.

Hedging is the management or elimination of foreign exchange risks. Various instruments (described below) may be used to lock-in future exchange rates, thus eliminating or reducing risk. A transaction which is a hedge for economic purposes may not always constitute a hedge for accounting purposes. This is discussed further in Chapter 20.

Strategies and Policies

The strategy of the company and its appetite for potential gains or losses from assuming foreign exchange risk must be set by senior management. (In practice, it would be proposed by the treasurer — in writing — and ratified by senior management, and probably the Board of Directors.)

To determine the appropriate level of risk, it is important to undertake appropriate quantitative analysis to quantify the likely risks and rewards as market exchange rates vary. From time to time, corporations have suffered large losses due to unanticipated market movements.

The magnitude of currency exposure taken by the company should be appropriate given the size of its resources and its appetite for risk. The risk management techniques used should be consistent with the method utilized for evaluating company performance. For example, it may not be appropriate to focus on managing strategic exposure if the company's performance is evaluated based only upon its accounting results.

Characteristics of Foreign Exchange Management Products

Custom or generic

Foreign exchange management products may be divided between *over the counter* and *exchange traded*.

Over the counter products are generally purchased from banks. They are custom products and contain terms and conditions, amounts, dates and other details as agreed to between the customer and the bank. As a result, there is complete flexibility as to the terms of the contract.

PART D

477

However, the corporation may require credit approval in order to enter into contracts with a bank. In the case of a foreign exchange contract, banks will be concerned about two types of credit exposure.

One is the "forward risk". If a company enters into a forward exchange contract with a bank, and rates move in the corporation's favour, the net result of settling the transaction upon maturity will be a cash inflow to the company. In that case, the company has the credit risk of the bank not fulfilling its obligation. Banks tend not to worry about this: there is no credit exposure to the bank itself.

If foreign exchange rates move in favour of the bank, then upon settlement of the forward contract, the value of the amount due from the corporation to the bank will exceed the value of the amount due from the bank to the corporation. Therefore, there is credit risk to the bank. The forward risk to the bank is the amount that it would cost to replace the foreign exchange contract in the market.

The other type of credit risk (from the perspective of the bank) is "settlement" or "payment" risk. This is the risk that the bank will disburse funds and then not receive funds from the corporation to effect the other side of the foreign *exchange* transaction. It is because of these forward and settlement risks that banks require credit lines be in place.

Exchange traded contracts are traded on a public exchange. Corporations can purchase and sell exchange traded instruments through brokers. The exchange acts as a clearing house and insures an orderly market. The corporate customer will be required to put up margin to ensure that the exchange has no credit risk from its activity. The market value of the customer's position is reviewed daily and compared to the margin posted. Any deficiency would require that the customer produce additional margin. Excess over the required margin may be repaid to the customer upon its request. Foreign exchange futures trading on various exchanges are examples of exchange traded foreign exchange risk management products.

Certainty or insurance

Foreign exchange forwards, futures and derivative products represent binding contracts to both parties. In other words, a corporate customer alters its risk profile in both directions — whether it gains from the transaction or not. Exposure to an adverse movement in the foreign currency is eliminated but the benefit from a favourable movement is also eliminated.

A fundamentally different type of instrument offers *insurance*. The purchaser of such an instrument may, at its option, decide whether to exercise its rights under the agreement. The protection provided is analogous to that of a conventional insurance policy. The corporation is protected from adverse movements but will still benefit from favourable movements in exchange rates. As is the case with conventional insurance, a premium is charged for this protection. Foreign exchange options including caps, floors and collars are all examples of foreign exchange management products that offer insurance.

Derivatives

In addition to foreign exchange contracts and foreign exchange futures, various other "synthetic" foreign exchange instruments have been developed. They are also called "derivatives" because their value is derived from foreign exchange rates. These can be seen as bundles of foreign exchange contracts with or without option (insurance) characteristics. Forward exchange agreements

PART D

479

and exchange rate agreements are examples of derivatives or synthetic foreign exchange contracts.

Description of Foreign Exchange Management Products

Spot and forward foreign exchange

In any foreign exchange transaction, each party agrees to pay the other an agreed amount of a specified currency, on a particular date. Most foreign exchange transactions are between U.S. dollars and another currency. Thus, a reference to the pound sterling rate, for example, means an exchange of pounds for U.S. dollars. "Cross" rates are also available. These are between two currencies other than U.S. dollars.

In a spot foreign exchange transaction, the agreed payment date or value date is normally two business days after the day the transaction has originated (the deal date). (For Canadian dollars and Mexican pesos, spot deals settle the next business day. Canadian banks will also settle spot deals on the same day if requested.)

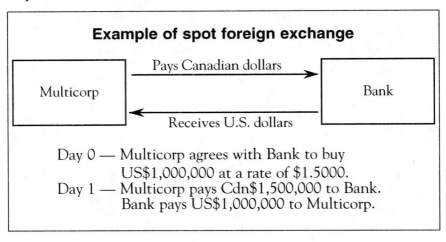

Example of spot foreign exchange

Multicorp → Pays Canadian dollars → Bank

Multicorp ← Receives U.S. dollars ← Bank

Day 0 — Multicorp agrees with Bank to buy
US$1,000,000 at a rate of $1.5000.
Day 1 — Multicorp pays Cdn$1,500,000 to Bank.
Bank pays US$1,000,000 to Multicorp.

Under a forward foreign exchange contract, each party agrees to pay the other at an exchange rate fixed at the time that the contract is made (the deal date), at a value date which is more than two business days in the future. A forward foreign exchange contract may mature in a few days, a few months or even in several years.

Forward foreign exchange contracts

A forward foreign exchange contract is an agreement between two parties to exchange two currencies at an exchange rate fixed at the time the contract is made at a value date which is more than two business days in the future. Note that the exchange rate is fixed at the time that the transaction is entered into even though the actual cash flows representing the exchange of currencies do not transpire until the stipulated future date.

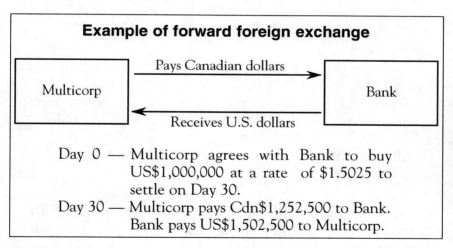

Example of forward foreign exchange

Pays Canadian dollars →

Multicorp   Bank

← Receives U.S. dollars

Day 0 — Multicorp agrees with Bank to buy US$1,000,000 at a rate of $1.5025 to settle on Day 30.
Day 30 — Multicorp pays Cdn$1,252,500 to Bank. Bank pays US$1,502,500 to Multicorp.

There are two basic types of foreign exchange forward contracts. The simplest are *outright* forward transactions which are simply the purchase or sale of foreign currency for a value date in the future.

A *swap* is a simultaneous purchase and sale of an amount of foreign currency for two different value dates. Unlike the spot or outright forward transaction, the swap transaction does not create net foreign exchange exposure as each party both pays and receives foreign currency at different dates. (Note that a foreign exchange swap is different from a currency swap or cross currency interest rate swap. Interest rate swaps are discussed in Chapter 18. Currency swaps and cross currency interest rate swaps are discussed later in this chapter.)

The two value dates in a foreign exchange swap can be any two future dates. One common type of swap is the "spot against forward" swap where the trader buys a currency for its spot value date and simultaneously sells it back for a value date some time later (or sells then buys). Another type of swap is a "forward-forward" in which the foreign currency is bought for one future date and sold for another future date (or sold, then bought).

Currency futures

A currency future is a specific type of futures contract. A futures contract is an agreement on an exchange to buy or sell a standard amount of a specified currency at a fixed price on a particular date.

All futures contracts trade on an organized exchange. Futures markets involve standardized contracts: that is what distinguishes these markets from the "over the counter" market in foreign exchange forwards (and other custom products). Every futures contract has particular specifications, including the size of the contract, the termination date of the contract, means of settlement, the quotation and minimum price movement of the contract.

Every futures exchange operates a clearing house to hold all positions and facilitate clearing and settlement. To eliminate credit risk, the clearing house requires an *initial margin* deposit from all market participants for every contract they trade. The actual amount required depends upon the particular futures contract as well as market volatility. Generally, the initial margin represents the maximum likely price fluctuation in one day.

Every day, all open positions are marked-to-market. At the daily close of business a settlement price is announced by the futures exchange for all contracts that are outstanding. Profits and losses are settled, so that there is no further credit risk to the exchange — or for that matter, to the participants. The daily settlement is called the *variation margin*.

Foreign exchange derivatives

Derivative or synthetic agreements are widely available in the foreign exchange markets. The primary derivatives are forward exchange agreements (FXA) and exchange rate agreements (ERA).

FXAs and ERAs are the equivalent in the foreign exchange forward market to the forward rate agreement (FRA) in the money market. They allow a counterparty to hedge a foreign forward exchange exposure with flexibility as to the settlement dates but much less credit exposure.

The forward exchange agreement is an agreement between two parties to settle the difference (on the first value date of the contract) between the dealing price and the market price. The forward price is then discounted to present value and the difference is settled.

These derivative products have an advantage over conventional foreign exchange forward contracts since no cash flows are exchanged. Thus there is considerably reduced credit risk and only one payment is necessary: the net amount to be settled.

PART D

483

Currency swaps

Currency swaps are also called *swap deposits*. They refer to an investment denominated in a foreign currency along with a foreign exchange swap, so that the investor can acquire the currency at the start of the term and exchange back to the home currency when the investment matures. In fact, *a swap deposit is not a foreign exchange management product at all*, since the investor receives the same currency back that it paid out at the beginning.

Cross currency interest rate swaps

In this section the terms cross currency interest rate swaps and cross currency swaps are used interchangeably. (Note that a currency swap is different — see the section immediately above.)

A cross currency swap is a transaction denominated in two currencies where one party pays interest in one currency and the other party pays interest denominated in a second currency. They generally involve two exchanges of principal, which are also essentially foreign exchange transactions, at the beginning and at the end of the term of the swap.

There are many variations on the basic structure of a cross currency swap. The interest rates exchanged may be fixed rates in different currencies, fixed for floating in different currencies, and there may be timing differences so that one party may make annual payments and the other pays quarterly or semi-annually.

Other variations include zero-coupon cross currency swaps, asset swaps, annuity or coupon swaps and differential swaps.

Example of cross currency interest rate swap

Multicorp has financed its Canadian dollar-based operations with a U.S. dollar loan. Thus it is exposed to foreign exchange risk. This cross-currency interest-rate swap allows it to eliminate this exposure.

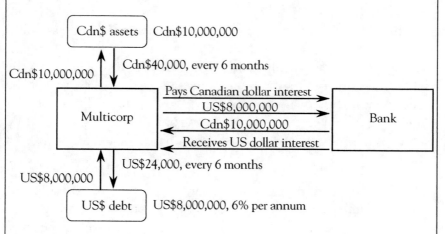

The cross currency interest rate swap is essentially a series of foreign exchange transactions:

Inception of swap — Multicorp receives Cdn$10,000,000 (which it uses to finance assets).

Multicorp pays US$8,000,000 (which it received from proceeds of debt).

At every semi-annual interest payment — Multicorp receives US$ interest flow (which it uses to pay interest due on US$ debt. (3% 2 $8,000,000 = US$24,000.)

Multicorp pays Cdn$ interest flow. Effectively, it has converted its interest obligation into Canadian dollars.

End of swap — Multicorp repays Cdn$10,000,000, and receives US$8,000,000, which it uses to discharge U.S. dollar debt.

PART D

Foreign currency options

Over the counter options (purchased from a bank) involving foreign exchange are sold under different names depending upon the needs of the purchaser. The most common are caps, floors, collars and swaptions. Exchange traded options are also available.

The holder (purchaser or owner) of an option has the right, but not the obligation, to buy or sell a particular underlying asset at a specific price, on (or before) a specified future date. The amount paid for the option is called the premium. A *call option* gives the holder the right to buy the asset, a *put option* is the right to sell the asset. In the case of foreign exchange, the distinction is not that important: a right to buy pounds sterling at a rate of Cdn$2.00/£1.00 is the same as a right to sell Canadian dollars at a rate of £1.00/Cdn$2.00.

Options involving foreign exchange can be viewed as "insurance" because the corporate purchaser is able to protect itself against adverse rate movements while benefitting from positive fluctuations in the exchange rate. This is in contrast to a future or forward where, although risk is eliminated (or reduced), potential upward gains are also lost.

CHAPTER 20

Accounting Issues in Treasury Management

Overview

Recent years have seen accounting scandals, massive financial statement corrections, and an extraordinary amount of news about accounting in treasury management. This chapter provides some perspective on accounting issues in treasury management.

Three developments are having a significant impact on accounting for treasury operations:

- Accounting for derivatives that is evolving rapidly, and becoming more complex, particularly in the United States;

- The fallout from Enron and other "accounting failures"; and
- Harmonization of Canadian and American accounting standards.

These are discussed later in the chapter. First, there is a discussion of some of the concepts and principles that underlie accounting for treasury products.

Introduction

We have recently seen an extraordinary amount of news about accounting issues in treasury management. Accounting seems to have evolved from being the domain of introverted bookkeepers to a discipline that can — and has — caused great companies to collapse. But there is nothing new under the sun: the Securities and Exchange Commission in the United States was set up in 1931 in response to perceived accounting abuses in the 1920s. And in the 1970s, a literature had already developed enumerating the deficiencies in corporate accounting. (Abraham Brilloff wrote three particularly good books: *More Debits and Credits, Unaccountable Accounting,* and *The Truth About Corporate Accounting.*)

Understanding accounting has always been vital to understanding and controlling risk and evaluating corporate performance. This has become a more complicated exercise as accounting in Canada is moving from the traditional historic cost model, to a hybrid with elements of both historic cost and market value.

Historic cost has the virtue of being objective and sometimes very accurate. Unfortunately, it is not very useful for most purposes. Market value approaches add subjectivity and volatility, but tend to be more useful. This is discussed in more detail later. First, we examine some of the principles underlying accounting.

Trade-offs

Accounting does not concern itself with trifles: it is about how to reflect economic reality concisely and accurately. The art of accounting is in dealing with trade-offs.

Information can be very relevant *or* very reliable — rarely can it have both attributes at the same time. Relevant information is timely and provides appropriate information for making decisions. Reliable information is unbiased, accurate and can be verified or audited. Improvement in one characteristic results in degrading the other. For example, faster generation of financial statements (increase in relevance) may require the use of estimates in their preparation (decrease in reliability). More accurate financial information (increase in reliability) may require delays in its release (decrease in relevance).

The purpose of accounting is to provide useful information to help the users of the information make decisions. This sounds fairly straightforward, but it actually contains the germ of a powerful and important concept. The production of useful information requires tradeoffs.

Several fundamental issues arise in accounting for treasury products. Many of them are not necessarily inherent in the financial instruments themselves, but rather result from the use of the historical cost model, normally required under generally accepted accounting principles ("GAAP").

Note that the "accounting" referred to in this chapter is *financial accounting* — that is, accounting for external reporting purposes. *Management accounting* for internal (management) reporting has considerable flexibility and need not be constrained by external reporting rules and conventions. In an ideal world, there would be convergence between the two, since both have the objective of reporting economic reality.

PART D

489

Generally Accepted Accounting Principles

A cartoon from *The New Yorker* in the 1970s shows one man in a dark suit addressing three other men in dark suits, saying: "In examining our books, Mr. Mathews promises to use generally accepted accounting principles, if you know what I mean." What are these generally accepted accounting principles?

The *CICA Handbook* of the Canadian Institute of Chartered Accountants provides a definition:

> The term generally accepted accounting principles encompasses not only specific rules, practices and procedures relating to particular circumstances but also broad principles and conventions of general application, including the underlying concepts described in this Section. Specifically, generally accepted accounting principles comprise the Accounting Recommendations in the Handbook and, where a matter is not covered by a Recommendation, other accounting principles that either:
>
> (a) are generally accepted by virtue of their use in similar circumstances by a significant number of entities in Canada; or
>
> (b) are consistent with the recommendations in the Handbook and are developed through the exercise of professional judgement, including consultation with other informed accountants where appropriate, and the application of the concepts described in this Section. In exercising professional judgement, established principles for analogous situations dealt with in the Handbook would be taken into account and reference would be made to:

(i)   other relevant matters dealt with in the Handbook;

(ii)   practice in similar circumstances;

(iii)   Accounting Guidelines published by the Accounting Standards Steering Committee;

(iv)   Abstracts of Issues Discussed by the CICA Emerging Issues Committee;

(v)   International Accounting Standards published by the International Accounting Standards Commit-tee;

(vi)   standards published by bodies authorized to establish financial accounting standards in other jurisdictions;

(vii)   CICA research studies; and

(viii)   other sources of accounting literature such as textbooks and journals.

The relative importance of these various sources is a matter of professional judgement in the circumstances.

Thus, accounting principles apply at various levels, from broad general concepts to detailed rules of application. The broad principles are very important because where there is no specific pronouncement on a particular issue, the appropriate treatment must be determined by reasoning by analogy from pronouncements dealing with similar issues. This is particularly important in accounting for financial instruments since established practices do not exist where the products themselves are new. (See the section "Sources of Accounting Guidance" below.)

As noted above, the primary objective of financial accounting is to communicate useful information. Therefore, appropriate recognition of the *economic substance* of the events and balances reported is critical. This requires that the preparers *understand* that economic substance. In the balance of this chapter, there is a very simple — but recurring — theme: accounting should reflect reality, and not be constrained by arcane rules.

PART D

491

Canadian GAAP, U.S. GAAP and Harmonization

Financial accounting should reflect economic substance. In fact, external reporting has often degenerated into a game played between management and shareholders. Often, the objective seems to be to disclose as little as possible, or to overwhelm the reader with data.

In theory, there has long been a difference between the application of Generally Accepted Accounting Principles in Canada and the United States. In Canada, GAAP has traditionally been focused on the substance of the transaction, which may be supported or not supported by referring to quantitative benchmarks.

In fact, the definition of GAAP set out in the *CICA Handbook* (section 1000.61) clearly provides that the detailed rules in the Handbook should not be followed if the result is not reasonable:

> In those rare circumstances where following a Handbook Recommendation would result in misleading financial statements, generally accepted accounting principles encompass appropriate alternative principles. When assessing whether a departure from a Handbook Recommendation is appropriate, consideration would be given to:
> (a) the objective of the Handbook Recommendation and why that objective is not achieved or is not relevant in the particular circumstances;
> (b) how the entity's circumstances differ from those of other entities which follow the Handbook Recommendation; and
> (c) the underlying principles of accounting alternatives by referring to other sources (see paragraph 1000.60).

The identification of these circumstances is a matter of professional judgment. However, there is a strong presumption that adherence to Handbook Recommendations results in appropriate presentation and that a departure from such Recommendations represents a departure from generally accepted accounting principles.

The American approach is the opposite: quantitative benchmarks determine the accounting treatment, with the substance of the transaction being a secondary consideration. This has been referred to as a "cookbook" approach: given these ingredients, this is the result. This results in an attempt to exploit perceived "loopholes" in accounting requiremnents, with the substance of the transactions left as an irrelevancy. An example of the ultimate result of applying this approach is the Enron debacle (more on that later), where the rules may have been combined legitimately, but the result was illogical. Arguably, the absurd result was actually required by U.S. GAAP. The classic Canadian approach would be to ask, "What are we trying to achieve and why?"

In practice, the Canadian and U.S. approaches have become similar. In Canada, accounting firms have endeavored to reduce the choices available under the rubric of "professional judgement." Consequently, quantitative benchmarks have tended to be used, with less scope for focusing on the "economic substance." In addition, when Canadian guidance is limited, accountants have referred to the U.S. rules.

In the United States, the accounting profession has become acutely aware of the sometimes contradictory rules that attempt to prescribe in detail specific accounting treatments. Consequently, there has been a movement to focus on principles rather than detailed rules. Nonetheless, for various reasons, include the threat of litigation, detailed rules will not disappear from U.S.-style GAAP.

PART D

Another peculiarity of the U.S. environment is the extent to which accounting standards have been influenced by politics. One example of this is accounting for the cost of employee stock options. In 1993, the Financial Accounting Standards Board (FASB), an independent private-sector organization that sets United States GAAP, proposed that companies be required to record the fair value of stock options as an expense. Since options have value to the recipients and a cost to other shareholders, that seemed quite sensible to the FASB. Extraordinary protests ensued . . . from lobbyists, the high-tech industry, CPA firms, and it seemed, most of the U.S. business world. Bills were proposed in the House and Senate to forbid the SEC from enforcing the proposed rule, and even to strip the FASB of its authority and require the SEC to approve all accounting rule changes. The FASB backed down and did not require the expensing of employee stock options. (Fast forward to 2002 and the business press is wailing that the inadequate accounting for employee stock options contributed significantly to the stock market bubble of the late 1990s, and the bust of 2002.) Regardless of the merits of the FASB proposal on stock options, this was an odd way for due process to operate. It is now recognized that politics is not the right forum to debate complex accounting rules.

Superimposed on U.S. and international accounting developments is a trend towards harmonization. Canadian accounting regulators are embarked on a program of conforming Canadian to American rules, except where the U.S. rules are so odd, complex, or irrational that differences must be preserved. Concurrently, while U.S. accounting regulators have no interest in Canadian GAAP, they are aware of worldwide International Accounting Standards (which often approximate Canadian GAAP) and are examining differences between the US rules and the international standards, with a view to eliminating differences. Canadian accounting regulators are embarking on the same quest. So the Canadian, U.S., and "International" GAAP are slowly being conformed.

Harmonization of Canadian with U.S. GAAP is, in principle, a very positive development. Many large Canadian companies need to report under Canadian GAAP under Canadian securities law and stock exchange requirements, and must also report under U.S. GAAP because of a U.S. stock exchange listing, or for U.S. bankers. There are several different acceptable ways of reporting and reconciling between the two GAAPs, but the result is always confusing. However, harmonization had to proceed at a measured pace, because in some cases U.S. GAAP was so clearly nonsensical that the Canadian accounting regulators were not able to adopt it, and had to wait for U.S. GAAP to change. (Recent examples include accounting for business acquisitions, and earnings per share calculations.)

Accounting Standards

Section 3860 of the *CICA Handbook*, "Financial Instruments— Disclosure and Presentation", sets out requirements for presentation and disclosure of financial instruments. It is very much part of a larger work in progress.

In 1991, the CICA released an exposure draft dealing with a wide range of recognition, measurement, presentation and disclosure issues related to financial instruments. Following comments and concerns from many interested parties, the document was substantially revised and released as a re-exposure draft in 1994. As a result of continuing concern over the complexity and length of the material, the project was divided into two parts. "Disclosure and Presentation" was released as section 3860 of the *CICA Handbook* in late 1995. "Recognition and Measurement" issues have not yet been released as *CICA Handbook* recommendations. The "Disclosure and Presentation" standards in section 3860 of the *CICA Handbook* are very broad and cover many areas. Interestingly, although the standards are stated to comprise

PART D

"Disclosure and Presentation" issues, in some places they implicitly specify the treatment of "Recognition and Measurement" issues as well. For example, debt or equity instruments must be reclassified if necessary to reflect their substance rather than legal form. This may result in changes in measurement. Similarly, split accounting is required for the individual components of financial instruments, which affects measurement as well as presentation.

In early 1997, the Canadian Institute of Chartered Accountants and the International Accounting Standards Committee (IASC) jointly issued a Discussion Paper, *Accounting for Financial Assets and Financial Liabilities*. The response to the Discussion Paper strongly supported the need for comprehensive international standards on accounting for financial instruments. However, there was considerable concern over the direction of the Discussion Paper towards a fair value accounting approach to valuation. A subsequent document with proposals for a fair value approach was issued in December 2000 by the "Financial Instruments Joint Working Group." Again, many critical comments were received, so further analysis is being carried out.

In January 2002, the Canadian accounting regulators started a project to develop standards for recognition and measurement of financial instruments that would conform to the standards developed in the United States. They issued an exposure draft in early 2003, and have announced the intention of requiring implementation for fiscal years starting after September 30, 2004.

Meanwhile, in June 1998, the FASB issued Statement of Financial Standards No. 133 ("SFAS 133"), *Accounting for Derivative Instruments and Hedging Activities*. While the standard is 33 pages long, with its appendices, it occupies 245 pages.

SFAS 133 defines a derivative as a financial instrument that has all of the following characteristics:

- It has one or more underlyings and one or more notional amounts or payment provisions or both. An underlying is a price or price index such as an interest rate, an exchange rate, etc.
- It requires either no initial investment or a smaller investment than would normally be expected given the way in which it is expected to respond to price changes.
- Its terms require or permit net settlement, or it provides for the delivery of an asset that puts the recipient in a similar position as net settlement.

Examples of derivatives include swaps, options, futures, and swaptions. In addition, convertible debt owned, commodity purchase agreements, and many structured transactions would appear to meet the definition of derivative.

SFAS 133 requires that derivatives be recorded on the balance sheet at fair value, and establishes special accounting treatment for different types of hedges.

Recognition Criteria

Recognition is the inclusion of an item in financial statements. If an item can be measured, and the economic benefits and obligations (or "risks and rewards of ownership") associated with it have been transferred, then the item should be recognized.

The CICA Handbook sets out the formal criteria for recognition as follows:

(a) the item has an appropriate basis of measurement and a reasonable estimate can be made of the amount involved; and
(b) for items involving obtaining for giving up future economic benefits, it is probable that such benefits will be obtained or given up. (CICA Handbook, 1000.44)

GAAP follows the *accrual basis* of accounting. This means that transactions and events are recorded in the period in which they occur, regardless of whether there has been a receipt or payment of cash. Note that under the new exposure draft, most financial instruments will be marked-to-market, not recorded at historic cost.

Recognition criteria for financial instruments are consistent with the general principles set out above. A financial instrument that is an asset or liability should be recognized on the balance sheet when:

(a) substantially all of the risks and rewards associated with the asset or liability have been transferred to the entity; and

(b) the cost or fair value of the asset to the entity or the amount of the obligation assumed can be measured reliably.

In June 1998, the FASB issued Statement of Financial Standards No. 133 ("SFAS 133"), *Accounting for Derivative Instruments and Hedging Activities*. It requires that derivatives be recognized as assets or liabilities on the balance sheet, and that they be recorded at fair value. It also establishes special accounting treatment for different types of hedges.

Historic Cost and Mark-to-Market

Measurement paradigms

The paradigm, or framework, for financial accounting has long been the so-called *historic cost* model. This model focuses on recognizing transactions between independent parties. Income is recorded when something is sold to another entity. Revenues are not recorded if an asset held has simply become more valuable, but has not been sold. The historic cost paradigm has the advantage of being objective, auditable and reliable. "Objective" means that the numbers are not subjective, and "reliable" means that a given set of facts will always result in the same number for accounting purposes.

Recording almost everything at cost is so entrenched that even the double-digit inflation of the 1970s failed to depose the principle. However, financial instruments are designed to protect or exploit changes in market prices. This raises the issue of how to account for a financial instrument within the historic cost framework when it is used to protect the market value of an asset or liability that is recorded in the financial statements at historic cost. A further difficulty is that historic cost is not a useful measure for recording assets and liabilities that are purchased for resale and for which there exists an active market.

As a result, there has been a piecemeal drift away from pure historic cost accounting. Financial instruments, other than derivatives, are normally recorded at cost. However, in certain areas, current practice is to record them on a *mark-to-market* basis, that is, at their fair market value (with unrealized gains and losses being recorded in the current income statement). The inventory of a bank or investment dealer in the business of buying and selling financial instruments records its trading inventory a fair market value. Financial instruments that are derivatives and are entered into (by any type of company) for trading or speculative purposes are also recorded at their fair market value unless they are:

- a hedge;
- a loan or deposit commitment;
- a letter of credit;
- a financial guarantee;
- a contract related to stock-based compensation;
- a contract that is classified as equity;

- a contract issued as contingent consideration in a business combination.

(See Emerging Issues Committee, EIC-128, "Accounting for trading, speculative or non-hedging derivative financial instruments.")

The mixture of historic cost and mark-to-market accounting creates new problems. Conventional historic cost accounting does permit the notion of *hedging*. Since a hedge reduces the risk in an underlying asset or liability, it must be accounted for in a way that reflects this. However different rules are now required in dealing with the hedge of an item carried at cost as opposed to the hedge of an item recorded at its market value. (And there are other complications: how to account for a hedge of something carried at the lower of cost and market?)

The exposure draft issued in March 2003 by the CICA proposes that most financial instruments will be recorded at their fair market values. If enacted, it will change accounting standards for fiscal years starting after September 30, 2004.

Initial recognition

When a financial asset is first recognized, it should be recorded at the fair value of the consideration given or received for it. For financial instruments such as bonds, loans, or promissory notes, the fair value is equal to the present value of the expected future payments, discounted at an appropriate interest rate. That fair value may differ from the face value of the instrument, or the principal amount due at maturity. Similarly, a financial liability is recorded at the present value of the payments that will be required to discharge it, or at the amount received in exchange for incurring the liability.

When an item is acquired in the course of an exchange, the fair value may not be readily apparent. In that case, the fair value is determined by considering either the item received, or that given up in exchange, depending upon which value is more clearly evident.

Subsequent to initial recognition

The "historic cost" and "fair value" approaches yield different results when applied to the measurement of financial instruments after initial recognition. At present, GAAP requires that most entities account for financial instruments on the historic cost basis. However, financial institutions, mutual funds and investment companies have generally accounted for their trading portfolios at fair market value.

The U.S. rules, under SFAS 133, require that if certain conditions are met, a derivative may be designated as:

- a hedge of the exposure to changes in the fair value of a recognized asset or liability or an unrecognized firm commitment,

- a hedge of the exposure to variable cash flows of a forecasted transaction, or

- a hedge of the foreign currency exposure of a net investment in a foreign operation, an unrecognized firm commitment in a foreign currency, an available for sale security denominated in a foreign currency, or a foreign currency denominated forecasted transaction.

For a derivative designated as hedging the exposure to changes in the fair value of a recognized asset or liability or an unrecognized firm commitment, the gain or loss is recognized in the income statement in the period it occurs together with the offsetting loss or gain on the hedged item attributable to the risk being hedged.

501

The result will be to recognize in the income statement the extent to which the hedge is not effective. This type of hedge is referred to as a *fair value hedge*.

For a derivative designated as a hedge of the exposure to variable cash flows of a forecasted transaction, the effective portion of the derivatives gain or loss is initially reported as a component of "other comprehensive income," and subsequently transferred into income when the forecasted transaction affects income. The portion of any gain or loss which is not an effective hedge is recognized in income when it occurs. The concept of "other comprehensive income" does not (yet) exist under Canadian GAAP. This type of hedge is referred to as a *cash flow hedge*.

For a derivative designated as a hedge of the foreign currency exposure of the net investment in a foreign operation, the gain or loss is reported as a component of "other comprehensive income," as part of the cumulative translation adjustment. The other foreign currency hedges are accounted for as described above. A derivative designated as a hedge of a foreign currency exposure of an unrecognized firm commitment or an available for sale security is accounted for as a fair value hedge. A derivative designated as a hedge of the foreign currency exposure of a foreign currency denominated forecasted transaction is accounted for as a cash flow hedge.

Finally, for a derivative not designated as a hedging instrument, as noted earlier, any gain or loss (change in its fair value) is recorded in the income statement when it occurs.

Hedging

Hedging refers to the reduction or elimination of the effect of risk. In the case of financial instruments, market risk is hedged. That may refer to interest rate risk, currency risk, basis risk, price risk or some other form of market risk. A transaction to hedge risk is entered into with the expectation that it will reduce the exposure to loss that would otherwise result. In March 2003, the CICA issued an exposure draft on hedges that proposes to change the accounting for hedges for fiscal years starting after September 30, 2004. The discussion below is based upon current GAAP.

When a transaction is accounted for as a hedge, the gains or losses from the hedge position are recognized in the same period as gains or losses on the item being hedged. For example, if the hedged item is recorded at cost, the hedge would also be recorded at cost so that recognition of changes in its value would be deferred. Conversely, if the item being hedged is marked-to-market so that unrealized changes are recorded in income, changes in the value of the hedged item would also be recorded in income as they occur.

To qualify for hedge accounting, the following conditions must be met:

(a) the hedge must be designated as a hedge by management;
(b) the position to be hedged must expose the entity to some form of risk: interest rate risk, foreign exchange risk, basis risk or other price risk that may result in loss; and
(c) there must be a high probability that changes in the market value of the hedge will offset changes in the market value of the item being hedged.

PART D

Hedge accounting is always optional. If management of an enterprise does not designate a particular transaction to be a hedge, then it may not be accounted for in accordance with hedge accounting principles.

A financial asset or liability may be classified as a hedge of a future position when it is highly probable that the future position will materialize. A high degree of probability would likely exist if the company has a contractual commitment or when the characteristics and expected terms of the future transaction giving rise to the exposed position have been identified and there is persuasive evidence that the transaction will occur as expected.

Portfolio Approach

Most accounting is based on the aggregation of data. Through the process of bookkeeping, individual transactions are combined and summarized. The aggregation process culminates in the generation of financial statements. The underlying premise is that transactions and balances can be added together appropriately to present the user with more useful information.

Many financial instruments simply do not work that way. That is, the characteristics of individual items cannot simply be added together to determine the nature of the portfolio. This is particularly clear in the case of synthetic instruments or synthetic assets which are produced by combining individual financial instruments. The risk and reward characteristics of synthetics often differ markedly from their underlying constituent instruments.

For example, if a company purchases a call option and sells a put option on the same underlying asset at the same expiry date and strike price, the result is economically the same as owning outright that underlying asset, at least until the options expire. The effect is not simply that of adding up two options. Instead, the result is the creation of a different *synthetic* position.

A related problem is that it is generally assumed that information speaks for itself. For example, companies disclose in their notes to the financial statements the components of their long-term debt obligations. Normally, maturities, interest rates and other material information related to their long-term debt obligations would be disclosed. The sum of all the individual obligations equals the total debt payable shown on the balance sheet.

It is difficult to see how this sort of information should be provided for more complex off balance sheet instruments. For example, a company may have a variety of interest rate swaps outstanding. It is not at all clear how they should be disclosed, what data about each should be disclosed and how the amounts can be aggregated. The risk profile on debt with a particular coupon of a particular maturity is fairly straightforward. The risk profile on an interest rate swap can be simple or can be very complex. The question arises as to what should be disclosed to the readers.

Transactions and Commitments

As noted earlier, the traditional accounting paradigm is based on actual transfers of assets and liabilities. The key concept is that of a transfer of the risks and rewards of ownership. Most transactions represent the exchange of cash or the promise to eventually pay cash, for an asset or to satisfy an obligation. For financial instruments that have a market value when transacted this presents no difficulty. The purchaser of an option records the option at the amount paid for it. The seller of a bond records the proceeds of sale as the amount received. The seller is left with an obligation (liability) and the purchaser with an asset for that amount.

PART D

505

However, many financial instruments represent off balance sheet activities. They are promises to do something in the future: there is no immediate transfer of cash or other assets and, for that matter, there is nothing "owned", so the risks and rewards of ownership do not seem to be necessarily transferred. (Risk transfer has been separated from ownership by these instruments.) For example, a foreign exchange forward contract is an agreement to exchange cash flows in different currencies at a future date. Similarly, an interest rate swap is an agreement to calculate two interest payments on different bases and pay or receive the net amount, at various future dates.

These are *executory contracts*, that is, contracts not requiring immediate performance. A related characteristic is that at the moment of the transaction, these contracts have no net market value. In the case of the foreign exchange forward and the interest rate swap noted here, from the perspective of the customer, promises made for future delivery by either side are worth the same amount. (In the case of a market maker, the situation is a little more complex because a dealer may price his or her portfolio, for valuation purposes, based on bid or offer or some other price point between the two.)

Conventional accounting does not always handle in a satisfactory manner situations where there has been no performance by either party. As noted above, historic cost accounting generally relies upon the transfer of assets and liabilities to recognize a transaction. When an asset or liability is not actually transferred, accountants look for evidence of the transfer of an ownership interest. Transfer of the risks and rewards of ownership may be proven by the transfer of title, or by other evidence that risk transfer has taken place.

To determine the ownership interest involved in the case of a financial instrument, we need to determine just what sort of beast it is. But what are interest rate swaps or foreign exchange forwards? They are *not* deposits, securities or loans. Are they *arrangements*, *transactions* or *economic events*? If they are arrangements, how do we treat them in our accounting system that is based on transactions?

The notion of the transfer of ownership interests is central to existing accounting. For example, the sale of a bond represents the promise to deliver a bond (now, or at a future date) in exchange for the promise to deliver cash (or equivalent). An ownership interest is transferred, and there clearly is a value to it. The cost of the bond equals its market value which equals the cash due.

A foreign exchange forward is different. The two parties have agreed to an exchange in the future that has zero net present value. It has no value because both parties are acting rationally and are agreeing to an exchange at a price that equalizes the value today of the two future cash flows. Most interest rate swaps are similar in that they have no net present value when transacted.

Some financial instruments which are otherwise "off balance sheet" involve an initial payment such as an upfront fee. This represents an exception to the situation of no market value at the time of the transaction. Such fees can generally be considered as similar to loans, which are then, in effect, repaid over the life of the instrument. This still leaves the problem of how to account for the instrument itself.

The materiality of the financial instruments has accentuated the problem. In the case of a bond, fluctuations in its market value (which are generally disregarded if unrealized, under historical cost accounting) are relatively small compared to the accounting value

PART D

507

(cost) of the bond. In the case of the foreign exchange forward, any change in market value away from zero is large relative to the accounting value, which is zero. This is a simplification of course, and there are many complexities. The point is that conventional accounting does not cope very well with future commitments.

Risk and Uncertainty

Existing accounting principles were formulated when the world was simpler. This can be seen by the simple approach to dealing with contingencies. A contingent loss is recorded in the financial statements if it is likely to occur. A contingent gain that is likely to occur is not recorded in the financial statements themselves but merely disclosed in the notes to the financial statements.

In general, events are only recognized for accounting purposes when they result from dealings with third parties. In those cases, the amounts of the transactions (by definition) represent fair market value. An exception is made on the grounds of *conservatism* if there is a probable overstatement of the benefit resulting from such an event. However, there is no concern if the benefit may be understated. These principles can be seen in operation in accounting for accounts receivable.

Accounts receivable are recorded at actual amounts owed by customers less an allowance for doubtful accounts. The amount owing to a customer is generally not difficult to determine: it equals the amount of the sale that gave rise to the receivable. There may be an allowance for doubtful accounts, which is subject to uncertainty. The allowance may be calculated in various ways but it is intended to be a "best estimate" of those receivables that will ultimately be uncollectible. And there is little doubt as to the amount of the receivable before any allowance is determined.

Valuing an interest rate swap is more complex. Certainly, it will have a fair market value (which may be positive or negative) which represents the present value of the future cash flows, discounted at whatever rate the market deems appropriate, at a particular point in time.

Assume that the mark-to-market value on a $20-million (notional principal) interest rate swap, a month after it is transacted, is $10,000. Looking at likely interest rate movements over the life of the swap, it may be reasonable to believe that there is a 95 per cent chance that the market value will vary between minus $800,000 and plus $800,000 over its life. If these amounts are material to the entity, the question arises as to how to disclose this uncertainty in a manner that will be useful to readers. Of course, financial instruments will fluctuate in value based on many different risks in the market place: foreign exchange rates, interest rates, changes in implied volatility of options, time decay of options, and so on.

Derecognition

Most accounting is concerned with how to recognize items for financial accounting purposes. Derecognition refers to the removal of items from financial statements. In many cases, derecognition (referred to in the Re-Exposure Draft as "discontinuing recognition") is not remarkable. Assets are removed from a balance sheet when they are sold or disposed of, liabilities are removed when they are discharged. However, on occasion, an asset or liability is transferred to others in a manner that involves the retention of some element of risk by the original owner. It is these transactions that require analysis in order to determine whether the assets or liabilities may be derecognized.

One development that is changing the structure of the financial services industry is that of *securitization*. This is the purchase and sale of loans and debt by means of their conversion into a tradeable financial instrument. One area of derecognition is in the sale of an asset such as a loan or account receivable. The question then arises as to the circumstances under which such a sale can be recorded as a sale for accounting purposes.

Another accounting problem also grouped under derecognition is *in-substance defeasance*. Defeasance refers to the setting aside of cash to retire corporate debt. *In-substance defeasance* is the setting aside of cash in a way that provides considerable assurance that the debt will be discharged but that does not in fact constitute a legal redemption of the debt. The question then arises as to the circumstances under which the debt and its related cash can be removed from the balance sheet.

The accounting treatment of derecognition issues may have a significant effect on the balance sheet and reported financial ratios. Sales of receivables and in-substance defeasance are discussed below.

Sale of receivables

In a sale of receivables, a creditor transfers an interest in its accounts receivable to another entity. The transferee may acquire an undivided interest in the receivables or may purchase units, shares or other securities in a special purpose entity set up to own the receivables. The transferor receives consideration for the receivables transferred and may also agree to service the receivables for a fee. The transferor may retain varying degrees of continuing involvement with the receivables in question.

Under what conditions would it be appropriate to reflect the transfer of receivables as a sale rather than as a financing? In March 2001, the Accounting Standards Board of the CICA released Accounting Guideline 12, *Transfers of Receivables*. This replaced the previous guidance issued by the Emerging Issues Committee of the CICA, EIC - 9. The new guidance focuses on control over the receivables that have been transferred, based on a financial components approach. Canadian GAAP regarding the transfer of receivables is now harmonized with United States GAAP and reflects the applicable portions of Statement of Financial Accounting Standards 140, Accounting for Transfers and Servicing of Financial Assets and Extinguishments of Liabilities.

In-substance defeasance

Defeasance refers to the removal of debt from the balance sheet by legally discharging it. In-substance defeasance refers to the removal of debt where the debt agreement contains no provision for defeasance, by depositing cash or securities in a trust solely to satisfy payments under the debt agreement. Recognition of extinguishment of debt determines when the debtor can recognize a gain or loss in the income statement.

The impetus for in-substance defeasance came during the last period of high interest rates. Many companies with low interest rate debt outstanding recognized that they could settle that debt for amounts considerably less than face value, giving rise to a gain. (In general, that gain should be deferred and recorded over the original term of the debt.) However, sometimes the debt could not be purchased in the open market, sometimes it carried call premiums above face value, and in other cases it was not callable at all due to the terms of the debt agreement. Therefore, those companies sought other means to take advantage of the opportunity to settle (and refinance) debt profitably.

PART D

511

The mechanism that was developed was a special-purpose trust that would assume responsibility for the debt and would be given the assets necessary to service it.

Many of the earlier instances of defeasance were inspired by their income statement impact. However, despite the current requirement to amortize any gain or loss over the remaining term of the bonds, defeasance transactions are still attractive to improve the debt/equity ratios on balance sheets.

The attractiveness of in-substance defeasance can be illustrated with an example. Assume that bonds are outstanding with a face value (and issue proceeds) of $5 million and bearing interest at 4 per cent. The bonds have a market value (present value of future cash flows) of $4.5 million because market interest rates have increased. The issuer of the bonds then purchases marketable securities of the same maturity as the bonds, bearing market interest rates of 8 per cent. If both the asset (the marketable securities) and the debt (the bonds) were transferred to a trust, the company could recognize a $0.5 million gain in its income statements. Normally, this gain will be deferred and amortized over the remaining term of the bonds.

The use of "Special Purpose Entities" to remove liabilities from the balance sheet is discussed below on page 518.

Liability vs. Equity

It is sometimes unclear whether a source of financing for a corporation is a liability or an equity instrument. To take advantage of income tax and other rules, instruments that have the characteristics of debt may legally constitute equity. For example, preferred shares that are redeemable and retractable and carry stated interest rates may legally be equity instruments but have many of the characteristics of liabilities. Similarly, instruments that have the characteristics of equity may legally constitute debt. For example, they may be deeply subordinated and there may be limited intention to ever redeem them. In addition, some financial instruments have both equity and debt elements.

The *CICA Handbook* requires that the substance of a financial instrument, rather than its legal form, governs whether it is classified as a liability or equity instrument (sections 3860.18 *et seq.*).

The primary means of determining whether the instrument is a liability or equity is whether there is a contractual obligation to deliver cash (or another financial instrument), or exchange for another financial instrument on terms that may be unfavourable to the issuer. When there is such an obligation, the instrument is a liability for accounting purposes, even if its legal form is that of an equity instrument. Otherwise the financial instrument is an equity instrument.

Thus, a preferred share that is redeemable by the issuer for a predetermined amount is a liability for accounting purposes. Similarly, if its terms do not require redemption by the issuer but make redemption very probable because, for example, of an accelerating dividend, or if redemption is at the option of the holder which is likely to occur, the instrument is classified as a liability.

A financial instrument that has both liability and equity elements should be divided for presentation purposes, with the liability and equity elements disclosed separately on the balance sheet.

PART D

The presentation required will affect the required measurement as well, notwithstanding section 3860 purports to exclude measurement issues. In EIC-69, the Emerging Issues Committee of the CICA confirmed this:

> The Committee reached a consensus that the issuer of a financial instrument should determine the instrument's balance sheet presentation under CICA 3860 and then recognize and measure it, or its components, in accordance with its balance sheet presentation. The issuer would apply the same accounting treatments to all financial instruments or components thereof in the same balance sheet class.

As a result, addressing presentation of various debt or equity items will imply (and require) dealing with measurement issues as well. For example, redeemable preferred shares may be classified as a liability. If they are redeemable at other than their stated redemption amount, the premium or discount would be accounted for in the same manner as the premium or discount on a bond. Similarly, the debt and equity components of convertible bonds must be presented separately, and any issue discount or premium on the liability component must be accounted for as a discount or premium on non-convertible debt.

Interest, dividends, and other income or expense related to a financial instrument classified as a liability should be reported in the income statement. Thus, a dividend on a redeemable preferred share issued that is classified as a liability must be shown as a deduction in the income statement. Conversely, distributions to holders of financial instruments classified as equity should be reported in the statement of changes in equity and not in the income statement.

Disclosure

GAAP requires that any information required for fair presentation of financial information must be included in the financial statements (which include notes and supporting schedules). To the extent that financial instruments are not recognized as financial assets or liabilities on the balance sheet, disclosure in notes to the financial statements is required by GAAP to ensure that the readers of the financial statements are fully informed. As is the case with any disclosure under generally accepted accounting principals, immaterial items need not be disclosed.

Section 3860 of the *CICA Handbook* provides considerable guidance on the disclosures required for financial instruments:

> The purpose of the disclosures . . . is to provide information that will enhance understanding of the significance of recognized and unrecognized financial instruments to an entity's financial position, performance and cash flows and assist in assessing the amounts, timing and certainty of future cash flows associated with those instruments. In addition to providing specific information about particular financial instrument balances and transactions, entities are encouraged to provide a discussion of the extent to which financial instruments are used, the associated risks and business purposes served. A discussion of management's policies for controlling the risks associated with the financial instruments, including policies on matters such as hedging of risk exposures, avoidance of undue concentrations of risk and requirements for collateral to mitigate credit risks, provides a valuable additional perspective that is independent of the specific instruments outstanding at a particular time. Some entities provide such information in a commentary that accom-

PART D

panies their financial statements rather than as part of the financial statements.

Transactions in financial instruments may result in an entity assuming of transferring to another party one or more of the financial risks described below. The required disclosures provide information that assists users of financial statements in assessing the extent of risk related to both recognized and unrecognized financial instruments.

(a) Price risk — There are three types of price risk: currency risk, interest rate risk and market risk. Currency risk is the risk that the value of a financial instrument will fluctuate due to changes in foreign exchange rates. Interest rate risk is the risk that the value of a financial instrument will fluctuate as a result of changes in market interest rates. Market risk is the risk that the value of a financial instrument will fluctuate as a result of changes in market prices whether those changes are caused by factors specific to the individual security or its issuer or factors affecting all securities traded in the market.

(b) Credit risk — Credit risk is the risk that one party to a financial instrument will fail to discharge an obligation and cause the other party to incur a financial loss.

(c) Liquidity risk — Liquidity risk, also referred to as funding risk, is the risk that an entity will encounter difficulty in raising funds to meet commitments associated with financial instruments. Liquidity risk may result from an inability to sell a financial instrument quickly at close to its fair value.

(d) Cash flow risk — Cash flow risk is the risk that future cash flows associated with a monetary financial instrument will fluctuate in amount. In the case of a floating rate debt instrument, for example, such fluctuations result in a change in the effective interest rate of the financial instrument, usually without a corresponding change in its fair value. (paragraphs 3860.43 – 44)

Interestingly, not all of the financial risks discussed in Chapter 17 are covered by the discussion in the *CICA Handbook*, although the risks that are more readily quantified are included.

An entity should disclose information about the extent and nature of each type of financial instrument, whether recognized on the balance sheet or not recognized. For each type of financial instrument, the following information should be disclosed:

- Extent and nature, including significant terms and conditions that may affect the amount, timing and uncertainty of future cash flows.
- Exposure to interest rate risk, including repricing or maturity dates and effective rates.
- Exposure to credit risk, including maximum exposure and significant concentrations.
- Fair value of the financial instruments.

In the case of financial instruments accounted for as a hedge of an anticipated future transaction, the following should be disclosed:

PART D

- A description of the future transactions, including when they are expected to occur.
- A description of the hedging instrument.
- The amount of any deferred or unrecognized gain or loss, and the expected timing of its recognition as income or expense.

The disclosure provisions are complex and lengthy: the reader is advised to review section 3860 of the *CICA Handbook* and consult his or her chartered accountant.

Enron Corporation and Special Purpose Entities

The demise of Enron Corporation in December 2001 shocked the financial community. Enron had been held up as a stellar example of novel approaches to business and treasury activity. Many press reports, magazine articles, and even business school case studies reported on Enron's success and suggested that this represented the birth of a new kind of company.

It turned out that Enron's success was built on doubtful accounting, as well as apparent frauds that resulted in the personal enrichment of various executives. In some cases, the accounting rules were simply disregarded, but in others they appear to have been carefully followed but in a way that produced a misleading result. Among the myriad of problems unearthed at Enron was the use of "Special Purpose Entities" (SPEs).

Special Purpose Entities are nominally independent entities (corporations or partnerships). The SPE can be treated as independent, and not included in a company's consolidated financial statements if certain conditions are met. First, an independent investor must make an equity investment of at least 3 per cent of the SPE's assets. This is to ensure that losses in the SPV are at the risk of the outside independent investor. Second, the independent investor must exercise control of the SPE. These rules are designed to ensure that the SPE is independent of the company and is financed independently. If these rules are not me, the SPE must be included in the company's consolidated financial statements. (The 3 per cent equity requirement was raised to 10 per cent after the Enron bankruptcy.)

Enron used hundreds of SPEs, one example follows. In early 1998, Enron invested $10 million (all figures here are in U.S. dollars) to acquire shares of Rythms NetConnections Inc. ("R"), an internet service provider, at $1.85 per share. In April 1999, R went public at $21.00 per share, and after the first day of trading the share price reached $69.00. By the end of May 1999, the price was around $55.00 per share, resulting in an unrealized gain of about $300 million to Enron. Due to a lock-up agreement, Enron was unable to sell its investment before the end of 1999. Enron accounted for its investment by recording it at fair value, so the increase in the value of its investment in R was recorded as a gain on Enron's income statement. Enron then attempted to hedge its investment in R against declines in value by taking advantage of accrued but unreported gains on forward contracts that gave Enron the ability to buy shares of its own stock at prices well below market value. A company is prohibited from recording gains from buying its own shares. (Enron had previously acquired the forwards to hedge the dilution caused by the issuance of employee stock options. Due to the rise in Enron's share price, these forwards had large unrealized gains.)

Enron then created a limited partnership SPE that was financed with the forward contracts. A series of complex transfers of shares, notes, swaps, puts and calls ensued, with the intention of transferring the risk of fluctuation in the shares of R to the SPE. To

PART D

meet the technical requirements for non-consolidation, the SPE needed to have outside equity equal to a value of at least 3 per cent of its assets. However, when it was formed, the SPE had negative equity because its liabilities (primarily a put on the shares of R) exceeded its assets (cash and some restricted shares of Enron). The accounting firm Andersen (which imploded soon after Enron exploded) said in December 2001:

> In evaluating the 3% residual equity level required to qualify for non-consolidation, there were some complex accounting issues concerning the valuation of various assets and liabilities. When we reviewed this transaction again in October 2001, we determined that our team's initial judgement that the 3% test was met was in error.

On November 8, 2001, Enron issued a press release indicating that the SPE was not properly capitalized with outside equity and that it should have been consolidated. As a result, Enron restated its 1999 and 2000 financial statements. (As a postscript, the process of unwinding the structure in 2000 lead to further complexity and weirdness.)

In this case, the 3 per cent requirement for external equity was not met, hence the structure failed to achieve its accounting objective. But even if the 3 per cent requirement had been met, it fails a reasonability test: the SPE was not independent of Enron, it had no purpose other than to allow Enron to use appreciation in its own shares to hedge against losses in an investment (and possibly to personally enrich some Enron employees). This account has been vastly simplified, the actual mechanics are mind-boggling, and this is only one of scores of examples of dubious accounting that surfaced from Enron.

An accounting environment that focused on the economic substance of a transaction would have ensured that a transaction such as the one above would never be contemplated. When accounting is seen as disparate rules that may be enforced blindly and is subject to loopholes, the inevitable result is accounting that makes no sense and invites abuse.

Sources of Accounting Guidance

Generally Accepted Accounting Principles

To assess the appropriate accounting treatment of a financial instrument, it is necessary to determine the broad accounting principles involved, as well as any specific rules in place that relate to the particular facts. These are collectively referred to as "Generally Accepted Accounting Principles".

The *CICA Handbook* of the Canadian Institute of Chartered Accountants is the recognized authority that specifies Canadian accounting principles and practices.

Authoritative sources

The *CICA Handbook* actually contains three different sources of accounting guidance. In order of importance they are: Accounting Recommendations, CICA Accounting Guidelines, and Abstracts of Issues Discussed by the Emerging Issues Committee.

If there is insufficient guidance in the Handbook, other sources should be consulted, based on the list of sources set out in the book and reproduced above on pages 490 and 491.

PART D

Emerging Issues Committee

Numerous accounting issues related to financial instruments have been discussed by the Emerging Issue Committee of the Canadian Institute of Chartered Accountants. The Terms of Reference of the Emerging Issues Committee are as follows:

> To provide a forum for the timely review of emerging accounting issues that are likely to receive divergent or unsatisfactory treatment in practice in the absence of some guidance.

The Ontario Securities Commission has stated (Staff Accounting Communique No. 1, June 23, 1989) that it "would expect reporting issuers to comply with the CICA Accounting Guidelines and the consensus views of the CICA Emerging Issues Committee since these sources represent considered views of informed accountants on areas for which there are no specific standards." The Direction de l'information of the Commission des valeurs mobilieres du Quebec expressed similar sentiments in its Accounting Communiqué No. 1 (April 20, 1990).

Guidance on financial instruments

Section 3860 of the *CICA Handbook* provides guidance primarily on the **disclosure and presentation** of financial instruments and derivatives. Canadian practice for the **measurement and valuation** of financial instruments and derivatives is not well defined. Eventually it will be consistent with the American rules. However, those rules are very complex and in some cases almost unworkable, so they are likely to continue their evolution.

Following is a list of sources for guidance on accounting for financial instruments. For measurement and valuation issues in many cases where Canadian GAAP is silent, companies have the choice of following Canadian GAAP (which may be fairly flexible) or the U.S. rules.

ACCOUNTING ISSUES IN TREASURY MANAGEMENT

CICA Accounting Recommendations

Section

1000	Financial statement concepts
1500	General standards of financial statement presentation
1501	International accounting standards
1508	Meaurement uncertainty
1520	Income statement
1650	Foreign currency translation
3050	Long term investments
3065	Leases
3280	Contractual obligations
3290	Contingencies
3400	Revenue
3820	Subsequent events
3830	Non-monetary transactions
3860	Financial instruments — disclosure and presentation
4100	Pension plans

CICA Exposure Drafts

March 2003	Financial Instruments — Recognition and Measurement
March 2003	Hedges
March 2003	Comprehensive income

CICA Accounting Guidelines

Number

4	Fees and costs associated with lending activities
12	Transfers of receivables
13	Hedging relationships

PART D

Emerging Issues Committee — Abstracts of Issues Discussed

121 Accounting for wash sales
122 Balance sheet classifications of callable debt obligations and debt obligations expected to be refinanced
128 Accounting for trading, speculative or non-hedging derivative financial instruments
131 Disclosure of accounting policies for derivative financial instruments and derivative commodity instruments

Where guidance is lacking in accounting, including accounting for financial instruments, there is a variety of other material available. Two sources are particularly useful, either for specific guidance, or for help in reasoning by analogy:

Accounting Standards in Evolution by R.M. Skinner and J.A. Milburn (2nd edition, 2001, Prentice Hall, Toronto) remains the authoritative text on Canadian accounting theory. The work is clear and insightful, and often very useful in identifying the critical issues.

Statements of the Financial Accounting Standards Board (FASB), in the United States, address many issues regarding financial instruments. The following may be relevant:

Statement
Number

12 Accounting for certain marketable securities
49 Accounting for product financing arrangements
65 Accounting for certain mortgage banking activities
76 Extinguishment of debt
77 Reporting by transferors for transfers of receivables with recourse
80 Accounting for futures contracts
84 Induced conversions of convertible debt
91 Accounting for non-refundable fees and costs associated with originating or acquiring loans and initial direct costs of leases

PART D

105 Disclosure of information about financial instruments with off-balance-sheet risk and financial instruments with concentrations of credit risk

107 Disclosures about fair value of financial instruments

115 Accounting for certain investments in debt and equity securities

119 Disclosure about derivative financial instruments and fair value of financial instruments

125 Accounting for transfer and servicing of financial assets and extinguishment of financial liabilities (superceded by No. 140)

127 Deferral of the effective date of certain provisions of FASB Statement No. 125

129 Disclosure of information about capital structure

133 Accounting for derivative instruments and hedging activities

134 Accounting for mortgage-backed securities retained after the securitization of mortgage loans held for sale by a mortgage banking enterprise

138 Accounting for certain derivative instruments and certain hedging activities

140 Accounting for transfers and servicing of financial assets and extinguishments of liabilities (a replacement of FASB Statement No. 25)

Many other sources of information are available, although they will often be less helpful in addressing specific queries. CICA Research Studies, Canadian accounting textbooks, other U.S. material and magazine and journal articles may all be of assistance. Several of the major chartered accountancy firms publish newsletters and other information on accounting issues including financial instruments.

21

Legal Issues in Treasury Management

Overview

When unusual transactions occur, the lawyers are called in, but legal issues are often not considered during the day-to-day pressures of routine business activity. It can be useful to review legal implications of routine transactions such as billing, as well as less common actions such as negotiating a new banking arrangement.

This chapter reviews some legal issues for the treasurer to consider, for transactions ranging from routine business dealings to initial public offerings. Of course, this material covers a vast area: its objective is as much to raise questions as to provide all of the answers. Legal counsel should be consulted where appropriate.

527

Dealing with Customers

Identifying customers

The first critical legal issue to address when dealing with customers is fundamental, namely, properly identifying the parties. Proper legal names should be used in documenting a transaction, whether the entity involved is a corporation, partnership or a natural person. When dealing with a corporation or a partnership, it is possible to conduct a search with the appropriate government registry to determine the legal name. In the case of a natural person, the only way to ascertain the proper legal name is by reviewing a copy of a birth certificate. The use of the proper legal name is necessary should legal action be required, and is essential to perfect a security interest (discussed below) against the entity.

In addition, it is important to ensure that the legal entity involved is an operating company with assets and not simply a holding company (that is, a company whose only assets are shares in the capital of other companies).

Corporate authority

An agreement with another party is only binding against the other party if the person signing the agreement has the capacity or is authorized to bind the other party. It can be assumed that a natural person has the capacity to enter into an obligation binding him or herself. However, there are exceptions to this rule. Minors do not have the capacity to contract nor do persons who are mentally incompetent.

Persons authorized to sign on behalf of corporations are established by a resolution of the shareholders or directors or by agreement of the shareholders. Accordingly, in dealing with a corporation, it is important to ensure that the person executing the document on behalf of the corporation has been granted the authority to bind the corporation. A copy of the authorizing resolution should be obtained. One general exception to this rule is established by statute and is known as the indoor management rule. The indoor management rule means that a person with apparent authority to bind a corporation will in fact bind the corporation regardless of whether the person actually had the authority to do so. There are some limitations to this rule, so it should only be relied on for routine transactions.

Each partner of a general partnership has the authority to bind the partnership and its assets in respect of partnership business. In dealing with a partnership, therefore, it is only necessary to ensure that the person being dealt with is in fact a partner or has the apparent authority of a partner.

Limited partnerships act through the general partner and usually only the general partner is authorized to bind the limited partnership. Limited partnerships must be registered with the provincial authority, and a search of the registry will disclose the identity of the general partner and each limited partner.

Trusts are entities created by a settlement of trust. Trusts act through trustees who are vested with authority in the trust agreement. A trustee only has the power granted to it by the trust agreement. Accordingly, when transacting business with a trust, the trust agreement must be reviewed to determine the identity of the trustee and the authority of the trustee to bind the trust or otherwise deal with trust assets.

PART D

529

Invoicing and billing

A properly drafted invoice accurately describes all relevant business terms including a clear description of goods sold or services provided, the terms for payment, interest rate payable on unpaid amounts including the date from which interest starts to accrue, and the amount of interest due to the date of the invoice. The interest rate should be expressed as an annual rate.

In order to receive a security interest (discussed below) from the customer to secure the receivable created by the invoice, the invoice should include charging language in which the customer expressly grants a security interest in the goods purchased. The customer must also sign the invoice.

If possible, a delivery confirmation system that provides evidence of, among other things, the date of delivery and the condition of goods on delivery should be implemented.

Securing receivables

It may be desirable to secure payment of an invoice by taking a security interest in the property which is the subject of the invoice or even additional personal property of the customer. To create a valid security interest in personal property, the creditor must grant a security interest and the security interest must be properly *perfected* under applicable personal property security legislation. In the common law provinces of Canada, a security interest is *perfected*, subject to certain preconditions, by registering a financing statement in the appropriate government registry system. The financing statement includes the customer's proper legal name, as discussed above, the birth date if the customer is a natural person, the customer's address, company's name and address, and a brief description of the collateral. Use of a name other than a proper legal name on a financing statement registered under provincial personal property security legislation renders the registration invalid. A security interest becomes effective from the time it is registered. Priority of competing security interests is generally governed by the order of registration, with the earliest registration having priority over all subsequent registrations. One notable exception to this general rule, the *purchase money security interest*, is discussed below.

The second requirement to the creation of a perfected security interest, the granting of a security interest, is usually accomplished through a written agreement between the company and the customer (e.g., an invoice signed by the customer) in which the security interest is specifically granted, the collateral is clearly described, and the respective rights and obligations of the parties are detailed.

A financing statement is valid for the registration period specified in the financing statement and may be indefinitely renewed by the filing of financing change statements prior to expiry.

One of the exceptions to the general priority rules described above is the *purchase money security interest*. This is a special priority security interest granted in an asset to the seller of the asset or a lender that lends the purchase money for the asset. The creation of a purchase money security interest requires technical compliance with applicable statutory provisions. A purchase money security interest in inventory requires registration of a financing statement prior to delivery of the inventory to the customer (or its agent). In addition, there must also be notification to any other secured party with an interest in the inventory of the customer that there is the intention to acquire a purchase money security interest in the inventory, with a description of the inventory by item or type. This notice must be delivered before delivery of the invento-

PART D

ry to the customer. A purchase money security interest in assets other than inventory is created by registering a financing statement prior to or within 10 days after the customer obtains possession of the collateral. There is no notice requirement.

Internal Controls

Books and records

All books and records should be maintained and kept up-to-date. If the company were to enter into an unusual transaction such as a sale or a loan arrangement, the due diligence process will include a requirement that books, records and information be delivered for review by the opposite transacting party or its counsel. In particular, the following information will likely be required to be produced and should therefore be readily available:

- material contracts, such as supply agreements;
- equipment leases;
- real property leases ;
- inventory listings;
- receivables listings categorized by age;
- employee listings;
- labour contracts;
- copies of pension plans and other benefit plans;
- a listing of intellectual property including trademarks, patents and copyright;
- a summary of outstanding claims pending to which the corporation is a party;
- tax returns, notices of assessment, and other evidence that the company is current in payment of its taxes, including income taxes and property taxes.

The gathering of this information and documentation could be extremely time-consuming if it is not maintained currently, and coordinating delivery of these items may delay closing or hinder completion of the contemplated transaction.

Tickler system

A diary or tickler system should be established to ensure that time-sensitive obligations are met. Security interests perfected under personal property security legislation will cease to be effective unless a financing change statement is filed prior to the expiry date of the current registration. Accordingly, it is essential to establish a system to track expiry dates of financing statements. As well, a tickler system will help to ensure that any reporting obligations to the lenders are fulfilled, whether quarterly, annually, monthly, weekly or even daily. Failure to report within the timeframes established in the credit documentation is generally an event of default allowing the lender to accelerate the obligations. In addition, lenders often impose a notice requirement to borrow under established credit facilities. The notice requirements should be readily retrievable to avoid unexpected delays in borrowing. Finally, for a regulated business, there may be reporting obligations to the governing authority and the timing of these reporting requirements should be diarized.

Dealing with Third Parties

Related parties

Related party transactions should be managed and documented in the same manner as third party transactions. For example, any corporate actions should be authorized by resolution. In particular, intercorporate transfers of assets, including funds, should be properly recorded in the books and records of both the transferor and the transferee. Evidence of indebtedness, such as promissory notes which should include the repayment terms and interest obligations, if any, should be issued. Consideration should be given to taking security to secure indebtedness. Failure to treat related party transactions in this manner may nullify any benefits of corporate structure involving separate and distinct corporate entities, should any of the members of the corporate groups experience financial difficulty.

Care should also be taken to ensure that related party transactions are undertaken in a manner permitted by the lenders. Credit agreements frequently impose restrictions on the ability to deal with non-arm's length persons and usually require that any such dealings be conducted on terms no more favourable to the related party than those made available to non-related parties.

Dealings with intermediaries

Care should be taken when engaging intermediaries such as financial advisors. In particular, no proprietary information of a confidential or privileged nature relating to the affairs of the business should be disclosed to any intermediary until the intermediary signs confidentiality agreements or non-disclosure agreements in which it agrees to keep the information acquired in the course of their engagement or in the course of due diligence confidential. In addition, the scope of the relationship with the intermediary should be clearly established before the commencement of the engagement in order to ensure that the intermediary does not exceed its authority or undertake initiatives not contemplated. Further, exclusivity issues should be dealt with before any formal engagement of the intermediary. Financial advisors may request exclusivity regarding matters beyond the scope of the engagement, in which case it may be appropriate to refuse.

Dealing with Lenders

Bank accounts

One of the most significant relationships for any company is its relationship with its bankers. The documents governing the basic banking relationship are the current account documents. These include the operation of account agreements which establish the general rules as to the deposit of money, chequing privileges and the operation of the bank accounts; signature cards; a certificate of incumbency outlining the officers and directors; and the banking resolution authorizing particular officers and directors to undertake banking business.

Borrowing from banks

Traditionally, if companies needed to borrow money, they would turn to their banker for the loan. With the maturity of the Canadian lending market and the entry into the market by non-traditional lenders, there is now the ability to select a lender to provide credit facilities most suitable to the business needs.

Traditional lenders, the banks listed in Schedules 1 and 2 of the *Bank Act*, continue to provide traditional operating and term loans. Operating loans are generally structured as revolving loans bearing floating interest rates that are utilized for working capital purposes. Such loans are payable upon demand by the lender. A portion of the operating facility may be advanced by way of Canadian or U.S. dollar overdrafts. Maximum borrowings are usually governed by a borrowing base, generally calculated as a percentage of good quality accounts receivable and eligible inventory less priority payables. Term loans are usually non-revolving and payable over a specified term either by regular installments or by way of a lump sum on maturity. The proceeds of term loans are generally utilized to purchase capital assets such as land and equipment. Term loans are generally not subject to acceleration unless an event of default has occurred.

Commitment letters

The terms and conditions pursuant to which a lender is prepared to make credit facilities available are initially set out in a commitment letter. In more complex transactions the commitment letter is usually superseded by a loan agreement that expands upon the rights and obligations of the parties. Regardless of whether the commitment letter is to be replaced by a loan agreement, it is critical that the commitment letter accurately describe the business deal. It is often believed that inaccuracies will be worked out in negotiation of the final closing documentation. However, it is often very difficult to persuade a lender to agree to accept terms other than terms outlined in the commitment letter, and the lender is not obliged to accept any proposed amendment. Accordingly, before any commitment fees or other non-refundable payments are made to any lender in connection with the issuance of the commitment letter, the company and its counsel should be satisfied that the proposed transaction is acceptable if closed in accordance with the commitment letter without amendment.

Loan agreements

A typical loan agreement will require the company, as well as guarantors, to restrict their business activities or operate in a manner satisfactory to the lender. This will be effected through extensive covenants, both positive and negative. Typically, these include covenants relating to financial reporting obligations, payment of taxes, maintenance of books and records, maintenance of adequate insurance coverage, the use of proceeds of the credit facility, notice requirements, protection of assets, restrictions on incurring indebtedness or further encumbering assets, restrictions on related party dealings and restrictions on payments to third parties. As well, a senior lender will impose financial covenants based upon the financial statements and cash flow such as debt/equity ratios, interest coverage ratios, current ratios, minimum tangible net worth requirements, debt coverage ratios and similar financial tests. Compliance with the financial ratios are strictly monitored by lenders, as a failure to comply is usually interpreted as an early warning sign of potential financial difficulties. Care should be taken when negotiating these covenants to ensure that the terms are properly defined and that, assuming normal business operations, the tests may be satisfied.

The loan agreement will also include extensive representations and warranties, including representations and warranties as to corporate existence, power and authority, title to and locations of assets, solvency, payment of taxes, and the existence and status of third party relationships including labour matters, pensions, franchises, and customer and trade relations. The loan agreement or commitment letter will provide that loans are not available until specific conditions precedent are satisfied or waived. Usual conditions precedent include completion of due diligence, payment of fees including work fees and legal fees, delivery of security, and supporting corporate documentation including resolutions and certificates and delivery of satisfactory legal opinions. If the credit arrangement includes a term loan, the loan agreement or the commitment letter will also include a list of events of default usually including the failure to pay principal or interest, breach of covenant, misrepresentation, insolvency, unauthorized transfer of assets, change in voting control and default under material contracts. Except with respect to defaults that cannot be cured, or payment defaults, lenders are generally amenable to providing reasonable grace periods that would allow a default to be remedied before it becomes an event of default entitling the lender to accelerate payment of the loans. In addition, lenders

PART D

often attempt to include broad, catch-all events of default such as the occurrence of a "material adverse change". Material adverse change defaults should be resisted as they lack certainty and grant excessive discretion to the lender.

Non-bank lenders

Alternatives to traditional bank lenders include asset-based lenders, leasing companies and factors. Asset-based lenders, not surprisingly, lend against the value of assets, particularly current assets. Asset-based lenders may be appropriate if there is difficulty with complying with extensive covenants, in particular financial covenants. Asset-based lenders usually attribute higher lending values to receivables and inventory, but because they primarily rely upon asset values as opposed to covenant compliance to manage their risk, they monitor collateral value much more extensively than would a traditional lender. Reporting by providing receivables listings and inventory lists may be required as frequently as weekly or even daily. Since the cash value of the current assets is the basis upon which the asset-based lender agrees to make funds available, cash receipts are tightly controlled. This may be done through the establishment of lockboxes in which customers are directed to remit any payments, or by blocked account arrangements in which the bank managing the current account agrees to hold monies received in the designated account for the benefit of the asset-based lender.

Another alternative to borrowing from traditional bank lenders is to finance equipment through operating or capital leases. Rather than tying up credit available under term credit facilities or operating credit facilities, a lease financing company may be used to finance the cost of acquisition of equipment. The title to the equipment remains with the leasing company, and the company enters into a lease agreement for a fixed period of time at a predetermined rental cost per month. The company may negotiate the right to return the equipment to the lessor, extend the term of the lease or purchase the equipment at the end of the term of the lease. Such leases can be structured as on-balance sheet or off-balance sheet for accounting and tax purposes. From a documentary point of view, lease agreements are typically in standard form, not heavily negotiated, and do not typically attract significant legal costs. Most traditional lenders will typically include limitations on the dollar amount of leases permitted in any given year. From a security point of view, the leasing company typically has a purchase money security interest in the equipment being leased, and would have a priority that ranks ahead of general bank security over that particular piece of equipment.

Another form of non-bank financing is factoring, in which receivables are sold to a financing company at a discount. Depending upon the arrangement, the factoring company may have complete control over receivable collections and even receive remittances directly, or the arrangement may be invisible to customers. In the latter case, it may be similar to an asset-backed loan, described above.

Other Lending Issues

Indemnities

Loan agreements often contain yield protection provisions that require the lender be indemnified if there is a change in circumstances, or a change in tax or similar legislation that reduces the rate of return to the lender. In addition, the company will likely be required to indemnify its lenders against claims arising against them as a result of their relationship with the company, in respect of environmental matters or any failure to comply with obligations in the credit documentation.

PART D

539

Withholding taxes

The loan agreement will often include a *gross up clause* in connection with withholding taxes. This normally provides that in the event that a lender is required to pay tax on any interest received from the company to a taxing authority, the payment must then be increased so that the amount actually received by the lender after the payment of the withholding tax is equal to the amount that it would have received but for the requirement to pay the withholding tax.

Security documentation

Most loans are secured. Senior lenders usually take security over all of the company's assets. Other types of lenders may only take security over particular assets. Typical security documents include:

- mortgages of land;
- general security agreements in which the company grants its lenders a security interest in all present and after acquired personal property;
- intellectual property security agreements, in which the company grants its lenders a security interest in any trade-marks, copyrights and patents;
- general assignments of accounts in which the company grants its lenders a security interest in accounts receivable and other book debts;
- assignment of material contracts in which contracts critical to the operation of the business are assigned in favour of the lenders, including assignment of insurance proceeds and the pledge of shares of subsidiaries;
- assignment of real estate leases, in the event that the company owns leased property.

It is often a requirement that any assignment of third party contracts, such as an assignment of material contracts or an assignment of leases, be accompanied by an acknowledgement from the third party that the contract is in good standing, and confirming certain terms of the contracts. It is often difficult to persuade a third party to provide these acknowledgements, as usually there is no economic benefit to them in providing the confirmation required. If the business is operated on leased premises, the lender will also usually require a non-disturbance agreement with the landlord of the premises to ensure that the landlord does not interfere with operations and which, among other things, grants the lender the right to enter the premises to realize on security and, in some cases, to operate the business. Landlords' non-disturbance agreements are usually subject to significant negotiation and often not provided by the landlord. Failure to obtain a landlord non-disturbance agreement may be a major impediment to closing a deal particularly when dealing with asset-based lenders. This is because asset-based lenders must be satisfied that they can take possession of the collateral against which it is lending should the company default in its obligations to its landlord. In certain situations, the failure to obtain a third party's acknowledgement or consent may be resolved by reserving an amount against availability so that the full amount is not actually borrowed.

Intercreditor agreement

Lenders will also want to insure that their security interests and collateral have priority over other security interests. Relative priorities of security are often determined through intercreditor agreements in which various creditors agree to deal with the assets in an agreed-upon manner. The terms of the intercreditor agreements will vary depending upon the nature of the competing creditors.

PART D

The closer that a subordinated loan is to equity, the greater will be the restrictions placed on the subordinated lender. Sometimes the subordinated lender is prohibited from taking any action in connection with its security for up to 180 days.

Estoppel letters

If assets are encumbered in favour of equipment lessors or other similar entities, the lender will usually require the equipment lessor to confirm that its registrations are limited to creating a security interest in particular assets, and will not be relied upon to perfect security interests in any other assets. This is usually done by estoppel letters addressed to the lender. Compiling estoppel letters is a time-consuming and sometimes fruitless exercise that often delays the closing of a transaction. The difficulty arising from the pursuit of estoppel letters can be minimized if the company ensures that its creditors properly limit their personal property security act registrations by describing the collateral or properly classifying the collateral in the financing statement.

Rights and Remedies after Default

When a company sells its goods or supplies its services to a customer on credit until the receivable is paid, it will be a creditor of the customer, and the customer will be the company's debtor. Conversely, when the company borrows money from its bank or another lender, it will be the debtor, and the bank the creditor. The rights and remedies available and the obligations imposed by statute on creditors and debtors are set out in this section.

Rights and remedies of a creditor

The rights and remedies available to a creditor after default by a debtor will depend on whether or not the creditor has taken any form of security for the debt owing. When the creditor has not taken security, its rights and remedies will be considerably more limited than when it has taken security.

Unsecured creditor

Court action

The principal remedy available to an unsecured creditor is to commence a court action in order to obtain a judgment against the debtor that can then be enforced against the debtor's property, pursuant to statutory remedies for such purpose.

A court action is normally commenced by the issuance of a statement of claim that must then be served personally on the defendant debtor. Where the defendant is served in Ontario, it has 20 days after the service of the statement of claim (30 days if it first delivers a notice of intent to defend) within which to deliver a statement of defence.

In bringing a court action, the creditor would attempt to obtain a summary judgment, without the need for a lengthy (and costly) trial. The creditor would anticipate that either the debtor does not deliver a statement of defence, or, if the debtor does deliver a statement of defence, the creditor would be successful in satisfying the court on a motion that there is no genuine issue for trial and the creditor should be granted judgment immediately.

PART D

When the creditor obtains judgment, the creditor will have several remedies available to it for enforcement of the judgment. The main remedies are:

- seizure and sale of assets; and
- garnishment.

Using the former remedy, the creditor would direct the local sheriff to seize the debtor's assets and sell them to satisfy the judgment. Using the latter remedy, the creditor would cause the court to send notices to parties that owe money to the debtor and direct them to make the payment to the court rather than to the debtor.

Bankruptcy petition

In an appropriate case, a creditor might consider issuing a petition against the debtor under the *Bankruptcy and Insolvency Act*, in order to have the debtor adjudged bankrupt. It would be an abuse of process to attempt to use a petition in order to collect a debt, but where the creditor is aware that the debtor is not paying other creditors or believes that the debtor is dealing improperly with its property, the issuance of a petition may be appropriate. Bankruptcy is discussed further below.

Secured creditor

Where a creditor holds security for its loan, the creditor does not first have to obtain a court judgment. The creditor's rights and remedies are determined by the provisions of the security documents, but subject to the requirements imposed by statute. Both federal and provincial/territorial legislation govern the enforcement of security by a secured creditor.

Notice of intention to enforce security

Under the *Bankruptcy and Insolvency Act*, before a secured creditor can enforce a security on all or substantially all of the inventory, accounts receivable or other property of a debtor used in a business, the secured creditor must give the debtor a statutory form of notice of its intention to enforce the security. Then, unless the debtor consents to earlier enforcement, it must wait until the expiry of the 10-day period after sending the notice before doing anything further. After the 10-day notice period has expired without the debtor commencing a proceeding for restructuring, as outlined below, the secured creditor may then begin to enforce its security.

The notice requirement applies only where security covers all or substantially all of the property used in a business. Consequently, where a company has security over just the property sold to a customer, and not over any other property of the customer, it is not necessary to give a notice of intention to the customer. Similarly, where a creditor has security over just the property that it has leased or sold to the company, the creditor may exercise its rights or default without giving the statutory notice. This is not a hard and fast rule, however. Many institutional creditors give notice as standard practice, regardless of the scope of their security.

Sale of debtor's property and appointment of receiver

The principal remedy available to a secured creditor is the sale of the debtor's property, which is subject to the security and application of the sale proceeds towards satisfaction of the indebtedness. Although security documents will normally empower the secured creditor to sell the debtor's secured property, the secured creditor will frequently appoint a receiver or a receiver/manager to do so, particularly where it is necessary to take possession of the debtor's property and/or to carry on its business.

PART D

A secured creditor initiates a private appointment of a receiver or receiver/manager simply by delivering a letter or other written instrument authorizing the receiver or receiver/manager to exercise all of the rights and remedies of the secured creditor set out in the security documents. If a more limited mandate is desired, it would enumerate the specific powers that the receiver or receiver/manager is to have. Alternatively, in an appropriate case, the secured creditor may seek the appointment by the court of a receiver or a receiver/manager pursuant to the applicable provincial or territorial statute (in Ontario, the *Courts of Justice Act*) or of an interim receiver pursuant to the *Bankruptcy and Insolvency Act*.

Before a secured creditor, receiver or receiver/manager may sell the property of a debtor, it must first send notices of the intended sale to the debtor and certain other parties as required under the applicable provincial or territorial statute. In Ontario, this would be the *Personal Property Security Act* (where the debtor's property includes personal property) or the *Mortgages Act* (where the debtor's property includes real property). Statutes are similar in other provinces and territories. The notice periods in Ontario are 15 days and 35 days, respectively. Upon expiry of the applicable notice period, the secured creditor, receiver or receiver/manager may then sell the debtor's property by the most appropriate method (private sale, public auction or public tender). In selling the debtor's property, the secured creditor, receiver or receiver/manager has an obligation to act in a commercially reasonable manner.

Foreclosure

A second remedy available to a secured creditor is foreclosure or becoming the owner of the debtor's property that is subject to the security in satisfaction of the indebtedness. A foreclosure of real property is obtained by a court action, and requires the issuance of a statement of claim and its service in the usual way on the debtor and on other persons who have an interest in the property and are named as defendants. Where the debtor or another defendant wishes to redeem the property, it must file a request to redeem. There will be a court hearing and the court will fix a redemption period (which in Ontario is not less than 60 days after the hearing). If no person redeems the mortgage, the secured creditor may obtain a final order of foreclosure and become the owner of the real property.

Foreclosure of personal property does not require recourse to the court. The secured creditor simply sends a notice to the debtor and other parties as required under the applicable provincial or territorial statute (in Ontario, the *Personal Property Security Act*). This will give them a period of time as stipulated by the statute (in Ontario, 30 days) within which to deliver a written objection to the creditor's intention to accept the property in satisfaction of the indebtedness. Upon expiry of the notice period without any objection, the secured creditor automatically becomes the owner of the debtor's personal property.

Bankruptcy petition

There may be cases in which a secured creditor desires to have the debtor become bankrupt, in addition to enforcing its remedies as set out above. A secured creditor may issue a petition provided that it can establish that it is unsecured for at least $1,000 and that an act of bankruptcy has occurred. Two situations in which bankruptcy may be advantageous to a secured creditor are the following:

- Where the debtor occupies leased premises, bankruptcy will prevent the landlord from terminating the lease or exercising its right to seize the debtor's property and sell it for unpaid rent. It will also give the trustee in bankruptcy the right to occupy the leased premises for up to three

PART D

547

months after the date of bankruptcy and to assign the lease subject to certain conditions.

- Where the debtor owes amounts for goods and services tax, retail sales tax and certain other taxes, and for vacation pay to employees, bankruptcy renders in-effective the pre-bankruptcy statutory priorities for such claims.

Rights and remedies of a debtor

General rights

The debtor is entitled to insist on compliance by the creditor with all obligations imposed on it both by statute and by contract (in the loan agreement, and, if there is security, in the security documents). For example, the loan agreement or the security documents may require the creditor to give to the debtor notice of default and a period of time within which the debtor may cure the default before the creditor may demand payment or enforce its security. Such a notice period would be in addition to and be given before any statutory notice period as described in the preceding section.

Where a creditor has commenced a court action, the debtor may defend the action, and, where the debtor feels that it has a grievance against the creditor, it may counterclaim for the damages that it has incurred as a result of the creditor's acts.

Reorganization or restructuring

A debtor may commence proceedings for the reorganization or restructuring of its financial affairs. Such proceedings may be informal or statutory, and may begin before or, subject to two qualifications, after a creditor has commenced the exercise of its rights and remedies as set out in the preceding section.

Informal proceedings

Informal proceedings for reorganization or restructuring simply involve the negotiation between the debtor and its creditors of amended terms of payment. The amended terms may encompass a reduction of the amount owing, an extended period of time for payment, or a combination of the two. Informal proceedings do not involve the court and therefore may be implemented at a lower cost than formal proceedings, but they are not without disadvantages. For one thing, the creditors will want assurance that each of them is receiving the same treatment. Where there are a large number of creditors, providing such assurance is very difficult for the debtor. A second disadvantage is that there is no stay of proceedings imposed on creditors. There is nothing to prevent one creditor or several creditors from pursuing their remedies to collect the debts owed to them even while the debtor is attempting to reorganize its affairs. The existence of such proceedings normally makes it difficult if not impossible for the debtor to reorganize successfully.

Because of the disadvantages of informal proceedings, formal proceedings under statute are more common. The applicable statutes are the *Bankruptcy and Insolvency Act* (Part III) and the *Companies' Creditors Arrangement Act*.

Proposal under the *Bankruptcy and Insolvency Act*

Under Part III of the *Bankruptcy and Insolvency Act*, insolvent individuals, corporations, partnerships and other entities may make a "proposal" to their creditors. The proposal will normally provide for one or more of the following elements: a percentage reduction of each creditor's claim, an extension of time for payment of claims, or, for corporate debtors, a conversion of claims or a portion of them into shares.

PART D

A debtor may initiate the process by filing a notice of intention to make a proposal. There is no need for a court order at this stage. The notice states the debtor's intention to make a proposal to its creditors and identifies the person who has consented to act as trustee. Attached to the notice is a list of the names of the known creditors with claims of $250 or more and the amounts of their claims. A copy of the notice is filed with the court and is sent to each known creditor.

As noted above, there are two qualifications regarding the timing of the filing. Where a secured creditor has served a notice of intention to enforce security more than 10 days before the filing, or where it has taken possession of secured assets for the purpose of realization before the filing, the stay of proceedings, mentioned below, will not apply to that secured creditor.

Upon filing the notice, the debtor will have 30 days within which to file a proposal. If it requires more time, it must apply to the court for an extension. The court has the power to grant extensions for a limited period of time. Failure to file a proposal within the required time (as it may have been extended) results in automatic bankruptcy. Instead of filing a notice of intention, a debtor may initiate the process by filing a proposal itself.

Upon filing a proposal or a notice of intention, the debtor obtains three significant benefits:

1. a stay of proceedings by creditors, including secured creditors (except those mentioned above to which the stay does not apply) and governments;
2. a prohibition against enforcement of "insolvency" clauses in agreements under which the other party may terminate or amend the agreement or accelerate the payment of indebtedness; and

3. subject to certain conditions, a right to disclaim commercial leases.

Part III expressly states, however, that parties to agreements with the debtor may require immediate payment for goods, services and use of leased or licensed property provided after the filing, and may not be required to make any further advance of money or credit.

A proposal must be made to all unsecured creditors. It may also be made to secured creditors. The proposal must be accepted by unsecured creditors at a meeting called for that purpose, and it must be approved by the court. Refusal results in automatic bankruptcy. For creditor acceptance, all classes of unsecured creditors must accept the proposal by a majority in number and two-thirds in value of the unsecured creditors of each class present at the meeting and voting on the proposal. If so accepted, the debtor applies to the court for approval of the proposal. To approve the proposal, the court must be satisfied that the terms of the proposal are reasonable and calculated to benefit the general body of creditors. Once accepted by the creditors and approved by the court, the proposal is binding on all unsecured creditors (and on any secured creditors that have accepted the proposal).

When a proposal has been fully performed, the trustee issues a certificate to that effect. Where there is a default that has not been remedied by the debtor or waived by the creditors, the creditor or the trustee may apply to the court for an order annulling the proposal. If the proposal is annulled, there is a deemed assignment in bankruptcy by the debtor.

PART D

Compromise or arrangement under the *Companies' Creditors Arrangement Act*

Under the *Companies' Creditors Arrangement Act*, an insolvent corporation may seek the court's assistance in making an arrangement with its creditors, where the total of claims against the corporation or affiliated corporations exceeds $5,000,000. The debtor applies to the court for an order that will typically grant the following relief:

- a declaration that the debtor is a company to which the act applies;
- a stay of proceedings by creditors (secured and unsecured), including governments, for up to 30 days;
- a prohibition against termination of contracts with the debtor by other parties to those contracts;
- authorization to file with the court a plan of compromise or arrangement between the debtor and its unsecured creditors and, if desired its secured creditors; and
- the appointment of a monitor to assist the debtor with the formulation of its plan.

The monitor must send a copy of the initial order to every known creditor with a claim of more than $250.

The debtor will undoubtedly require more than 30 days to prepare a plan, and will need to apply to the court for an extension of time. There are no provisions in the Act that limit the length of an extension or the number of extensions that a debtor may obtain. If the debtor does not present a plan within the required time (as it may have been extended), there will not be an automatic bankruptcy. However, the stay of proceedings by creditors will dissolve and they will be free to enforce their claims.

After the filing of a plan, the debtor will normally apply to the court for a further order that will normally establish a procedure for the submission of claims, the acceptance or disallowance of claims, and the resolution of disputes, and will schedule a meeting of creditors to vote on the plan.

Acceptance by creditors of a plan requires the same majority as for a proposal under the *Bankruptcy and Insolvency Act*. If the creditors accept the plan, the debtor applies for the court's sanction. If the court sanctions the plan, it becomes binding on the debtor and on all the creditors or the class of creditors, as the case may be. The plan thereby replaces the original agreement between the debtor and each creditor.

The Act makes no provision for the monitor to issue a certificate of performance when a debtor performs its obligations under the plan. Where the debtor defaults in performing the plan, unless the debtor makes an assignment in bankruptcy, the proper procedure is to seek an order declaring the compromise or arrangement void and adjudging the debtor bankrupt.

Bankruptcy

Introduction

Although the words "bankruptcy" and "insolvency" are synonymous to non-lawyers, they have different meanings in law. Insolvency is a financial condition; bankruptcy is a legal status.

Insolvency as defined in the *Bankruptcy and Insolvency Act* is:

- The condition of a debtor that is unable to meet its obligations as they generally become due; or
- That has ceased paying its current obligations in the ordinary course of business as they generally become due; or

PART D

- Whose property is not sufficient to enable payment of all its obligations, due and accruing due.

Bankruptcy is the legal status of an insolvent debtor that has become a "bankrupt" pursuant to a formal proceeding under the *Bankruptcy and Insolvency Act*. A bankrupt person is always insolvent, but an insolvent person does not necessarily have to become a bankrupt.

Ways to become bankrupt

There are three ways by which a debtor may become bankrupt: (i) petition for a receiving order, (ii) assignment and (iii) deemed assignment.

Petition for receiving order

A creditor may commence bankruptcy proceedings in Canada by filing a petition against a debtor. The petitioning creditor must be owed at least $1,000 (on an unsecured basis) by the debtor and must allege in the petition that the debtor has committed an act of bankruptcy within the six months preceding the date of the petition. The most common act of bankruptcy relied on is that the debtor has ceased to meet its liabilities generally as they become due. A secured creditor may initiate a bankruptcy petition if it can establish that it is unsecured for at least $1,000 and that an act of bankruptcy has occurred.

Like a statement of claim, a petition must be served personally on the debtor. If the petition is not contested by the debtor, a bankruptcy receiving order may be obtained 10 days after the service on the debtor of the petition. The receiving order declares the debtor to be bankrupt and appoints a trustee in bankruptcy to administer the estate. The debtor's assets will vest in the trustee in bankruptcy, subject to the rights of secured creditors.

If the debtor contests the petition, the debtor must file with the court a notice setting out the contested allegations contained in the petition and the grounds for contesting them. In that event, a receiving order will be made only after a trial at which the creditor proves the allegations set out in the petition.

Assignment

A debtor may initiate bankruptcy proceedings by making a voluntary assignment for the general benefit of its creditors. The debtor's liabilities to creditors must amount to $1,000, and the debtor must satisfy one of the following requirements:

- It is unable to meet its obligations as they generally become due;
- It has ceased paying its current obligations in the ordinary course of business as they generally become due; or
- The aggregate of its property is not, at a fair valuation, sufficient, or, if disposed of at a fairly conducted sale under legal process, would not be sufficient to enable payment of all its obligations due and accruing due.

The debtor becomes bankrupt when the assignment is filed with the official receiver. A debtor that has made a voluntary assignment is in the same position as a debtor that has been adjudged bankrupt by a receiving order.

PART D

Deemed assignment

A debtor will be deemed to have made an assignment in bankruptcy after it has filed a notice of intention to make a proposal (discussed in Part 2(b)(ii) above) in the following circumstances:

- If the debtor fails to file with the official receiver, within 10 days after filing the notice of intention, a cash flow statement indicating its projected cash flow, together with the prescribed reports thereon by the trustee and the debtor itself; or
- If the debtor fails to lodge a copy of its proposal with the trustee and the trustee fails to file a copy with the official receiver within 30 days after the filing of the notice of intention (or any extension of that period granted by the court).

A debtor will also be deemed to have made an assignment in bankruptcy after filing a proposal in the following circumstances:

- If the unsecured creditors fail to accept the proposal by the necessary majority at the creditors' meeting held for such purpose;
- If the court refuses to approve the proposal at the hearing of the proposal; or
- If, after the unsecured creditors and the court have approved the proposal, the debtor subsequently defaults in performing the proposal, and the court, on the application of the creditors or the trustee, annuls the proposal.

A debtor that becomes bankrupt by a deemed assignment is in the same position as a debtor that becomes bankrupt by a receiving order or an assignment.

Administration of bankrupt estate

When bankruptcy occurs by any method, the debtor's property passes to and vests in the trustee named in the receiving order, assignment, proposal or notice of intention, subject to the rights of secured creditors. The trustee's role is to dispose of the debtor's unencumbered property and to distribute the proceeds among the creditors in accordance with the *Bankruptcy and Insolvency Act*.

The property of a bankrupt vests in the trustee subject to the rights of secured creditors. Secured creditors therefore are generally free to enforce their security without interference by the trustee (although they are subject to compliance with certain statutory requirements in enforcing their security, both federal and provincial/territorial, which are outlined above).

Equity Financing

Raising funds to operate a business can be accomplished in a number of ways. Typically, when a business commemces operations, money is raised through friends and family. If the business is successful, the investor base may be expanded beyond that close circle. High net worth individuals that are private investors or persons in a similar line of business who perceive possible synergies often assist start-up companies in this next phase of financing. This type of investment is referred to as "angel money" or "seed money". As the business expands and develops further, financing can be obtained from venture capital funds. These funds typically require a certain amount of control over management and the direction of the business in exchange for their investment and always limit the time frame of their investment. Therefore, it is essential that the venture capital funds have some form of exit mechanism through an initial public offering, a merger, acquisition or buy-out. More established companies that need to progress beyond venture capi-

PART D

tal financing may consider equity financing through a public offering by way of a prospectus.

Financings can also be accomplished by way of private placement. This method relies on available exemptions from the prospectus requirements of applicable securities legislation. Institutional or high net worth investors generally participate in private placements. Because there are certain restrictions on the resale of the securities they acquire, such securities are often priced at a discount to market. Private placement financing may be favoured by a company because it is less expensive and time-consuming than a public prospectus offering.

Public equity

Before commencing any sort of public offering, the company must ensure that all the necessary organizational steps have been taken. Such steps may include revision (simplification) of its capital structure, dealing with corporate governance issues including the composition of the board of directors and board committees, amendments to any existing contracts, and tax planning. The company will then engage one or more investment dealers to act as underwriters and assist in the public offering, in particular, finding purchasers for the securities offered for sale. When selecting an underwriter, it is important to take into consideration not only the ability of the underwriter to place the securities with institutional investors, but also their ability to sell to a sufficiently large retail component to permit the successful application for and maintenance of a listing on a stock exchange, if desired. An engagement letter or a term sheet is generally entered into between the company and the underwriters, which will set out the terms of the offering, as well as any conditions to closing. These terms will be the basis for a more comprehensive underwriting agreement later on in the offering process.

Preliminary prospectus

A public offering is offered by way of a prospectus, which may be in short-form or long-form. The use of a short-form prospectus is reserved for senior issuers that have met the qualification criteria set out in National Instrument 44-101 — *Short-Form Prospectus Distributions*. These criteria include having fulfilled certain continuous disclosure requirements and having a minimum public float of not less than $75 million, among other considerations. Issuers using a short-form prospectus may incorporate by reference certain documents on their public record. In addition, issuers may take advantage of an abridged review period by the securities regulators permitting completion of the financing more quickly.

Initial public offerings are always offered by way of a long-form prospectus. A long- form prospectus is a collaborative effort among the company, its auditors and legal counsel, the underwriters and the underwriters' counsel. The contents of the prospectus are prescribed by regulation, and extensive disclosure — including a description of the business, competition, risk factors, financial statements, capitalization, forecasts and executive compensation — is required.

A preliminary prospectus will identify the underwriters and provides information on the type of security being offered, any application made to list on a stock exchange, the amount of compensation to the underwriters, and whether the underwriters have been granted an "over-allotment option" that permits them to sell securities in excess of the actual number of securities being offered. The over-allotment option permits the underwriters to stabilize the market after the completion of the offering. Ontario Securities Commission Rule 41-501 — *General Prospectus Requirements* ("Rule 41-501") came into force on December 15, 2000, and contains Form 41-501F1, which prescribes the contents of the prospec-

PART D

tus. This form is accepted by all the securities commissions in Canada.

One important decision is to decide in which provinces to offer the securities. The underwriters may require certain provinces to be included if they have prominent or institutional investors in those jurisdictions. The company may identify strategic investors in a particular province. However, the company will become subject to ongoing continuous disclosure requirements in every province in which the prospectus if filed.

The main part of the prospectus begins with a description of the corporate structure, including name and incorporation, as well as details of any intercorporate relationships (typically set out in a chart form). Following the corporate structure should be a description of the general development of the business, which must consist of a three-year history of the company, as well as disclosure with respect to any significant acquisitions and/or dispositions. If the company has completed any significant acquisitions or dispositions, it may be required to file *pro forma* financial statements to reflect the state of the company before and after such transactions. Rule 41-501 sets out the various significance tests applied to determine whether additional disclosure is required.

The prospectus should contain a narrative description of the business as well as a disclosure on the use of the proceeds from the offering. Also included will be selected consolidated financial information together with management's discussion and analysis of the financial statements. In the case of any debt securities being offered, disclosure on earnings coverage and ratios is also required. A description of the securities being distributed and the plan of the distribution are included in the prospectus. A chart outlining the company's capitalization before and after the offering is required. Other disclosure items include a description of any options to purchase securities, any sales of securities within the previous 12 months, any escrow conditions, the identity of the directors and officers, along with details of compensation paid to the five highest paid executives during the past three years. The financial statements will also form an integral part of the prospectus. Securities regulators require that financial data be provided for each of the last three completed financial years and any period subsequent to the most recently completed financial year. The management's discussion and analysis must cover all those financial periods.

Because the prospectus is the document with which the investor will decide whether or not to invest, risk factors involved in purchasing the securities must be disclosed. Risk factors that are material to the business that a reasonable investor would consider relevant must be discussed. Risk factors can include limited operating history, cash flow and liquidity problems, management experience, general business risks, environmental and health risks, reliance on key personnel, regulatory constraints, economic or political conditions, financial history, intellectual property risks and any other issues that could likely influence an investor's decision to purchase securities. Risks should be disclosed in the order of their significance.

Once a draft of the prospectus is completed, it is crucial that the board of directors review the document thoroughly to ensure that there is full, true and plain disclosure of all material facts relating to the company and the securities being offered. The chief executive officer, the chief financial officer and two directors, representing the board, will be required to sign a certificate certifying that the prospectus constitutes full, true and plain disclosure of all material facts relating to the securities offered. Once a prospectus is completed and approved by the audit committee and the board of directors, it is filed with the applicable securities commissions in each of the provinces in which the offering is to take place. If the offering

PART D

is to take place in the province of Quebec, the prospectus must be translated into French. Translation of the document must be completed before the filing of the prospectus. The company must select a principal regulator to take the primary role in reviewing the prospectus. The principal regulator will generally be the securities commission in the province in which the company's head office is located or in which the majority of its business is conducted.

Once the prospectus and any supporting documents are filed, a preliminary decision document (essentially a receipt) for the prospectus will be issued by the principal regulator on behalf of all jurisdictions. The Ontario Securities Commission ("OSC") requires that all documents must be filed by noon Eastern Standard Time on the day that the decision document is required. If the documents are filed after noon, the decision document will generally be issued on the next business day. Once the decision document is issued the prospectus is printed commercially and distributed for investors to consider.

More often than not, the preliminary prospectus does not contain the size or pricing of the offering as that is determined as the solicitation process goes on and the underwriters acquire a sense of what pricing would be most attractive to the investors. There are circumstances in which the underwriters will commit to purchasing a certain fixed amount, known as a bought deal wherein the risk of selling the offered securities passes to the underwriters. In a "bought deal" the underwriters purchase the entire offering but are permitted to find "substituted purchasers" to buy the securities. If the underwriters are unable to place the full amount of the offering, they are obliged to take up the balance themselves. Initial public offerings are rarely completed on a bought deal basis.

Regulatory review

Securities commissions select prospectuses for either full, selective or no review. The securities commissions will always conduct a full review in the case of an initial public offering. The principal regulator has 10 business days to review the prospectus and provide comments. Thereafter, the other securities commissions will review the principal regulator's comments and add any of their own comments within five business days. During the review period, the principal regulator will deal with the company, its legal counsel and auditors, and the underwriters to resolve any issues raised with respect to the prospectus. The review undertaken by the principal regulator, as well as the other securities commissions, does not evaluate the quality of the securities being offered, but rather is to ensure that the regulations have been complied with and adequate disclosure has been made. The regulators may identify issues such as insufficient disclosure, positioning of information in the document, support for certain claims or statements, as well as questions regarding accounting policies or additional disclosure in the financial statements.

CUSIP number

If this is the first time the class or type of securities is being issued, an application for an identification number must be made. The Canadian Depository for Securities Limited will assign a CUSIP number to the securities for use on the book-based system through which the majority of public securities in Canada trade or are held. The book-based system is computerized, holdings are recorded electronically and physical certificates are not required. Nonetheless, the registrar and transfer agent will require a certain number of physical certificates to keep in inventory, and therefore the company should arrange for the printing of a certain number of share certificates. Shareholders are entitled to acquire a certificate representing their shares if they choose. In addition, in certain situations such as private placement financings, restrictions may be placed on the securities and a certificate is necessary to stipulate the conditions. Restricted securities may not be held through the book-based system.

Soliciting "expressions of interest"

There is an absolute prohibition on any sales of securities during the review period. However, underwriters may actively solicit "expressions of interest" in the securities through what are commonly known as "roadshows" and other meetings with prospective investors. This type of solicitation is permitted by the securities regulators, but is very restricted. The preliminary prospectus serves as the sole marketing document for the offering. A distribution list of potential investors must be maintained to ensure that any marketing of the securities is accomplished by way of the preliminary prospectus and that no extraneous literature or information is disseminated. This includes press releases and interviews with the media. As the solicitation process progresses, the underwriters will build a book of tentative orders at the various prices indicated by the investors.

Underwriting agreement

Once comments on the preliminary prospectus have been resolved and underwriters have reviewed their order book and determined the demand for the securities, the size of the offering as well as the price will be fixed. The price and maximum number of securities offered for sale will be reflected in an underwriting agreement executed at this time between the company and its underwriters. The underwriting agreement is a detailed document that sets out the legal obligations between the parties and includes a number of representations and warranties made by the company with respect to its business and condition. It contains conditions to closing as well as certain "market out" conditions upon the occurrence of which the underwriters may elect to terminate the offering. The Investment Dealers Association provides guidelines for acceptable "market out" conditions. The company will also be required to indemnify the underwriters for any material misrepresentations in the prospectus (except for information provided by the underwriters).

Due diligence

Due diligence is the review of and investigation into the company's business, financial and legal affairs, and prospects. The primary purpose of due diligence is to gather information necessary to prepare the prospectus, verify information provided, evaluate the offering and determine appropriate valuation, and establish a proper due diligence defence in the event of a purchaser exercising his rights of action. In a public offering, counsel for the company and the underwriters will conduct a substantial amount of due diligence. The lawyers will work in conjunction with the company's senior management as well as its auditors to verify information contained in the prospectus. The underwriters will focus on business due diligence to assess the viability of the business and determine the pre-IPO valuation of the company. Counsel for the underwriters will focus on matters that involve legal analysis and an assessment of the impact of such matters on the offering. Both forms of due diligence are also performed by the underwriters and their counsel to establish a due diligence defence against liability for misrepresentations in the prospectus.

Documentary due diligence may include a review of:

- all constating documents such as articles of incorporation (and amendments) and by-laws;

PART D

- corporate searches on the company performed, including PPSA and *Bank Act* registrations, bankruptcy filings, pending litigation and sheriff's executions;
- all minute books, including those of any subsidiaries;
- all material contracts;
- documentation with respect to any prior financings, both debt and equity;
- any litigation documents;
- any pension, benefits, stock purchase or other similar types of plans;
- any licenses or permits;
- intellectual property, including searches on trademarks and patents, as well as a review of any confidentiality agreements.

Final prospectus

Once preliminary prospectus comments have been resolved, a final prospectus is prepared that contains the price and size of the offering and reflects any comments made by the securities regulators. The final prospectus is then filed with the securities commissions together with the underwriting agreement and certain other ancillary documents. Upon review of the final prospectus, the director of the principal regulator will issue a final decision document for the final prospectus. The final decision document must be issued within 90 days after the issuance of the receipt for the preliminary prospectus. In order to have the final decision document issued on a timely basis, it is strongly recommended that the principal regulator be kept up-to-date on the amendments to the preliminary prospectus. A blackline showing all of the cumulative changes between the preliminary and final prospectus is to be filed with the final prospectus.

Upon issuance of the final decision document, the underwriters will contract for the sale of the securities to investors who indicated an interest. A confirmation of trade together with a copy of the final prospectus must be sent to each purchaser. There is a "cooling off" period of two business days from the date of receipt by the purchaser of the final prospectus. During that time, purchasers may choose to rescind their purchase and withdraw from the offering. Closing of the public offering typically takes place approximately two weeks after the receipt for the final prospectus is issued. Once the final receipt is issued, the company becomes a "reporting issuer" and is subject to certain continuous disclosure requirements, discussed further below.

Rights and remedies of the purchaser

In addition to the two-day statutory waiting period described above, subsection 130(1) of the *Securities Act* (Ontario) provides further protection to the purchaser. If the prospectus contains a misrepresentation, a purchaser during the initial distribution period will be deemed to have relied upon such misrepresentation as if it was a misrepresentation at the time of purchase, and has a right of action for damages against the company, the underwriters, and every director of the company at the time the prospectus was filed. While the underwriters may establish a "due diligence defence" the only defence available to the company under the *Securities Act* (Ontario) would be to prove that the purchaser purchased the securities with prior knowledge of the misrepresentation.

A "misrepresentation" means an untrue statement of a material fact or an omission to state a material fact that is required to be stated or that is necessary to make a statement in the prospectus or amendment to the prospectus not misleading in light of the circumstances in which it was made. Damages recoverable by a purchaser can be up to the full amount of their purchase.

PART D

567

Escrow requirements

The principals or founders of the company will be required to place their shareholdings into escrow at the time the initial public offering is completed. This is to ensure their interests are aligned with those of the new shareholders, sustain investor confidence in the company, and prevent them from destabilizing the price of the shares by dumping large quantities of stock into the market.

On June 30, 2002, the OSC and the other members of the Canadian Securities Administrators (the "CSA"), with the exception of Quebec, adopted National Policy 46-201 — Escrow for Initial Public Offerings ("NP 46-201"). NP 46-201 provides a single, uniform escrow regime across Canada and supplements the regimes imposed by the TSX and TSX-V.

NP 46-201 divides issuers into three categories: (1) exempt issuers, (2) established issuers and (3) emerging issuers. Escrow requirements are imposed based upon the classification of the issuer. No escrow requirements are imposed upon exempt issuers; less onerous requirements are imposed upon established issuers, and more onerous upon emerging issuers. Principals of established issuers will have their securities released over an 18-month period, and principals of emerging issuers will have their securities released over a three-year period. However, securities regulators, as well as any stock exchange on which the shares are listed, have the authority to impose more onerous terms.

Stock exchange listing

A stock exchange listing provides visibility, attracts analysts and institutional investors, and improves access to a larger capital pool than would otherwise be available. When an application to list the shares is made concurrently with a prospectus offering, the stock exchanges will accept their form of listing application attached to or "wrapped" around the preliminary prospectus (which contains most of the information they require) rather than requiring a separate application.

Listing on the Toronto Stock Exchange

The premier stock exchange in Canada is the Toronto Stock Exchange ("TSX"). Companies listing on the TSX must comply with certain financial, public distribution and management requirements, and have a sponsor.

The TSX divides its issuers into three separate industry sectors: industrial, oil and gas, and mining. Each sector has its own separate financial criteria. Within each sector, there are two levels of financial standards. *Exempt issuers* are established companies that meet certain prescribed levels of pre-tax profitability and cash flow, based on their previous financial year. *Non-exempt issuers* are smaller companies with lower levels of net tangible cash flow or profit. These companies are subject to closer supervision by the TSX and are required to obtain consent of the TSX before making any material change to the their business or financial affairs. A non-exempt issuer in the industrial sector is subject to different listing requirements, depending on whether it is (i) profitable, (ii) not profitable but forecasting profitability, (iii) a technology company, or (iv) a research and development company.

As part of the listing application process, each director, officer and shareholder owning more than 10 per cent of issued and outstanding shares must complete a Personal Information Form which requires them to provide details of their background (including education and previous employment), board experience and industry knowledge. Each individual is subject to a security check by the TSX. Management quality and expertise are key factors the TSX

PART D

takes into account when assessing a listing application. Management (including the board of directors) must have relevant business experience as well as public company experience. There must be at least two Canadian directors on the board of directors.

The TSX requires the company to have and maintain a minimum public float of not less than one million free shares with an aggregate market value of $4 million (or $10 million for issuers qualifying under the Technology Company criteria). These shares must be held by at least 300 public shareholders each holding one or more board lots. A board lot consists of 100 shares.

A TSX Participating Organization, typically the lead underwriter in the public offering, must sponsor the listing of a non-exempt issuer. The investment dealer will write a sponsorship letter to the TSX confirming that the company satisfies the listing requirements and commenting on its ability to meet its obligations as a TSX-listed company. The TSX requires the sponsor to comment on all visits or inspections of principal facilities and offices, any financial forecast that has been included in the application, and management's experience and technical expertise relevant to the business.

Listing on the TSX Venture Exchange Inc.

Companies that do not meet the requirements for listing on the TSX may consider listing on the TSX-V, a national exchange for venture class securities. The TSX-V is the result of the amalgamation of the Vancouver Stock Exchange and the Alberta Stock Exchange. The TSX-V provides a flexible two-tiered system for emerging companies. Each tier is broken down into industry segments, with minimum listing requirements based on financial performance, resources and stage of development. These requirements vary from segment to segment depending upon the industry. Both tiers classify companies by the following industry segments:

- mining;
- oil and gas;
- technology or industrial;
- research and development;
- real estate or investment.

Once listed on TSX-V, the company is required to meet minimum tier maintenance requirements on a continuous basis. These requirements relate to financial condition and shareholder base. Companies that mature can elect to "graduate" to the TSX or other senior stock exchange.

Multi-jurisdictional disclosure system

The multi-jurisdictional disclosure system ("MJDS") is a securities filing system that permits a company to offer its securities in both Canada and the United States, using the Canadian form of offering documents and filing procedures. MJDS is available for use depending on the type of securities, the company's continuous disclosure record, and its market capitalization. Canadian companies wishing to use MJDS must prepare and file a prospectus in compliance with applicable securities legislation in their resident province. The only exception is that financial statements in certain types of prospectuses must contain U.S. GAAP reconciliations. The prospectus is also filed with the United States Securities Exchange Commission ("SEC") together with a "wrapper" that is an additional cover document to the prospectus containing information pertinent to U.S. investors. The SEC typically does not review an MJDS filing other than to verify eligibility to use the system, and relies, instead, upon the review by the principal regulator in Canada. There are separate U.S. requirements concerning marketing activities, including the issuance of press releases and other public announcements, the timing and content of "roadshows" and other meetings with prospective U.S. investors, and the delivery to potential U.S. investors of materials other than the prospectus.

Continuous disclosure obligations

A company is subject to a number of filing and reporting requirements once it is subject to continuous disclosure requirements. The continuous disclosure requirements imposed by securities legislation are designed to protect the integrity of the capital markets by ensuring that timely disclosure of information relating to the company is made to the public.

The System for Electronic Document Analysis and Retrieval ("SEDAR") was developed by the CSA to provide for the transmission, receipt, acceptance, review and dissemination of documents filed with securities regulatory authorities in Canada. Filing under SEDAR is mandatory for most reporting issuers in Canada. Documents filed through SEDAR are available for review by the public on its Web site at *www.sedar.com*.

Continuous disclosure and other reporting requirements include:

- financial reporting;
- mandatory solicitation of proxies and delivery of an information circular to each shareholder prior to shareholders' meetings;
- preparation and filing of an annual information form and management's discussion and analysis;
- timely disclosure of material information relating to the business and affairs of the company; and
- insider trade reporting.

Annual financial statements and annual reports

Public companies are required to file via SEDAR audited comparative annual financial statements prepared in accordance with generally accepted accounting principles which report on the last two financial years. Before filing on SEDAR, the annual financial statements must be reviewed by the audit committee who must then report the findings of their review to the board of directors. The financial statements should then be approved by the board of directors, which approval is evidenced by the signatures of two directors. Annual financial statements must not be filed, published or circulated until they have been so approved. Annual financial statements must also be sent to all shareholders no later than 21 days before the annual shareholders' meeting. Many companies also prepare an annual report to send to shareholders and include the annual financial statements and management's discussion and analysis in that report.

Interim financial statements

Public companies are required to file through SEDAR unaudited quarterly financial statements consisting of an income statement and a statement of changes in financial position. The interim statements must be comparative to the corresponding three-, six- or nine-month period in the previous fiscal year, and may include additional financial information for the most recent three-month period that may be comparable to the corresponding three-month period in the previous fiscal year. The interim financial statements must also be sent to shareholders concurrently with such filing. The interim financial statements must be accompanied by the management's discussion and analysis for the quarter. Interim financial statements must be reviewed by the directors prior to their filing and delivery to shareholders, but the board may delegate the responsibility for such review to the audit committee.

PART D

Although it is not required, the OSC has expressed the view that issuers should consider engaging an external auditor to review their interim financial statements.

Management's discussion and analysis

OSC Rule 51-501 *AIF and MD&A* ("Rule 51-501") requires that the company file via SEDAR a Management's Discussion and Analysis ("MD&A") for each annual and interim period. MD&A is supplemental to the financial statements. It provides management with an opportunity to explain the current financial situation and the future prospects in narrative form with particular emphasis on liquidity and capital resources. MD&A must accompany annual and interim financial statements, and it is also customary to include MD&A in the annual report, as well as to provide a cross-reference to such disclosure in the annual information form.

Annual information form

Rule 51-501 requires certain public companies to file an annual information form ("AIF") for a particular fiscal year if it exceeds certain financial thresholds. The AIF filing requirement is applicable if shareholders' equity or revenues exceed $10 million, or if the aggregate market value of equity securities was $75 million. The AIF includes information such as the general development of the business over the previous five years (or any shorter period in which the company has been in existence) along with any expected changes, the extent and seasonality of the industry segment, an assessment of competitive position, and certain financial data for the previous five fiscal years. A company that is not required to file an AIF under Rule 51-501, may wish to do so if it has been a reporting issuer for at least 12 months and its securities are listed on a stock exchange. This filing would fulfill the "current AIF" requirements under Ontario securities legislation and permit it to become a "Qualifying Issuer". This designation enables a reduction in the length of time resale restrictions are imposed on any securities sold on a private placement basis.

Insider trading report requirements

Insiders of a public company are required to file insider reports disclosing their direct or indirect beneficial ownership of or control over the securities of the company. Generally, an "insider" is defined to include, among others, directors and senior officers of the company, its subsidiaries, or a company which it beneficially owns, directly or indirectly, or exercises control or direction more than 10 per cent of the issued and outstanding voting securities of the company. A "senior officer" is defined as the Chairman or Vice Chairman of the board of directors, the President, any Vice President, secretary, treasurer, chief financial officer, general manager or general counsel of the company or any other individual who performs the functions of those offices including each of the five highest paid employees.

Insider reports must be filed under three circumstances. First, when a person or company becomes an insider, an initial insider report must be filed within 10 calendar days of the date that person became an insider. No report is required to be filed if the insider does not own any securities of the company. Second, when the insider purchases or sells any of the securities held, an insider report must be filed disclosing the details of the purchase and/or sale and disclose the balance of that person's holdings after completion of the transaction. Such report must be filed within 10 calendar days of the completion of the transaction. Third, unless the insider is transferring his or her securities for the purpose of giving collateral for a *bona fide* debt, he or she is prohibited from transferring any of the securities owned into the name of an agent, nominee or custodian unless a report is filed disclosing such transfer of title. Penalty fees imposed for late filings.

In addition to SEDAR, the CSA has introduced the System For Electronic Disclosure By Insiders ("SEDI"). SEDI is available over the Internet and replaces the paper-based reporting of insider trading data. Insiders are required to file their insider reports electronically through the SEDI Web site. Before an insider report can be filed, the insider must ensure he or she is registered on SEDI by filing an Insider Profile. The public has access to the public information filed on the Web site. An Issuer Event Report must be filed by the company in the case of a stock dividend, split, consolidation or similar event.

Material change reports

Securities legislation requires a disclosure of any material change by filing a report on SEDAR as soon as reasonably practicable, and in any event within 10 calendar days. Material changes include:

- changes in corporate structure;
- changes in capital structure;
- changes in financial results;
- changes in business and operations;
- acquisitions and dispositions;
- changes in credit arrangements; and
- any other developments relating to the business and affairs of the company that would reasonably be expected to significantly affect the market price or value of any securities, or would be reasonably expected to have a significant influence on a reasonable investor's investment decision.

A press release should be issued and a material change report filed with the applicable securities regulatory authorities. This is in addition to the SEDI Issuer Event Report, which may be required depending upon the nature of the material change.

Disclosure standards

It is a fundamental tenet of the capital markets in Canada that all persons investing in securities of publicly listed companies have equal access to information that may affect their investment decisions. Timely disclosure of material information concerning the business and affairs of the company is vital to upholding that principle. The CSA had concerns about the selective disclosure of material corporate information by companies to analysts, institutional investors, investment dealers and other market professionals. Selective disclosure occurs when a company discloses material non-public information to one or more individuals or companies and not broadly to the investing public. Selective disclosure can create opportunities for insider trading and also undermines retail investors' confidence in the marketplace as a level playing field.

The CSA therefore adopted National Policy 51-201 *Disclosure Standards* ("Policy 51-201"). It is not prescriptive, but is intended to constitute guidance and to be implemented flexibly. Policy 51-201 recommends that companies consider implementing the following disclosure practices:

- establish a written disclosure policy that promotes informative, timely and broadly disseminated disclosure of material information to the market place;
- establish a committee of company personnel or an individual with senior rank to monitor the effectiveness of the company's disclosure policy;
- limit the number of people authorized to speak on behalf of the company to analysts, the media and investors;

PART D

- adopt an "open access" policy for analyst conference calls by permitting any interested party to listen by telephone and/or through a webcast;
- establish a policy on commenting on draft analyst reports;
- observe a "quiet period" around the end of the quarter and prior to the release of quarterly earnings announcements;
- adopt an insider trading policy to monitor the trading of insiders in the company's securities, including trading "blackout periods" that may mirror quiet periods;
- ensure the company's Web site is up-to-date and accurate and use current technology to improve investor access to corporate information;
- do not participate in, host or link to Internet chat rooms or bulletin boards;
- adopt a "no comment" policy on market rumours that are not attributable to the company, ensure that the policy is applied consistently and if the rumours relate to information that has leaked, disclose the information broadly and on a timely basis.

Private placements

Canadian securities laws generally require that any sale of securities must be by way of a prospectus in order that a purchaser has full disclosure, which has been reviewed by the appropriate securities authorities. Prospectus offerings, however, can be time-consuming and costly. Often companies may choose to complete their financings by way of private placement, which is less expensive and faster. Securities regulators have recognized that certain investors may not require the level of protection offered by applicable securities legislation in public offerings. Companies are permitted to offer securities to sophisticated investors provided that such purchase of securities is based on publicly available information or an offering memorandum that provide rights of action for misrepresentations.

Securities offered by way of private placement are not qualified by a prospectus and therefore are subject to resale restrictions or "hold periods". Securities sold in this manner are often priced at a discount to market to compensate for the restrictions.

Private placements can be accomplished either with or without the assistance of an investment dealer. Companies are permitted to issue their own securities without registering under applicable securities legislation. In order to gain access to a wider pool of investors, however, they do generally engage an investment dealer to act as agent or underwriter. If the investment dealer is retained as an underwriter, it will make a firm commitment to sell the full amount of the offering. In an agency situation the investment dealer will act as agent (usually on an exclusive basis) and agree to use either "best efforts" or "commercially reasonable efforts" to place the securities with investors. An engagement letter or term sheet is entered into that is subsequently followed up by an agency or underwriting agreement detailing the relationship. The form of this agreement is similar to an underwriting agreement for a public offering.

Securities may be offered through an offering memorandum. There are no specific form requirements for an offering memorandum in most of the provinces in Canada. Misrepresentation in an offering memorandum, which includes a mistaken material fact or the omission of a material fact that may lead to misrepresentation, carries the same liability as that in a prospectus or information circular. Therefore, offering memoranda typically provides prospectus level disclosure in order to avoid inadvertent misrepresentations due to the omission of any facts.

The agent or underwriter would conduct similar due diligence as it would for a public offering in order to determine the pre-financing valuation of the company, verify the contents of the offering memorandum (if one is used), and establish a due dili-

PART D

579

gence defence. While there is no statutory liability imposed on an underwriter or agent with respect to an offering memorandum, mistakes in the disclosure to potential investors can impact an investment dealer's reputation with its clients.

If its securities are listed on a stock exchange such as the TSX or the TSX-V, the company is required to file a notice of the private placement prior to the completion of the offering. This is a notice only and does not typically result in any further inquiry by the stock exchange. Because securities are subject to a resale restriction, they are generally offered at a discount to market price. The stock exchanges, however, prescribe maximum discount levels and stipulate that warrants may not be offered at any discount. In order to preserve a discounted price, company's counsel will file a notice of price protection that will fix the sale price regardless of the fluctuation in the market price of the securities for a period of up to 45 days to allow time to complete the financing.

Exemptions from prospectus requirements

The available exemptions from prospectus requirements vary from province to province. Traditionally, securities regulators have assumed that an investor capable of subscribing for a prescribed minimum amount in a private placement is a sophisticated investor. Recently, Ontario, British Columbia and Alberta have moved away from the concept of a threshold exemption and have established prospectus exemptions similar to those in the United States. The remaining provinces and territories continue to have threshold exemptions ranging from $97,000 to $150,000.

Ontario

OSC Rule 45-501 *Exempt Distributions* (the "Rule 45-501") came into effect on November 30, 2001, and regulates private placements in Ontario. Two main types of prospectus exemptions most commonly used are the closely-held issuer exemption and the accredited investor exemption.

Closely-held issuer exemption

The closely-held issuer exemption permits closely-held issuers to raise up to $3 million from a limited number of investors in any number of offerings. A company qualifies as a closely-held issuer if it has 35 or fewer securityholders, excluding securityholders that are "accredited investors," as discussed below, and its officers, directors and employees. Distributions can be made under the exemption without regard for the qualifications or sophistication of the purchasers.

The company must provide a standard form of Information Statement to investors at least four days prior to the date of the sale unless, subsequent to the sale, it will have fewer than five beneficial securityholders. The Information Statement describes the types of information a potential investor may want to review before making an investment and warns investors about the risks of investing in small businesses.

Rule 45-501 does not mandate the provision to potential investors of disclosure material such as an offering memorandum. However, if disclosure material is provided to an investor and the disclosure material constitutes an offering memorandum, an investor has statutory rights of action for damages and rescission for any misrepresentation contained in the offering memorandum. "Offering Memorandum" is broadly defined in Ontario securities law to include any material that describes the business and affairs of the issuer prepared primarily for review by potential investors.

PART D

The closely-held issuer exemption is available if one of the promoters has acted as a promoter of any other company that issued securities under exemption within the last twelve months. In addition, the exemption prohibits the company from incurring selling or promotional expenses in connection with trades made in reliance on the exemption.

Accredited investor exemption

The accredited investor exemption permits raising any amount of capital in any number of financings from investors meeting certain qualifications. The classes of investors that qualify as "accredited investors" include the following:

- certain regulated institutions such as banks, loan or trust corporations, credit unions, insurance companies and securities dealers;
- the federal, provincial and territorial governments, and their crown corporations, instrumentalities and agencies;
- a Canadian municipality or a provincial or territorial capital city;
- federally or provincially regulated pension funds;
- registered charities;
- individuals who, either alone or jointly with their spouses, own financial assets net of related liabilities having an aggregate realizable value before taxes that exceeds $1 million;
- individuals who had net income before taxes exceeding $200,000 in each of the two most recent years or whose net income together with their spouses' exceeded $300,000 in each of the preceding two years, and where the individuals have a reasonable expectation of exceeding the income level in the current year;
- individuals that are currently or were formerly registered under the *Securities Act* (Ontario) or the securities legisla-

tion of another province or territory as a representative of an adviser or dealer;

- officers, directors and promoters of the issuer or any affiliated entity of the promoter of the issuer;
- spouses, parents, grandparents or children of officers, directors or promoters of the issuer;
- a person or company that is part of a control block in respect of the issuer and persons or companies that are affiliated entities of the issuer;
- companies, limited partnerships, limited liability partnerships, trusts and estates, other than mutual funds or non-redeemable investment funds, which have net assets of at least $5 million;
- persons or companies recognized by the Commission as accredited investors;
- mutual funds or non-redeemable investment funds that, in Ontario, distribute securities only to accredited investors;
- mutual funds or non-redeemable investment funds that, in Ontario, distribute securities by prospectus;
- managed accounts that are not acquiring securities of mutual funds or non-redeemable investment funds; and
- persons or companies in respect of which all of the legal and beneficial interests are owned by accredited investors.

There is no requirement to provide the Information Statement, an offering memorandum or any other disclosure material to investors acquiring securities under the accredited investor exemption. Disclosure materials may be provided to investors, but statutory rights of action will be available to investors if such materials constitute an offering memorandum and contain a misrepresentation. There is no restriction on the involvement of promoters with trades made in reliance on the exemption. Further, there is no prohibition in incurring selling or promotional expenses in connection with trades made in reliance on this exemption.

British Columbia and Alberta

British Columbia and Alberta enacted Multilateral Instrument 45-103 — *Capital Raising Exemptions* ("MI 45-103") on April 3, 2002, and March 30, 2002, respectively. MI 45-103 provides four types of exemptions.

Private issuer exemption

Under the definition of "private issuer" under MI 45-103, sales of securities can be made to certain specified persons including:

- a director, officer, employee or control person;
- a spouse, parent, grandparent, brother, sister or child of a director, senior officer or control person;
- a close personal friend of a director, senior officer or control person of the issuer;
- a close business associate of a director, senior officer or control person;
- a spouse, parent, grandparent, brother, sister or child of the selling security holder;
- a current holder of the class of securities being offered;
- an accredited investor;
- a person or company that is wholly-owned by any combination of persons or companies described above; or
- a person or company that is not the public.

The definition of private issuer requires that there be less than 50 "designated" securityholders (excluding employees). Since the term "designated securities" excludes debt securities, in calculating the number of designated securityholders, holders of non-convertible debt securities would generally be excluded.

If designated securities are distributed to a person or company that does not fall within one of the categories above even under another exemption, the company will no longer be considered a private issuer and will no longer be able to use the private issuer exemption. For example, if securities are distributed under the offering memorandum exemption, the company will no longer be a private issuer. It may be able to use the other exemptions provided under securities legislation, including the family, friends and business associates exemption, the accredited investor exemption and the offering memorandum exemption, but will be required to report the distributions to the securities regulatory authority in each jurisdiction in which the distribution took place. The private issuer exemption does not require that an offering memorandum or other disclosure document be provided to a potential investor. If an offering document is provided, it is not required to be in a prescribed form, nor does it trigger statutory rights of action for purchasers.

Family, friends and business associates exemption

This family, friends and business associates exemption permits trades in securities to directors, officers and control persons, as well as certain family members, close personal friends, and close business associates of directors, senior officers or control person, or to any company that is wholly owned by such persons. There is no prescribed limit on the number of purchasers under this exemption. However, if securities are sold to a large number of persons under this exemption, that may create a presumption that not all of the purchasers are family, close personal friends or close business associates, and the exemption may not be available.

The exemption does not require that an offering memorandum or other disclosure document be provided to an investor. If an offering document is provided, it is not required to be in a prescribed form, nor does it trigger statutory rights of action for purchasers.

PART D

Offering memorandum exemption

This exemption permits the sale of securities to a purchaser who obtains an offering memorandum in the required form and completes a prescribed risk acknowledgement form.

Investor protection provisions have been added giving purchasers almost identical rights to those they receive under a prospectus. The rights include a two-day right to cancel the purchase and broader rights to cancel or sue for damages if there is a misrepresentation in the offering memorandum. The offering memorandum must be filed with the securities regulators in each of the jurisdictions in which securities are distributed.

If relying on the offering memorandum exemption, it must be prepared in the required form. The chief executive officer, chief financial officer, two directors and all promoters must sign the offering memorandum certificate. The offering memorandum must be kept current to reflect any material changes. The Alberta Securities Commission has added some additional restrictions to the offering memorandum exemption in its version of the rule.

Accredited investor exemption

This exemption permits securities to be sold in British Columbia or Alberta to any person or company that qualifies as an "accredited investor", generally financial institutions, pensions, investment dealers, established companies and wealthy individuals. There is no minimum or maximum dollar subscription. The exemption does not require that an offering memorandum or other disclosure document be provided to an investor. If an offering document is provided, it is not required to be in a prescribed form, nor does it provide statutory rights of action to purchasers. The accredited investor categories under MI 45-103 are substantially the same as under Rule 45-501.

Subscription agreement

Because investors must meet certain requirements before they are eligible to purchase securities under a prospectus exemption, typically a subscription agreement is completed and executed by the investor and then accepted by the company. In the subscription agreement potential investors will make certain representations and warranties as to their eligibility to purchase the securities including their "accredited investor" status if applicable. Often accredited investors are asked to complete a certificate certifying their category of accredited investor. If the shares being sold are listed on the TSX, the subscription agreement will also contain a private placement questionnaire and undertaking that must be completed by the investor and filed with the TSX after completion of the sale.

Reporting requirements

While private placements do not require pre-approval by the securities regulators, there are post-closing filing requirements. In most provinces, a form outlining the amount of securities sold, the purchase price and the identity of the purchasers is required to be filed together with the appropriate fee within 10 calendar days after closing. In addition, if the private placement constitutes a material change for the company, it will be required to file a material change report and issue a press release regarding the closing of the private placement.

PART D

Resale of securities acquired in a private placement

Securities acquired through a private placement carry with them a restriction on resale that can range from four months to indefinitely, depending upon the company's status as a reporting issuer. Such securities do not trade through the book-based system but rather are evidenced by a physical certificate which bears a legend detailing the restrictions that apply. Once the restrictions have ended, the securities can then be placed into the book-based system. A securityholder holding restricted securities may not sell those securities unless the hold period on the securities has expired or pursuant to a prospectus exemption.

Multilateral Instrument 45-102 *Resale of Securities* ("MI 45-102") came into force on November 30, 2001. It harmonizes the resale requirements across most Canadian jurisdictions and permits more lenient hold period conditions under certain circumstances.

Private placements outside Canada

Often underwriters will have prospective investors resident in jurisdictions outside of Canada. Any offering of securities outside the country must be completed in accordance with the securities laws of that jurisdiction. Some jurisdictions do not have rules applicable to the sale of securities. In other jurisdictions, including the United States, there are rules and restrictions but there may be exemptions available for accredited or sophisticated investors.

Convertible debt

The issuance of convertible debt securities does not differ significantly from that of an equity offering, as described above. Issuance of a debt instrument involves the determination of its nature and characteristics, review of the status of other intercreditor arrangements, other competing registered security if security is to be taken, and the drafting of the contractual arrangement. The structure of a debt instrument for public issue does not differ significantly from that of a debt instrument for a bank financing.

The documentation for the convertible debt is typically a trust deed or indenture, which sets out the relationship between the company and the debtholders. The document establishes the terms and conditions governing the debtor-creditor relationship, the characteristics of the debt instrument, the conversion features of the debt into equity, redemption features, if any, and the capability of the representative (typically a trust company) to undertake action on the part of the debtholders. The trust deed will also specify events of default and the consequences thereof. Procedures for meetings of debtholders are also set out in the trust deed. A trust company is appointed to act as trustee for the debtholders and the terms of its appointment including an indemnity and certain protections for the trustee are stipulated in the trust deed.

When structuring convertible debt, it is important to review the accounting treatment of debt with equity features. Depending upon its nature, the convertible debt may be treated entirely as debt or it may also be treated as a blend of debt and equity. This can have an impact on any debt-equity ratios that the company is required to maintain.

Disclosure documents for the offering of convertible debt are substantially the same as any other type of equity offering. Debt can be offered by way of prospectus in a public offering or by way of private placement with or without an offering memorandum. The securities rules governing the sale of convertible debt are generally the same as those governing the sale of equity securities.

PART D

C H A P T E R **22**

Evaluating Treasury
Performance

Overview

The role of the treasury department is to provide effective risk management of the financial assets and liabilities of the company. This normally entails managing cash, bank relations, financial investments and debt (including loans and leases). The objective is to maximize the return (or minimize the cost) while achieving a predetermined level of risk.

In this chapter, the role, objectives and responsibilities of the treasury department are reviewed, as well as how its performance may be measured and evaluated.

Role of the Treasury Department

The corporate treasury department plays an important role in managing risks and rewards in the corporation. Treasury is responsible for access to and the effective use of financial resources. Normally, the Treasury Department is responsible for:

- Banking and banking relationships;
- Cash management;
- Working capital management;
- Short- and long-term borrowings, including capital leases;
- Investing excess funds;
- Foreign currencies;
- Risk management and insurance.

The actual responsibilities of the Treasury Department will depend upon the corporate culture and organizational structure. In a smaller organization, the chief financial officer or controller may be responsible for the functions set out in this chapter. In a larger organization, there will be a controller and a treasurer reporting to the chief financial officer (not necessarily with those exact titles). The controller will be responsible for accounting and management reporting, while the treasurer will be responsible for the bulleted items listed above.

The structure will also depend upon the industry: in a financial services company, treasury is integral to the operations of the organization, and there will be a complex risk management infrastructure in place. But in any company, an effective treasury department will provide an early warning of problems and opportunities in operational areas. This is because of the central role of cash within the organization. A problem with customer service, production or other areas may frequently manifest itself as a cash flow problem or opportunity.

How the Treasury Department Can Make a Difference

The role of the treasury department is often constrained by culture and tradition. In many companies, this has evolved over time as it has become recognized that treasury can add value by serving an advisory function to the core operating areas. As the discipline of risk management has become embraced by senior management as a necessary corporate function, treasury has had additional opportunities to involve itself in operations.

A contemporary corporate treasury department will be active in the following areas:

- *Manage liquidity and cash.* Within the organization, there are many conflicting objectives. For example, do we keep high inventory levels to satisfy customers or lower levels to minimize the investment required in inventory? Do we push customers for speedy payment, or focus on customer service and condone deferred payments until any issues are resolved? These need to be dealt with at a senior management-policy level. Treasurers can play an important role in identifying where policies are required, then ensuring that processes are in place to implement the policies.
- *Anticipate varying levels of cash.* An effective cash forecasting process will make borrowing, investing and banking easier to anticipate and reduce the risk level associated with varying needs for cash.
- *Manage your banker.* An effective relationship with your bank and bankers can prevent problems ahead of time. The inevitable errors, frauds and other problems that arise from time to time will be settled more easily and smoothly if there is a trusting relationship between the company and the bank. Even more important, dealing with financial

PART D

593

emergencies is much easier if the banker is on your side and not stuck in an adversarial relationship with a "problem" client.

- *Maximize income earned on short-term investments.* In today's interest rate environment, squeezing out returns on short-term excess funds can be challenging. An effective treasury department will have specific guidance on permitted risk levels and permitted investments. It will also be proactive in following up new investments, analyzing them and recommending (or not) approval to utilize them.

- *Understand risk management issues.* Traditionally, the treasurer has been responsible for coordinating insurance coverage throughout the company. This has expanded to the responsibility for identifying and coordinating risk management issues throughout the enterprise. Often, creating formal written policies and guidelines will identify cracks in coverage that should be filled, or explicitly accepted by senior management and perhaps the Board of Directors. This is a broader interpretation of the treasurer's traditional function of safeguarding assets by arranging for insurance.

- *Understand foreign currency and foreign exchange issues.* The question of whether and how to hedge foreign exchange risk often does not have a simple answer. No hedge is costless: the cost may be the opportunity cost of giving up any upside win, or an actual cost in buying an option. Financial services companies have been quick to package apparently costless solutions, but it is incumbent on the treasury department to analyze what the cost really is. You can be confident that your bank is not servicing you for free.

- *Watch the environment.* An effective contemporary treasury department will provide intelligence to senior management on developments inside and outside the business. These include changes in financial markets to the regulatory environment, technology used in treasury, and the competition.

- *Other activities.* Depending upon the organization, there are other activities that may be explicitly or implicitly under the purview of treasury. Often, they are not the clear responsibility of any particular area. These include:

  - Capital and resource allocation analysis;
  - Tax planning;
  - Trade finance;
  - Benchmarking studies and consulting;
  - Project evaluation.

If these functions are not being performed already, they can represent significant opportunities for the treasury department to contribute to the organization.

Measuring and Evaluating Performance

Most treasury departments do not measure their performance, except perhaps by comparing costs or profit to budget. This is due to the difficulty in defining appropriate measures and benchmarks. The quantitative nature of treasury operations means that performance parameters are usually quantitative, rather than qualitative such as the level of service provided.

Measuring performance of treasury departments can have two benefits:

- Assess the effectiveness of treasury strategy.
- Assess the efficiency of treasury operations.

The first is important in providing feedback to senior management and the Board of Directors as to the appropriateness of the strategic direction, and should also include a measure of the risks assumed. The second is important in assessing the performance of the treasurer and others within the treasury department.

PART D

A fair measurement system should have the following characteristics:

- It should be objective and preferably quantitative.
- It should be within the control of those being evaluated.
- It should be communicated appropriately so that those being evaluated understand what is expected.

Each of the accountabilities that pertains to the treasury department should have one or more measurements applied to it. For example, under "Manage Liquidity and Cash," some or all of the following measurements could be used:

- Average cash balance (or average overdraft).
- Forecast daily cash versus actual.
- Bank charges for unanticipated overdraft.
- Net working capital.
- Accounts receivable measures such as days sales outstanding.

In measuring interest revenue and interest expense, the measurement process should separate the cash or loan balance from market interest rates (that cannot be controlled). Actual interest rates should be compared to an appropriate market index rate (Bankers' Acceptances, bank prime or something similar) to assess how well interest revenues or expenses are managed. If derivatives such as swaps or forward rate agreements are used, their impact and risk should be identified.

The measurement system should be focused on controllable items. Non-controllable items and events should be identified and their impact assessed separately.

Benchmarking is the process of comparing various metrics to those in comparable organizations. Similarly, it can be used to track costs over time within the treasury department. In back-office processing areas, metrics such as labour costs per transaction can be tracked. At the very least, back-office costs can be compared to the company's total sales and tracked over time or compared to those of other companies.

Conducting an Operations Review

An operations review of treasury can provide some insight into areas where improvements are required. Even if operations are stable and efficient, the discipline of an independent review and a fresh look may be very beneficial.

There are four steps involved in conducting an operations review:

- Identify potential problems.
- Analyze and investigate the problem.
- Propose a solution.
- Implement the solution.

The checklist below covers the first step. It should not be rigidly applied to all situations. Some questions may need to be changed or added, and judgment will be required to evaluate the significance of the responses.

The other steps will depend on the nature of the problem uncovered. Often, the process is iterative: based upon analysis a tentative solution is proposed that must then be modified after further study. Since cash is the lifeblood of the entire organization, problems diagnosed through a review of treasury operations may have their origins elsewhere in the organization.

PART D

Appendix 22A

Treasury operations checklist

The following checklist can be used to diagnose problems in the treasury process. It may reveal symptoms in the treasury area that need to be addressed elsewhere in the organization to deal with the underlying causes. The checklist should be tailored to the specific reader of the company.

Sales and Receivables	Yes	No	N/A	Comments
1. Are invoices sent out as soon as possible, rather than at month-end?				
2. Are there controls to ensure that all goods and services are billed?				
3. Are there controls to ensure that invoices are accurate?				
4. Are payment terms, including due date and charges for overdue accounts, clearly stated on the invoice?				
5. Are customers' special instructions followed?				
6. Are old accounts reviewed?				
7. Is credit approved before goods are shipped?				
8. Does credit evaluation consider credit history, references, credit agencies rating?				
9. Are monthly statements sent out?				
10. Is interest charged on overdue accounts?				
11. Is there a process in place for dealing with delinquent accounts?				
12. Is Days' Sales Outstanding calculated regularly and tracked over time?				

EVALUATING TREASURY PERFORMANCE

Sales and Receivables	Yes	No	N/A	Comments
13. Is an aging of accounts receivable reviewed by management monthly?				
14. Are accounts receivables metrics compared to other companies in the same industry?				
15. Are accounts receivable write-offs approved by management?				
16. Is there a process in place to control, approve and track credit notes?				
17. Are cash (currency) receipts controlled by a cash register or similar device?				
18. Is the accounts receivable subledger balanced to the general ledger monthly?				
19. Does someone independent of the processing of cash receipts review the accounts receivable subledger to general ledger reconciliation?				
20. Is there adequate division of duties in the processing of cash receipts?				
21. Are there controls in place for recording sundry cash receipts such as sale of pallets or scrap?				
22. Is the credit department completely independent of the sales department?				
23. Are credit files maintained for each customer?				
24. Is senior management involved, where appropriate, in the collection process?				

Banking and Cash Management	Yes	No	N/A	Comments
1. Are cash receipts deposited daily?				
2. Are there controls to ensure that all cash receipts are deposited?				

PART D

CANADIAN TREASURY MANAGEMENT

Banking and Cash Management	Yes	No	N/A	Comments
3. Is activity through the bank accounts reviewed daily?				
4. Is positive pay or negative pay used to prevent or detect fraudulent items?				
5. Do cheques have anti-forgery features?				
6. Does the bank respond to queries quickly?				
7. Are bank charges reviewed at least annually?				
8. Do all cheques require two signatures?				
9. Are signing officers independent of cheque preparation?				
10. Are there special procedures for approving large cheques?				
11. Is interest paid (or credited against bank charges)?				
12. Are excess funds automatically transferred to reduce overdrafts daily?				
13. Are there adequate controls over non-Canadian-dollar bank accounts?				
14. Is there a cash forecasting process in place?				
15. Are all bank accounts reconciled monthly?				
16. Are no reconciling items carried forward from month to month?				
17. Are all reconciliations approved independently?				
18. If a line of credit is used, does it fluctuate considerably so that it is not a substitute for a loan or equity?				
19. Is there a positive relationship with the bank?				

EVALUATING TREASURY PERFORMANCE

Banking and Cash Management	Yes	No	N/A	Comments
20. Are bank charges reasonable?				
21. Is the bank proactive in suggesting ways to improve the banking process?				
22. Are there good controls over petty cash?				
23. Are there good controls over employee expense reimbursements?				
24. Is direct deposit used for payroll payments?				
25. Is electronic access used to monitor all bank accounts?				
26. Are bank accounts linked so that transfers can be made readily?				
27. Can wire payments and automated transfers be done electronically?				
28. Are there strong controls over electronic banking?				

Accounts Payable and Disbursements	Yes	No	N/A	Comments
1. Are vendors' invoices received directly by accounts payable?				
2. Are vendors' invoices checked against purchase orders and receiving reports?				
3. Are statements from vendors reviewed?				
4. Are interest charges on vendors' statements not paid?				
5. Are all discounts for prompt payment taken?				
6. Is there a process to review pricing of major or frequent purchases?				
7. Are vendors' invoices cancelled after they are paid?				

PART D

Accounts Payable and Disbursements	Yes	No	N/A	Comments
8. Are all disbursements, other than petty cash, made by cheque?				
9. Are vendors' invoices not paid before their due date?				
10. Are there adequate approvals from management before items are ordered from suppliers?				
11. Are there adequate approvals from management for items not in the ordinary course of business (such as fixed assets, one-off items, etc.)?				
12. Is the accounts payable subledger balanced to the general ledger monthly?				
13. Does someone independent of the processing of accounts payable review the accounts payable subledger to general ledger reconciliation?				
14. Is there adequate division of duties in the processing of disbursements?				
15. Is an aging of accounts payable reviewed by management monthly?				
16. Are accounts payable metrics compared to other companies in the same industry?				

Working Capital and Operations Management	Yes	No	N/A	Comments
1. Does the budget process include the balance sheet and cash flows?				
2. Are rolling forecasts of the balance sheet and cash flows prepared?				
3. Does the company have a written cash management and risk policy?				

EVALUATING TREASURY PERFORMANCE

Working Capital and Operations Management	Yes	No	N/A	Comments
4. Has the cash management and risk policy been approved by the Board of Directors?				
5. Are all major items not in the normal course of business approved by the Board of Directors?				
6 Is there a written investment policy?				
7. Is the investment policy approved by the Board of Directors?				
8. Is a monthly analysis of operating results prepared, and reviewed by senior management?				
9. Is a monthly analysis of cash flows and balance sheet changes prepared, and reviewed by senior management?				
10. Is a checklist maintained to ensure that government filings, remittances and reports are all made as required?				
11. Are monthly financial statements and management reports prepared promptly?				
12. Is insurance coverage reviewed at least semi-annually?				
13. Is there an internal audit process in place?				
14. Are monthly management reports derived from or reconciled to the general ledger?				
15. Are statistics such as sales, gross margin and profit per employee tracked monthly and compared to budget?				
16. Are statistics such as gross margin by product line or department tracked monthly and compared to budget?				

Working Capital and Operations Management	Yes	No	N/A	Comments
17. Does each business manager prepare a monthly report explaining variances to budget?				
18. Is there a process in place for analyzing and reviewing proposed capital expenditures?				
19. Are there controls in place over the hiring of consultants?				
20. Does the annual audit or review of the company's financial statements by chartered accountants produce value added information?				
21. Is planning carried out with regard to income taxes, GST/GST and provincial sales taxes?				

PART

Reference

This section includes information on the Treasury Management Association of Canada, international treasury associations, Canadian historical treasury statistics, and a glossary of finance and treasury terms.

PART E

Treasury Management Association of Canada

Overview

The Treasury Management Association of Canada (TMAC) provides a forum for information and networking for Canadian treasury professionals. TMAC is the umbrella organization representing its 14 regional treasury associations. This chapter includes information on TMAC, including a directory of staff, officers and directors, and regional contacts. TMAC can be reached at (416) 367-8500, or (800) 449-8622, or through its Web site, *www.tmac.ca.*

PART E

Introduction

The Treasury Management Association of Canada (TMAC) is a federation of 14 regional associations of professional treasury managers responsible for administering the corporate treasury function in Canada. TMAC members are involved in such areas as short- and long-term borrowing and investing, foreign exchange and risk management. They average about seven years experience in their profession, and 83 per cent work in organizations with annual revenues of $100 million or more.

TMAC consists of its regional associations, each with its own specific mandate and membership requirements. Treasury professionals who join a regional association are recognized as members of TMAC. The national organization is directed by a board consisting of Vice-Presidents from each of the regional associations, who elect a President, First Vice-President, and Secretary for a one-year term. Association members are also encouraged to participate in the committees that oversee TMAC's activities.

Through membership in TMAC, treasury practitioners stay abreast of current trends and developments in their profession. Activities include seminars, luncheons, and information sessions at the regional level, as well as an annual national conference and a bi-monthly magazine. Of equal importance, TMAC provides an environment of informal networking among treasury professionals.

Programs and Services

- **Conference** — TMAC's annual conference attracts over 500 participants from corporate treasury departments and other areas of the financial community. In addition to more than 30 formal presentations on all aspects of the treasury function, the conference also provides an opportunity to meet and exchange ideas with other treasury managers, suppliers, and financial professionals.

- **Magazine** — TMAC's bi-monthly magazine, *The Canadian Treasurer* carries a wide selection of articles on topics relevant to treasury management. Readers include treasurers and treasury professionals in corporate, institutional, and government organizations, including the top 1,000 companies in Canada. *The Canadian Treasurer* also carries news about people and events within the Canadian treasury community.
- **Education** — Throughout the year, TMAC holds one- and two-day seminars at various locations throughout the country on topics of importance to treasury managers. In addition, TMAC promotes the Certified Cash Manager (CCM) designation.

Seminars available
- Introduction to Cash Management
- Cash Flow Forecasting
- Introduction to Foreign Exchange
- Introduction to Money Markets
- Essentials of Electronic Commerce
- Advanced Electronic Commerce Payments
- Derivatives Demystified
- Managing Banking Relationships

- **Professional liaison** — TMAC maintains close ties with other organizations in the financial community. It also maintains links with international treasury organizations in the United States, United Kingdom, Ireland, Europe, Australia and New Zealand.

PART E

TMAC Regional Associations

TMAC British Columbia	Vancouver
TMAC Calgary	Calgary
TMAC Edmonton	Edmonton
TMAC Regina	Regina
TMAC Saskatoon	Saskatoon
TMAC Manitoba	Winnipeg
TMAC Southwestern Ontario	Waterloo
TMAC York Region	York Region
TMAC Insurance Chapter	Toronto
TMAC Toronto	Toronto
TMAC Ottawa	Ottawa
TMAC Montreal	Montreal
TMAC Maritimes	Halifax
TMAC Newfoundland	St. John's

TMAC 2003 Directory

Treasury Management
Association of Canada
8 King Street East
Suite 1010
Toronto, Ontario
M5C 1B5

Tel: (416) 367-8500
Toll free: (800) 449-8622
Fax: (416) 367-3240
E-mail: info@tmac.ca
Web site: *www.tmac.ca*

Executive Director
Blair McRobie
Tel: (416) 367-8501, ext. 2
E-mail: bmcrobie@tmac.ca

Director, Finance & Communication
Belinda Espley
Tel: (416) 367-8501, ext. 3
E-mail: bespley@tmac.ca

Manager, Administration
Riina Koppel
Tel: (416) 367-8501, ext. 1
E-mail: rkoppel@tmac.ca

Coordinator, Member Services
Rose Ficco
Tel: (416) 367-8501, ext. 4
E-mail: rficco@tmac.ca

Managing Editor, *The Canadian Treasurer*
Bruce McDougall
Tel: (416) 920-2668
E-mail: brucer@rogers.com

Director of Marketing, *The Canadian Treasurer*
Peter Stamp
Tel: (416) 367-8501, ext. 6
E-mail: pstamp@rogers.com

Western Sales Manager, *The Canadian Treasurer*
Gordon Smart
Tel: (604) 733-6896
E-mail: keegongroup@attglobal.net

TMAC 2003 Officers

President
Bill Edwards
SaskTel
Regina, Saskatchewan

Vice President
Irene Nicol
Scotiabank
Markham, Ontario

Treasurer
Peter Honeyborne
City of Brampton
Brampton, Ontario

Secretary
Laurie Benson
Bank of Montreal
Edmonton, Alberta

**Board Effectiveness
Committee Chair**
Irene Nicol
Scotiabank
Markham, Ontario

Directors
Paul Atterton
District of Vancouver
Vancouver, British Columbia

Jannette Baxter
Prudential of America
Toronto, Ontario

Marleen Church
Manitoba Hydro
Winnipeg, Manitoba

Juanita Flynn
Maritime Life Assurance
Halifax, Nova Scotia

Paul Pohl
Regional Municipality of
Waterloo
Kitchener, Ontario

Rick Rackal
Province of Manitoba
Winnipeg, Manitoba

Daphne Rixon
WHSC Commission
St. John's, Newfoundland

Gail Somers
Scotiabank
Ottawa, Ontario

Jon Verleih
BMO Nesbitt Burns
Calgary, Alberta

Mike Whiston
Magnet Communications Inc.
Sunderland, Ontario

Don Zealand
Royal Bank Financial Group
Saskatoon, Saskatchewan

TMAC Regional Association Contacts

TMAC British Columbia
President: Gavin Julius
City of Richmond
Tel: (604) 276-4216
VP Membership: Brenda
Cameron
RBC Capital Markets
Tel: (604) 257-7744

TMAC Calgary
President: Don Ogg
RBC Global Services
Tel: (403) 503-6178
VP Membership: Don Harlam
Glenbrian Technologies
Tel: (403) 233-7303

TMAC Edmonton
President: Ron Crosby
Alberta Gaming and Liquor
Commission
Tel: (780) 447-8668
VP Membership: Glen
Buchner
Liquid Capital West Limited
Tel: (780) 450-3519

TMAC Regina
President: Daniel Johnson
CUCORP Financial Services
Tel: (306) 566-1785
VP Membership: Jerry Irwin
RBC Financial Group
Tel: (306) 780-2501

TMAC Saskatoon
President: Marion Van Impe
University of Saskatchewan
Tel: (306) 966-2439

TMAC Manitoba
President: Dean Lash
Manitoba Civil Service
Superannuation Board
Tel: (204) 957-8722, ext. 229

TMAC Southwestern Ontario
President: Michael Cummins
CIBC Wood Gundy
Tel: (519) 883-5336
VP Membership: John Stilo
Equitable Life of Canada
Tel: (519) 886-5210

TMAC York Region
President: Mike Whiston
Tel: (905) 952-4294
VP Membership: John Lyles
iTrade Finance Inc.
Tel: (416) 492-7773

TMAC Insurance Chapter
President: Jannette Baxter
RBC Insurance
Tel: (905) 606-1458

PART E

TMAC Toronto
President: Robert Fisher
Robert Fisher Consulting Inc.
Tel: (416) 686-2538
VP Membership: Francis
Lindayen
Celestica Inc.
Tel: (416) 448-5844

TMAC Ottawa
President: Gail Somers
Scotiabank
Tel: (613) 564-5393
Membership VP: Sye Mincoff
Sye Mincoff Consulting
Tel: (613) 224-4820

TMAC Montreal
President: Claude Desautels
Bank of Montreal
Tel: (514) 282-5960
VP Membership: Anthony
Porraccio
Aclon Finance
Tel: (514) 935-8776

TMAC Newfoundland
President: Jim Mayo
Workplace Health, Safety and
Compensation Commission
Tel: (709) 778-1368
VP Membership: Lew
Andrews
Urquhart MacDonald &
Associates
Tel: (709) 753-4447

TMAC Maritimes
President: Geoff Baldwin
Oxford Frozen Foods
Tel: (902) 447-2100
VP Membership: Blaine
Recker
Emera Inc.
Tel: (902) 428-6813

CHAPTER 24

International Treasury Management Associations

Australia
The Finance and Treasury Association Limited
formerly The Australian Society of Corporate Treasurers (ASCT)
22 William Street
Melbourne, Victoria 3000
Australia

Contact: Marilyn Forde
Tel: 39 629 7954
Fax: 61 03 9629 7881
E-mail: info@fta.asn.au
Web site: *www.fta.asn.au*

Austria
Austrian Society of Corporate Treasurers
Rockhgasse 6
Vienna A-1014
Austria

Contact: Wilhelm Stejskal
Tel: 253 386 3631
Fax: 253 386 3673
E-mail: office@opwz.com
Web site: *www.opwz.com*

Belgium
Association des Trésoriers d'Entreprises en Belgique
c/o Chrysler Europe SA
Boulevard de la Woluwe 106-108
1200 Brussels
Belgium

Contact: Paul Deruyter
Tel: 32 2 775 4352
Fax: 32 2 775 4496
E-mail: pd6@chrysler.com

Canada
Treasury Management Association of Canada
8 King Street East, Suite 1010
Toronto, Ontario M5C 1B5
Canada

Contact: Blair McRobie
Tel: 416 367 8501, ext. 2
Fax: 416 367 3240
E-mail: bmcrobie@tmac.ca
Web site: *www.tmac.ca*

Costa Rica
Intituro Costarricense de Electricidad (ICE)
Avenida las Americas, Sabana Norte
San Jose
Costa Rica

Contact: Victor Fernandez
E-mail: ViFern@msmail.ice.go.cr

England
Association of Corporate Treasurers (UK)
Ocean House
10/12 Little Trinity Lane
London, England EC4V 2AA
United Kingdom

Contact: Richard Raeburn
Tel: 0207 213 9728
Fax: 0207 248 2591
E-mail: rraeburn@treasurers.co.uk
Web site: *www.corporate-treasurers.co.uk*

France
Association Française des Trésoriers d'Entreprise
20 rue d'Athenes
75442 Paris, Cedex 09
France

Contact: Carole D'Armaillé
Tel: 01 42 81 53 98
Fax: 01 42 80 18 90
E-mail: afte@wanadoo.fr
Web site: *www.afte.com*

PART E

Germany
Gesellschaft fuer Finanzwirtschaft in der Unternehmensfuehrung
e.V. (GEFIU)
c/o KPMG
Barbarossaplatz 1a
D-50674 Cologne
Germany
Tel: +49 221 2073 1565
Fax: +49 221 2073 218

Contact: Professor Felix Liermann
Tel: 49 69 1533 2938
Fax: 49 69 1533 2903
E-mail: liermann@fbw.fh-frankfurt.de

Greece
BP Hellas SA

Contact: Vassilis Tzortzis
Tel: 0030 1 6887 510
Fax: 0030 1 6887 892
E-mail: tzortzv@bp.com

Hong Kong
Association of Corporate Treasurers (Hong Kong)
c/o Hong Kong Land Limited
81F, One Exchange Square
Central
Hong Kong

Contact: Nick Sallnow-Smith
Tel: 2 843 8388
Fax: 2 521 5351

India

The Association of Certified Treasury Managers (IACT)
44 Nagarjana Hills
Nyderabad 500082
India

Contact: Ravi Kumar
Tel: 040 335 3748
Fax: 040 335 0193
E-mail: lcawin@hd2venl.net.in

Ireland

Irish Association of Corporate Treasurers (IACT)
19 Fitzwilliam Place
Dublin
Ireland

Contact: Susan Nonan – Administrator
Tel: 3 531 676 9411
Fax: 3 531 676 9415
E-mail: iact@indigo.ie

Italy

Italian Association of Corporate Treasurers
c/o ABB Finanziaria S.r.i.
P.le Lodi, 3
20137 Milano
Italy

Contact: Cino Ricci
Tel: 39 25 797 2545
Fax: 39 25 797 2450
E-mail: cino.ricci@ittrc.mail.abb.com

PART E

Luxembourg
Association des Trésoriers d'Entreprises à Luxembourg (ATEL)
c/o CLT-UFA
45, boulevard Pierre Frieden
L-1543 Luxembourg

Contact: Jonas Jeannot
Tel: 352 43 881 602
Fax: 352 42 93 82
E-mail: jeannot.jonas@mat.dyckerhoff.de

Malaysia
Malaysian Association of Corporate Treasurers (MACT)
9th Floor, Balai Felda
Jalan Gurney Satu
54000 Kuala Lumpur
Malaysia

Contact: Anne Rodrigues
Tel: 603 240 5201
Fax: 603 298 2677
E-mail: anne.r@felda.net.my

Morocco
c/o AKCE Finance
213 Rond-Point d'Europe
Mers Saltan, Casablanca
Morocco

Contact: Mohamed El Hajjouji
Tel: 212 248 4550
E-mail: akcefinance@elan.net.ma

Netherlands
Dutch Association of Corporate Treasurers (DACT)
P.O. Box 1483
5602 BL Eindhoven
Netherlands
Contact: Wim van Winden
Tel: 3 140 242 1744
Fax: 3 140 242 9425
E-mail: licht@iaehv.nl
Web site: *www.dact.nl*

New Zealand
New Zealand Society of Corporate Treasurers
P.O. Box 11-817 Wellington
New Zealand

Contact: Helen Walshaw
Tel: 644 479 2387
Fax: 644 479 5504
E-mail: info@corptreas.org.nz

Singapore
Association of Corporate Treasurers (Singapore)
c/o Hexa-Team Planners Pte. Ltd.
26 Duxton – Hill
089609 Singapore

Contact: Ang Thiam Huat
Tel: 65 227 8110
Fax: 65 227 8113

South Africa
Association of Corporate Treasurers of South Africa (ACTSA)
c/o Deloitte & Touche (ACTSA)
Private Bag X11
Gallo Manor
2092 South Africa

PART E

Contact: Lily Mitchell
Tel: 27 11 806 5584
Fax: 27 11 806 5558
E-mail: actsa@altavista.net
Web site: *www.actsa.org.sa*

Spain
ASSET
Asociacion Espanola de Tesoreros de Empresa
Aribau
195 5 Derecha
08021 Barcelona
Spain

Contact: Ricardo Fernandez Esteban
Tel: 34 93 414 1214
Fax: 34 93 414 0106
E-mail: asset@asset.es

Sweden
SSAB Finance Stockholm
Box 26208 S-100 40 Stockholm
Sweden

Contact: Goran Fritzell
Tel: 46 8 454 5700
Fax: 46 8 454 5777
E-mail: goran.fritzell@ssab.se

Switzerland
Swiss Association of Corporate Treasurers (SwissACT)
c/o Electrowatt Management Corp.
Bellevestrasse 36
CH-8002 Zurich
Switzerland

Contact: Roland C. Kofer
Tel: 411 385 2556
Fax: 411 385 3159

United States
Association For Financial Professionals (formerly TMA)
7315 Wisconsin Avenue, Suite 600 West
Bethesda, Maryland 20814
USA

Contact: James A. Kaitz
Tel: 301 907 2862
Fax: 301 907 2864
E-mail: AFP@AFPonline.org
Web site: *www.afponline.org*

PART E

CHAPTER 25

Key Canadian Historical Statistics

Overview

This chapter includes historical information on exchange rates, interest rates and other economic statistics.

Canadian Interest Rates (%)
1983-2002

| At end of | Bank rate | Bankers' acceptances 30 day | Conventional Mortgage | | Chartered Bank Administered Rates | | | |
			One year	Five year	Non-chequable savings deposits	Guaranteed Investment Certificates five year	Prime business	Overnight Target Rate
1983	10.04	9.57	10.25	12.50	6.75	8.50	11.00	9.07
1984	10.16	10.10	11.25	12.50	6.75	10.25	11.25	10.05
1985	9.49	9.45	9.75	11.50	5.50	9.25	10.00	9.84
1986	8.49	8.23	9.75	11.00	5.25	7.75	9.75	8.16
1987	8.66	8.62	10.25	11.75	4.75	7.25	9.75	8.50
1988	11.17	10.63	12.00	12.25	7.00	9.00	12.25	10.35
1989	12.47	12.31	12.75	11.75	8.25	9.50	13.50	12.17
1990	11.78	11.88	12.50	12.50	7.50	9.50	12.75	11.62
1991	7.67	7.48	8.50	9.88	3.00	7.25	8.00	7.40
1992	7.36	6.84	7.75	9.50	1.50	6.00	7.25	6.79
1993	4.11	3.76	6.25	7.75	0.50	5.00	5.50	3.79
1994	7.43	6.25	9.50	10.50	0.50	8.38	8.00	5.54
1995	5.79	5.67	7.25	8.45	0.50	6.38	7.50	5.71
1996	3.25	3.08	5.20	6.95	0.50	4.38	4.75	3.01
1997	4.50	4.50	6.65	7.05	0.50	4.63	6.00	4.34
1998	5.25	5.07	6.20	6.60	0.10	3.98	6.75	5.11
1999	5.00	5.33	7.70	8.35	0.10	5.43	7.00	5.25
2000	6.00	5.80	7.70	7.95	0.10	4.28	7.50	5.75
2001	2.50	2.18	4.60	6.85	0.10	3.53	4.00	2.25
2002	3.00	2.79	4.90	6.70	0.05	3.93	4.50	2.75

Source: *Bank of Canada Weekly Financial Statistics.*

Canadian Interest Rates (%) (cont'd)
1983-2002

| At end of | Prime Corporate Paper | | | Treasury Bills | | | Average yields on corporate bonds | |
	One month	Three month	Three month	Six month	One year	Mid-term	Long-term
1983	9.55	9.85	9.71	9.86	NA	12.21	12.95
1984	10.20	10.00	9.84	10.16	NA	11.91	12.40
1985	9.45	9.40	9.24	9.26	NA	10.26	10.86
1986	8.25	8.35	8.24	8.48	NA	10.02	10.13
1987	8.70	8.90	8.41	9.01	NA	10.87	11.13
1988	10.70	11.10	10.94	11.40	NA	11.12	11.13
1989	12.34	12.34	12.21	12.14	NA	10.90	10.82
1990	11.92	11.73	11.51	11.42	11.21	11.50	11.74
1991	7.58	7.55	7.43	7.28	7.39	9.48	10.17
1992	7.00	7.25	7.01	7.01	7.13	9.36	9.70
1993	3.81	3.94	3.87	4.04	4.23	7.05	8.02
1994	6.27	7.22	7.14	8.12	8.79	9.71	9.95
1995	5.72	5.67	5.54	5.64	5.74	7.33	8.12
1996	3.10	3.13	2.85	3.24	3.61	6.33	7.35
1997	4.50	4.80	3.99	4.56	4.99	6.11	6.42
1998	5.08	5.02	4.66	4.76	4.80	5.77	6.06
1999	5.27	5.27	4.85	5.16	5.63	6.96	7.22
2000	5.81	5.71	5.49	5.46	5.41	6.58	7.04
2001	2.18	2.08	2.00	2.06	2.35	6.27	7.05
2002	2.79	2.83	2.67	2.79	2.89	5.60	6.73

Source: *Bank of Canada Weekly Financial Statistics.*

PART E

627

Canadian Interest Rates (%) (cont'd) 1983-2002

At end of	Average yields on Government of Canada bonds (cont'd)				Average yields on provincial bonds	
	One to three year	Three to five year	Five to ten year	Over ten years	Mid-term	Long-Term
1983	10.39	10.84	11.41	12.02	NA	12.86
1984	10.44	10.76	11.24	11.66	NA	12.27
1985	9.10	9.33	9.67	10.06	NA	10.76
1986	8.63	8.81	8.89	9.23	NA	9.82
1987	9.69	9.95	10.04	10.34	NA	11.08
1988	10.58	10.40	10.17	10.36	NA	10.92
1989	10.99	10.36	9.83	9.80	NA	10.41
1990	10.77	10.50	10.28	10.51	11.23	11.47
1991	7.65	7.95	8.37	8.97	9.00	9.69
1992	7.20	7.35	8.03	8.54	8.76	9.34
1993	4.57	5.47	6.33	7.12	6.63	7.71
1994	8.86	9.00	9.09	9.16	9.59	9.78
1995	5.98	6.51	6.92	7.43	7.05	7.98
1996	4.24	5.20	6.02	6.77	5.94	7.22
1997	5.22	5.37	5.54	5.80	5.70	6.19
1998	4.84	4.81	4.88	5.08	5.18	5.67
1999	5.86	6.14	6.19	6.25	6.49	6.75
2000	5.29	5.32	5.35	5.59	5.72	6.18
2001	3.28	4.54	5.25	5.75	5.59	6.29
2002	3.23	3.93	4.60	5.37	4.84	5.81

Source: *Bank of Canada Weekly Financial Statistics.*

U.S. Dollar Interest Rates (%) 1983-2002

At end of	Commercial Paper		Federal funds rate	Prime bank rate	U.S. Treasuries		Forward premium (discount) of U.S. dollars in C$	
	One month	Three month			Five year	Long-term	One month	Three month
1983	9.85	9.90	8.96	11.00	11.56	NA	NA	(0.39)
1984	8.14	8.33	7.95	10.75	10.97	NA	NA	1.39
1985	7.99	7.97	8.02	9.50	8.56	NA	NA	1.22
1986	7.65	6.48	9.20	7.50	6.81	NA	NA	2.14
1987	7.11	7.22	6.81	8.75	8.32	NA	NA	1.18
1988	9.43	9.31	8.86	10.50	9.22	NA	NA	1.53
1989	8.53	8.44	8.51	10.50	7.78	NA	NA	3.76
1990	9.45	8.54	7.16	10.00	7.78	8.30	3.15	3.39
1991	5.09	4.20	4.22	6.50	6.01	7.53	2.52	3.01
1992	3.41	3.43	2.86	6.00	5.98	7.38	3.45	3.48
1993	3.46	3.40	2.99	6.00	5.12	6.26	0.55	0.52
1994	5.98	6.35	5.45	8.50	7.81	7.83	0.09	0.66
1995	5.70	5.60	5.48	8.50	5.46	6.01	(0.09)	0.00
1996	5.62	5.55	5.18	8.25	6.13	6.58	(2.76)	(2.44)
1997	6.06	5.97	5.45	8.50	5.71	5.92	(1.36)	(1.08)
1998	5.29	4.93	4.48	7.75	4.55	5.09	(0.31)	(0.18)
1999	5.55	5.76	5.01	8.50	6.32	6.45	(1.00)	(0.89)
2000	6.53	6.31	6.48	9.50	4.99	5.45	(0.97)	(0.72)
2001	1.99	1.89	1.77	4.75	4.55	5.22	(0.30)	(0.20)
2002	1.35	1.33	1.23	4.25	2.92	3.95	1.42	1.47

Source: Bank of Canada Weekly Financial Statistics.

PART E

629

Average Spot Exchange Rates
1983-2002

Average (Note 1)	U.S. Dollar	British Pound	Euro	French Franc	German Mark	Japanese Yen	Swiss Franc
1983	1.2324	1.8683		0.1624	0.4834	0.005190	0.5873
1984	1.2948	1.7300		0.1487	0.4564	0.005457	0.5527
1985	1.3652	1.7701		0.1533	0.4677	0.005767	0.5615
1986	1.3894	2.0388		0.2010	0.6425	0.008300	0.7769
1987	1.3260	2.1725		0.2208	0.7384	0.009190	0.8905
1988	1.2309	2.1929		0.2072	0.7028	0.009610	0.8443
1989	1.1842	1.9415		0.1858	0.6304	0.008610	0.7246
1990	1.1668	2.0808		0.2147	0.7234	0.008090	0.8430
1991	1.1458	2.0275		0.2039	0.6934	0.008520	0.8027
1992	1.2083	2.1302		0.2288	0.7757	0.009550	0.8627
1993	1.2898	1.9372		0.2279	0.7804	0.01165	0.8734
1994	1.3659	2.0929		0.2469	0.8444	0.01139	1.0024
1995	1.3726	2.1671		0.2754	0.9591	0.01470	1.1633
1996	1.3636	2.1283		0.2667	0.9068	0.01255	1.1051
1997	1.3844	2.2682		0.2375	0.7994	0.01145	0.9548
1998	1.4831	2.4587		0.2520	0.8450	0.01139	1.0258
1999	1.4858	2.4038	1.5847	0.2416	0.8102	0.01311	0.9901
2000	1.4852	2.2499	1.3704	0.2089	0.7007	0.01378	0.8793
2001	1.5928	2.2845	1.4070	0.2145	0.7194	0.012383	0.9534
2002	1.5593	2.4730	1.5883	—	—	0.212787	1.0830

Source: *Bank of Canada Weekly Review Statistics.*

Notes:

1. Average of noon spot rates.

Credit Outstanding
1983-2002

Credit, seasonally adjusted (in $millions)

At end of	Business credit	Consumer credit	Residential mortgage credit
1983	234,995	40,631	73,278
1984	251,273	44,271	78,449
1985	270,191	50,146	87,916
1986	289,524	56,181	103,090
1987	313,293	63,108	123,201
1988	397,237	83,840	186,623
1989	441,652	93,494	216,885
1990	467,778	99,688	248,415
1991	484,521	99,060	268,935
1992	490,428	97,707	294,066
1993	495,677	104,882	313,707
1994	522,363	112,868	332,675
1995	556,596	121,843	341,205
1996	586,214	132,225	358,436
1997	661,350	149,138	380,884
1998	714,592	160,578	401,227
1999	757,445	175,977	415,617
2000	810,389	195,459	433,625
2001	849,905	205,576	462,493
2002	862,918	221,209	492,761

Source: *Bank of Canada Weekly Finance Statistics.*

PART E

Glossary

This glossary defines commonly used treasury and finance terms. To locate more detailed discussions and descriptions of treasury instruments, please refer to the index.

Acceleration clause — Allows a creditor to demand immediate payment in the event of default.

Accept-reject approach — An approach to evaluating capital expenditure proposals to determine whether the project meets the minimum criteria established by management.

Accounts payable — Amounts owing to suppliers for goods and services.

Accounts receivable — Amounts owed to a business by customers for merchandise or services sold on open account.

Accounts receivable financing — Obtaining a short-term loan from a bank, factor or finance company to finance working capital, collateralized by accounts receivable.

Accounts receivable turnover — The ratio obtained by dividing total sales on credit by average accounts receivable. It indicates how many times the receivables portfolio has been collected during the period.

Accretion — An increase. It can refer to asset growth, an increase in the value of a bond as a discount is amortized, or in general, anything that increases. For example, an accreting swap is a swap where the notional principal amount increases over time.

Accrued interest — Interest that has accumulated since the last payment was made. When a bond is purchased or sold, the accrued interest is taken into account in determining the amount paid upon settlement.

Actuals — Physical commodities such as those underlying commodity futures contracts.

Ad valorem — Means "according to value". Generally refers to assessment of taxes or duties on goods or property based on the value of the property rather than for example, on its weight or quantity.

Agency — Refers in general to a relationship between two parties: one a principal and the other an agent who represents the interest of the principal in transactions with a third party. An employee of a corporation generally acts as an agent in entering into binding contracts on behalf of the corporation.

Allotment — Securities assigned to a participant in an investment banking syndicate to underwrite and distribute a new issue.

Alpha — The net risk-adjusted premium rate of return from taking a position or holding a portfolio. It is equal to the difference between the actual return and the risk-adjusted return based upon the beta or the theoretical return based on the capital asset pricing model market line.

Amortization — The reduction in the valuation or book value of an asset. The accounting procedure of amortization is intended to allocate cost of an asset over its estimated useful life. For fixed assets the term depreciation is used. For wasting assets, such as natural resources, the term is depletion.

Amortization also refers generally to any reduction in an asset or liability such as the reduction of debt by regular payments of interest and principal to discharge it by its maturity date. Similarly, an amortizing swap is a swap with a notional principal reduced over time.

Amount at risk — In a swap agreement, this refers to the present value of a replacement swap or the present value of future cash flows under the swap.

Annuity — A fixed rate instrument that pays the investor an equal amount of cash each year over its life. Individual payments contain increasing amounts of principal and correspondingly smaller amounts of interest.

Annuity swap — This can refer to either a currency swap with an exchange of interest payments only but no exchange of principal, or another name for a swap where the notional principal amount amortizes over time (also called an amortizing swap).

Arbitrage — In general, this refers to activity that attempts to buy relatively underpriced financial instruments and sell a related relatively overpriced instrument with an expectation of profit. In the futures markets, arbitrage refers to purchasing a commodity or security in one market for immediate sale in another in order to lock in a gain.

PART E

Arbitrage is also used to discuss specific methodologies that attempt to lock in gains. Tax arbitrage refers to transactions undertaken to share the benefit of differential tax rates among two or more parties. Risk arbitrage refers to purchasing shares in a company that is a takeover target and selling shares in a bidding company whose shares are expected to fall. It also refers to the action of purchasing shares in the takeover of a company with the expectation that the indicated takeover price will be raised. Regulatory arbitrage refers to the provision of access to a market where one party is denied direct access due to regulatory or other restrictions.

Swap-driven arbitrage transactions are inspired by the comparative advantage that swap counterparties enjoy in different debt or currency markets.

Arbitrage Pricing Theory (APT) — Theory of portfolio behaviour that states that if the returns of a portfolio of assets can be described by a factor structure or model, the expected return of each asset in the portfolio can be described by combination of the covariances of the factors with the returns of the asset. The resulting models are used to create portfolios that track market indices, or assess the risk profile of a portfolio.

Appreciation — An increase in the market value of an asset or security.

Arrangement fee — A commission paid to a financial intermediary such as a securities firm, for its role in initiating or implementing a transaction.

Arrears swap — An interest rate swap where the floating rate is set in arrears, that is based on the reference rate at the end of the reset period, applied retroactively, rather than based on the floating index at the beginning of the reset period. As with a conventional interest rate swap, payments are made at the end of each period.

GLOSSARY

Ask — The lowest price acceptable to a prospective seller at a particular time.

Asset — Anything owned by or owed to an entity. In accounting, an asset is that which adds future value to the firm.

Asset allocation — The division of investment funds among different categories of assets such as cash, shares and fixed income instruments. The term can also apply to subcategories such as different entity groups of shares or different types of bonds (federal government, provincial government, corporate).

Asset-backed securities — Notes that are backed by underlying loans, accounts receivable, or other assets. The assets provide collateral for the securities issued. The owner of the loans or receivables may sell the paper to a trust which repackages them as securities, which are then underwritten or sold.

Asset financing — The conversion of particular assets into working capital by giving up a security interest in those assets. An example would be a borrowing secured by accounts receivable.

Asset-liability management — Managing the relative terms to maturity of assets and liabilities.

Asset swap — An interest rate swap that is based upon altering the payment basis of assets rather than liabilities. Its actual mechanics do not differ from a conventional swap based upon a liability.

Assignment — Notice to the seller of an option that an option has been exercised by the option holder. In general, assignment refers to the transfer of rights to settle an obligation. In that sense, it can also refer to the transfer of ownership in a structured product, private placement or financial instrument to another counterparty, with the consent of the original issuer.

637

At the money — Means at the current market price. For example, an option with an exercise price equal to the current price of the underlying instrument is at the money.

Auction rate note — A floating rate note where the interest rate is reset based upon bids received at a Dutch auction. A Dutch auction sets a high opening price and then lowers the bids until a buyer is found.

Average rate cap — A cap on the average interest rate over a period of time, rather than based upon the rate on a particular date.

Average rate of return — Evaluating proposed capital expenditures by dividing after-tax profits into the net assets required or capital employed. Can also refer to the rate of return on a portfolio of securities which includes both capital gains and income.

Average rate option — Also referred to as average price option. An option that pays the difference between the average rate of the underlying and the predetermined strike price.

Averaging down — Normally applied to the purchase of additional shares at a lower price than that of those originally held, which results in a lower average cost. Sometimes alleged to be an important investment principle. Actually, it is more of an arithmetical truism.

Back contract — Refers to future contracts that have the most distant expiration dates.

Back office — The area in a bank or securities dealer not directly involved in selling or trading. The back office handles administration, accounting, compliance with regulatory requirements and settlement procedures. Recently the concept of a "mid-office" to handle risk management and management accounting has become popular among some dealers.

Back-to-back loan — The original prototype for a simple cross-currency swap which was designed to overcome currency restrictions. Back-to-back borrowing and lending arrangements refer to offsetting loans between two parties in different currencies.

Back-to-back swap — A swap that reverses the cash flow patterns of another swap, altering the paying and receiving positions of the counterparties. Such swaps can be used to extend the effective maturity of an issuer's fixed rate debt.

Backwardation — A situation where the forward price on the futures market is lower than the spot price. The opposite is *contango*.

Balance sheet — Financial statement showing the nature and amounts of an entity's assets, liabilities and owner's or shareholder's equity. Also referred to as statement of financial position or statement of capital employed.

Balloon — Where the final payment on debt is much larger than the preceding payments. For example, where there is no repayment of principal before maturity of a bond, the final balloon payment would equal the amount of the debt.

Bank Act — The federal statute that regulates the operations of the chartered banks. It is revised approximately every ten years. It was last amended in 1991.

Bank draft — In effect, a cheque issued by a bank in its own name.

Bank guarantee — A form of credit enhancement in which a bank guarantees the timely payment of the obligations of another party.

Bank of Canada — The central bank responsible for Canada's monetary policy. It also manages the national debt, invests funds for government agencies, advises the minister of finance on economic policies, and controls the printing of bank notes. The *Bank of Canada Act* provides that it is responsible for regulating "credit and currency in the best interest of the economic life of the nation".

PART E

Bank rate — The minimum rate of interest that the Bank of Canada charges chartered banks and other financial institutions for loans from the Bank of Canada. These loans are relatively rare and the bank rate is more important as a signal to the banking system of current monetary policy. Since 1980, the bank rate has been formally fixed at 25 basis points above the average yield on 91-day Government of Canada Treasury Bills at their auctions each Tuesday.

Bankers' acceptance — Negotiable commercial paper issued by a non- financial corporation but guaranteed as to principal and interest by a chartered bank. The bank normally charges a "stamping fee" for the guarantee. Most Canadian dollar interest rate swaps use the bankers' acceptance rate as the reference rate for floating rate side.

Barrier option — A path dependent option that is either cancelled or activated if the underlying instrument reaches a predetermined price. Also referred to as knock out, knock in, trigger, down-and-out, up and in, or early exercise trigger options.

Basis — The difference between the price of a futures contract and the underlying cash instrument. In the sense of basis risk, it refers to the relationship between the price or rate in two related but not identical markets.

Basis point — Used to quote yields on interest rate instruments. One basis point is $\frac{1}{100}$ of 1 per cent of yield. Thus, changing a yield from 7 per cent to 8 per cent represents a change of 100 basis points.

In foreign exchange, a basis point, for most currencies, is $\frac{1}{10,000}$ of the currency. This is also referred to simply as a "point". For example, a change in the Canada/U.S. exchange rate from $1.53 to $1.54 (that is from $1.5300 to $1.5400) is a change of 100 foreign exchange points.

Basis risk — The risk of loss from imperfectly matched positions in two related but not identical markets.

Bear — A position that will be profitable if the market declines, or a person who expects the market to decline.

Bear floaters — A floating rate note which is reset at a rate equal to a multiple of the floating rate index minus a fixed rate. For example, a bear floater may call for a variable rate payment equal to twice LIBOR minus 7 per cent. If floating rates rise, the floating rate receiver benefits.

Bear spread — An option strategy predicated upon a bearish view of the market. Bear strategies have limited upside potential but also limited risk.

Bear trap — A downward move in market rates that stops and then turns into an upward move, trapping the bears.

Beta — A measurement of the relative volatility of a financial instrument. Beta represents the covariance of a financial instrument relative to the market as a whole. For example, a share with the same volatility as the market as a whole has a beta coefficient of one. Shares with a higher beta are more volatile than the market and can be expected to rise and fall rapidly. Beta is also referred to as systematic risk because it is risk that cannot be diversified away.

Bid — The highest price that a prospective buyer is prepared to pay at a particular time.

Big board — Refers to the New York Stock Exchange (NYSE), the largest stock exchange in the United States, established in 1792.

Big figure — In foreign exchange, refers to 100 foreign exchange points. A change in the Canada/U.S. exchange rate from a $1.33 to a $1.34 is a change of one big figure.

PART E

Binary option — An option that pays out a fixed amount if the underlying reaches a predetermined strike price. This is in contrast to simple options which have continuous pay out profiles. In the case of a simple option, once it is in the money, its pay out increases as the price of the underlying increases or decreases. The pay out under a binary option is a fixed amount.

Black-Scholes options pricing model — The model developed by Fischer Black and Myron Scholes in 1973 to determine prices for option contracts. It offers a solution to the pricing of European-style options on assets with interim cash payouts over the life of an option. The model calculates a theoretical value for the option based on constructing a riskless hedge whose performance is the mirror image of the payout of the option. Therefore, the combination of the hedge and the option should earn the risk-free rate of return.

The model is based upon the price of the underlying, the level of interest rates, the strike price and volatility. The model assumes that market returns are normally distributed, that is, that prices are log normally distributed, there are no transaction costs and that volatility and market interest rates remain constant through the life of the option.

Blue-sky law — U.S. term that refers to legislation enacted to protect investors against securities fraud. Blue-sky laws require promoters of new share issues or mutual funds to register their offerings and provide for financial information to investors.

Bond — An IOU from the borrower to the lender. It refers to any interest-bearing government or corporate security that obligates the issuer to pay a particular sum of money at specified intervals and to repay the principal amount of the loan upon maturity. A secured bond is backed by collateral which may be sold by the bond holder if the bond issuer fails to pay interest and principal as due. A debenture or unsecured bond is not backed by any specific collateral.

Bond rating — An evaluation of the likelihood of default by a bond issuer. Canada Bond Rating Service and Dominion Bond Rating Service are the primary bond rating agencies in Canada. Standard and Poors, Moody's and Fitch are American bond rating firms that also rate some Canadian issuers.

Each agency uses slightly different ratings, but the ratings vary in general from AAA, for an issuer that is highly unlikely to default to D minus for an issuer that is in default. Bonds rated below A are not investment grade. This means that entities with fiduciary responsibilities in investing (banks, life insurance companies, trust companies, etc.) are restricted in their ability to invest in them.

Book entry — Refers to securities records being maintained on computer records rather than by paper certificates.

Bought deal — A firm commitment to purchase an entire issue of securities from the issuing company.

Break even analysis — An analysis of the relationship between revenues and costs taking into account fixed costs and variable costs. The break even point represents the volume of sales at which total costs equal total revenues so that gross profit is zero.

Break forward — The sale of an underlying forward at a discount below the prevailing forward rate. The discount pays for the purchase of an option that cancels the forward if the underlying rises above a predetermined value. The transaction is generally constructed so that there is no cost to the purchaser because the discount on the forward is sufficient to pay for the option.

Bretton Woods — Refers to the Bretton Woods International Monetary Conference which in 1944 established a system of fixed exchange rates between currencies. This system collapsed in the early 1970s.

Broken dates — Settlement dates for forward currency contracts that fall within the standard futures contract periods.

PART E

Budget — An estimate of revenues and expenditures for a particular period. Depending on the context, it may refer to a financial plan that is an objective for management to achieve, or it may refer to a most likely estimate of revenues and expenditures.

Bull — One who expects the market to rise, or a position that will be profitable if the market rises.

Bull floater — A floating rate note in which the rate paid increases as market floating rates decline. A bull floater reset rate might be 14 per cent minus LIBOR. Also referred to as a reverse floating rate note.

Bull spread — Generally, refers to an options strategy that will be profitable if the underlying security rises in value. For example, a vertical bull spread is the simultaneous purchase and sale of option of the same security at different strike prices but with the same expiration date.

Bullet maturity — A bond with no repayment of principal until maturity.

Bunds — Bonds issued by the Government of Germany, denominated in Deutschmarks.

Business Development Bank of Canada (BDC) — A Crown corporation established in 1975 charged with assisting the growth of small and medium sized businesses in Canada. It provides loans, loan guarantees and financing for export receivables.

Butterfly spread — A structure based on buying and selling options that produces profits, if the price of the underlying remains relatively unchanged, and limited losses in the event that the price of the underlying changes significantly in either direction. This is normally accomplished through the sale of an at-the-money straddle and the purchase of an out-of-the money strangle, otherwise known as vertical bull spread and vertical bear spread.

Cable — The exchange rate between Pound Sterling and the United States Dollar.

Cage — A securities dealer's back office where funds and securities are received and disbursed.

Calendar Roll — A trade where a futures or option contract is sold or closed in one contract month, then purchased for a more distant date.

Call — Refers the right of the issuer of a security to redeem bonds or preferred shares before maturity. The result is that the security has embedded in it an option, that can be valued using normal option valuation techniques.

Call option — An option to buy. *See* Option.

Call price — The price at which a callable security can be called by the issuer. This term can also be used to refer to the market price of a call option.

Call protection — A provision in a bond or stock indenture that provides that the issuer cannot call an issue for a particular period of time or that the issuer must pay a premium over issue price to retire the issue.

Callable — Means redeemable by the issuer before scheduled maturity.

Callable swap — A swap agreement in which the fixed rate receiver has the right to terminate the swap prior to its maturity. This provision has the effect of protecting the fixed rate receiver from an increase in fixed interest rates.

Canada Savings Bonds — Bonds sold to the public in October of every year, since 1946. The Bonds are sold by the Bank of Canada through a network of chartered banks, investment dealers and other authorized sales agents. Canada Savings Bonds can be redeemed by the holder before maturity but may not be sold to other investors.

PART E

Canadian Venture Exchange (CDNX) — Founded in 1999 through the merger of the Alberta Stock Exchange and the Vancouver Stock Exchange. Its predecessors were founded in 1913 and 1907 and were known for their speculative or higher risk companies listed.

Cap — An agreement that puts a ceiling or "cap" on an interest rate. This may be part of a debt agreement assumed by a borrower or sold as a separate option. An embedded cap will actually impose a maximum level of interest rates payable. A separate option contract would normally be structured to pay the owner of the cap an amount equal to the excess of market rates over the cap rate times the notional principal.

The cap is actually a strip of interest rate guarantees or options that put a ceiling on the rates for each reset period over the life of the cap.

Capacity — Refers to the legal capacity to enter into a binding contract. This has become an issue in the case of derivative contracts since the *Hammersmith and Fulham* case. In 1991, the British House of Lords decided that U.K. municipalities ("local authorities") did not have the contractual capacity to enter into interest rate swap contracts.

Capital asset — Generally, an asset other than intangible assets or working capital. A capital asset is not purchased or sold in the normal course of business. Capital assets include fixed assets such as land, buildings and equipment as well as capital leases on fixed assets.

Capital Asset Pricing Model (CAPM) — Usually refers to the theory that there is a correlation between risks and rewards. Investors demand and receive higher returns for taking greater risk. Strictly speaking, the Capital Asset Pricing Model states that the return on an asset is equal to the risk-free return plus a risk premium. Unfortunately, while the concept is intuitively sensible, some recent research has failed to support it.

Capital expenditure — Disbursements to acquire or improve capital assets.

Capital gain — The excess of the proceeds of sale of an asset over its original cost.

Capital structure — The mix of various types of debt and equity capital maintained by a firm. A firm with more debt in its capital structure is more highly levered.

Capped swap — An interest rate swap that has an embedded cap on the floating rate payments.

Caption — An *option* to buy a *cap*.

Cash — In the sense of "cash market", refers to an underlying financial instrument, such as a bond, rather than one traded in a forward or futures market.

Cash budget — A summary of expected cash receipts and disbursements, often on a monthly basis. The purpose of a cash budget is to determine when financing will be required and when cash surpluses will occur.

Cash cycle — The period of time from making an outlay to purchase raw materials to the point that cash is collected as a result of the sale of finished goods.

CATS — Certificate of account on treasury securities. U.S. Treasury zero coupon bonds.

Central bank — The bank in a particular country that issues currency, administers monetary policy, and acts as a banker to other banks for example, by holding their deposits. The central bank in Canada is the Bank of Canada. In the United States, the function is carried out by the Federal Reserve System.

Cheapest To Deliver (CTD) — In the futures markets, various bonds or notes may be delivered to satisfy a commitment. Similarly, various grades of commodities can be delivered to any of several

PART E

delivery points. The market price of the future is based upon the assumption that the delivery requirement will be met in the form of the instrument that can be delivered at the least total cost.

Cherry picking — Refers to the concern that in bankruptcy proceedings, courts may enforce contracts favourable to the bankrupt entity and leave unfavourable contracts to be settled as part of the residue of the estate of the bankrupt. The corollary of this is the enforceability of netting agreements.

Chooser option — Permits the holder to select between a put option and a call option. While payouts are similar to those of a straddle, chooser options are cheaper because purchasers must select either a put or a call before expiry.

Clearing — The process of receiving credit for the funds represented by a cheque by presenting the item at the bank that it is drawn upon.

Collar — The simultaneous purchase of a call option that is out-of-the-money and the sale of a put option, that is out-of-the-money. In the case of an interest rate product, this would be the purchase of a cap and the sale of a floor. The net premium is the cost of the call less the proceeds of selling the put. In many cases, a caller will be structured so that no net premium is payable.

Collateral — An asset pledged to a lender until a loan is repaid. If the borrower defaults, the lender has the legal right to seize the collateral and sell it to discharge the loan.

Collateralized mortgage obligation — An asset backed security that is secured by mortgage payments.

Commitment — Commitment fee is charged by a bank for agreeing to make credit available when required.

Commodity swap — A swap in which counterparties exchange cash flows based on a commodity price on one side.

Compound option — An option on an option, for example, a call on a call or a call on a put.

Confirmation — A printed statement from a financial institution to its customer setting out the details of the purchase or sale of a security.

Contango — A case where the price of a future is higher than the spot price for a particular instrument. The "normal" upward sloping forward curve is an example of contango. The reverse is called backwardation.

Convexity — The convexity of a bond measures the amount by which its price changes as interest rates change. Convexity is also referred to as *gamma.*

Corporation — An artificial entity that is a legal person in its own right. A corporation has most of the powers of a natural person. The advantages of the corporate form of organization include: committed liability to owners, transferability of ownership, perpetual existence and (perhaps) some income tax benefits.

Correspondent bank — A bank that serves as a depository and performs banking services for other banks, generally in another country.

Cost of carry — Costs incurred by an investor to have an investment. These costs include interest payable on margin accounts, dividends which must be made up or lost due to short positions, and other expenses.

Coupon — The interest rate on a bond that the issuer promises to pay the holder until maturity, expressed as a percentage of face value at an annual rate.

Coverage ratios — Financial ratios such as times interest earned and total debt coverage that measure the ability of a firm to meet its fixed financial obligations.

PART E

Cox-Ingersoll-Ross Model — A model used to calculate prices for zero-coupon bonds and consequently, put and call options on interest rate instruments.

Credit risk — The risk that an obligation will not be repaid.

Cross currency interest rate swap — A swap that involves the exchange of cash flows in one currency for those of another. Cross currency swaps usually require an exchange of principal at the beginning and the end of the contract period, unlike single currency swaps.

Cum dividend — Means with dividend. Refers to a share where a buyer is eligible to receive a dividend that has already been declared. Shares trade cum dividend for transactions that settle by the record. Trades after that date go ex dividend.

Current assets — Assets of the company that management expects will be converted into cash within a year.

Current liability — Debt or other obligation payable by the company within a year of its current business cycle, whichever is longer.

Current ratio — Current assets divided by current liabilities. The current ratio indicates the company's ability to meet its current obligations from current assets.

Cylinder — The purchase of an out-of-the-money put option on a currency and the simultaneous sale of an out-of-the-money call option on the same currency at different strike prices. Also known as a *range forward.*

 aisy chain — A series of linked trades or contracts.

Dead cat bounce — A brief rally after a long market decline.

Debt/equity ratio — The measure of a firm's financial leverage. The debt/equity ratio is calculated by dividing a corporation's long-term debt into its shareholders equity. A higher ratio represents higher leverage.

Defeasance — This is generally used in the context of *in-substance defeasance*, a technique for removing debt from a company's balance sheet without redeeming or cancelling it. This is generally done by establishing an irrevocable trust which would be funded with sufficient assets to discharge the debt. At present, it is uncertain whether this would enable the debt to be reflected as discharged for financial reporting purposes.

Deferred swap — A swap that starts at a date after the transaction date.

Delivery — The date on which an exchange of funds takes place.

Delta — In general, refers to the rate at which the price of a financial instrument changes as underlying market rates change. For example, the delta of a bond is the rate at which the bond price changes as interest rates change. Frequently used in the context of options: the delta of an option reflects the rate at which the market price of an option changes as the price of the underlying changes.

Direct placement — Also called a *private placement*. The sale of financial instruments directly to the ultimate investors, for example, life insurance companies.

Discounted cash flow — The valuation of future expected cash flows at a common date by taking into account the time value of money.

Disintermediation — For investors, refers to the trend away from deposits (and similar instruments) in financial institutions to direct investment in the financial markets. For example, purchase of a treasury bill or corporate commercial paper rather than a bank-issued guaranteed investment certificate. From the perspective of a borrower, disintermediation refers to borrowing directly from the investor rather than from a financial intermediary.

Draft — A written order, signed by the drawer, instructing the drawee to pay a specified sum to a third party (the payee). The payee and drawer are often the same person. A cheque is a type of draft. A bill of exchange is a draft used for a foreign transaction.

Duration — The weighted average life of the present values of cash flows. Modified duration measures the effect of a change in interest rates on the price of a bond.

Dutch auction — An auction that sets a high opening price and then lowers the bids until a buyer is found.

ECN — Electronic Communication Network. An alternative securities trading system that allows trade outside the normal U.S. stock markets such as the NYSE or Nasdaq.

Efficient market — The efficient market hypothesis (EMH) is that market prices reflect all information about the entity. If the EMH is correct, then it is futile to attempt to beat the market or forecast market movements. The EMH exists in various forms: this definition applies to the so-called "strong" form of the EMH. The semi-strong form is that prices reflect all publicly available information.

Eigenvalue — A measure of the position of the variations in a rate of return that is caused by a particular factor.

Electronic Communications Network (ECN) — A trading system that allows automated transactions with a conventional financial market.

Embedded option — An option embedded in another financial instrument such as an interest rate option embedded in a callable bond or mortgage-backed security.

Euro-currency — Refers to money denominated in any currency, outside the home country of that currency. In its most common usage, U.S. dollars in Europe are referred to as Euro dollars. In fact, Euro-currency does not mean that either the currencies or the locations of the funds is European. Japanese yen deposited in an Australian bank are considered to be Euro-currency.

European-style option — An option in which the holder has the right to exercise only at the expiration date.

Event risk — The risk that the market price of a financial instrument will change because of a non-financial event, that is, a risk other than interest rate risk, liquidity risk, currency risk, etc. Event risk often refers to takeovers, political changes, legal and regulatory changes, and so on. By definition, event risk cannot be forecast.

Ex dividend — Without dividend. Refers to a share trading without the buyer receiving a dividend that has been declared but not paid. Shares trade ex dividend for transactions that settle after the record date. *See* Cum dividend.

Extendible swap — A swap where one or both counterparties have an option to extend the swap for an additional period beyond the stated maturity date.

Face value — Value of a bond or other debt instrument at maturity. May also refer to the notional principal amount of an off balance sheet financial instrument.

Fail — A trade that does not clear on the settlement date, normally because one of the parties has not performed its side of the transaction.

Fair market value — The amount for which a buyer would buy and a seller would sell in a free market. In the financial markets, fair market value is equivalent to the present value of all future cash flows.

Fixed cost — An expense that does not vary with the level of output, for example, property taxes and interest expense. Of course, in the long run there is no such thing as a truly fixed cost.

Float — Refers to the total time a cheque is in transit before being charged to the payor's account. Thus, the float depends upon the length of time the banking system takes to clear the cheque as well as time in the mail, etc. Float in the banking system relates to the time between a cheque being deposited and the payor's account being charged. Cheques drawn on a Canadian bank and deposited at a Canadian bank will normally clear the same day.

Floating-rate note (FRN) — A financial instrument with a fixed principal amount, a long life, with a yield reset periodically by reference to a short or medium-term interest rate.

Forecast — A best guess as to what the future will bring. A projection is an estimate as to future results using stated assumptions. A forecast is an estimate as to future results using assumptions which represent the most likely scenarios.

Forward Exchange Agreement (FXA) — A contract, the value of which is based upon the difference between the forward exchange rate on its start date and the spot rate at settlement. FXAs are settled with one net cash flow (in one currency) in contrast with foreign exchange contracts which are settled with two offsetting cash flows upon maturity.

Forward start — Applied to a financial instrument, refers to a start date at some future time. A forward swap is a swap agreement with a delayed start date.

Fraption — An option on a forward rate agreement, i.e., an interest rate guarantee.

Futures contract — A type of forward contract trading on an organized exchange. The futures contract is an agreement to buy or sell a specific amount of an financial instrument or commodity at a designated price at a stipulated time.

Gamma — The rate of change in the price sensitivity (or delta) of a financial instrument or a small change in interest rates or the underlying instrument. In the case of options, gamma refers to the rate of change in the delta of an option for the small change in the underlying. In the case of bonds, gamma refers to the rate of change in the price sensitivity of a bond to changes in interest rates as interest rates change.

Garch — Stands for generalized autoregressive conditional heteroscedasticity. Used in some option valuation models, this is an assumption that variance depends upon the variance of previous observations.

Gearing — Refers to leverage.

Gensaki rate — The repo rate on Japanese Government Bonds. An alternative to yen LIBOR as an indicator of short-term rates in yen instruments.

Grandfather clause — A legislative provision that exempts existing activity or an existing situation from falling under the new legislation. For example, the Free Trade Agreement between Canada and the United States grandfathered existing Canadian and American restrictions on foreign investment in broadcasting, communications and transportation.

Gross profit — Net sales less cost of good sold.

Gross sales — Total cash and credit sale as invoiced, not reduced by allowances, returns or other adjustments.

655

Group Of Seven (G7) — Seven major industrial countries that have held formal summits since 1975. The group consists of Canada, the United States, Britain, France, Germany, Italy and Japan.

Group Of Thirty — A group based in Washington D.C. comprising leading bankers, economists and financial officials. They developed a plan for faster and standardized clearance and settlement of international securities transactions, and in 1993 prepared a report on derivatives.

Guaranteed Investment Certificate (GIC) — A debt instrument issued by a chartered bank or trust company, that pays a fixed rate of interest until maturity. GICs are not transferable.

Heath-Jarrow-Morton Model — A model for interest rate options that is constructed based on an interest rate term structure rather than one interest rate for all periods. It also uses a volatility function rather than a point estimate of volatility.

Hedge — In general, an instrument or strategy used to reduce financial risk. A perfect hedge has the same effect as selling the instrument being hedged. Hedging a complex portfolio is generally a dynamic process so that a position which appears to be perfectly hedged at one point will become unhedged as the market moves.

Hedge fund — A term used in the United States for a private pool of assets overseen by a fund manager. Hedge funds are often managed quite aggressively and fund managers may be paid a percentage of any profits made. At one time, hedge funds attempted to lock in arbitrage profits, hence the name. Hedge funds now normally do little or no hedging and may in fact be highly leveraged.

Herstatt risk — Refers to the risk that one party to a currency exchange will default after the other side has met its obligation. The name comes from a German bank that failed.

Heteroscedasticity — A random variable whose variance is not constant.

High coupon swap — An interest rate swap where the fixed rate is set above market interest rates. The receiver of the high coupon normally would pay a fee up front to offset the higher cash flow.

Historical cost accounting — This is the basic premise underlying generally accepted accounting principles which requires that financial statement items be recorded at original cost. Traders or dealers in financial instruments may record their portfolio of marketable securities or financial instruments at market value and thus record gains and losses as the market moves, and market value changes, rather than when realized (that is when the security is sold).

Historical volatility — Actual volatility of the financial instrument underlying an option during a specified prior period. There has been considerable debate as to whether historical volatility is a useful indicator of future volatility.

Homoscedasticity — A random variable whose variance is constant. The Black-Scholes Option Pricing Model assumes homoscedasticity.

Hybrid security — A complex security consisting of a combination of two or more basic financial instruments.

Hypothecate — To pledge assets as collateral for a loan. Title to the assets being hypothecated remains with the owner (borrower). In the event of default, the creditor is entitled to sell the hypothecated assets and use the proceeds to retire the debt.

Implied forward curve — The forward curve consisting of zero-coupon interest rates calculated from the incremental period return in adjacent instruments on the yield curve.

Implied volatility — Volatility used to calculate the price of an option.

In-arrears swap — An interest rate swap where the floating rate is set in arrears, that is based on the reference rate at the end of the reset period applied retroactively, rather than based on the floating index at the beginning of the reset period. As with a conventional interest rate swap, payments are made at the end of each period.

In-the-money — Refers to an option that has intrinsic value because there would be a gain to the holder of the option if it were exercised.

Instinet — The world's largest agency brokerage firm, a subsidiary of Reuters PLC. Using Istinet, investors can trade directly and anonymously with each other.

Interest — The cost of using money, generally expressed as a rate per annum. Interest is expressed in notional annual terms even when the payment period is less than a year. For example, the rate for a three-month treasury bill multiplied by four is quoted as an annual rate of interest. Similarly, bond coupon payments payable every six months are converted to an annual equivalent equal to twice the rate of each coupon rate.

Interest only obligation — A tranche of an asset-backed security whose holder is entitled to only the interest paid on financial instruments in the underlying pool.

Interest rate differential — The interest rate difference between two comparable debt instruments denominated in different currencies.

Internal Rate Of Return (IRR) — The discount rate at which the present value of the future cash flows equals zero. In other words, the present value of future cash flows in is equal to the present value of future cash flows out. Often used to evaluate a capital project: if the project's IRR is greater than hurdle rate or the cost of capital, the project is acceptable; otherwise, it is rejected.

Intrinsic value — The amount by which an option is in the money, that is the amount a holder could receive for exercising the option .

Inverse floater — A floating rate note which is reset at a rate equal to a fixed rate minus a floating rate index. For example, an inverse floater may call for a variable rate payment equal to 12 per cent minus LIBOR.

Inverted yield curve — Also referred to as *negative yield curve*. Refers to the situation in which the interest rates on short-term securities is higher than those on longer-term securities of the same quality.

Junk bond — A bond carrying a high yield and a relatively high risk of default.

Kappa — Change in the price of an option due to a one percentage point change in implied volatility.

Kondratieff wave — Refers to the theories of Nikolai Kondratieff, a Soviet economist of the 1920s, that Western economies were prone to major cycles lasting about 60 years. Low points of economic cycles have occurred in the 1810s, 1870s, 1930s, and 1990s.

Kurtosis — A measure of how fast the tails of a probability distribution approach zero, compared to a normal probability distribution. Markets are often seen to be leptokurtic, that is the tails are fatter than would normally be expected. A fatter tail means that there is a higher probability that a variable will reach an extreme value. Thus, risk management practices and models such as option pricing models that are premised upon normal distributions underestimate the likelihood of unusually large changes in value.

Lambda — The change in option price divided by the change in the underlying price. Lambda indicates the leverage factor of an option.

PART E

659

Leptokurtic — *See* Kurtosis.

LIBOR — Stands for London Inter Bank Offered Rate. A rate determined by market forces (unlike prime rates, which are administered and set by each chartered bank) which is technically the rate that large international banks charge each other for large Euro-dollar loans contractual rates are often set with reference to LIBOR: for example, 40 basis points over LIBOR. Note that there are actually different LIBORs, depending upon the currency and term.

LIBOR used without modification generally means a loan in United States funds where the interest rate is determined ("reset") every three months.

Liquid yield option note (LYON) — A zero-coupon convertible bond that is callable by the issuer and puttable by the investor.

Liquidation value — The value of a firm, if all of its assets are valued at their liquidation price and the resulting proceeds are reduced by the amount necessary to discharge debts and other obligations. The liquidation price of a business is its estimated price assuming that each asset is sold separately from the organization. Liquidation value assumes that the business is being dismantled and so is distinguished from going concern value, which may be higher.

Liquidity — Refers generally to the ability to convert assets into cash or cash equivalents without significant loss in value. May also be defined as "the ability to pay bills as they come due".

Liquidity is also applied to markets to refer to sufficient securities or commodities traded and outstanding so that large transactions do not significantly affect the price.

Long — To be long is to own an assets.

Long-term equity anticipation securities (LEAPS) — Exchange-traded options that are created with a life of about two years. As they approach maturity, they are indistinguishable from conventional short-term exchange-traded options.

Look back option — An option that gives the holder the right to buy or sell the underlying at its minimum or maximum price within the look back period. A call would give the holder the right to buy at the lowest price, a put would give the purchaser the right to sell at the highest price.

Low coupon swap — An interest rate swap with fixed coupon rates below market rates at the date that the swap is entered into. The fixed rate receiver normally receives a fee to compensate for the reduction in future cash flows.

Magnetic Ink Character Recognition (MICR) — Magnetic characters encoded at the bottom of a cheque to permit the use of automated cheque clearing equipment. A fully encoded micro line specifies the cheque number, the payor bank number, transit or branch number, account number, and the dollar amount of the cheque.

Margin — The amount a customer deposits with an investment dealer when in borrowing from the dealer to purchase shares. Margin also refers to the deposit a customer must put up when buying or selling a contract trading on a futures exchange to allow for future changes in its market value. The amount of margin required is set by the by-laws of the stock or futures exchange.

Mark-to-market — To record the value of a financial instrument at current market value. This has the effect of recognizing increases or decreases in market prices even if the financial instrument has not been disposed of.

PART E

Market discontinuity — Also referred to as *market gapping*. Refers to market prices failing to follow a continuous path. In other words, a graph of market prices jumps or gaps between two points rather than moving continuously.

Market maker — A dealer prepared to buy or sell an item depending upon the wishes of a customer. A market maker will quote a "two-way price" — that is buy or sell or bid and asked, and will then be prepared to buy or sell at the indicated price.

Market price — The price at which buyers and sellers trade in an open market place.

Market value — If there is a market, the market value is equal to the market price. If there is no market in the item, market value is the highest price a buyer would be likely to pay and a seller likely to accept, provided both parties were fully informed and acting voluntarily.

Medium-term bond — A bond maturing in three to 10 years.

Medium-term notes — A debt instrument normally issued by an investment grade corporate borrower that generally matures in less than seven years.

Model risk — A variation in return resulting from a failure to model the behaviour of the instrument correctly.

Montreal Exchange (ME) — Founded in 1874 as the Montreal Stock Exchange. In 1926, the Montreal Cash Exchange was founded which in 1953 changed its name to the Canadian Stock Exchange. The Montreal Stock Exchange and the Canadian Stock Exchange merged in 1974 to become the Montreal Exchange. In 1999 most share trading was transferred to other stock exchanges and the Montreal Exchange now trades futures and options.

Naked option — An option for which the writer (seller) has no underlying financial instrument. For example, the writer of a naked call option does not own the instrument on which the option has been written.

Negative carry — When the cost of funds borrowed to finance securities is higher than the yield on the securities. Borrowing at 8 per cent to purchase a bond yielding 6 per cent means that the bond would then have a negative carry.

Net assets — The difference between a company's total assets and total liabilities, also equal to owner's equity or net worth.

Net income — Also referred to as net earnings, or net profit or loss. The amount remaining after all expenses have been taken into account and deducted. It is the amount that can be distributed to the owners without impinging on capital or retained earnings.

Net sales — Total sales less returns, allowances and other adjustments.

Nondiversifiable risk — Systematic risk, that is, risk that cannot be eliminated by diversification.

Non systematic risk — The element of market price risk that can be eliminated by diversification.

Not rated — Means that no bond rating has been assigned by a bond rating service (such as Dominion Bond Rating Service in Canada or Standard and Poors or Moody's in the U.S.).

Novation — An agreement to replace one or more existing contracts with a new contract. The old contracts are effectively cancelled and the new contract replaces them.

Off balance sheet instrument — A contractual agreement that changes the risk structure of both parties without appearing as an asset or liability on a balance sheet.

Offer — The price at which a seller offers to sell an instrument. Also referred to as the *asked price*.

PART E

Office of the Superintendent Of Financial Institutions (OSFI) —The federal agency that supervises federally regulated financial institutions: banks, trust companies and insurance companies.

Open interest — The number of specified futures or options outstanding at a particular time.

Open market operations — Activity undertaken by the Bank of Canada to influence the Canadian money supply and interest rates. These are carried out through the purchase and sale of government securities such as government bonds and treasury bills.

Operating lease — A lease which is in essence a short-term rental of property. The intention is that the risks and rewards of ownership remain with the owner and the lessee is paying for the ability to use the property for a relatively short period of time.

Opportunity cost — Measurement of the benefits forgone resulting from taking one course of action instead of an alternative.

Option — The right, without any obligation to buy or sell an instrument at a particular price until a particular expiration date. If the option is not exercised by its expiry date, the option expires, worthless.

Option writer — The entity that sells an option.

Orthogonal factors — Factors that are not related to each other.

Out of the money — Refers to an option that has no intrinsic value because the price of the underlying is below the strike price of a call or above the strike price of a put.

Over the counter (OTC) — Refers to a one-off transaction negotiated between a bank and a customer, as opposed to "exchange traded" when the terms of the contract are predefined by the exchange. For example, an over the counter foreign exchange forward agreement with a bank will have the amount, currency, settlement instructions and all other aspects as agreed to between the customer and the bank. An exchange traded foreign exchange future will be in the parameters set by the exchange for example, a fixed delivery date and with a contract representing a fixed amount of currency.

Over the counter also refers to the market in which securities transactions are conducted through a computer network or over the telephone, etc., connecting the dealers rather than through an organized exchange.

Oversubscribed — A new share issue for which there are more willing buyers than available shares. May be an indication that the underwriter has priced the issue too low. Normally, an issue which is oversubscribed will increase in price immediately after issue to satisfy the unfilled demand.

Par — The face value or nominal value of a financial instrument.

Parallel shift — A movement of each point on an interest rate yield curve up or down by the same amount.

Partnership — An agreement between two or more parties to conduct business together and share in the profits and losses of the enterprise.

Path dependent option — An option where the payout is effected by movements in the price of the underlying during the life of the option. This defers from a standard option where its value at its exercise date is determined solely by the price of the underlying at that date.

Pay out ratio — The proportion of an entity's profits that is distributed to shareholders by way of dividends.

Payback — Refers to the length of time required for a firm to recover an initial investment in a project, from the cash flows generated by the project. It can be used as an approximate measure of the risk being undertaken. A shorter payback denotes relatively less risk.

PART E

Paying agent — The agent, generally a trust company or bank, that receives funds from an issue of shares or bonds and in turn remits interest in dividends to bond holders and shareholders.

Perpetual bond — A bond with no maturity date that is not redeemable.

Point — Generally, refers to a 1 per cent change in the yield of an instrument. Thus, for interest rate products, one point equals 100 basis points.

In foreign exchange, a point is generally the same as a basis point: that is $1/10,000$ of the unit of the currency. A change in the Canada/U.S. exchange rate from $1.38 to $1.39 (1.3800 to 1.3900) is a change of 100 points. Sometimes the context will make it clear that point is used in the sense of 100 basis points as in "the rate has moved a full point".

Positive carry — When the cost of funds borrowed to finance securities is lower than the yield on the securities. Borrowing at 6 per cent to purchase a bond yielding 8 per cent would mean that the bond has a positive carry.

Positive yield curve — Also referred to as *normal yield curve*. The case where interest rates are higher on longer-term securities than on shorter-term securities of comparable quality.

Present value — The value today of a future stream of cash receipts or disbursements, discounted at an appropriate rate of interest (or discount rate). A present value method is also called *a discounted cash flow method*.

Prime interest rate — The rate of interest charged by the chartered banks on business loans to their most creditworthy customers. The prime rate fluctuates within market interest rates although it is itself a rate set by the banks. This is in contrast to rates such as treasury bill, bankers' acceptance or commercial paper yields, which are determined by the market.

Private placement — Also called a direct placement. The sale of financial instruments directly to the ultimate investors, for example, life insurance companies.

Proprietorship — An unincorporated business owned by a single individual. The simplest form of business organization in which the owner has unlimited personal liability for debts of the business.

Puttable swap — An interest rate swap in which the fixed rate payer has the right to terminate after a specified period. Therefore, if interest rates decline, the swap would be put back to the fixed receiver. In effect, the fixed rate payer is buying an embedded swaption and consequently, pays the higher fixed rate.

Quantise, quanto — An asset or liability denominated in a currency other than the one in which it is usually traded. An example might be option on yen interest rates payable in U.S. dollars.

Quick ratio — Cash, marketable securities plus accounts receivable divided by current liabilities. The quick ratio excludes inventories and, therefore, focuses on an entity's liquid assets.

Ratio analysis — Examining the relationship of numbers in financial statements to evaluate the risks and rewards for investing in a firm. Normally involves a comparison of such ratios to those of prior periods and with other entities. Properly done, ratio analysis is an iterative process that in its early stages yields more questions than answers.

Real — In a context such as *real income, real rate of return, real wages or real interest rate* refers to the notional amount adjusted for changes in purchasing power caused by inflation.

Real property — Land and all physical property on it and attached to it. This is distinct from movable property which is also tangible, and intangible property which cannot be touched (such as patents, goodwill and similar deferred assets).

PART E

Retained earnings — Net income retained in the business after dividends have been paid out.

Return On Equity (ROE) — The rate of return on the owner's investment, determined by dividing net income, after preferred share dividends, into shareholders' equity (which is the same as net assets).

Reverse floater — A floating rate instrument that bears coupons that fluctuate inversely with interest rates, for example, a floating rate may be set at 12 per cent minus LIBOR.

Risk — A measure of the possibility of gain or loss. Risk is traditionally differentiated from uncertainty because risk is measurable whereas uncertainty is not measurable.

Typical risks include:

- *Credit risk*, the risk that a borrower or debtor will not repay an obligation when it is due.
- *Foreign exchange risk*, the risk (gain or loss) due to foreign exchange fluctuations.
- *Interest rate risk*, the risk that a fixed rate debt instrument will change in value due to a change in interest rates.
- *Liquidity risk*, the risk that an investor will not be able to buy or sell an instrument quickly.

Risk arbitrage — Normally, refers to simultaneous purchase and sale of shares in two companies based upon their expected takeover or merger. Conventional arbitrage is relatively riskless in that the resulting return is guaranteed regardless of other events. In the case of risk arbitrage, losses are likely if the expected event (takeover) does not materialize.

Risk premium — In modern portfolio theory, the difference between a risk free return and the total return on an investment.

Rocket scientist — According to folklore, the original mathematicians and scientists that devised ways of measuring innovative financial securities were actually laid off by Lockheed from their missile program in the 1970s. Hence the term "rocket scientist" to refer to technical specialists and scientists that devise and analyze innovative securities.

Rollover risk — Risk of loss due to mispricing of an option or future when the old position is closed and a new position is opened.

Secondary distribution — The sale of previously issued securities. The proceeds of sale on a secondary distribution accrue to the previous owners of the securities rather than to the companies that originally issued the securities.

Secondary market — Stock exchanges and over the counter markets where shares and money market instruments are purchased and sold after their original issue.

Shares — A claim on the earnings and assets of a corporation, representing an ownership interest. Common shares entitle the shareholder to participate in the election of directors. Special or preference shares generally do not have voting rights but have prior claims on assets and income.

Short — To be short is to sell or owe an item.

Solvency — The ability to meet obligations as they fall due.

Sovereign risk — The risk that a foreign government will default on its debt or interfere with the ability of corporations and individuals under its jurisdiction to pay their obligations as they fall due.

Stand by commitment — A promise by a bank to lend funds in the event of a particular contingency. A fee is normally charged by the bank.

Stand by fee — Fee charged on the unused portion of the credit line under a line of credit arrangement with a bank.

PART E

Statement of changes in cash — Used to be called the statement of source and application of funds or statement of changes in financial position. Measures the inflows and outflows of cash between accounting periods. It distinguishes cash flows from operations, from investing activities, and from financing activities.

Straddle — The sale or purchase of a put option and a call option with the same strike price on the same underlying instrument with the same expiry date. Purchasers benefit if the underlying moves significantly in either direction. Sellers benefit if the underlying moves relatively little.

Strangle — Similar to a *straddle* in that it represents the sale or purchase of a put option and a call option on the same instrument with the same strike price and the same expiry date, but at strike prices that are significantly out of the money. Because both options are out of the money, a strangle costs less than a straddle but only generates profits for the purchaser if the underlying moves very significantly.

Strip — A separation of a bond into its coupon payments and principal repayment which are all then sold separately as zero-coupon securities.

Dividend stripping is the practice of purchasing shares to collect their dividends and then reselling the shares.

Subscription — An agreement to purchase newly issued securities. Thus, a subscription right is that granted to existing shareholders to subscribe to a new issue of common shares.

Suspend trading — A temporary halt in the trading of a security (normally a share) in anticipation of a major announcement. Occasionally, may be ordered by a stock exchange or securities commission, if a listed company has been remiss in filing timely information to its shareholders.

Synthetic Agreement for Forward Exchange (SAFE) — Another term for a *forward exchange agreement (FXA)*. A contract, the value of which is based upon the difference between the forward exchange rate on its start date and the spot rate at settlement. SAFEs are settled with one net cash flow (in one currency) in contrast with foreign exchange contracts which are settled with two offsetting cash flows upon maturity.

Systematic risk — Risk resulting from market movements in general. Systematic risk cannot be diversified away within a particular market or market segment.

Systemic risk — Risk related to the overall health and liquidity of the financial system.

Tangible asset — An asset having physical existence such as cash, real estate or machinery, as well as a monetary asset that is expected to be realized in monetary terms such as accounts receivable or bonds.

Tangible net worth — Net assets less intangible assets. May also be calculated as total assets less intangible assets including non material items such as copyrights, trademarks and goodwill.

Tax credit — A direct dollar for dollar reduction in tax liability, as opposed to a tax deduction which reduces taxable income and hence, reduces taxes only by the percentage of the tax bracket. Most credits are non-refundable which means that they cannot reduce taxes payable to a negative amount. Refundable tax credit can result in a cash refund to the taxpayer.

Tenor — The term or life of a financial instrument.

Thin market — The situation in which there is little competition in the market due to limited trading volumes.

Tick — The minimum price change available in a market place.

PART E

Tombstone — An advertisement placed in newspapers by investment dealers to announce an offering of securities or similar financial transaction. Usually done after the securities have been sold to call the attention of the investment community to the transaction.

Toronto Stock Exchange (TSX) — Founded in 1852 and incorporated in 1878 as the Toronto Stock Exchange. In 1899, the Toronto Stock and Mining Exchange was established as a second exchange to provide a market for speculative mining shares. It eventually became the Standard Stock and Mining Exchange which merged in 1934 with the Toronto Stock Exchange. The TSX is Canada's primary stock exchange in terms of share value and volumes traded.

Tranche — One of a series of related security issues, with different payback patterns, expiry dates and other features. Asset-backed securities and collateralized mortgage obligations are often created in tranches to meet differing investor needs.

Treasurer — Corporate officer responsible for the receipt, custody, disbursement and investment of funds as well as for borrowings and relationships with banks. In smaller companies, the treasurer may also function as the controller with accounting, budgeting and internal audit responsibilities.

Treasury shares — Shares reacquired by the issuing company and available for cancellation or resale. Treasury shares are issued but not outstanding. Therefore, they are excluded from ratios that measure amounts per share. Under several corporations acts, shares repurchased by the issuing company are deemed to be cancelled. Therefore, under those acts treasury shares cannot exist.

Ultra vires — Refers to activities beyond the scope of that which are permitted. Often refers to an artificial entity such as a corporation doing something beyond its legal powers.

Under all Canadian corporations' acts, business corporations have the rights and abilities of a natural person. However, non-business and other corporations — that is those incorporated under an act of parliament or provincial legislature, or those incorporated under a special purpose act, may be restricted in their business activities if they are not specifically authorized to carry out certain actions. For example, if the corporation does not have the rights and abilities of a natural person, it might not be able to engage in certain treasury activities unless its charter specifically authorizes it.

Examples of activity that might be *ultra vires* include buying and selling foreign exchange and treasury activity that could be interpreted as speculative.

Unbundling — The trend in banking toward separating costs for different services provided permitting the payment of higher rates of interest on various types of deposits.

Uncertainty — *See* Risk.

Underlying — The instrument or variable upon which a futures or option contract is based.

Unit Trust — Term for mutual fund used outside North America.

Value at risk — The loss an investor would experience in the event of a two-standard deviation advance move in market rates. Note that this will understate the actual risk due to issues such as liquidity.

Vertical spread — An option strategy based upon the difference in premium between two options on the same underlying, with the same maturity, but different strike prices.

Volatility — A statistical measure of the tendency of a market price or yield to vary over time.

PART E

Warrant — An instrument giving the purchaser the right, but not the obligation, to purchase a specified amount of an asset at a particular price over a specified time period. Warrants differ from options in that they are issued for periods exceeding a year and they may be listed on an exchange.

Writer — For options, refers to the entity that sells options. In general, refers to the party that sells an instrument.

Yankee Bond — A U.S. dollar-denominated bond issued by a non-U.S. company in the United States.

Yield — The interest rate that will make the present value of future cash flows from an asset equal to the price or market value of the asset. In effect, the same as the internal rate of return.

Yield curve — A graph indicating the term structure of interest rates by plotting the yield for instruments with similar characteristics but different maturities.

Zaitech — A Japanese term meaning financial engineering.

Zero coupon — Refers to a security that makes no periodic interest payments but only a payment upon maturity. Such an instrument is sold at a discount to its maturity value.

Zero coupon swap — A swap in which a counterparty makes one payment at maturity. This swap may be appropriate to hedge a zero-coupon bond or a project for which payment will not be received until its completion. It is functionally equivalent to a loan.

Index

The following references appear with their corresponding page numbers in Canadian Treasury Management. Additional references and definitions may be found in Chapter 26 ("Glossary") on page 633.